Wisdom on the Move: Late Antique Traditions in Multicultural Conversation

Supplements to Vigiliae Christianae

TEXTS AND STUDIES OF EARLY CHRISTIAN LIFE AND LANGUAGE

Editors-in-Chief

D.T. Runia
G. Rouwhorst

Editorial Board

B.D. Ehrman
K. Greschat
J. Lössl
J. van Oort
C. Scholten

VOLUME 161

The titles published in this series are listed at *brill.com/vcs*

Wisdom on the Move: Late Antique Traditions in Multicultural Conversation

Essays in Honor of Samuel Rubenson

Edited by

Susan Ashbrook Harvey
Thomas Arentzen
Henrik Rydell Johnsén
Andreas Westergren

BRILL

LEIDEN | BOSTON

The Library of Congress Cataloging-in-Publication Data is available online at http://catalog.loc.gov

Typeface for the Latin, Greek, and Cyrillic scripts: "Brill". See and download: brill.com/brill-typeface.

ISSN 0920-623X
ISBN 978-90-04-43069-3 (hardback)
ISBN 978-90-04-43074-7 (e-book)

Copyright 2020 by Koninklijke Brill NV, Leiden, The Netherlands.
Koninklijke Brill NV incorporates the imprints Brill, Brill Hes & De Graaf, Brill Nijhoff, Brill Rodopi, Brill Sense, Hotei Publishing, mentis Verlag, Verlag Ferdinand Schöningh and Wilhelm Fink Verlag.
All rights reserved. No part of this publication may be reproduced, translated, stored in a retrieval system, or transmitted in any form or by any means, electronic, mechanical, photocopying, recording or otherwise, without prior written permission from the publisher.
Authorization to photocopy items for internal or personal use is granted by Koninklijke Brill NV provided that the appropriate fees are paid directly to The Copyright Clearance Center, 222 Rosewood Drive, Suite 910, Danvers, MA 01923, USA. Fees are subject to change.

This book is printed on acid-free paper and produced in a sustainable manner.

For Samuel

Contents

The Editors' Preface IX
Abbreviations X
Notes on Contributors XII

Wisdom on the Move: An Introduction   1
   Thomas Arentzen, Henrik Rydell Johnsén and Andreas Westergren

PART 1
Wisdom in Transmission: Egypt and Palestine

1   Wisdom in Fragments: The Earliest Manuscript of the First Greek *Life of St Pachomius*   13
   Peter Toth

2   Producing Pachomius: The Role of Lower Egypt in the Creation, Reception, and Adaptation of the Pachomian *Vita* Tradition   35
   James E. Goehring

3   The Wisdom of the Fathers: The Use of the *Apophthegmata* in the Correspondence of Barsanuphius and John of Gaza   54
   Lorenzo Perrone

PART 2
Wisdom in Translation: Apophthegmata in New Languages

4   The Unmentionable Apophthegm: An Overview of the Pagan Greek Tradition   75
   Denis M. Searby

5   Between East and West: Cassian the Roman in Greek and Latin   97
   Britt Dahlman

6 The *Apophthegmata Patrum* in the Slavonic Context: A Case Study of Textual Doublets 119
   Karine Åkerman Sarkisian

7 The Armenian Transmission of the *Apophthegmata Patrum* 147
   Anahit Avagyan

8 The Monk as Storyteller? On the Transmission of the *Apophthegmata Patrum* among Muslim Ascetics in Basra 166
   Ute Pietruschka

PART 3
Wisdom in Transition: Hellenic, Jewish, Christian and Islamic Worlds

9 "Wise Elders" and "Nursing Infants": Wisdom Extended to the Gentiles in the Pseudo-Clementine *Homilies* 187
   Karin Hedner Zetterholm

10 Training the Women's Choir: Ascetic Practice and Liturgical Education in Late Antique Syriac Christianity 203
   Susan Ashbrook Harvey

11 Universal Wisdom in Defence of the Particular: Medieval Jewish and Christian Usage of Biblical Wisdom in Arabic Treatises 224
   Miriam L. Hjälm

Rubenson on the Move: A Biographical Journey 247
   Thomas Arentzen, Henrik Rydell Johnsén and Andreas Westergren

List of Publications by Samuel Rubenson 251
Index 260

The Editors' Preface

This volume is dedicated to the scholarly work of Samuel Rubenson. His friends are numerous, and numerous indeed are those who had wished to contribute to a festschrift in his honor. Since the scope of the current book is focused and particular, it cannot represent the entirety of Rubenson's indebted friends and colleagues. We trust that those who are not included will find other apt ways to celebrate his scholarship.

Apart from the unfailing effort of the various authors, the completion of this book has depended on the whole-hearted work of Ute Possekel, whose thorough, devoted and efficient copy-editing brought the chapters to their final form. We are deeply grateful for the many intense hours she spent with the manuscript. We should also like to thank Terry Wright for his work on the index and Marjolein van Zuylen at Brill.

The publication has been supported financially by Lunds Missionssällskap and the Birgit and Sven Håkan Ohlsson Foundation.

Epiphany 2020

Abbreviations

ACW	Ancient Christian Writers
AnBoll	*Analecta Bollandiana*
ANF	The Ante-Nicene Fathers
CSCO	Corpus Scriptorum Christianorum Orientalium
	Copt. = Scriptores Coptici; Subs. = Subsidia; Syr. = Scriptores Syri
CSEL	Corpus Scriptorum Ecclesiasticorum Latinorum
CSS	Cistercian Studies Series
DOP	*Dumbarton Oaks Papers*
EI^2	*Encyclopaedia of Islam*, 2nd edition
EI^3	*Encyclopaedia of Islam*, 3rd edition, online
ETSE	Estonian Theological Society in Exile
FC	Fathers of the Church
HTR	*Harvard Theological Review*
Hugoye	*Hugoye: Journal of Syriac Studies*
JAC	*Jahrbuch für Antike und Christentum*
JECS	*Journal of Early Christian Studies*
JEH	*Journal of Ecclesiastical History*
JTS	*Journal of Theological Studies*
LCC	Library of Christian Classics
MCPL	*Meddelanden från Collegium Patristicum Lundense*
MKHA	Meddelanden från Kyrkohistoriska Arkivet i Lund
NPNF	Select Library of Nicene and Post-Nicene Fathers
OCA	Orientalia Christiana Analecta
OCP	*Orientalia Christiana Periodica*
OCT	Oxford Classical Texts
OECS	Oxford Early Christian Studies
OLA	Orientalia Lovaniensia Analecta
OLP	*Orientalia Lovaniensia Periodica*
OrChr	*Oriens Christianus*
ParOr	*Parole de l'Orient*
PETSE	Papers of the Estonian Theological Society in Exile
PG	Patrologia Graeca
PL	Patrologia Latina
PO	Patrologial Orientalis
PTS	Patristische Texte und Studien
RAC	*Reallexikon für Antike und Christentum*
RE	*Paulys Realencyklopädie der classischen Altertumswissenschaft* (Stuttgart 1894–1980)

SChr	Sources chrétiennes
STAC	Studien und Texte zu Antike und Christentum
StAns	Studia Anselmiana
StPatr	*Studia Patristica*
SubsHag	Subsidia Hagiographica
SVigChr	Supplements to Vigiliae Christianae
TTH	Translated Texts for Historians
TU	Texte und Untersuchungen zur Geschichte der altchristlichen Literatur
ZAC	*Zeitschrift für Antikes Christentum / Journal of Ancient Christianity*
ZNW	*Zeitschrift für die neutestamentliche Wissenschaft*

Notes on Contributors

Thomas Arentzen
received his PhD in Church History from Lund University in 2014, and earned his habilitation in Church History at the same institution in 2018. During the academic year 2018–2019 he was a Fellow in Byzantine Studies at Dumbarton Oaks. Currently he is Researcher at Uppsala University, where he conducts the project "Beyond the Garden: An Ecocritical Approach to Early Byzantine Christianity," funded by the Swedish Research Council. His research focuses on Christian hymns and hagiography in relation to corporeality and ecology. His publications include *The Virgin in Song: Mary and the Poetry of Romanos the Melodist* (University of Pennsylvania Press, 2017) and *The Reception of the Virgin in Byzantium: Marian Narratives in Texts and Images* (Cambridge University Press, 2019).

Anahit Avagyan
studied theology at Yerevan State University (Armenia) and received her PhD degree from the Friedrich-Alexander-University Erlangen-Nuremberg. She has conducted research on Medieval Armenian translations for many years. Her interest focuses on the Armenian translations of the Church Fathers, especially Athanasius of Alexandria and the Armenian collections of *Vitae Patrum*. Currently she is a researcher in the Mashtots Matenadaran Research Institute of Ancient Manuscripts in Yerevan; she also teaches Patristics and Church History at the Gevorgian Theological Seminary in Etchmiadzin.

Britt Dahlman
received her PhD in Greek in 2007 from Lund University. Since then she has worked as a research fellow within three larger projects on Greek manuscripts containing monastic literature. In the collaborative project, "Formative Wisdom. The Reception of Monastic Sayings in European Culture: Scholarly Collaboration on a Digital Platform," her work included the digital editing and encoding of manuscripts for a relational database of apophthegmatic and monastic literature. Currently she participates in the project "Cultural Evolution of Texts" at Uppsala University. Her publications include *Saint Daniel of Sketis* (2007) and several studies on and editions of the *Apophthegmata Patrum* (*Paradiset*, vols. 4–9 and 15).

James E. Goehring
is Professor Emeritus of Religion at the University of Mary Washington in Fredericksburg, Virginia. His research interests focus on early Egyptian monasti-

cism in general, and Upper Egyptian Pachomian monasticism in particular. He was an Alexander von Humboldt fellow and is a past president on the North American Patristics Society. His publications include *The Crosby-Schøyen Codex* (1990), *Ascetics, Society and the Desert* (1999), and *Politics, Monasticism, and Miracles in Sixth Century Upper Egypt* (2012). In retirement he has become an avid birder.

Susan Ashbrook Harvey
is the Willard Prescott and Annie McClelland Smith Professor of Religion and History at Brown University, where she has also served as Royce Family Professor of Teaching Excellence and, presently, as Director of the Program in Early Cultures. A specialist in Syriac and Byzantine Christianity, she has received honorary doctorates from Grinnell College (Iowa), the University of Bern (Switzerland), and Lund University (Sweden), and is a past-President of the Orthodox Theological Society in America and of the North American Patristics Society. She has published widely in academic venues on women in ancient Christianity, asceticism, the cult of saints, hagiography, hymnography, and religion and the senses.

Miriam L. Hjälm
holds a PhD in Semitic languages from Uppsala University (2015) and has been a postdoctoral research fellow in the *Biblia Arabica* project at Ludwig Maximilian University of Munich (2015–2017). She is currently employed as an Assistant Professor in Easter Christian Studies at the Stockholm School of Theology/Sankt Ignatios College. Her research focuses on Christian Arabic literature in general, and in particular on various aspects of Bible translations as well as the perception and use of the Bible among early Arabic-speaking Christians. Her research interests also include religious encounters as reflected in shared traditions and tacit borrowing among Arabic-speaking Jews and Christians in the Islamic world.

Henrik Rydell Johnsén
received his PhD in Church History from Lund University, Sweden. Since 2017 he is senior lecturer and researcher at Stockholm University. His research focuses on late antique monasticism in Palestine and Egypt and includes studies of early monasticism in light of late antique philosophy and education, as well as literary studies of the early monastic genre of chapters. His publications include *Reading John Climacus* (2007) and various articles on early Egyptian monasticism and late antique philosophy.

Lorenzo Perrone
is Professor Emeritus of Early Christian Literature at the University of Bologna. He has studied the history of the Church and monasticism in the Holy Land during Late Antiquity. In the last two decades he mainly worked on Origen and the history of biblical interpretation. Moreover, an ongoing subject of his scholarly interest has been the doctrine of prayer in ancient Christianity. In 1995 he created the international journal *Adamantius* that specializes in the study of Origen and the Alexandrian tradition. After their discovery in Munich in 2012, he directed the critical edition of twenty-nine new *Homilies on the Psalms* by Origen (Berlin 2015).

Ute Pietruschka
is senior researcher at the Academy of Sciences Göttingen (Germany), where she currently focuses on the project "Cataloguing Oriental Manuscripts in Germany." She is a lecturer at the University of Halle and the Freie University Berlin. She received her PhD from the University of Halle (Germany). Since 2009 she has directed the project "Corpus of Arabic and Syriac Gnomologia." Her academic interests include Christian-Arabic and Islamic studies, manuscript studies, the transmission of Greek knowledge in the Islamicate world and Digital Humanities.

Karine Åkerman Sarkisian
holds a PhD in Slavonic Languages from Uppsala University. Her research concentrates on the reception of Byzantine hagiography among the Slavs. Her publications include a linguistic analysis and critical edition of the *Life of St. Onuphrios*, as well as translation studies. In recent years she has explored the reception and text evolution of monastic sayings on Slavic soil within two projects: "Formative Wisdom. The Reception of Monastic Sayings in European Culture: Scholarly Collaboration on a Digital Platform" at Lund University, where she contributed to the development of the relational database by digital editing of apophthegmatic literature; and the project "Cultural Evolution of Texts" at Uppsala University, which integrates phylogenetic network analysis with studies of textual evolution.

Denis M. Searby
received his BA and MA in Classics from Columbia University, New York, and his PhD from Uppsala University, Sweden. He was named professor of ancient Greek at Stockholm University in 2012. His research has included studies and editions of Greek gnomologia and anthologies, editorial theory, as well as theological and philosophical interactions between the Latin West and Greek East,

especially focused on the statesman and humanist Demetrios Kydones. He has also translated the works of Birgitta of Sweden from Latin into English (4 vols., Oxford University Press).

Peter Toth
earned his MA in Egyptology and Classics and his PhD in Classics at the University of Budapest. He worked and published on the various versions and translations of the late-fourth-century monastic collection *Historia monachorum*. After a ten-year curatorship of medieval manuscripts at the University Library Budapest, he conducted various research projects at The Warburg Institute and King's College, London before he joined the British Library in 2016 as Curator of Ancient and Medieval Manuscripts. His main interest is in the cultural interaction between Late Antiquity and the Middle Ages via translations of texts and ideas.

Andreas Westergren
is Researcher and Lecturer at the Centre for Theology and Religious Studies at Lund University. He holds a PhD in Church History from Lund University. After completing his dissertation in 2012, he participated in the long-term research project on "Early Monasticism and Classical Paideia" at Lund University, where his work focused on hagiographical and historiographical sources in light of communal and civic ideals. He published some of the results in "The Monastic Paradox: Desert Ascetics as Founders, Fathers, and Benefactors in Early Christian Historiography," *Vigiliae Christianae* 72 (2018). Currently he is part of the research project "Integration and Tradition: The Making of the Syrian Orthodox Church in Sweden," funded by the Swedish Research Council.

Karin Hedner Zetterholm
is Associate Professor of Jewish Studies at Lund University. She is the author of *Jewish Interpretation of the Bible: Ancient and Contemporary* (Fortress Press, 2012); *Portrait of a Villain: Laban the Aramean in Rabbinic Literature* (Peeters, 2002); and various articles on the relationship between the Pseudo-Clementine *Homilies* and Judaism and the impact of Jesus-oriented groups on the emergence of a rabbinic Jewish identity.

Wisdom on the Move: An Introduction

Thomas Arentzen, Henrik Rydell Johnsén and Andreas Westergren

How many times have you heard that you cannot enter the same river twice?[*][1] No one knows for sure who first heard these words from Heraclitus in Ephesus. A hundred years later, however, Plato quoted them in Athens.[2] Plutarch repeated a similar statement 400 years after that in Delphi.[3] Indeed, people still allude to these words. Interviewed by the *New York Times* in 2009, President Barack Obama was asked whether he thought Afghanistan might be a new Vietnam for him. He replied: "You have to learn lessons from history. On the other hand, each historical moment is different. You never step into the same river twice. And so Afghanistan is not Vietnam."[4] Ironically, Obama is hardly stepping into the same sagacious river as Heraclitus; the President's usage yields a much less complex or paradoxical interpretation, and we may be quite sure that his application of the saying diverges from the intention of the Ephesian's own. Yet he employs approximately the same expression, albeit 2500 years later and in a different language. It is as if Heraclitus' words represent a comment upon themselves: the words mean different things in different contexts. No one can step into this same stream twice.

Words of wisdom are often flexible. In a collection of the Sayings of the Desert Fathers, Abba Evagrius is recorded to have said: "Take away temptations and nobody is being saved."[5] In another apophthegm, in the same collection, the same statement recurs in a new combination but now attributed to Abba Antony: "'Nobody who has not been tempted will be able to enter the Kingdom of Heaven for, take away temptations,' he says, 'and nobody is being saved.'"[6] To

---

[*] This introduction has been written with funding from the Åke Wiberg foundation.
[1] Heraclitus, fragment 12 (ed. Diels and Kranz): ποταμοῖσι τοῖσιν αὐτοῖσιν ἐμβαίνουσιν ἕτερα καὶ ἕτερα ὕδατα ἐπιρρεῖ· καὶ ψυχαὶ δὲ ἀπὸ τῶν ὑγρῶν ἀναθυμιῶνται. There are several versions of the saying, but most scholars regard fragment 12 as the most genuine one. For the debate, see Daniel W. Graham, "Once More unto the Stream," in *Doctrine and Doxography: Studies on Heraclitus and Pythagoras*, ed. David Sider and Dirk Obbink (Berlin: de Gruyter, 2013), 303–320.
[2] *Cratylus* 402a8–10 (ed. Burnet): Λέγει που Ἡράκλειτος ὅτι "πάντα χωρεῖ καὶ οὐδὲν μένει," καὶ ποταμοῦ ῥοῇ ἀπεικάζων τὰ ὄντα λέγει ὡς "δὶς ἐς τὸν αὐτὸν ποταμὸν οὐκ ἂν ἐμβαίης."
[3] *De E apud Delphos* 392b; *Aetia physica* 912a.
[4] John Harwood, "Obama Rejects Afghanistan–Vietnam Comparison," *New York Times*, September 15, 2009.
[5] AP/G Evagrius 5 (tr. Wortley): Εἶπε πάλιν· Ἔπαρον τοὺς πειρασμούς, καὶ οὐδεὶς ὁ σωζόμενος.
[6] AP/G Antony 5 (tr. Wortley): Ὁ αὐτὸς εἶπεν· Οὐδεὶς ἀπείραστος δυνήσεται εἰσελθεῖν εἰς τὴν βασιλείαν τῶν οὐρανῶν. Ἔπαρον γάρ, φησί, τοὺς πειρασμούς, καὶ οὐδεὶς ὁ σωζόμενος.

reuse a saying, to rewrite it, to combine it with new material, or to reattribute it to a different sage are all recurring features in sayings traditions. Even the message of the saying itself is flexible. Even when Abba Antony, in another saying, offers critique of his own specific generation by stating, "God does not allow there to be battles against this generation such as there were in the time of those of old; for he knows these are weak and cannot sustain it,"[7] it is not difficult to read any period into such statement. Laconic sayings and enigmatic statements often come with open ends.

More often than not, religious sagacity and insightful claims give practical guidance. Rather than fixed eternal truths, they provide advice, not seldom in direct and personal ways. Men and women pass on their insight from one person to another. If convincing, their words may travel from the one who first hears them to new people, through new or existing webs of relations. The process of transmission may take oral or written form; the modes are fluid.[8] When anecdotes and insightful words migrate to new places, new periods and new audiences, the words themselves shift meaning and start to communicate in unexpected ways. As wisdom travels, wisdom changes.

This book brings together articles that focus on the complexity and flexibility of wisdom traditions at the crossroads of late antiquity, and literature which has traveled along the road to or from that historical intersection. Sayings and texts passed from Jewish or pagan sources into Christian corpora, while Jewish and Christian sayings passed into Islamic traditions. Even within a narrower Christian focus, the same words of wisdom were attributed to a number of sages and appeared in diverse literary contexts. Not least did expressions of spiritual insight travel across linguistic and cultural borders, a process which naturally changed the way they were heard or read. Drawing together various cultural and religious contexts on one large map and resisting the temptation to eclipse what are often dubbed "peripheries," *Wisdom on the Move* explores how, why and in what ways the transmission of wisdom took place in the late antique Mediterranean world.

---

7   *AP*/G Antony 23 (tr. Wortley): ὁ Θεὸς οὐκ ἀφίει τοὺς πολέμους ἐπὶ τὴν γενεὰν ταύτην, ὥσπερ ἐπὶ τῶν ἀρχαίων. Οἶδε γὰρ ὅτι ἀσθενεῖς εἰσι καὶ οὐ βαστάζουσιν. On textual fluidity in the *Apophthegmata Patrum*, see Samuel Rubenson, "Textual Fluidity in Early Monasticism: Sayings, Sermons and Stories," in *Snapshots of Evolving Traditions: Jewish and Christian Manuscript Culture, Textual Fluidity, and New Philology*, ed. Liv Ingeborg Lied and Hugo Lundhaug (Berlin: de Gruyter, 2017), 178–200.

8   Dan Ben Amos, "Transmission," in *Folklore: An Encyclopedia of Beliefs, Customs, Tales, Music, and Art*, vol. 3, ed. Charlie T. McCormick and Kim Kennedy White (Santa Barbara: Clio, 1997), 807–811.

1 Wisdom in the Late Antique Mediterranean

Wisdom and wisdom literature permeate many religious traditions and cultures. A precise meaning of the concept of wisdom itself is impossible to frame; rather, the concept varies over time and culture, covering with various emphases practical as well as theoretical knowledge and skills.[9] The Sanskrit Vedas have conveyed Indian wisdom for more than two and a half millennia, while the *Prajñāpāramitā* sutras represent but one example from Mahayana Buddhism. Pagan Scandinavians composed the sagacious poems of *Hávamál*, and the sura of the Qur'an called Luqman may be considered a typical example of early Islamic wisdom. Even pre-Socratic Greek philosophy, such as that of Heraclitus, was often passed on in the form of wise sayings or *apophthegmata*. And, significantly for the current volume, most of the *Ketuvim* of the Hebrew Scriptures, such as the Psalms, the Book of Proverbs and Ecclesiastes, consist of wisdom literature. The same can be said of other Jewish and Christian works; the Book of Wisdom and the Odes of Solomon both echo earlier sapiential works.

Jewish and Christian wisdom, like wisdom in the ancient Mediterranean in general, appears in the earliest literary remains for these communities. These traditions were a crucial current across cultures and religious borders, covering a range of literary genres and literary forms: maxims and sayings, poetry and prose, pithy aphorisms as well as longer stories, gathered in collections,[10] or incorporated as part of wisdom instructions or other literary works.[11]

The two main variants of wisdom literature—collections of sayings and collections of maxims—were often loosely organized without apparent order except for, occasionally, shorter thematic sections. They varied greatly in form and structure.[12] It was a multifaceted type of literature, but also one with

---

[9]   Franco Volpi et al. "Wisdom," in *Brill's New Pauly* (online), accessed 1 April 2019.
[10] On ancient wisdom literature, see J. Barns, "A New Gnomologium: With Some Remarks on Gnomic Anthologies", *Classical Quarterly* 44 (1950): 126–137; 45 (1951): 1–19; Dimitri Gutas, "Classical Arabic Wisdom Literature: Nature and Scope," *Journal of the American Oriental Society* 101 (1975): 49–86; John S. Kloppenborg, *The Formation of Q: Trajectories in Ancient Wisdom Collections* (Philadelphia: Fortress Press, 1987), 264–316; Walter T. Wilson, *The Mysteries of Righteousness: The Literary Composition and Genre of the Sentences of Pseudo-Phocylides* (Tübingen: Mohr Siebeck, 1994), 15–41; Andrea W. Nightingale, "Sages, Sophists, and Philosophers: Greek Wisdom Literature," in *Literature in the Greek and Roman Worlds: A New Perspective*, ed. O. Taplin (Oxford: Oxford University Press, 2000), 156–191.
[11] See Wilson, *Mysteries of Righteousness*, 18–25, 33–39; Kloppenborg, *Formation of Q*, 264–289, 295.
[12] For the variety in form and structure, see Kloppenborg, *Formation of Q*, 295–299, 306–311; Wilson, *Mysteries of Righteousness*, 26, 28–31.

porous borders; one cannot always draw clear distinctions between wisdom expressed in maxims and sayings, and wisdom expressed in other literary genres. Sayings and biographies (*bioi*), for instance, often resemble one another; "the distinction between the chriae collection and the *bios* is a fine one," as Jonathan S. Kloppenborg put it.[13] Psalms such as those in the Hebrew scriptures represent another genre related to such wisdom traditions.[14]

Not only individual sayings but also whole collections were ascribed to authoritative figures.[15] We have collections under the name of philosophers like Epictetus, Epicurus and Pythagoras, or other figures like Menander, Aesop or the Seven Sages. Such attributions clearly legitimized the teaching, but were also easily changed or dropped when sayings travelled into new contexts.

The main social setting for these wisdom traditions was clearly education. Teachers used wisdom sayings to teach basic reading and writing skills, while various schools of philosophy gathered them into collections as summaries of doctrines or ethical principles.[16] The purpose of such collections was not simply to convey knowledge, but also to provide students and readers with useful wisdom to adapt for practical benefit, or examples of appropriate behavior to imitate and implement.[17]

Even if these manifold traditions of wisdom stretched far back in time, they were by no means static. Rather, as Walter T. Wilson puts it, "over the course of centuries any number of additions, abridgements, or rearrangements could be made to a collection, all at the hands of anonymous writers and editors according to their particular needs."[18] Adaptability belonged to the very nature of the genre itself; ethical norms and attitudes with a broad and basic relevance facilitated transmission both to new generations and to new cultures.[19] Greek and Roman wisdom traditions offered a continuous recycling of older traditions, and similar procedures took place in the Jewish and Christian

---

13 Kloppenborg, *Formation of Q*, 316.
14 For a discussion of the Psalms and the wisdom tradition, see Susan Gillingham "'I Will Incline My Ear to a Proverb; I Will Solve My Riddle to the Music of the Harp' (Psalm 49.4): The Wisdom Tradition and the Psalms," in *Perspectives on Israelite Wisdom: Proceedings of the Oxford Old Testament Seminar*, ed. J. Jarick (London: Bloomsbury, 2016), 277–309.
15 See Kloppenborg, *Formation of Q*, 292–294, 301–302.
16 Teresa Morgan, *Literate Education in the Hellenistic and Roman Worlds* (Cambridge: Cambridge University Press, 1998), esp. 120–151; Kloppenborg, *Formation of Q*, 289–290, 299–301, 313–315; Wilson, *Mysteries of Righteousness*, 17, 31–33.
17 Kloppenborg, *Formation of Q*, 302–304, 315–316.
18 Wilson, *Mysteries of Righteousness*, 28.
19 Wilson, *Mysteries of Righteousness*, 32.

traditions and cultures. Late antiquity brought an especially fruitful time for such transmission and exchange.

From early on, biblical wisdom literature contributed to the shaping of both Jewish and Christian ethics,[20] and it served a similar purpose during later periods. Jews and Christians, however, also combined their biblical heritage with Greek and Roman traditions, forming new Jewish and Christian maxims and sayings. The *Sentences of Pseudo-Phocylides* or the tractate *Avot* are well-known Jewish examples of adaptions of Greco-Roman traditions and literary forms.[21] The *Sentences of Sextus*, the earliest example of Christian wisdom literature, is even more clearly based upon earlier collections, notably the *Clitarchi sententiae* and the *Sententiae Pythagoreorum*.[22]

Late antique monasticism, especially in Egypt and Palestine, provided perhaps the most important context for the production of new Christian wisdom. Works of short gnomic chapters (*kephalaia*) appeared already from the late fourth century, starting with Evagrius Ponticus,[23] and even more numerous sayings collections attributed to the so-called Desert Fathers (the *Apophthegmata Patrum*), were compiled from late fifth century onwards.[24]

---

20 John J. Collins, *Jewish Wisdom in the Hellenistic Age* (Edinburgh: T&T Clark, 1997); Frances Young, "Wisdom in the Apostolic Fathers and the New Testament," in *Trajectories Through the New Testament and the Apostolic Fathers*, ed. Andrew F. Gregory and C.M. Tuckett (Oxford: Oxford University Press, 2005), 85–104; Robert L. Wilken, "Wisdom and Philosophy in Early Christianity" in *Aspects of Wisdom in Judaism and Early Christianity*, ed. Robert L. Wilken (Notre Dame, IN: University of Notre Dame Press, 1975), 143–168.

21 Walter T. Wilson, *The Sentences of Pseudo-Phocylides* (Berlin: de Gruyter, 2005), esp. 14–17; Amram Tropper, *Wisdom, Politics, and Historiography: Tractate Avot in the Context of the Graeco-Roman Near East* (Oxford: Oxford University Press, 2004), esp. 157–188.

22 See Daniele Pevarello, *The Sentences of Sextus and the Origins of Christian Asceticism* (Tübingen: Mohr Siebeck, 2013); Walter T. Wilson, *The Sentences of Sextus* (Atlanta: Society of Biblical Literature, 2012); Henry Chadwick, *The Sentences of Sextus: A Contribution to the History of Early Christian Ethics* (Cambridge: Cambridge University Press, 2003).

23 See Paul Géhin, "Les collections de *kephalaia* monastiques: Naissance et succès d'un genre entre création originale, plagiat et florilège," in *Theologica minora: The Minor Genres of Byzantine Theological Literature*, ed. Antonio Rigo (Turnhout: Brepols, 2013), 1–50; Columba Stewart, "Evagrius Ponticus on Monastic Pedagogy," in *Abba: The Tradition of Orthodoxy in the West (Festschrift for Bishop Kallistos of Diokleia)*, ed. Andrew Louth et al. (Crestwood, NY: St. Vladimir's Seminary Press, 2003), 241–271; Joel Kalvesmaki, "Evagrius in the Byzantine Genre of Chapters," in *Evagrius and his Legacy*, ed. Joel Kalvesmaki and Robin Darling Young (Notre Dame, IN: University of Notre Dame Press, 2016), 257–287.

24 For the variety of collections and their complex textual history, see Samuel Rubenson "The Formation and Re-Formations of the Sayings of the Desert Fathers," *StPatr* 55 (2013): 5–22, with further references. The studies on the collections, especially in the Greek and Latin tradition, are numerous, see, e.g., Douglas Burton-Christie, *The Word in the Desert: Scripture and the Quest for Holiness in Early Christian Monasticism* (New York: Oxford Uni-

The monastic sayings have sometimes been treated as a Christian innovation,[25] but we now know that the sayings and maxims continue a broader spectrum of Greek, Roman, Jewish and Christian wisdom traditions.[26]

Earlier in the twentieth century, scholars attempted to sort the vast material of the *Apophthegmata Patrum* into an ordered set of original collections. In recent research, however, it has become increasingly clear that this model fails to capture what is more like a continuously fluid situation, where each manuscript is a new collection, slightly altered to suit a new social context and a new set of readers,[27] or, in the words of Samuel Rubenson: "the texts were constantly rearranged, reattributed, rephrased, divided and recombined. Sayings were culled from other texts, and material from sermons, letters and hagiographical texts were 'apophthegmatized.' i.e. made into sayings."[28] This

versity Press, 1993); Graham Gould, *The Desert Fathers on Monastic Community* (Oxford: Clarendon, 1993); James E. Goehring, "Monastic Diversity and Ideological Boundaries in Fourth-Century Christian Egypt," *JECS* 5 (1997): 79–82; Lillian I. Larsen, "Ørkenfedrenes Apophthegmata og den klassiske retoriske tradisjon," *MCPL* 16 (2001): 26–35; eadem, "Pedagogical Parallels: Re-Reading the Apophthegmata Patrum" (PhD diss., Columbia University, 2006); eadem, "The *Apophthegmata Patrum* and the Classical Rhetorical Tradition," *StPatr* 39 (2006): 409–415; eadem, "The Apophthegmata Patrum: Rustic Rumination or Rhetorical Recitation," *MCPL* 23 (2008): 21–30; eadem, "Early Monasticism and the Rhetorical Tradition: Sayings and Stories as Schooltexts," in *Education and Religion in Late Antiquity: Reflections, Social Contexts, and Genres*, ed. Peter Gemeinhardt and Peter Van Nuffelen (London: Routledge, 2016), 13–33; Henrik Rydell Johnsén, "Doctors, Teachers and Friends: Lower Egyptian Desert Elders and Late Antique Directors of Souls," in *Teachers in Late Antique Christianity*, ed. Peter Gemeinhardt, Olga Lorgeoux and Maria Munkholt Christensen (Tübingen: Mohr Siebeck, 2018), 184–205; idem, "Repentance and Confession: Teaching in Ancient Philosophy and Early Monasticism," in *Pratiche didattiche tra centro e periferia nel Mediterraneo tardoantico: Atti del convegno di studio (Roma, 13–15 maggio 2015)*, ed. G. Agosti and D. Bianconi (Spoleto: Fondazione CISAM, 2019), 141–170. See also the sayings collections in the "Monastica" digital library available online: http://monastica.ht.lu.se. For dating of the earliest collections, see Lucien Regnault, "Les Apophtegmes en Palestine aux Vᵉ–VIᵉ siècles," *Irénikon* 54 (1981): 320–330.

25   See, e.g., Jean-Claude Guy, "Educational Innovation in the Desert Fathers," *Eastern Churches Review* 6 (1974): 44–51.

26   For the sayings tradition, the work of Lillian I. Larsen has been crucial, see n. 24 above. For maxims or the *kephalaia* genre, see especially Endre von Ivánka "ΚΕΦΑΛΑΙΑ: Eine byzantinische Literaturform und ihre antiken Wurzeln," *Byzantinische Zeitschrift* 47 (1954): 285–291, and more recently Henrik Rydell Johnsén, "Reading John Climacus: Rhetorical Argumentation, Literary Convention and the Tradition of Monastic Formation" (PhD diss., Lund University, 2007), 30–162, and Kalvesmaki, "Evagrius in the Byzantine Genre of Chapters," 261–263, with further references.

27   For an overview of previous scholarship, see Rubenson, "Formation and Re-Formations."

28   Rubenson, "Textual Fluidity in Early Monasticism," 180, with reference to Chiara Faraggiana di Sarzana, "*Apophthegmata Patrum*: Some Crucial Points of their Textual Transmission and the Problem of a Critical Edition," *StPatr* 30 (1997): 455–467.

continuous refashioning of sayings and collections also took place from early on in similar ways in other languages—Latin, Syriac, Georgian, Armenian, Arabic and Slavonic—adding further dimensions to an already complex pattern of transmission. We know something about the impact of these other traditions and their adaptions, especially for the Latin West,[29] but far less about how these traditions traveled within cultures and languages in the eastern Mediterranean, and how the sayings and the collections changed when entering these other linguistic spheres.[30] How this floating tradition of monastic wisdom traveled across the ancient Mediterranean, scholars are just beginning to learn.

2 This Book

This book journeys through late ancient wisdom traditions, from the monastic cradle of Egypt via manuscript fragments and folios, across linguistic and cultural barriers, through Jewish expressions of biblical wisdom, to Christian monastic sayings and Muslim interpretations. Particular attention is paid to the *Apophthegmata Patrum*, which is arguably the most important body of wisdom literature in the Christian world. Because early Christian wisdom literature often emerged from monastic communities, this book draws heavily on research regarding Christian monasticism and asceticism. How did wisdom change when traveling into and out of these contexts? Why? With what results? The following pages explore these questions and more. The book does not trace linear or chronological developments as much as it pursues the very processes of transition and adaption that took place.

The essays are divided into three sections: "Wisdom in Transmission" explores ways in which monastic traditions in Egypt and Palestine were transmitted. "Wisdom in Translation" focuses on linguistic border crossings. Finally, "Wisdom in Transition" engages exchanges between broader cultural and religious realms, through which wisdom entered multicultural conversations.

---

29 E.g., Hans-Oskar Weber, *Die Stellung des Johannes Cassianus zur ausserpachomianischen Mönchstradition: Eine Quellenuntersuchung* (Münster: Aschendorff, 1961).

30 For the collections of *Apophthegmata Patrum* in oriental languages, see Samuel Rubenson, "The Apophthegmata Patrum in Syriac, Arabic and Ethiopic: Status Questionis," *ParOr* 36 (2011): 319–328; Bo Holmberg, "The Syriac Collection of *Apophthegmata Patrum* in MS Sin. syr. 46," *StPatr* 55 (2013): 35–57; Jason Zaborowski, "Greek Thought, Arabic Culture: Approaching Arabic Recensions of the *Apophthegmata Patrum*," in *Monastic Education in Late Antiquity: The Transformation of Classical Paideia*, ed. Lillian I. Larsen and Samuel Rubenson (Cambridge: Cambridge University Press, 2018), 326–342.

Bibliography

Primary Sources

AP/G = *Apophthegmata Patrum. Greek Alphabetical Collection*. Ed. Jean Baptiste Cotelier, *Ecclesiae Graecae monumenta*. Vol. 1, pp. 338–712. Paris, 1677. Reprinted in PG 65 (1858), 71–440. English transl. John Wortley, *Give Me a Word: The Alphabetical Sayings of the Desert Fathers*. New York: St. Vladimir's Seminary Press, 2014.

Hereclitus. *Fragments*. Ed. Diels and W. Kranz, *Die Fragmente der Vorsokratiker*. 6th ed. Vol. 1, pp. 150–182. Berlin: Weidmann, 1951.

Plato. *Cratylus*. Ed. J. Burnet, *Platonis opera*. Vol. 1, pp. 383–440. Oxford: Clarendon, 1900.

Plutarch. *De E apud Delphos*. Ed. W. Sieveking, in *Plutarchi Moralia*. Vol. 3, pp. 1–24. Leipzig: Teubner, 1929.

Plutarch. *Aetia physica*. Ed. C. Hubert, in *Plutarchi Moralia*. 2nd ed. Vol. 5.3, pp. 1–26. Leipzig: Teubner, 1960.

Secondary Sources

Barns, John. "A New Gnomologium: With Some Remarks on Gnomic Anthologies (I)." *Classical Quarterly* 44 (1950): 126–137; 45 (1951):1–19.

Ben Amos, Dan. "Transmission." In *Folklore: An Encyclopedia of Beliefs, Customs, Tales, Music, and Art*, ed. Charlie T. McCormick and Kim Kennedy White, vol. 3, pp. 807–811. Santa Barbara: Clio, 1997.

Burton-Christie, Douglas. *The Word in the Desert: Scripture and the Quest for Holiness in Early Christian Monasticism*. Oxford: Oxford University Press, 1993.

Chadwick, Henry. *The Sentences of Sextus: A Contribution to the History of Early Christian Ethics*. Cambridge: Cambridge University Press, 2003.

Collins, John Joseph. *Jewish Wisdom in the Hellenistic Age*. Edinburgh: T&T Clark, 1997.

Faraggiana di Sarzana, Chiara. "*Apophthegmata Patrum*: Some Crucial Points of their Textual Transmission and the Problem of a Critical Edition." *StPatr* 30 (1997): 455–467.

Géhin, Paul. "Les collections de *kephalaia* monastiques: Naissance et succès d'un genre entre création originale, plagiat et florilège." In *Theologica minora: The Minor Genres of Byzantine Theological Literature*, ed. Antonio Rigo, 1–50. Turnhout: Brepols, 2013.

Gillingham Susan. "'I Will Incline My Ear to a Proverb; I Will Solve My Riddle to the Music of the Harp' (Psalm 49.4): The Wisdom Tradition and the Psalms." In *Perspectives on Israelite Wisdom: Proceedings of the Oxford Old Testament Seminar*, ed. J. Jarick, 277–309. London: Bloomsbury, 2016.

Goehring, James E. "Monastic Diversity and Ideological Boundaries in Fourth-Century Christian Egypt." *Journal of Early Christian Studies* 5 (1997): 79–82.

Gould, Graham. *The Desert Fathers on Monastic Community*. Oxford: Clarendon Press, 1993.

Graham, Daniel W. "Once More unto the Stream." In *Doctrine and Doxography: Studies on Heraclitus and Pythagoras*, ed. David Sider and Dirk Obbink, 303–320. Berlin: de Gruyter, 2013.

Gutas, Dimitri. "Classical Arabic Wisdom Literature: Nature and Scope." *Journal of the American Oriental Society* 101 (1975): 49–86.

Guy, Jean-Claude. "Educational Innovation in the Desert Fathers." *Eastern Churches Review* 6 (1974): 44–51.

Holmberg, Bo. "The Syriac Collection of *Apophthegmata Patrum* in MS Sin. syr. 46." *StPatr* 55 (2013), 35–57.

Ivánka, Endre von "ΚΕΦΑΛΑΙΑ: Eine byzantinische Literaturform und ihre antiken Wurzeln." *Byzantinische Zeitschrift* 47 (1954): 285–291.

Johnsén, Henrik Rydell. "Doctors, Teachers and Friends: Lower Egyptian Desert Elders and Late Antique Directors of Souls." In *Teachers in Late Antique Christianity*, ed. Peter Gemeinhardt, Olga Lorgeoux and Maria Munkholt Christensen, 184–205. Tübingen: Mohr Siebeck, 2018.

Johnsén, Henrik Rydell. "Reading John Climacus: Rhetorical Argumentation, Literary Convention and the Tradition of Monastic Formation." PhD diss., Lund University, 2007.

Johnsén, Henrik Rydell. "Repentance and Confession: Teaching in Ancient Philosophy and Early Monasticism." In *Pratiche didattiche tra centro e periferia nel Mediterraneo tardoantico: Atti del convegno di studio (Roma, 13–15 maggio 2015)*, ed. G. Agosti and D. Bianconi, 141–170. Spoleto: Fondazione CISAM, 2019.

Kalvesmaki, Joel. "Evagrius in the Byzantine Genre of Chapters." In *Evagrius and his Legacy*, ed. Joel Kalvesmaki and Robin Darling Young, 257–287. Notre Dame, IN: University of Notre Dame Press, 2016.

Kloppenborg, John S. *The Formation of Q: Trajectories in Ancient Wisdom Collections* Philadelphia: Fortress Press, 1987.

Larsen, Lillian I. "Ørkenfedrenes Apophthegmata og den klassiske Retoriske Tradisjon." *MCPL* 16 (2001): 26–35.

Larsen, Lillian I. "Pedagogical Parallels: Re-Reading the Apophthegmata Patrum." PhD diss., Columbia University, 2006.

Larsen, Lillian I. "The *Apophthegmata Patrum* and the Classical Rhetorical Tradition." *StPatr* 39 (2006): 409–415.

Larsen, Lillian I. "The Apophthegmata Patrum: Rustic Rumination or Rhetorical Recitation." *MCPL* 23 (2008): 21–30.

Larsen, Lillian I. "Early Monasticism and the Rhetorical Tradition: Sayings and Stories as Schooltexts." In *Education and Religion in Late Antiquity: Reflections, Social Contexts, and Genres*, ed. Peter Gemeinhardt and Peter Van Nuffelen, 13–33. London: Routledge, 2016.

Morgan, Teresa. *Literate Education in the Hellenistic and Roman Worlds*. Cambridge: Cambridge University Press, 1998.

Nightingale, Andrea W. "Sages, Sophists, and Philosophers: Greek Wisdom Literature." In *Literature in the Greek and Roman Worlds: A New Perspective*, ed. O. Taplin, 156–191. Oxford: Oxford University Press, 2000.

Pevarello, Daniele. *The Sentences of Sextus and the Origins of Christian Asceticism*. Tübingen: Mohr Siebeck, 2013.

Regnault, Lucien. "Les Apophtegmes en Palestine aux Ve–VIe siècles." *Irénikon* 54 (1981): 320–330.

Rubenson, Samuel. "Textual Fluidity in Early Monasticism: Sayings, Sermons and Stories." In *Snapshots of Evolving Traditions: Jewish and Christian Manuscript Culture, Textual Fluidity, and New Philology*, ed. Liv Ingeborg Lied and Hugo Lundhaug, 177–200. Berlin: de Gruyter, 2017.

Rubenson, Samuel. "The Apophthegmata Patrum in Syriac, Arabic and Ethiopic: Status Questionis." *ParOr* 36 (2011): 305–313.

Rubenson, Samuel. "The Formation and Re-Formations of the Sayings of the Desert Fathers." *StPatr* 55 (2013): 5–22.

Rubenson, Samuel. "Wisdom, Paraenesis and the Roots of Monasticism." In *Early Christian Paraenesis in Context*, ed. James Starr and Troels Engberg-Pedersen, 521–534. Berlin: de Gruyter, 2005.

Stewart, Columba. "Evagrius Ponticus on Monastic Pedagogy." In *Abba: The Tradition of Orthodoxy in the West (Festschrift for Bishop Kallistos of Diokleia)*, ed. Andrew Louth et al., 241–271. Crestwood, NY: St. Vladimir's Seminary Press, 2003.

Tropper, Amram. *Wisdom, Politics, and Historiography: Tractate Avot in the Context of the Graeco-Roman Near East*. Oxford: Oxford University Press, 2004.

Volpi, Franco, et al. "Wisdom." In *Brill's New Pauly* (online). Leiden: Brill, 2006.

Weber, Hans-Oskar. *Die Stellung des Johannes Cassianus zur ausserpachomianischen Mönchstradition: Eine Quellenuntersuchung*. Münster: Aschendorff, 1961.

Wilken, Robert L. "Wisdom and Philosophy in Early Christianity." In *Aspects of Wisdom in Judaism and Early Christianity*, ed. Robert L. Wilken, 143–168. Notre Dame, IN: University of Notre Dame Press, 1975.

Wilson, Walter T. *The Sentences of Sextus*. Atlanta: Society of Biblical Literature, 2012.

Wilson, Walter T. *The Mysteries of Righteousness: The Literary Composition and Genre of the Sentences of Pseudo-Phocylides*. Tübingen: Mohr Siebeck, 1994.

Wilson, Walter T. *The Sentences of Pseudo-Phocylides*. Berlin: de Gruyter, 2005.

Young, Frances. "Wisdom in the Apostolic Fathers and the New Testament." In *Trajectories Through the New Testament and the Apostolic Fathers*, ed. Andrew F. Gregory and C.M. Tuckett, 85–104. Oxford: Oxford University Press, 2005.

Zaborowski, Jason. "Greek Thought, Arabic Culture: Approaching Arabic Recensions of the *Apophthegmata Patrum*." In *Monastic Education in Late Antiquity: The Transformation of Classical Paideia*, ed. Lillian I. Larsen and Samuel Rubenson, 326–342. Cambridge: Cambridge University Press, 2018.

PART 1

Wisdom in Transmission: Egypt and Palestine

∴

CHAPTER 1

Wisdom in Fragments: The Earliest Manuscript of the First Greek *Life* of St Pachomius

Peter Toth

Studying unidentified fragments is like hunting in an unknown forest: anything can be found, but still nothing achieved. The most puzzling pieces can eventually turn out to be mediocre witnesses of well-known texts, unsolvable mysteries, or unique survivals of long-lost works. It was with this mixed fascination that I embarked upon the study of two recently acquired Greek items in the British Library, described in the *Catalogue* as ninth-century fragments "possibly from the *Apophthegmata Patrum*."[1]

Since—apart from one single codex in the Protaton Monastery on Mount Athos and some scattered palimpsest pages elsewhere—there are no ninth-century manuscripts surviving of any Greek versions of the *Apophthegmata Patrum*,[2] I was hoping to enrich the Lund Database of Monastic Paideia with a new and fascinating text. What I found in the fragments, however, was not the *Sayings* of the desert fathers, but sections from the *Life* of one them, Pachomius of Tabennesi. The following paper contains a presentation, edition, and evaluation of the newly identified fragments, and places them in the context of the transmission of the Greek monastic literature of Egypt.

---

1 *The British Library Catalogue of Additions to the Manuscripts. New Series, 1986–1990* (London: British Library, 1993), 601–604. Reprinted in Tom Pattie and Scot McKendrick, eds., *Summary Catalogue of Greek Manuscripts* (London: British Library, 1999), 276–277.
2 The earliest extant manuscript of the Greek *Apophthegmata Patrum*, and the only one written in uncials, is the systematic collection in MS Protaton 86, dating from the ninth century. See Jean-Claude Guy, *Recherches sur la tradition grecque des Apophthegmata Patrum*, SubsHag 36 (Brussels: Société des Bollandistes, 1962), 120, and the detailed study by Britt Dahlman and Per Rönnegård, *Paradiset. Ökenfädernas tänkespråk: Den systematiska samlingen 8; Om att inte göra något för syns skull* (Sturefors: Silentium, 2017). For two eighth-century folios in Athens (National Library MS 842), see Zisis Melissakis, "Οἱ Παλίμψηστοι Κώδικες Τῆς Ἑλληνικῆς Βιβλιοθήκης Τῆς Ἑλλάδος. Προκαταρτικὰ Συμπεράσματα Μιᾶς "Ερευνας," *Σύμμεικτα* 16 (2013): 191–192. For two further folios from the ninth century in Grottaferrata (Biblioteca Statale del Monumento Nazionale fonds principal A. δ. 004 (gr. 095), fols. 73, 89), see Edoardo Crisci, *I palinsesti di Grottaferrata: Studio codicologico e paleografico* (Naples: Edizioni Scientifiche Italiane, 1990), 66–67.

1   The Fragments

Today, the two fragments constitute folios 84 and 85 of a bound collection of fragments, a volume now inventoried as manuscript BL Add MS 70516 (Figures 1.1 and 1.2). They are not more than the lower half of two parchment folios of the original manuscript, with fol. 84 measuring 180 × 160 mm, and fol. 85 measuring 160 × 160 mm respectively. The ruling system, as far as it is visible on fol. 85^r, is the very common type 20C1 of Leroy, with an interlinear distance of 7 mm shown clearly by prickings on the left-hand margin of fol. 85^r. Lines usually have about 25 letters. Calculated on the basis of the amount of text missing between the end of the *recto* and first legible lines of the *verso*, pages may have contained thirty lines on average. As the surviving portion of the folios preserves 17–18 complete lines—approximately half of the original text space, covering an area of about 120 mm in height—the full height of the text on the page was probably twice as large, that is about 240 mm, which, together with the margins, means that the manuscript would have been an average-sized book of 250/260 × 160 mm.

The script of the Greek text is the characteristic sloping majuscule of the ninth century, which is rather hard to date and localize precisely. The script appears very close to majuscule scripts such as BL Add MS 26113, an eight- or ninth-century liturgical codex from Sinai,[3] and the famous Paris manuscript of the *Corpus Dionysiacum* (Paris Gr. 437) dating from about 827.[4]

In contrast to the heavy and bulky shapes of the Oriental form of the sloping majuscules, manifested in BL Add MS 26113, however, the general *ductus* of the script of the fragments seems a bit lighter.[5] This feature, along with the angle of its slope (about 110°–113°)—a feature often used to localize this script[6]—brings it closer to Constantinopolitan examples. In addition to Paris Gr. 437 and 510 (the latter a famous illuminated copy of the homilies of Gregory of Nazianzus),

---

3   There is a striking similarity between how the letter ξ is written in the two manuscripts. See the online images of Add MS 26113, accessed 29 September 2019, http://www.bl.uk/manuscripts/Viewer.aspx?ref=add_ms_26113_fs001r. Evaluation with literature in Pasquale Orsini, "La maiuscola ogivale inclinata: contributo preliminare," *Scripta* 9 (2016): 90.
4   For this most famous witness of the Dionysian corpus, see the online images of Paris Grec. 437, https://gallica.bnf.fr/ark:/12148/btv1b6000953x, and the survey of literature by Orsini, "La maiuscola ogivale inclinata," 107–108.
5   For the Oriental type of the sloping majuscule, see Dieter Harlfinger, "Beispiele der Maiuscula ogivalis inclinata vom Sinai und aus Damaskus," in *Alethes Philia: Studi in onore di Giancarlo Prato*, Collectanea 23 (Spoleto: Centro italiano di studi sull' alto medioevo, 2010), 461–477.
6   See Guglielmo Cavallo, "Funzione e strutture della maiuscola greca tra i secoli VIII–XI," in *La paléographie grecque et byzantine: Paris, 21–25 octobre 1974* (Paris: Éditions du Centre national de la recherche scientifique, 1977), 95–137. A recent review in Orsini, "La maiuscola ogivale inclinata," 107–108.

both from Constantinople, the script of the fragments shows similarity to an undated ninth-century manuscript of the homilies of St Basil the Great (Vat. Gr. 428), which is also generally located to Constantinople.[7] Thus we are probably not mistaken if, on the basis of their script, we date the two fragments to the first half or the middle of the ninth century and assume that the manuscript which they derive from may also have been of Constantinopolitan origin.

The fragments bear clear signs of having been folded in half, probably to support the binding of a book or a manuscript. Reuse of the parchment sheets presumably took place in a Greek-speaking area. There are scattered notes in Greek on each side of the two fragments, surrounding but never touching the text. There are also a number of doodles preserved on the margins, one of them even coloured (fol. 84^r, see Figure 1.2).

The notes consist of pen trials experimenting with the alphabet (fol. 84^r, upper left hand side, see Figure 1.2) or the letter α (fol. 85^r, upper right hand corner, see Figure 1.1), and are not very helpful for tracing provenance. The only longer note with some coherent text is on fol. 84^v (see Figure 1.3), but—despite my repeated efforts—I have been unable to decipher it. As these later notes, pen trials, and drawings are present on both sides of each fragment, on the lower margin as well as across the side margins of the pages, we can assume that the two leaves probably served as flyleaves in a bound volume in which both sides of the fragments would have been accessible to write on.

2   The Origin of the Fragments

There is no apparent information about the book that used to preserve the fragments. The two leaves are currently bound in a volume comprising some ninety manuscript fragments, five of them in Greek, and the remaining ones in Latin or English. The volume forms part of a large collection, known today as the Portland Papers, which was offered to the British Library by the Portland family from their estate at Welbeck Abbey (Nottinghamshire) in lieu of Capital Transfer Tax in 1967.[8]

The volume preserving the fragments still bears the heraldic bookplate of William Arthur Cavendish-Bentinck (1857–1943), the 6th Duke of Portland.

---

7 For this manuscript and its Constantinopolitan provenance, see Orsini, "La maiuscola ogivale inclinata," 115, n. 10, with extensive bibliography, and the online images of Vat. Gr. 428, accessed 29 September 2019, https://digi.vatlib.it/view/MSS_Vat.gr.428.
8 On the Portland Papers in general, see R.J. Olney, "The Portland Papers," *The Archives* 19 (1989): 78–87.

There are a number of notes accompanying some of the fragments, offering information on their text, date, and origin. These notes, dating from the early 1930s, are all signed by a certain E. Lobel from Oxford, who is probably the Romanian-born papyrologist Edgar Lobel (1888–1982), curator of the Bodleian Library. Lobel was probably approached by the duke or his librarian to provide information on the fragments in their collection. It was Lobel who, on a little label preserved next to the two Greek fragments, described them as remains of a ninth-century manuscript of the *Apophthegmata Patrum*, which seems to have served as the basis of the description in the British Library's printed catalogues.

The fact that Lobel provided information about almost all the fragments collected in the volume around the same time, indicates that the librarian at Welbeck Abbey may have found them all in the Portland collection (probably unbound). In an attempt to arrange the fragments, the librarian may have asked Lobel to identify and date them before they were bound in a volume. This apparently occurred some time between the 1930s, the date of Lobel's notes, and 1943, when the 6th Duke, whose bookplate is found on the inside cover of the volume, died.

The family collection of the Dukes of Portland in Welbeck Abbey is one of the largest and most diverse aristocratic collections in Britain. It comprises not only private papers of the family and their estates, but also medieval charters and manuscripts, and a large corpus of documents illustrating the history of the famous Harley collection of manuscripts housed now at the British Library. In addition to a number of letters and papers by Robert Harley, 1st Earl of Oxford, and his son Edward Harley, the 2nd Earl of Oxford, owners and collectors of the Harleian manuscripts, the papers also preserve a considerable amount of material from Harley's famous librarian, Humfrey Wanley (1672–1726).[9]

In addition to Wanley's family papers (including letters to his wife, a family Bible etc.), the Portland Papers also contain his extensive correspondence with Robert Harley and various bookdealers in London and Europe. These documents illustrate Wanley's efforts to expand the Harley collection in various ways and directions.

Wanley's letters also testify to his keen interest in fragments of manuscripts. As early as 1698, he applied to the curators of the Bodleian Library for permission to remove fragments of manuscripts from the bindings of printed volumes for further study.[10] In a letter from 1699 he indicated that he owned a large col-

---

9   Clyve Jones, "The Harley Family and the Harley Papers," *The British Library Journal* 15 (1989): 128–130.
10 This letter was also preserved in the Portland Papers and was first edited and discussed by

lection of fragments, "some hundreds of such pieces and leaves," which were mainly supplied to him by one of the most notorious collectors of fragments, John Bagford (1650–1716).[11]

Bagford was an amateur scholar endeavouring to publish a full history of printing in England and Europe illustrated with an extensive collection of specimens. In his quest for examples of printing, he collected a number of important manuscript fragments, too. These he incorporated either in specimen collections of manuscripts or in volumes comprising printed material.

Wanley knew about Bagford's specimens of manuscripts because Bagford often contacted him for advice on his pieces. It is from one of these letters from Bagford to Wanley that we know that Bagford found and collected Greek fragments too.[12] Surprisingly, none of Bagford's extant volumes, neither those later acquired by Wanley for the Harley collection and now held at the British Library, nor the ones preserved elsewhere seem to contain any Greek fragments today.[13]

The most plausible explanation for their absence is provided by another letter from Wanley to Bagford, written in 1699. Here, Wanley, answering another query from Bagford about a Greek fragment, explicitly "entreats" him to send the fragment to him together with "all the Greek Fragments you can meet with."[14]

The fact that this may have happened, and that Bagford had probably sent his Greek fragments to Wanley, is confirmed by Bagford's autograph account-book where he records the transfer of various "Greek specimens" to Wanley in

---

Milton McC. Gatch, "Humfrey Wanley's Proposal to the Curators of the Bodleian Library on the Usefulness of Manuscript Fragments from Bindings," *Bodleian Library Record* 11 (1983): 94–98. It was later republished in Wanely's collected letters by Peter Heyworth, *Letters of Humfrey Wanley: Palaeographer, Anglo-Saxonist, Librarian, 1672–1726; With an Appendix of Documents* (Oxford: Clarendon, 1989), 479–480.

11 See Letter 63 (25 June 1699) in Heyworth, *Letters of Humfrey Wanley*, 123–124.

12 See Letter 39 in his edited collection from 1697, where he writes about a "shred of Greek" sent to him by Bagford, which he returned two months later (accompanied by Letter 42) to Bagford. The letters are published in Heyworth, *Letters of Humfrey Wanley*, 75–77.

13 For a survey on Bagford's fragments in the Harley collection, see Cyril Ernest Wright, *Fontes Harleiani: A Study of the Sources of the Harleian Collection of Manuscripts Preserved in the Department of Manuscripts in the British Museum*, British Museum Bicentenary Publications (London: The Trustees of the British Museum, 1972), 478–479. For other repositories, see Milton McC. Gatch, "John Bagford as a Collector and Disseminator of Manuscript Fragments," *The Library*, 6th ser., 7/2 (1985): 95–114, and Milton McC. Gatch, *"Fragmenta manuscripta* and *varia* at Missouri and Cambridge," *Transactions of the Cambridge Bibliographical Society* 9 (1990): 434–475.

14 Letter 56, in Heyworth, *Letters of Humfrey Wanley*, 110.

1706.[15] Whether these fragments were incorporated later in the Harley collection, together with many of Bagford's bound specimen collections, or became part of Wanley's private holdings is uncertain. However, we know from Wanley himself that, already by 1699, he had acquired a considerable collection of "some hundreds of such pieces and leaves" from Bagford.[16] Here he writes that he was planning to place them "in a book according to their Age, and the Countrey wherein they were written" and use it as a practical palaeographic manual for his own research.[17]

Whether this volume was ever produced is unsure, and some scholars even doubt the very survival of Wanley's fragments.[18] But since none of the relatively large number of *fragmenta manuscripta* relatable to Bagford seem to contain Greek fragments, and since the Greek and other fragments in BL Add MS 70516 were preserved together with Wanley's personal documents in the Portland Papers, it appears likely that the two Greek folios, along with the other Greek, Latin, and English fragments bound in the volume, were part of Wanley's own personal collection of what he called "shreads and scraps of parchment" that he had acquired either from Bagford or through his own personal research in bookbindings at the Bodleian Library in Oxford.

Identifying the actual source of the two fragments, that is the very book that preserved them, however, is very difficult. In an undated note from the early 1700s, Bagford records that by then he had looked through "most of the great Libraries that have been sold by Auction since the year 1686." Moreover, he was also granted

> opportunity in looking over such vast quantities of old books and not only in Sales but in the shop of ... Mr Christopher Bateman, who at all times hath given me the liberty of looking over when he hath bought any parcels, and for his time he hath had more good and Valuable books pass through his hands than all the Book-sellers in England. Besides he always gave me notice when he had any waste books to sell and freely gave me Liberty to take out of them what I thought fit, as the blank leaves at the beginning of them, old pieces of MSS. etc.[19]

---

15   London, British Library, Harley MS 5998, fol. 24ᵛ.
16   See note 11 above.
17   See his letter to Samuel Peps (24 June 1699, no. 63 in the collection), published in Heyworth, *Letters of Humfrey Wanley*, 120–131, 123–124.
18   Gatch, "John Bagford as a Collector and Disseminator of Manuscript Fragments," 97.
19   This report forms part of Bagford's undated note on the use of various inks in printing, preserved in his collected autographs in British Library, Harley MS 5910, vol. 3, fol. 120, and

Amongst this massive amount of material which Bagford went through from 1686 until his death in 1716, it is almost impossible to identify the book that once contained the two ninth-century Greek fragments.

The identification of the volume would be slightly more promising if the Greek fragments were found by Wanley himself during his own investigations at the Bodleian. However, although his 1698 application to pursue this research in the library seems to have been approved by the curators, there is no evidence that his proposal was ever put into effect.[20]

At present, therefore, one can only propose that the two Greek sheets were probably removed from their original manuscript somewhere in the Greek-speaking Mediterranean, as indicated by the Greek pen trials preserved on them. They were reused as flyleaves in the front and back cover of a (presumably printed) book. Later, this book reached England where, either at one of the London book sales of the late seventeenth or early eighteenth century, or, somewhat less likely, at the Bodleian Library in Oxford, the two fragments were removed from the binding and included in Humfrey Wanley's private collection of manuscript specimens. As his planned palaeographical handbook probably never realized, the fragments would have been left unbound amongst Wanley's personal papers, which later became part of the Portland collection. It was there that the librarians of the 6th Duke of Portland found them in the early 1930s. After seeking advice from Edgar Lobel, the librarians bound them, together with the other ninety fragments similarly found, into the large folio volume donated to the British Library in 1967 as part of the Portland Papers which eventually became Add MS 70516.

3   The Text

As mentioned above, Lobel's first impression of the fragments, an opinion later incorporated in the British Library's printed catalogues, was that the fragments contain a Greek monastic text from Egypt, "possibly from the *Apophthegmata Patrum*." The text preserved on the two ninth-century fragments is indeed a monastic text, but not the *Apophthegmata Patrum*. Instead, it turns out to preserve portions of an even rarer text: the first Greek version (*Vita prima*) of the *Life* of St Pachomius, with fol. 85 containing passages from §§ 53–54 and fol. 84 from §§ 65–67.

---

was published by Robert Steele, "John Bagford's Own Account of his Collection of Title-Pages," *The Library*, n. s., 8 (1907): 224.

20 Gatch, "*Fragmenta manuscripta* and *varia*," 443.

4 The Greek Lives of St Pachomius

The various *Lives* of St Pachomius form one of the most complex groups of monastic hagiographies that have come down to us from Late Antiquity. In addition to a number of *apophthegmata*[21] and a series of anecdotes arranged in a collection termed *Paralipomena* by its seventeenth-century editor,[22] the history of Pachomius and his monastic community survives in a large variety of biographies preserved in Coptic (Sahidic and Bohairic alike), Arabic, Syriac, and Greek.[23] The intertwined connections between these versions and recensions have long been debated in scholarship.[24] After painstaking analyses of generations of scholars, the current view, based mainly on Armand Veilleux's textual comparisons, is that the earliest version of Pachomius's life, which does not survive today, can be reconstructed from the consensus of the Arabic and Coptic (Bohairic) versions, and the so-called first Greek Life, the *Vita prima*.[25]

The Greek *Vita prima* (G1), thus named by its first editor Daniel Papebroch in 1680,[26] is one of six different Greek versions of the *Life* of St Pachomius. Apart from later Byzantine compilations known as G3, G4, G5, and G6, the two earliest and most important Greek versions of Pachomius's life are G1 and G2.[27]

G2, the *Vita altera*, is by far the most widespread and popular account of the history of Pachomius. Preserved in a relatively large number of manuscripts,

---

[21] Sayings related to Pachomius in the various versions of the *Apophthegmata Patrum* have been surveyed and analysed by Louis Théophile Lefort, *Les vies coptes de saint Pachôme et de ses premiers successeurs*, Bibliothèque du Muséon 16 (Louvain: Bureaux du Muséon, 1943), xxiv–xxvii; and Veilleux, *Liturgie*, 113–114.

[22] First published by Daniel Papebroch in *Acta Sanctorum Maii*, vol. 3 (1680), 51–62, and later by François Halkin, *Sancti Pachomii vitae graecae*, SubsHag 19 (Brussels: Société des Bollandistes, 1932), 122–165.

[23] A full list of text editions is provided by Armand Veilleux, *Pachomian Koinonia*, vol. 1, *The Life of Saint Pachomius and his Disciples*, CSS 45 (Kalamazoo, MI: Cistercian Publications, 1980), 477–480.

[24] A sharp-eyed overview of the century-long debate can be found in Philip Rousseau, *Pachomius: The Making of a Community in Fourth-Century Egypt* (Berkeley: University of California Press, 1985), 37–55. For an earlier, very concise presentation of the *status quo*, see Jozef Vergote, "La valeur des vies grecques et coptes de S. Pakhôme," *OLP* 8 (1977): 175–186.

[25] A full presentation of the thesis in Veilleux, *Liturgie*, 17–107. A revised and much shorter English version is available in his *Pachomian Koinonia*, vol. 1, pp. 1–21.

[26] *Acta Sanctorum Maii*, vol. 3 (1680), 25–51.

[27] A complete survey of the manuscripts and the interconnection of the later Greek *Lives* of St Pachomius (G3–G6) is found in Halkin, *Vitae graecae*, 62–88. For a reappraisal, see Veilleux, *Liturgie*, 32–35.

excerpts, and reworkings, its textual tradition goes back to the ninth century, and is represented by a manuscript in the Vatopedi Monastery on Mount Athos.[28] Although this codex contains only two larger portions of the *Vita altera* (§§ 1–13 and 88–90),[29] the history of the text can be traced back even further, to the sixth century, as it seems to be the basis of the Latin *Life*, a translation by the one of the most prolific translators of the period, Dionysius Exiguus (d. 567 CE).[30] The interconnection of these two texts, G2 and Dionysius's Latin version, has long puzzled scholars. They gave priority either to Dionysius, claiming that his text (or its Greek *Vorlage*) was reworked by the author of G2, or to G2, considering it as the hypothetical exemplar of Dionysius's version.[31] Whichever of these two hypotheses is correct, the present consensus is that both G2 and Dionysius's Latin text are based on material borrowed from an even earlier recension: the *Vita prima*.

5 The Greek *Vita Prima*

Compared to the Coptic (SBo) and Arabic lives (Am and Ag), the Greek *Vita prima* seems to be a compilation made from the same material that underlies the Oriental versions. It is based on a hypothetical composition (termed ξ), possibly written in Coptic, which unites an earlier and shorter Coptic *Life* of Pachomius (the so-called *Vita brevis*) with the Coptic *Life* of Theodorus (*Vita Theodori*). Translating this double biography into Greek, the translator complemented his text with information borrowed from the *Paralipomena* and the *Rule of Pachomius*.[32] Despite its general overlap with the Coptic and Arabic versions, the Greek *Vita prima* preserves material that is unique to it and absent from all other versions.[33] It is, therefore, an important and, being the main

---

28 Vatopedi Monastery, MS 84, fols. 65ʳ–70ᵛ. It is dated to the eleventh century by Halkin, *Vitae graecae*, 44. It was re-dated to the turn of 9/10th century in the new catalogue by Erich Lamberz, *Katalog der griechischen Handschriften des Athosklosters Vatopedi*, vol. 1, *Codices 1–102* (Thessaloniki, 2006), 353–357.
29 As the manuscript has no damaged or missing folios, the gap is probably due to the incomplete exemplar used by the scribe. Cf. Halkin, *Vitae graecae*, 44.
30 Edition by H. van Cranenburgh, *La vie latine de Saint Pachôme traduite du grec par Denys le Petit*, SubsHag 46 (Brussels: Société des Bollandistes, 1969).
31 For a detailed comparison of G2 with the Latin version, see Lefort, *Les vies coptes*, xxvii–xxxviii; Derwas J. Chitty, "Pachomian Sources Reconsidered," *JEH* 5 (1954): 55–59; Veilleux, *Liturgie*, 28–32; Veilleux, *Pachomian Koinonia*, vol. 1, pp. 12–14.
32 See the detailed explication and stemma in Veilleux, *Liturgie*, 83–107.
33 Short discussion of this material in Veilleux, *Liturgie*, 93.

source of the sixth-century G2 and—indirectly—of all later Greek versions, also a very early account of Pachomius's life.

The *Vita prima*, apparently the earliest of the extant Greek *Lives* of Pachomius, has come down to us in surprisingly few manuscripts. According to François Halkin's survey in his critical edition of the Greek biographies,[34] it is preserved in two recensions: an earlier, less sophisticated text in a very simple, almost vulgar Greek (G1a), represented by one single manuscript now at the Biblioteca Laurenziana in Florence,[35] and a revised and polished version thereof (G1b), preserved in an early-eleventh-century manuscript in Athens,[36] as well as in a later and very fragmentary copy at the Ambrosiana in Milan.[37] A common feature of these two recensions of the *Vita prima* is that they both survive as part of the same corpus of Pachomian texts that comprises the *Vita prima*, the *Letter of Ammon to Theophilus*, and Theophilus's reply, followed by the *Rule of Pachomius* and the *Paralipomena*, named *Ascetica* in the manuscripts.[38]

This structure of the corpus, shared by all three manuscripts, suggests that the two recensions G1a and G1b belong together, and that G1b is a revised and

---

34 Halkin, *Vitae graecae*, 10–18.
35 Florence, Biblioteca Medicea Laurenziana, Plut. XI. 9, described in Angelo Maria Bandini, *Fasciculus rerum graecarum ecclesiarum* (Florence, 1763), 123–133, and idem, *Catalogus codicum manuscriptorum Bibliothecae Mediceae Laurentianae*, vol. 1 (Florence, 1764), 502–507. It was also described by Albert Ehrhard, *Überlieferung und Bestand der hagiographischen und homiletischen Literatur der griechischen Kirche von den Anfängen bis zum Ende des 16. Jahrhunderts*, vol. 3, TU 52 (Leipzig: J.C. Hinrichs, 1952), 938–940.
36 Athens, National Library (EBE), MS 1015, described first by Ehrhard, *Überlieferung und Bestand*, vol. 3, pp. 903–904; see also François Halkin, *Catalogue des manuscrits hagiographiques de la Bibliothèque nationale d'Athènes*, SubsHag 66 (Brussels: Société des Bollandistes, 1983), 84–85.
37 Milan, Biblioteca Ambrosiana, D 69 sup. (third quarter of the fourteenth cent.), described by Cesare Pasini, *Inventario agiografico dei manoscritti greci dell'Ambrosiana*, SubsHag 84 (Brussels: Société des Bollandistes, 2003), 56–57. The *Life of Pachomius* is found on fols. 1–21 of the manuscript, but due to an early damage these leaves are mixed up and some folios are missing. As a result, there are only three portions of the *Life* preserved in this manuscript (§§ 33–54, 72–93, 143–150). For a reconstruction, see Halkin, *Vitae graecae*, 12, and Pasini, *Inventario agiografico*, 56.
38 A hitherto unrecorded manuscript of G1a has recently been identified at the Ecclesiastical Historical and Archival Institute of the Bulgarian Patriarchate in Sofia MS 839, ff. 287v–289r. The manuscript, an ascetic florilegium from the 13th century, apparently preserves a portion of the G1a recension of the Vita Prima as recorded in the catalogue by Dimitar Getov (*A Catalogue of the Greek Manuscripts at the Ecclesiastical Historical and Archival Institute of the Patriarchate of Bulgaria. I, Bačkovo Monastery*, Turnhout, Brepols, 2014, 149). I am currently working on the evaluation of this witness.

refined version of G1a. The connection between the two recensions of the *Life* was found so close by Halkin that, in his critical edition of the *Vita prima*, he created a composite text based on the two branches. Prioritizing variants of the Florence manuscript, he emendated its scribal errors and *lacunae* with readings taken from the Ambrosianus.[39] Due to some difficulties with acquiring microfilms from Athens, Halkin was unable to consult the Atheniensis in his 1932 edition of the *Vita prima*, so its readings are not incorporated into the critical apparatus. It was exactly 50 years later that he could finally fill this gap, and published a full edition of the Pachomian corpus of the Atheniensis in 1982.[40] This new edition, in addition to the fact that it provides us with a complete text of the entire corpus from this early-eleventh-century manuscript, makes it obvious that Ambrosianus and Atheniensis preserve the very same G1b recension of the *Vita prima* which is a later, reworked and more sophisticated version of G1a, as known from the Florence manuscript.

The earliest version of the earliest Greek *Life* of Pachomius (G1a), therefore, is apparently preserved in one single manuscript, the Florence Laurentianus XI.9 (F). This manuscript contains a monastic-ascetical collection of hagiographic, ascetical, and homiletical pieces in a rather random, and definitely not calendric order. According to various subscriptions in the manuscript (on fols. 103^v, 129^r, 282^v), the codex was copied by two scribes: Esaias copied its first half (fols. 1–215^r) and Lukas the second (fols. 215^v–282^r).[41] In his autograph note in form of a crucifix on fol. 282^v, Lukas explicitly dates the completion of his part of the manuscript to 6529 (= 1020/21 AD) and names Isidore, the abbot of the Monastery of St John in Apiro in Italy, as the commissioner of his work.[42] As Lukas's part follows that of Esaias in the manuscript, we can safely assume that the entire volume was written in Italy during the first quarter of the eleventh century and remains there until today.[43]

---

39 Between fols. 167 and 168 there are two leaves missing from the Florentinus, comprising §§ 31–34, which are fortunately preserved amongst the fragments of the Ambrosianus, and Halkin took the text of the missing portions from that manuscript.
40 François Halkin, *Le corpus athénien de saint Pachôme* (Geneva: P. Cramer, 1982).
41 For an attempt to identify Lukas, see Kurt Weitzmann, *Die byzantinische Buchmalerei des 9. und 10. Jahrhunderts* (Berlin 1935, reprint Vienna: Verlag der österreichischen Akademie der Wissenschaften, 1996), 86–87.
42 A full reproduction of this colophon is published in Bandini, *Fasciculus*, 132, and Bandini, *Catalogus codicum*, vol. 1, p. 506.
43 According to a note on fol. 198^v, the manuscript was sold in 1385 to a certain monk Ambrosius from Rhegino in Calabria. For a detailed presentation of the manuscript, see the description by M. Vicario in Sebastiano Gentile, ed., *Oriente cristiano e santità: Figure e storie di santi tra Bisanzio e l'Occidente* (Milan: Centro Tibaldi, 1998), 212–216.

The earliest version of the Greek *Lives* of Pachomius (G1a), preserved on folios 163ʳ–183ᵛ of F and copied by the monk Esaias some time before Lukas completed his part in 1020/21, is a rather crude text. As early as the seventeenth century, François Tillemont was already horrified by its Greek, which he found "full of obscurities, not to say barbaric."[44]

This peculiar feature of the language of G1a has been interpreted in various ways afterwards. Theodore Lefort and René Draguet regarded it as a manifestation of "Copticisms" in the Greek text, which they took as proof that the text is a translation of a Coptic original.[45] André-Jean Festugière, however, interpreted it as a marker of the specific Greek linguistic milieu in which the author created his work, which, in many ways, is represented by other Greek monastic texts of Egypt, such as the *Apophthegmata*.[46]

It is this early version G1a, hitherto known only from the early-eleventh-century Florence manuscript, that the two newly identified ninth-century leaves of the British Library represent. The edition of the two fragments below makes it very clear that the text they preserve is not only identical with G1a, as we know it from F, but also that the clumsy text of G1a is an independent recension of its own and not the result of errors by the incapable or uneducated scribe responsible for copying F or its *Vorlage*. Apart from some occasional, very obvious spelling mistakes, the text of the fragments corresponds closely to F: the BL fragments agree with F in each and every case where it differs from G1b. In order to highlight the position of the fragments in the textual history of G1, I have compared their text to both F and to G1b. I place the variants in the apparatus, using F for readings in Florence Laurentianus XI.9 and G1b for the shared readings of Atheniensis 1015 and Ambrosianus D 69sup. In order to make the text comprehensible, I have provided the missing text of the fragments from F in brackets set with smaller characters.

---

44   Sébastien Le Nain de Tillemont, *Mémoires pour servir à l'histoire ecclésiastique des six premiers siècles*, vol. 7 (Paris, 1700), 169: "beaucoup d'obscurite, pour ne pas dire de barbarie."
45   Lefort, *Vies coptes*, xliii–xlvi, and René Draguet, "Un morceau grec inédit des vies de Pachôme apparié à un texte d'Evagre en partie inconnu," *Le Muséon* 70 (1957): 277–279.
46   André-Jean Festugière, *Les moines d'Orient*, vol. 4/2, *La première vie grecque de saint Pachôme* (Paris: Cerf, 1965), 125–157.

6   Edition of the British Library Fragments

Fol. 85ᵛ (= *Sancti Pachomii Vita prima* § 53)[47]

ἦν γὰρ [τὸ σῶμα ἔχων ὀστοῦν μό-]
νον [τῷ χρόνῳ τῆς κακώσεως, καὶ μήπω θανέντος αὐτῷ, λέγει τινὶ Ἀδελφῷ· Κρατῶν με ἀπάγαγε πρὸς τὸν πατέρα ἡμῶν] Παχού-
[μιον. Καὶ πλησιάσας ἔρριψεν ἐπὶ]
πρόσωπον ἑαυτόν, λέγων τὴν
αἰτίαν.ᵃ Καὶ κατανοήσαςᵇ αὐτὸν
ἄξιον εἶναιᶜ τοῦ αἰτήματος ἀ-
νεστέναξεν. Καὶ τῇ ὥρᾳ τοῦ
φαγεῖν τοὺς ἀδελφοὺςᵈ καὶ αὐτῷ
ἠνέχθη, καθὼς πᾶσιν, τό τι ἂν
φάγοι.ᵉ Καὶᶠ μὴ φαγὼν λέγει· Προ-
σωποληπται, ποῦ τὸ γεγραμμέ-
νον, Ἀγαπήσεις τὸν πλησίον σου
ὡς σεαυτόν;ᵍ Οὐχ ὁρᾶτε τοῦτον
νεκρὸν ὄντα; διάτι ὅλως πρὸ
τοῦ αἰτῆσαι αὐτὸν οὐκ ἐφρον-
τίσατε αὐτοῦ ἀξίως; καὶ ζη-
τήσαντοςʰ αὐτοῦ τὸ αἴτημα

ᵃ τὸ αἴτημα G1b   ᵇ οὖν ὁ μέγας G1b   ᶜ ὄντα G1b   ᵈ τοὺς ἀδελφοὺς *om.* G1b   ᵉ τό τι ἂν φάγοι *om.* G1b   ᶠ Ὁ δὲ πατὴρ ἡμῶν G1b   ᵍ ἑαυτὸν F   ʰ Καὶ εἰπόντα G1b

---

47   As the text has not been identified previously, the foliation of the fragments does not reflect the actual position of the leaves in the original manuscript. It begins with fol. 85 and continues with fol. 84. Moreover, the text begins on the *verso* of fol. 85, so that the present fol. 85ʳ is the *verso*, and fol. 85ᵛ the *recto* of the original leaf.

Fol. 85ʳ (= *Sancti Pachomii Vita prima* §§ 53–54)

[διά τί παρεβλέψατε αὐτόν; Ἀλλ᾽ ἐρεῖτε, ὅτι, ἐπειδὴ μὴ ὄντος ἔθους τροφῆς τοιαύτης, ὑπερίδομεν αὐτόν. Οὐκ ἔστιν οὖν διαφορὰ νόσου; οὐ πάντα καθαρὰ τοῖς καθαροῖς; Κἂν οὐκ ἠδυνήθητε διακρῖναι, ὅτι καλὸν τοῦτο διχᾷ γνώμης ἡμῶν, διά τί οὐκ ἐδηλώσατέ μοι; Καὶ ταῦτα λέγων ἐδάκρυσεν· ἀεὶ γὰρ σημεῖον αἰσ]θή
[σεως δάκρυα. Κἂν ᾖ τις αἰσθ]ανόμε-
νο[ς μὴ δακρύων ἐν κ]αιρῷ καθ᾽ ὅ-
τι συμβαίνει, ἀλλ᾽ ἔστιν καὶ ἔσω τὸ
δακρύειν.ᵃ Καὶ ἀκούσαντες ταῦταᵇ
ἐσπούδασαν ἀγοράσαντες τὸ εἶδος,
ψωμῆσαι αὐτὸν τὸν κάμνοντα.
Ἔπειτα καὶ αὐτὸς ἔφαγεν λάχα-
νον ἑψητὸν, ὡς ἔθος πᾶσιν. [§ 54] Ἰ-
δὼν δέ, ἀδελφῶν πολλῶν γενομένων,ᶜ τὴν μονὴν στενοχορουμένην, μετήγαγέν τινας, αὐτῶν εἰς ἄλλην κώμην ἔρημον,
λεγομένην Πρώων,ᵈ καὶ οὕτως
σὺν αὐτοῖς ἐπλάτυνεν τὴν μονὴν οἰκοδομῶν, σκοπῶνᵉ πολλῶν εἶναι τὴν κλῆσιν παρὰ Κ(υρίο)υ.
Καὶ ἔταξεν οἰκονόμονᶠ σὺν δευ-
τέροις ἄλλοιςᵍ ἐκεῖ οἰκονομῆσαι
τοὺς ἀδελφούς, καὶ οἰκιακούς,
καὶ δευτέρους, κατὰ τοὺς θεσμοὺς

ᵃ sentence missing in G1b ᵇ ταῦτα *om.* G1b ᶜ ἀδελφῶν πολλῶν γενομένων *transp. post* στενοχορουμένην G1b ᵈ Πρόου F; Παβαῦ G1b ᵉ ἐσκόπει γὰρ G1b ᶠ οἰκονόμους G1b ᵍ *om.* G1b

Fol. 84ʳ (= *Sancti Pachomii Vita prima* §§ 65–66)

Καὶ ἀκού[σας Θεόδωρος ἐποίησεν]
οὕτως. [(§ 66) Καὶ ἦν τις ἀδελφὸς ἐν τῇ
μονῇ περίλυπος διὰ τὸ ἐλέγχεσθαι
αὐτὸν ὑπ' αὐτοῦ] σωτηρίας χάριν. Καὶ
γνοὺς Θεόδωρος ὅτι ἐξενίσθη[a] τῇ
καρδίᾳ ἐκεῖνος[b] ἐξελθεῖν τῶν ἀ-
δελφῶν[c] ἕνεκεν τούτου, φρό-
νημος τυγχάνων [καὶ] σοφός,[d]
λέγει αὐτῷ· Γινώσκεις [ἄρα][e] ὅτι
ὁ λόγος τοῦ γέροντος τούτου
ἀπότομός ἐστιν παρὰ [τὸ μέτρον],
καὶ οὐκ οἶδα εἰ[f] δύναμαι [μεῖναι ὧδε].
Καὶ ἀποκριθεὶς ὁ ἀδελφός, ἀπέθε-
το τὸ βάρος αὐτοῦ ἐπ' αὐτῷ λέγων·[g]
Καὶ σὺ τοῦτο πάσχεις; Καὶ λέγει αὐ-
τῷ·[h] Ἐγὼ μᾶλλον. Ἀλλὰ γενώμεθα
παραμυθούμενοι ἀλλήλους, ἕως πει-
ράσωμεν αὐτὸν ἔτι ἄλλο[i] ἅπαξ,
ἐὰν μὲν χρηστὸς πρὸς ἡμᾶς γένη-
ται,[j] μένωμεν· ἐὰν δὲ μή, ὑπάγω[μεν][k]

---

[a] ὅτι ἐξενίσθηα | παρακινηθέντα G1b   [b] τὸν ἀδελφὸν τοῦ G1b   [c] τῶν ἀδελφῶν | τῆς μονῆς G1b   [d] καὶ σοφὸς *om.* G1b   [e] Ἄρα οἶδας G1b   [f] καὶ τάχα οὐ G1b   [g] ἀπέθετο τὸ βάρος αὐτοῦ ἐπ' αὐτῷ λέγων | λέγει G1b   [h] αὐτῷ | Θεόδωρος G1b   [i] ἄλλο *om.* G1b   [j] χρηστὸς γένηται πρὸς ἡμᾶς F: Κἂν μὲν χρηστότερος γένηται πρὸς ἡμᾶς G1b   [k] εἰ δὲ μή, ἀπελευσόμεθά G1b

Fol. 84ᵛ (= *Sancti Pachomii Vita prima* §§ 66–67)

[πώποτε ἀναχωρεῖν ἑαυτοῖς μετὰ ἀναπαύσεως. Καὶ ταῦτα ἀκούσας ἐνίσχυσεν ἀπὸ ἀσθενείας. Καὶ ἀπελθόντος Θεοδώρου λάθρα ἐκείνου πρὸς τὸν πατέρα ἡμῶν Παχούμιον, καὶ τὴν ὑπόθεσιν εἰπόντος, λέγει αὐτῷ· Καλῶς. Ἀλλὰ, φέρε μοι αὐτὸν ὧδε, ὡς ἵνα μέμψησθέ με περὶ τούτου· καὶ ἐν ᾧ δίδωσιν ὁ Θεὸς πείθω αὐτόν.

Καὶ οὕτως ἐλθόντων αὐτ]ῶν, καὶ τοῦ [Θεοδώρου ὡς ἐλέγ]χοντος αὐτὸν, ἀπεκρίθη αὐτοῖς· Συν]χωρήσατέ μοι· [ἥμαρτον. Ο]ὐκ ὀφείλετε, ὡς τέκνα, φέρειν τὸν πατέρα ὑμῶν; Καὶ ἀρξαμένου πάλιν Θεοδώρου ὡς ἐλέγχειν αὐτὸν,ᵃ [νεύει αὐ]τῷ ὁ ἀδ[ελφὸςᵇ παῦσαι· Κάλω]ς [ἔχει· ἐγὼ γὰρ παρεκλήθ]η σφόδρα. [Καὶ οὕτως ὠφέλησεν τὸν] ἀδελφὸν [μετὰ παρουρ]γίας ἀγαθῆς.

[Βλέπων δὲ αὐτὸν ὁ] πατὴρ ἡμῶν [Παχούμιος, σοφὸν ὄντα] καὶ ἐπί-[κοον τ]ῇ ἀλη[θεί]ᾳ, ἔπεμψεν αὐ-τ[ὸ]ν [μετὰ] ἄλλου ἀδελφοῦ ποτε εἰς τὴν οἰκίανᶜ αὐτοῦ, αἰτοῦντος αὐτοῦ τοῦ ἐπισκέψασθαι τοὺς ἰδίους.ᵈ Καὶ μετὰ τὸ εἰσελθεῖνᵉ ἐκεῖ τῇ ὥρᾳ τοῦ φαγεῖν,ᶠ οἱ γονεῖς αὐτοῦ ἡτοίμασαν αὐτοῖς φαγεῖνᵍ

ᵃ ὡς ἐλέγχοντος ἔτι τὸν γέροντα G1b   ᵇ ἐκεῖνος G1b   ᶜ οἰκείαν F   ᵈ αἰτησαμένου τοὺς ἰδίους ἐπισκέψασθαι G1b   ᵉ ἀμφοτέρους *add.* G1b   ᶠ τῇ τοῦ ἀρίστου ὥρᾳ G1b   ᵍ ἡτοίμασαν αὐτοῖς φαγεῖν οἱ τοῦ ἀδελφοῦ γονεῖς G1b

FIGURE 1.1 © British Library Board Add MS 70518, fol. 85ʳ

FIGURE 1.2 © British Library Board Add MS 70518, fol. 84ʳ

FIGURE 1.3 © British Library Board Add MS 70518, fol. 84ʳ (details with faded Greek notes across the right margin)

7 Textual Value of the Fragments

As shown in the above edition, all the linguistic oddities of manuscript F that separate it from G1b, the other, later branch of the textual tradition of the Greek *Vita prima*, are present in this ninth-century witness. Although very little text is preserved on the fragments, it is sufficient to detect variants that may differ from the parallel passages in F. The scanty differences identified between the two in the apparatus make it rather unlikely that the British Library fragments derive from the manuscript *Vorlage* of F. The different provenance of the two witnesses also speaks for the independence of the manuscripts. F, as mentioned above, apparently derives from an Italo-Greek environment, presumably from the monastery of Apiro in Central Italy, whereas the script of the British Library fragments, as discussed previously, seems to suggest an Eastern, Constantinopolitan provenance. The textual agreement between these two potentially unrelated manuscripts, however little they actually overlap, seems to represent a textually rather homogenous recension, which differs considerably from G1b.

Supported by readings of these new, presumably independent ninth-century fragments, phrases peculiar to G1a, such as ἔτι ἄλλο ἅπαξ (once more again) which G1b corrects to ἔτι ἅπαξ (once again), or the characteristic wording τῇ ὥρᾳ τοῦ φαγεῖν (time to eat) changed occasionally in G1b, might lead us closer to the origins of the *Vita prima*. As highlighted by Lefort and later by Veilleux, a thorough linguistic examination of G1, especially of the differences between its two recensions G1a and G1b, may reveal more about the milieu of the compiler of this text, and also about the literary agenda of the redactor behind G1b. In a comparative textual analysis of the two recensions, the two British Library leaves, which provide an independent and early witness to G1a, may possibly serve as a helpful comparative tool. The relatively small amount of text they preserve, supporting specific variants of F, will help formulate conclusions about the general tendencies in rewriting the primitive G1a into a more sophisticated G1b.

The fragmentation of the British Library leaves is very unfortunate. Had the bookbinder of the unknown book in which these fragments survived reused the two leaves immediately preceding these in the original manuscript, we may have been provided with the original G1a version of §§ 33–43 of the *Vita prima*, a portion which, due to a loss of two folios between fols. 167–168 in F, is unknown to us in the original wording.

Although there is very little hope to discover these or any other leaves from the ninth-century manuscript from which the British Library leaves derive, the two fragments that have come down to us are important. Having travelled in the binding of a book to Humfrey Wanley's private collection of fragments, and eventually to the Portland family's papers with which they arrived in the British Library in 1967, the two leaves will now earn their place in the long and entangled history of Pachomian monastic literature as fragments of the earliest manuscript of Pachomius's first Greek *Life*.

Bibliography

Primary Sources

Cranenburgh, H. van, ed. *La vie latine de saint Pachôme traduite du grec par Denys le Petit*. SubsHag 46. Brussels: Société des Bollandistes, 1969.

Festugière, André Jean, ed. *Les moines d'Orient*. Vol. 4/2, *La premiére vie grecque de saint Pachôme*. Paris: Cerf, 1965.

Halkin, François, ed. *Le corpus athénien de saint Pachôme*. Vol. 2. Cahiers d'Orientalisme. Geneva: P. Cramer, 1982.

Halkin, François, ed. *Sancti Pachomii vitae graecae*. SubsHag 19. Brussels: Société des Bollandistes, 1932.

Lefort, Louis Théophile. *Les vies coptes de saint Pachôme et de ses premiers successeurs*. Bibliothèque du Muséon 16. Louvain: Bureaux du Muséon, 1943.

Veilleux, Armand, transl. *Pachomian Koinonia*. Vol. 1, *The Life of St Pachomius and his Disciples*. CSS 45. Kalamazoo, MI, 1980.

Secondary Sources

Bandini, Angelo Maria. *Catalogus codicum manuscriptorum Bibliothecae Mediceae Laurentianae*. Vol. 1. Florence, 1764.

Bandini, Angelo Maria. *Fasciculus rerum graecarum ecclesiarum*. Florence, 1763.

The British Library Catalogue of Additions to the Manuscripts. New Series, 1986–1990. London: British Library, 1993.

Cavallo, Guglielmo. "Funzione e strutture della maiuscola greca tra i secoli VIII–XI." In *La paléographie grecque et byzantine: Paris, 21–25 octobre 1974*, pp. 95–137. Paris: Éditions du Centre national de la recherche scientifique, 1977.

Chitty, Derwas J. "Pachomian Sources Reconsidered." *JEH* 5 (1954): 38–77.

Crisci, Edoardo. *I palinsesti di Grottaferrata: Studio codicologico e paleografico*. Naples: Edizioni scientifiche italiane, 1990.

Dahlman, Britt and Per Rönnegård. *Paradiset. Ökenfädernas tänkespråk: Den systematiska samlingen 8; Om att inte göra något för syns skull*. Sturefors: Silentium, 2017.

Draguet, René. "Un morceau grec inédit des vies de Pachôme apparié à un texte d'Evagre en partie inconnu." *Le Muséon* 70 (1957): 267–306.

Ehrhard, Albert. *Überlieferung und Bestand der hagiographischen und homiletischen Lit-*

eratur der griechischen Kirche von den Anfängen bis zum Ende des 16. Jahrhunderts. Vol. 3. TU 52. Leipzig: J.C. Hinrichs, 1943.

Gatch, Milton McC. "*Fragmenta manuscripta* and *varia* at Missouri and Cambridge." *Transactions of the Cambridge Bibliographical Society* 9 (1990): 434–475.

Gatch, Milton McC. "Humfrey Wanley's Proposal to the Curators of the Bodleian Library on the Usefulness of Manuscript Fragments from Bindings." *Bodleian Library Record* 11 (1983): 94–98.

Gatch, Milton McC. "John Bagford as a Collector and Disseminator of Manuscript Fragments." *The Library*, 6th ser., 7/2 (1985): 95–114.

Gentile, Sebastiano, ed. *Oriente cristiano e santità: Figure e storie di santi tra Bisanzio e l'Occidente*. Milan: Centro Tibaldi, 1998.

Guy, Jean-Claude. *Recherches sur la tradition grecque des Apophthegmata Patrum*. SubsHag 36. Brussels: Société des Bollandistes, 1962.

Halkin, François. *Catalogue des manuscrits hagiographiques de la Bibliothèque nationale d'Athènes*. SubsHag 66. Brussels: Société des Bollandistes, 1983.

Harlfinger, Dieter. "Beispiele der Maiuscula ogivalis inclinata vom Sinai und aus Damaskus." In *Alethes Philia: Studi in onore di Giancarlo Prato*, 461–177. Collectanea 23. Spoleto: Centro italiano di studi sull' alto medioevo, 2010.

Heyworth, Peter. *Letters of Humfrey Wanley: Palaeographer, Anglo-Saxonist, Librarian, 1672–1726; with an Appendix of Documents*. Oxford: Clarendon, 1989.

Jones, Clyve. "The Harley Family and the Harley Papers." *The British Library Journal* 15 (1989): 123–133.

Lamberz, Erich. *Katalog der griechischen Handschriften des Athosklosters Vatopedi*. Vol. 1, *Codices 1–102*. Thessaloniki, 2006.

Melissakis, Zisis. "Οἱ Παλίμψηστοι Κώδικες Τῆς Ἑλληνικῆς Βιβλιοθήκης Τῆς Ἑλλάδος. Προκαταρτικὰ Συμπεράσματα Μιᾶς Ἔρευνας." *Σύμμεικτα* 16 (2013): 159–216.

Olney, R.J. "The Portland Papers." *The Archives* 19 (1989): 78–87.

Orsini, Pasquale. "La maiuscola ogivale inclinata: contributo preliminare." *Scripta* 9 (2016): 89–116.

Pasini, Cesare. *Inventario agiografico dei manoscritti greci dell'Ambrosiana*. SubsHag 84. Brussels: Société des Bollandistes, 2003.

Pattie, Tom, and Scot McKendrick, eds. *Summary Catalogue of Greek Manuscripts*. London: British Library, 1999.

Rousseau, Philip. *Pachomius: The Making of a Community in Fourth-Century Egypt*. Transformation of the Classical Heritage 6. Berkeley: University of California Press, 1985.

Steele, Robert. "John Bagford's Own Account of his Collection of Title-Pages." *The Library*, n. s., 8 (1907): 223–224.

Tillemont, Sébastien le Nain de. *Mémoires pour servir à l'histoire ecclésiastique des six premiers siècles*. Vol. 7. Paris, 1700.

Veilleux, Armand. *La liturgie dans le cénobitisme pachômien au quatrième siècle*. StAns 57. Rome: Herder, 1968.

Veilleux, Armand. *Pachomian Koinonia* (see above under primary sources).

Vergote, Jozef. "La valeur des vies grecques et coptes de S. Pakhôme." *OLP* 8 (1977): 175–186.

Weitzmann, Kurt. *Die byzantinische Buchmalerei des 9. und 10. Jahrhunderts*. Berlin, 1935; reprint Vienna: Verlag der österreichischen Akademie der Wissenschaften, 1996.

Wright, Cyril Ernest. *Fontes Harleiani: A Study of the Sources of the Harleian Collection of Manuscripts Preserved in the Department of Manuscripts in the British Museum*. London: The Trustees of the British Museum, 1972.

CHAPTER 2

Producing Pachomius: The Role of Lower Egypt in the Creation, Reception, and Adaptation of the Pachomian *Vita* Tradition

James E. Goehring

The history of Pachomian scholarship, like the history of scholarship on Jesus, has been in large part a quest for origins. Sources that survive in multiple forms and editions are analyzed, judged, and arranged to indicate their proximity, by date or purity of form, to the founding figure in question. The history of research on the various *Lives* of Pachomius, for example, initially centered on establishing the priority of the earliest Greek or Coptic version.[1] Once it became clear that the two linguistic traditions developed separately,[2] the focus shifted to the interpretation of individual stories and units, seeking to move behind the *Lives* to the "historical" movement from which they drew. The later inclusion of the Arabic *Lives* in the debate added to its complexity. This led in turn to a complex stemma of the relationships among the various versions, a stemma that again allowed one to focus on the earliest version in each language group while generally ignoring the later texts.[3] While the aim of such research is admirable and remains vital to our understanding of the Pachomian movement's early years, I wish here to turn instead to external influences that through time participated in producing the literary images of Pachomius that survive. For a vol-

---

1 L.Th. Lefort and Derwas Chitty engaged in an animated debate over the priority of the Coptic or Greek version of the *Life* through the latter half of the twentieth century. For a history of research on the *Life*, see James E. Goehring, *The Letter of Ammon and Pachomian Monasticism* (Berlin: de Gruyter, 1986), 23; Armand Veilleux, *La liturgie dans le cénobitisme pachômien au quatrième siècle*, StAns 57 (Rome: Herder, 1968), 11–107; idem, *Pachomian Koinonia*, vol. 1, *The Life of Pachomius and his Disciples*, CSS 45 (Kalamazoo, MI: Cistercian Publications, 1980), 1–21.
2 Armand Veilleux, *Pachomian Koinonia*, vol. 2, *Pachomian Chronicles and Rules*, CSS 46 (Kalamazoo, MI: Cistercian Publications, 1981), 3; A.-J. Festugière, *Les moines d'Orient*, vol. 4.2, *La première vie grecque de saint Pachôme* (Paris: Cerf, 1965), 5–7; Goehring, *Letter of Ammon*, 23.
3 Veilleux, *Liturgie*, 104; idem, *Pachomian Koinonia*, vol. 1, p. 17. One can note, of course, a similar desire to distinguish the earliest layers with respect to the Pachomian *Rules*. See most recently, Christoph Joest, *Die Mönchsregeln der Pachomianer*, CSCO 660 / Subs. 124 (Leuven: Peeters, 2016); idem, "Die *Praecepta* Pachoms: Untersuchung zu dem größten Abschnitt der Pachom-Regeln," *ZAC* 13 (2009): 430–451.

ume in honor of Samuel Rubenson, whose seminal work in the field changed forever how we read and understand the *Life of Antony* and the *Apophthegmata Patrum*,[4] an essay exploring the impact of the world of Lower Egypt on the literary memory of the Upper Egyptian Pachomian movement seems most appropriate. It is a pleasure and honor to dedicate this contribution to him.

The impact of Lower Egyptian ideas on the framing of the Pachomian story likely began well before the earliest written versions of the story emerged. While earlier texts attributed to Pachomius and Theodore, and those later composed by Horsiesius,[5] surely participate in the larger flow of monastic ideas and spirituality throughout Egypt, it is the descriptive accounts in the various versions of the *Life*, the *Letter of Ammon*, and the *Ascetica* that offer the clearest evidence of the impact of Lower Egypt on the portrayal of the Pachomian movement.[6] The impact is apparent both in the creative moment of the texts' origin as well as in how they were used and employed in the later stages of the

---

4 His impact began with the publication of his Lund University dissertation in 1990 and has continued through numerous publications and an international project on "Early Monasticism and Classical Paideia" that he directed through Lund University; see Samuel Rubenson, *The Letters of Antony: Origenist Theology, Monastic Tradition and the Making of a Saint* (Lund: Lund University Press, 1990); idem, "Christian Asceticism and the Emergence of the Monastic Tradition," in *Asceticism*, ed. Vincent L. Wimbush and Richard Valantasis (New York: Oxford University Press, 1995), 49–57. Information on the research project can be found online at Lund University, "Monastica—a Dynamic Library and Research Tool"; and Lund University, "Early Monasticism and Classical Paideia."
5 Tito Orlandi, "Coptic Literature," in *The Roots of Egyptian Christianity*, ed. Birger A. Pearson and James E. Goehring (Philadelphia: Fortress Press, 1986), 60–63; James E. Goehring, "New Frontiers in Pachomian Studies," in *The Roots of Egyptian Christianity*, ed. Birger A. Pearson and James E. Goehring (Philadelphia: Fortress Press, 1986), 236–240, reprinted in idem, *Ascetics, Society, and the Desert: Studies in Early Egyptian Monasticism* (Harrisburg, PA: Trinity Press International, 1999), 162–166. For the sources themselves, see L.Th. Lefort, *Oeuvres de S. Pachôme et de ses disciples*, CSCO 159–160 / Copt. 23–24 (Louvain: Durbecq, 1956); Armand Veilleux, *Pachomian Koinonia*, vol. 3, *Instructions, Letters, and Other Writings of Saint Pachomius and his Disciples*, CSS 47 (Kalamazoo, MI: Cistercian Publications, 1982); Christoph Joest, *Die Pachom-Briefe: Übersetzung und Deutung*, CSCO 655 / Subs. 155 (Leuven: Peeters, 2014); idem, *Über den geistlichen Kampf: Katechesen des Mönchsvaters Pachom* (Beuron: Beuroner Kunstverlag, 2010); Heinrich Bacht, *Das Vermächtnis des Ursprungs: Studien zum frühen Mönchtum* (Würzburg: Echter, 1972).
6 For the various versions of the *Life*, see L.Th. Lefort, *S. Pachomii vitae sahidice scriptae*, CSCO 99–100 / Copt. 8 (Paris: E typographeo reipublicae, 1933; reprint Louvain: Secrétariat du CorpusSCO, 1965); idem, *Les vies coptes de saint Pachôme et de ses premiers successeurs* (Louvain: Bureaux du Muséon, 1943); François Halkin, *Sancti Pachomii vitae graecae* (Brussels: Société des Bollandistes, 1932); and Veilleux, *Pachomian Koinonia*, vol. 1; for the *Letter of Ammon* (*Epistula Ammonis*) and the *Ascetica* (also referred to as the *Paralipomena*), see Halkin, *Sancti Pachomii vitae graecae*, 97–165; Veilleux, *Pachomian Koinonia*, vol. 2, pp. 71–109; Goehring, *Letter of Ammon*.

expanding Greek Pachomian dossier.[7] One suspects that the ground was laid for the production of the earliest version(s) of the *Life*, at least in part, by the flow of ideas into the Pachomian monasteries from Lower Egypt. The various versions of the *Life* indicate considerable contact with Lower Egypt from early in the movement's history.[8] The tradition reports Pachomius's contact with the archbishop Athanasius during his visit to the Thebaid in 329–330 CE,[9] only six to seven years after Pachomius founded his first monastery at Tabennisi. Subsequent accounts report travel of Pachomian monks to and from Alexandria by boat, a practice that began already in Pachomius's lifetime.[10] While such contact allowed for the occasional flow of information between the Pachomian federation and Lower Egypt, I would suggest that it was the creation of a specific house in the central Pachomian monastery of Pbow dedicated to non-Coptic-speaking Alexandrians and foreigners (Ἀλεξανδρέων καὶ ξενικῶν)[11] that facilitated the most direct, enduring, and influential connection between the two monastic centers. Its origin is connected to the arrival of an Alexandrian named Theodore at Pbow circa 340 CE. He was a young reader in the Alexandrian church, who according to the Coptic tradition knew Athanasius. He led an ascetic life and when he heard about Pachomius, decided to join his movement. He took advantage of a visit by Pachomian monks to Alexandria to leave the city and travel back upriver with them to Pbow. As he spoke only Greek, Pachomius assigned him to a house with an old monk with whom he could communicate. His interest and ability led him to learn Coptic. Eventually Pachomius, recognizing his talent, made him head of a newly created house of Alexandrians and foreigners. The Bohairic and Greek *Life* both report that "the first spiritual fruits of that house among the Alexandrians were Ausonius the Great and [another] Ausonius, and a boy called Neon. Among the Romans there were the God-bearers Firmus and Romulus, Domnius the Armenian and

---

7   I have chosen not to address the complex situation of the Pachomian *Rules* in this essay. See above, n. 3.
8   For a detailed discussion, see James E. Goehring, "The Pachomian Federation and Lower Egypt: The Ties that Bind," in *Christianity and Monasticism in Northern Egypt: Beni Suef, Giza, Cairo, and the Nile Delta*, ed. Gawdat Gabra and Hany N. Takla (Cairo: The American University in Cairo Press, 2017), 49–60.
9   SBo 28; G¹ 30. SBo is basically the Bohairic version of the *Life* completed by Armand Veilleux (*Pachomian Koinonia*, vol. 1, pp. 1–4) using various Sahidic fragments. G¹ is the *Vita prima* or first Greek *Life of Pachomius*.
10 For references to boats, see SBo 30, 53, 56, 59, 89 96; G¹ 55, 60, 94, 109, 113; after Pachomius's death, SBo 204; G¹ 146; Pachomian *Rule*, *Praecepta* 118; Roger Remondon, "Le monastère alexandrin de la Métanoia était-il bénéficiaire du fisc ou à son service?" in *Studi in onore di Edoardo Volterra*, vol. 5 (Milan: Giuffrè, 1971), 779.
11 G¹ 95; Halkin, *Sancti Pachomii vitae graecae*, 63.

other holy men."[12] One assumes that an influx of foreign monks, chiefly from Alexandria, had created the need for the new house in the first place.

As the Pachomian federation grew and its fame spread, the flow of ascetics and prospective monks from Alexandria and Lower Egypt into the movement increased, aided no doubt by boat traffic between the two centers. An account of a prospective monk who had lived an impure life, for example, begins by noting that he was one of three men who, wanting to become monks, had boarded a Pachomian boat in Alexandria that had come to sell mats and buy provisions for the sick.[13] Ammon, who later penned the *Letter of Ammon*, offers another example from after Pachomius's death. In 352, having recently converted and joined the Alexandrian church of Pierius, he told his priest of his desire to embrace a monastic life. The priest, fearing his contact with heretical anchorites in the city, told him of the Pachomians and connected him with Theodore and Copres, Pachomian monks who had come to Alexandria with letters for the archbishop.[14] He traveled with them by boat to Pbow, where he entered the house of foreigners, which he describes as consisting of twenty Greek-speaking monks under the leadership of the Alexandrians Theodore and Ausonius.[15]

One can only imagine that such connections included a significant flow of information between the Pachomians and Alexandria. Clearly the Alexandrian Christian communities had learned and approved of the Pachomian movement. The resulting flow of Greek-speaking ascetic prospects from Alexandria to the federation in Upper Egypt surely brought with it knowledge and abilities gained from these recruits' years in the city. The pull of Alexandria within the Pachomian federation is further witnessed in its seemingly irresistible expansion northward. Apart from the sole example of the monastery of Phnoum in Latopolis, south of Pbow, each subsequent expansion of the federation occurred in a northward direction. Initial growth took place directly north of the first monastery at Tabennisi. It added the monasteries of Pbow, Sheneset, and Thmousons. A second northern cluster followed some ninety kilometers north of Pbow near Panopolis. It included the monasteries of Tse, Shmin, Tsmine, and Thbew. After Pachomius's death, his successor Theodore added three monasteries, two of which, Kaior and Oui, were located 160 kilometers nearer Alexandria. Eventually, during the reign of Archbishop Theophilus, the

---

12   G¹ 95 = SBo 90–91; English translation from Veilleux, *Pachomian Koinonia*, vol. 1, p. 362.
13   SBo 107.
14   *Epistula Ammonis* 2 and 29; Goehring, *Letter of Ammon*, 192.
15   *Epistula Ammonis* 7.

Pachomians incorporated the monastery of Metanoia, located in the Alexandrian suburb of Canopus, into their federation.[16]

One can note the increasing closeness of the connection as well through the federation's expanding contact with the ecclesiastical hierarchy in Alexandria. While one may debate the degree and nature of the contact between the federation and Athanasius during Pachomius's lifetime, it seems clear that Theodore, his ultimate successor as head of the federation, enjoyed a closer connection with the archbishop and Alexandria.[17] So in turn, his successor Horsiesius exchanged letters with Archbishop Theophilus (385–412), established the monastery of Metanoia in Canopus at the archbishop's request, and sent him a copy of the Greek *Life of Pachomius*.[18] Furthermore, Ammon, who had traveled from Alexandria to join the federation in 352 during Theodore's tenure as its head, moved back to Lower Egypt three years later, first as a monk in Nitria and eventually becoming a bishop. He composed his *Letter of Ammon*, which describes his years as a monk at Pbow, sometime after 385 at the request of Archbishop Theophilus (385–412).[19] Ammon thus offers an example not only of the more common movement of individuals from the Alexandrian church to Upper Egypt to become monks in the Pachomian federation, but of subsequent movement back in the opposite direction; namely, Ammon, the Pachomian monk, moves from the federation in Upper Egypt back to Lower Egypt where he then rises within the church hierarchy.

The pattern continues into the fifth and sixth centuries. The Pachomian archimandrite Victor corresponded with Archbishop Cyril of Alexandria and accompanied him to the Council of Ephesus in 431 CE.[20] A pseudonymous pan-

---

16 Goehring, "The Pachomian Federation and Lower Egypt," 51–52. For Metanoia, see Jean Gascou, "Monastery of Metanoia," in *The Coptic Encyclopedia*, vol. 5 (1991), 1608–1611.

17 Goehring, "New Frontiers," 244–246, reprinted in idem, *Ascetics*, 170–172; idem, *Chalcedonian Power Politics and Pachomian Monasticism*, Occasional Papers 15 (Claremont: Institute for Antiquity and Christianity, 1989), 14–16, reprinted in idem, *Ascetics*, 254–256; Henry Chadwick, "Pachomios and the Idea of Sanctity," in *The Byzantine Saint: University of Birmingham Fourteenth Symposium of Byzantine Studies*, ed. S. Hackel (London: Fellowship of St. Alban and St. Sergius, 1981), 19.

18 Walter E. Crum, *Der Papyruscodex saec. VI–VII der Phillippsbibliothek in Cheltenham: Koptische theologische Schriften* (Strasbourg: Trübner, 1915), 12–13, 65–66; Lefort, *Les vies coptes*, 389–390.

19 Goehring, *Letter of Ammon*, 103, 118–119, 183–184.

20 Cyril of Alexandria, *Letters* 107–109, transl. John I. McEnerney, *St. Cyril of Alexandria, Letters 51–110*, FC 76–77 (Washington, DC: Catholic University of America Press, 1987), 170–175. On the journey to the Council of Ephesus, see James E. Goehring, *Politics, Monasticism, and Miracles in Sixth Century Upper Egypt: A Critical Edition and Translation of the Coptic Texts on Abraham of Farshut*, STAC 69 (Tübingen: Mohr Siebeck, 2012), 52–53; Caroline

egyric attributed to Timothy of Alexandria indicates a connection between the church in Alexandria and the construction of the federation's great fifth-century basilica at Pbow.[21] And from the latter part of the fifth to the mid-sixth-century, three Alexandrian patriarchs, all pro-Chalcedonian, were drawn from the Lower Egyptian Pachomian monastery of Metanoia.[22] While the federation's increasingly close connection to the Alexandrian ecclesiastical hierarchy, particularly as fed in the later years through its Lower Egyptian monastery of Metanoia, led ultimately to its historical demise in the reign of the Byzantine emperor Justinian I,[23] the seeds of the connection were planted at the very beginning of the Pachomian movement.

The point in establishing this close connection between the Pachomian federation and Lower Egypt, a connection that dates back to the very beginnings of the movement, is to suggest that the influence of Lower Egypt on the portrayal of Pachomian monasticism found in the Pachomian sources in general, and in the *vita* tradition in particular, occurred already in the creative processes through which the Pachomian literature was generated. One wonders, in fact, if the idea of fashioning a *Life of Pachomius* arose within the federation as a result of its connections with Lower Egypt. Might the house of foreigners at Pbow, with its dominant Greek population, have advanced the idea or even initiated it in the first place? The Alexandrian Theodore, who first led the house of foreigners, for example, knew Athanasius before his departure for Pbow,[24] and given the continuing flow to and from Alexandria, I see little reason to doubt that the connection continued in some form. Athanasius's seminal *Life of Antony*, in turn, appears to have influenced the production of the Pachomian *vita* tradition. The first Greek life, or *Vita prima* (G¹), explicitly references Athanasius's *Life of Antony* in its opening, and the Bohairic, while not referring to the *Life* per se, does begin with a reference to "the virtuous life of our holy

---

T. Schroeder, *Monastic Bodies: Discipline and Salvation in Shenoute of Atripe* (Philadelphia: University of Pennsylvania Press, 2007), 122–123; Wilhelm Kraatz, *Koptische Akten zum Ephesinischen Konzil vom Jahre 431* (Leipzig: J.C. Hinrichs, 1904), 24. Victor appears frequently in this text.

21 Arn van Lantschoot, "Allocution de Timothée d'Alexandrie prononcée a l'occasion de la dédicace de l'église de Pachôme a Pboou," *Le Muséon* 47 (1934): 13–56; Goehring, *Politics*, 59; Schroeder, *Monastic Bodies*, 122–123.

22 Timothy II Salofaciolus (460–475 and 477–482), John I Talaia (482), and Paul of Tabenna (537–540); Gascou, "Monastery of Metanoia," 1609; James E. Goehring, "Remembering Abraham of Farshut: History, Hagiography, and the Fate of the Pachomian Tradition," *JECS* 14 (2006): 16.

23 Goehring, "Remembering Abraham of Farshut," 1–26; idem, *Politics*, 32–49.

24 G¹ 94; SBo 89.

father Apa Antony, like that of the great Elijah, of Elisha, and of John the Baptist."[25] Both the Bohairic and the Greek *Life* immediately connect this reference to Amoun of Nitria, who led a similar life. His story occurs in Palladius's *Lausiac History*, likewise composed in Greek.[26] The monastic recruits who moved from Alexandria into the Pachomian federation in Upper Egypt, some of whom at least were learned, would have brought with them ideas, perhaps books, and certainly abilities learned in their pre-monastic years. The fact that the Pachomian federation alone in Upper Egypt produced relatively early in its existence a *Life* of its founder begs the question of the idea's origin. It is interesting in this regard to note the absence of an early *Life of Shenoute* in his slightly later parallel Upper Egyptian federation. While it may simply be the case that Shenoute's own literary talent and greater involvement in ecclesiastical and local politics steered his federation's literary production elsewhere, it is noteworthy that his organization contained no house of foreigners and that his writings reference none as well.[27] While one cannot with certainty assert that the idea of a *Life of Pachomius* arose within the house of foreigners at Pbow, circumstantial evidence lends support to the hypothesis.[28]

Regardless of the origin of the *vita* tradition, there seems little doubt, given the opening references to Antony and Amoun, that it was influenced by the monastic ideology and imagery espoused in the earlier Lower Egyptian sources.[29] The limited emphasis on Pachomius's learning offers an interesting case in point. The accounts of his childhood in both the Greek and the Bohairic *Life* center on his pagan origin, miraculous encounters with demons when taken to sacrifices or fed sacrificial meat, his rejection of sexual overtures, and his conversion as a young conscript in the emperor's army.[30] There is no

---

25 G¹ 2; SBo 2; translation from Veilleux, *Pachomian Koinonia*, vol. 1, p. 24.
26 *Historia lausiaca* 8; cf., Veilleux, *Pachomian Koinonia*, vol. 1, p. 266 (SBo 2, n. 2).
27 Goehring, "The Pachomian Federation and Lower Egypt," 52 and 59, n. 11.
28 I do not see this argument as evidence of the priority of the Greek *Vita prima* over the earliest Coptic versions of the *Life*, but rather as suggestive of the path by which the idea of a *Life of Pachomius* entered the federation's literary community.
29 Compare my treatment of this topic in James E. Goehring, "The Persistence of Crafted Memories: The Nag Hammadi Cartonnage, Upper Egyptian Monasticism, and the Literary Sources," in *Envisioning God in the Humanities: Essays on Christianity, Judaism, and Ancient Religion in Honor of Melissa Harl Sellew*, ed. Courtney J.P. Friesen (Eugene, OR: Wipf and Stock, 2018), 153–172.
30 SBo 4–7; G¹ 3–5; The Bohairic *Life* expands on the more limited miraculous stories found in the Greek version. The account of Pachomius's reaction to sacrificial meat and his spurning of sexual advances occurs only in the Bohairic version. While the *vita* tradition links his conscription to the Christian emperor Constantine, it is generally assumed that he was conscripted by Maximinus Daia in 312 for his war against Licinius. See Veilleux, *Pachomian*

discussion of his education or learning prior to his entry into the monastic life in any of the sources, which one suspects reflects the downplaying of classical education in early Christian sources in general, and monastic sources in particular. Among the latter, of course, the *Life of Antony*, to which the authors of the Pachomian *vita* tradition tip their literary hat, looms particularly large.[31] When one turns to the Pachomian sources, however, and considers the development of the federation over time, it seems clear that an appreciation for education and literacy played a significant role from the movement's beginnings in the fourth century through its historical decline and eventual disappearance in the sixth century and beyond. As such, one suspects that its founder fostered such an orientation, which in turn suggests his educated background.

The early stage of monasticism in Upper Egypt when Pachomius embraced the ascetic life under Palamon offers little occasion or structure for his education there. The *vita* tradition reports that as a monk with Palamon his regimen included the memorization and recitation of long passages from scripture, which the Greek *Vita prima* reports he "read and wrote by heart."[32] Pachomius must have been literate when he joined Palamon's group of ascetics. In addition to his own surviving letters and instructions,[33] the *vita* tradition and the Pachomian rules support his interest in literacy. Pachomius undertook to learn Greek so as better to serve the Greek-speaking brothers,[34] and various rules emphasize the need for literacy. They require literacy of all the monks, establish a form of monastic schooling to insure it, and report that books were kept in each house within the monastery from which monks could borrow them to read.[35] While some of these developments, particularly with respect to the rules, postdate Pachomius, the overall trajectory of the movement in terms of literacy suggests its existence as a driving force from its inception.

The leadership of the federation over time likewise supports this conclusion. While the monasteries surely drew from a broad cross-section of the society, the leaders who followed Pachomius came from the wealthy, literate

---

        Koinonia, vol. 1, p. 267; Derwas Chitty, *The Desert a City: An Introduction to the Study of Egyptian and Palestinian Monasticism under the Christian Empire* (Oxford: Blackwell, 1966), 7, 17 n. 39; Christoph Joest, "Ein Versuch zur Chronologie Pachoms und Theodoros," *ZNW* 85 (1994): 144. Joest calls the entire story into question.

31   On this topic the work of Samuel Rubenson has been seminal; see his *The Letters of Antony*, especially 185–191.

32   SBo 15; G^1 9; Veilleux, *Pachomian Koinonia*, vol. 1, p. 304.

33   Lefort, *Oeuvres*, 159:1–36; Veilleux, *Pachomian Koinonia*, vol. 3, pp. 1–5, 13–89.

34   SBo 89; G^1 95.

35   *Praecepta* 25, 100, 139–140; G^1 59; *Praecepta et Instituta* 2. The educational training comes from a section of the rules that likely postdate Pachomius.

classes. Petronius and Theodore came from prominent families, where one would expect sons to be educated. The tradition, in fact, reports Theodore's schooling prior to his entry into the monastic life, as well as his reading and composition of letters, some of which, along with a few catecheses, survive.[36] While less is known of Horsiesius, his reported correspondence with Athanasius and Theophilus, as well as his own surviving writings, particularly his impressive *Testament*, underscore his literary abilities.[37] The membership of the house of foreigners at Pbow, as detailed above, further establishes this point. The Alexandrian Theodore, who first led the house, was clearly educated, and Ammon likewise came from educated circles in Alexandria to which he later returned.

The overall impression that the sources leave is of a community founded by an educated individual who sought to build it outward on a foundation of literacy and education. In so far as it accepted illiterate individuals into its ranks, it taught them to read. As such it furthered the Christian value of embracing all as equally children of God, it did so not by downplaying or rejecting classical forms of education, but rather by expanding the reach of education to all its members. The federation became, in a sense, a monastic school, a vehicle to expand education and literacy in Upper Egypt. The impact of literary sources like the *Life of Antony*, on the other hand, centered the presentation of Pachomian monasticism around values integral to the monastic life, values that reach back to the earliest stages of Christianity and its embrace of the apostle Paul. The emphasis on scripture, coupled with Paul's notion of becoming "fools for the sake of Christ,"[38] placed the focus elsewhere, even when education and literacy loomed large in a movement's origin and success. Monks and monastic success, including that of Pachomius, were due to God, a point that is only blurred through discussions of the saint's education and prior learning. The ascetic goals of the literary production required its focus on God-given success rather than educated, empowered players.

What I am suggesting here is that the literary portrayal of the ascetic enterprise that emerged in Lower Egypt early on shaped the portrayal of Pachomian monasticism through the creation of the *vita* tradition. While the tradition, along with the other Pachomian sources, preserves evidence of the value of education and literacy within the federation, it comes and goes in the background of a story centered on the traditional monastic values of humility, scrip-

---

36   Theodore: SBo 31; G¹ 33. Petronius: SBo 56; G¹ 80.
37   Lefort, *Oeuvres*, 159.63–104; Veilleux, *Pachomian Koinonia*, vol. 3, pp. 135–224; Bacht, *Vermächtnis*.
38   1 Cor 4:10.

ture, and the role of God. The impact shapes even our modern understanding of the movement over time. It looks decidedly different when one imagines it through the lens of an educated, experienced, and resourceful founder. I would suggest that Pachomius's initial ascetic foundation at Tabennisi, presented as a result of a vision in the *vita* tradition, represents rather a calculated move in reaction to local developments in the surrounding ascetic communities. He recognized, perhaps based on past experiences, the need for and advantages of a more organized system. The accuracy of his insight was borne out by his community's rapid growth, which led him to expand, creating the first monastic federation. This required education, the keeping of books, the organization and communication across and between individual monasteries, and the creation of a shared monastic practice. The latter, insured through the individual community's father or head in the past, required now a common written rule to which the heads of the individual conjoined monasteries could refer.[39] The role of education and literacy in such a system is self-evident. None of this is to deny the role of God, miraculously portrayed in the *vita* tradition, but only to suggest that such stories function as unconscious literary devices shaped by the times and goals of their authors. Seen through more secular eyes, no matter what role one envisions God playing in the origin and success of the Pachomian federation, it involved the work of educated men, whose training and experience accounts for the community's innovations and success.

In a similar vein, the inclusion of Pachomian monasticism in Athanasius's claim that "the desert was made a city by monks," epitomized most clearly in Derwas Chitty's history of early Christian monasticism entitled *The Desert a City*, is demonstrably false in terms of the geography of the federation's monasteries. In this case, the impact of the Lower Egyptian portrayal is perceptible less in the Pachomian sources themselves than in modern western scholarship. While the Pachomians did embrace the notion of withdrawal, the reality of their experience did not connect it with a spatial movement out of the *oikoumene* or inhabited region along the Nile into the desert. Pachomius rather withdrew into an alternate ascetic life within the *oikoumene*, establishing his monasteries in or near villages and towns.[40] While the inclusion of the move-

---

39 While Bentley Layton makes a case for a lost White Monastery rule book (*The Canons of Our Fathers: Monastic Rules of Shenoute* (Oxford: Oxford University Press, 2014)), I would suggest that Shenoute, given the geographically limited nature of his federation and his own control of it, relied, apart perhaps from a copy of the Pachomian rules, on the earlier pattern.

40 James E. Goehring, "Withdrawing from the Desert: Pachomius and the Development of Village Asceticism in Upper Egypt," *HTR* 89 (1996): 267–285.

ment in discussions of monasticism as a desert phenomenon arose in a post-Pachomian environment where the location of their monasteries was no longer apparent, the early linking of Pachomius's experiment to those of Antony and Amoun in the *vita* tradition made the assumption easy for those no longer reading the texts in their geography of origin.

When one moves on to the Pachomian literature as it traveled to and developed in Lower Egypt and beyond, one finds a continuing editorial influence in the production of the saint's image and the history of his federation. While the complex nature of the *vita* tradition complicates efforts to identify the origins and unravel patterns of influence, particularly in the earlier stages, one can nonetheless clearly see how, over time, the portrait of Pachomius and his movement are increasingly aligned with Alexandrian ecclesial ideology and what is expected of a saint. I will focus here on the Greek tradition,[41] which finds expression in the *Letter of Ammon*, the *Ascetica*, and the *vita* tradition. The latter arrived in Alexandria in the tenure of Archbishop Theodosius, who had requested a copy from Horsiesius, who then led the Pachomian movement.[42] One suspects that its acquisition, together with a Greek copy of the *Rules*, was connected to Theophilus's establishment of a Pachomian community at Canopus outside Alexandria.[43] While we cannot know if the Greek *Life* brought to Alexandria was the *Vita prima* as we know it, it seems safe to assume that if the latter is not the edition supplied by Horsiesius, it is as close to it as we can come.

Already in the Greek *Vita prima*, one can detect patterns of realignment in the portrayal of Pachomius and his federation. For example, while the Upper Egyptian Sahidic *vita* tradition, as it survived in Shenoute's White Monastery, preserved the account of Pachomius's first failed attempt to establish a communal monastery, it is not included in the Greek version as such. In the earli-

---

41   It is through the Greek tradition that the knowledge of the Pachomians initially moved beyond Egypt to the West. While the Coptic *vita* tradition did reach Lower Egypt as evidenced in the single surviving Bohairic manuscript, space and focus do not allow for its treatment here. In terms of the Coptic tradition more generally, it is worth noting that the Sahidic versions depend heavily on 9th- to 11th-century White Monastery manuscripts. One can only wonder how much of the editing evident in the Coptic *vita* tradition occurred later in the White Monastery. James E. Goehring, "Pachomius and his Successors in the Library of Deir Anba Shenouda," in *From Gnostics to Monastics: Studies in Coptic and Early Christianity in Honor of Bentley Layton*, ed. David Brakke, Stephen J. Davis, and Stephen Emmel (Leuven: Peeters, 2017), 409–427.

42   See above, n. 17.

43   It is from this monastery, Metanoia, that Jerome obtained the copy of the *Rules* he translated into Latin.

est Sahidic version (S1), Pachomius's call to establish a coenobitic monastery occurs only after he and his brother have established themselves as anchorites in Tabennesi. After Pachomius receives his vision, which he hides from his brother, they begin to expand the monastery together. Conflict emerges between the two, and then between Pachomius and the first influx of disciples, which leads to the initial failure of his experiment. While the later Coptic and Greek traditions preserve the stories in some form, they alter the sequence of events. They place Pachomius's vision before his brother joins him, a move that clearly differentiates Pachomius and precludes any suggestion that the brother may have played a role in the movement's origin. Furthermore, while the conflicts with his brother and the initial disciples survive, their shift to later in the story avoids the fact of Pachomius's initial failure in carrying out his vision.[44] The alterations participate in translating Pachomius's story into the story of a saint. For those in Lower Egypt, who came to know Pachomius through the Greek *Life*, it mattered little whether the changes occurred in *Upper* Egypt or took place after the *Life* came north to Alexandria. It is the Greek *Life*, as we find it in the *Vita prima*, that became the basis for the portrayal of Pachomius and his movement in the Greek-speaking ecclesiastical circles of Lower Egypt and beyond.

Proximity to the Alexandrian church in Lower Egypt likewise increased the focus on doctrinal concerns. While one must recognize changes in this regard already in the Upper Egyptian *vita* tradition, they become more specific in the Greek texts in Lower Egypt. In Upper Egypt, the changes reflect in general the increasing comfort of monasticism's relationship with the episcopal church, and more specifically the expression of that fact in the changing situation from the time of Pachomius to that of Theodore and Horsiesius. One sees in the Greek sources in Lower Egypt, however, an increasing specificity that underlines the movement's connection with the archbishop and his doctrinal concerns. The *Vita prima*, for instance, after an account of Athanasius's visit to the Thebaid which it shares with the Coptic tradition, adds an entire section on Pachomius's hatred of Origen, who it reports "was cast out of the church by Heracles, the archbishop of Alexandria, before Arius and Melitius, who uttered blasphemy against Christ."[45] The Coptic *vita* tradition not only does not include this section against Origen, but never in fact mentions him.

---

44 James E. Goehring, "The First Sahidic Life of Pachomius," in *Religions of Late Antiquity in Practice*, ed. Richard Valantasis (Princeton: Princeton University Press, 2000), 19–33.

45 G^1 30 = SBo 28 reports Athanasius's visit, after which G^1 adds section 31; translation from Veilleux, *Pachomian Koinonia*, vol. 1, p. 317. On the identity of the archbishop Heraclas, see Veilleux's note.

The only other condemnation of Origen in the Pachomian dossier occurs in the *Ascetica*, in a section that reports on Origenist anchorites who come to meet with Pachomius.[46] Their stench leads Pachomius to pray, after which their Origenism comes to light and he advises them to cast the heretical books into the river and never read them again. The *Ascetica*, a collection of Pachomian anecdotes, appears here to reflect Lower Egyptian concerns, a fact confirmed by Armand Veilleux's earlier analysis of this source. He noted that the text's reference to a liturgical night service (νυκτερινή σύναξις), a practice not found in Pachomian monasteries, its use of the Lower Egyptian monastic title of ὁ γέρων for Pachomius, and its introduction of the well-known Pachomian Theodore as "a certain Theodore," point to its origin in semi-anchoretic circles in Lower Egypt.[47]

The *Letter of Ammon* similarly heightens the movement's doctrinal connection with the episcopacy. Composed by an Alexandrian bishop who had in his youth spent three years (352–355 CE) as a Pachomian monk, the letter begins and ends with references to Athanasius. Ammon starts by connecting his resolve to embrace a monastic life to a sermon he heard Athanasius deliver in church, and he ends with an account of Athanasius's praise of Theodore, on whom the letter focuses, and his approval of Ammon's report.[48] The letter further includes a warning about heretical anchorites operating in Alexandria, an account of Theodore's prophecy concerning Arian and pagan persecutions, which are later transmitted by word and letter to Lower Egypt, an episode in which Theodore expels errant monks for "misleading those who are yet babes in Christ," a report of his correction of a monk's teaching against the resurrection of the flesh, and an account of a revelation he receives about the forgiveness of post-baptismal sins which is in turn supported by a letter from Antony.[49]

Again the point here is not that the Pachomians in Upper Egypt embraced, at least knowingly and/or universally, heretical teachings or what later became heretical teachings at any point in their history. Rather, it seems that the issue, however it played out in Upper Egypt, generated increased interest and hence space in the Greek Pachomian sources as they developed in Lower Egypt. This

---

46 *Ascetica* 7; Veilleux, *Pachomian Koinonia*, vol. 2, pp. 28–29.
47 Veilleux, *Liturgie*, 23–24 and 302–305. In a similar fashion, it has been suggested, the account of Theodore's catecheses found in the *Letter of Ammon* reflects the Lower Egyptian practice epitomized in Evagrius of Pontus's *Talking Back*, a practice Ammon would have come into contact with during his years in Nitria. *Epistula Ammonis* 3; James E. Goehring, "'Talking Back' in Pachomian Hagiography: Theodore's Catechesis and the Letter of Ammon," in *StPatr* 96 (2017): 257–264.
48 *Epistula Ammonis* 2, 34–35.
49 *Epistula Ammonis* 2, 5, 20, 26, 28–29, 32.

in turn focused the lens through which the other Pachomian sources were read, conforming the memory of the Upper Egyptian movement to the experience of the increasingly church-affiliated monasticism centered in Lower Egypt. While geographical proximity to the episcopacy and the more general advance of ecclesiastical power throughout Egypt played a significant role in this process, the development was enhanced and furthered in the case of Pachomian monasticism through the production of the Greek sources outlined above. This shift in perspective, and eventually behavior and belief, is perhaps best represented in later developments centered in the Pachomian Monastery of Metanoia. The connection of this Lower Egyptian Pachomian monastery to episcopal politics becomes increasingly clear in the post-Chalcedonian era when the episcopacy drew a series of pro-Chalcedonian archbishops from its members, a move that eventually set them and the Pachomian movement they came to control on the wrong side of Egyptian church history.[50]

The impact of these modifications continued in the Greek *vita* tradition as it developed beyond the *Vita prima*, most likely outside of Egypt. The influence of the *Letter of Ammon* and the *Ascetica* on the understanding of the *vita* tradition, for example, was realized in part by the inclusion of these texts alongside the *Vita prima* in the manuscript tradition that transmitted them. The assembling of these three texts into a Pachomian collection, which likely occurred in Lower Egypt, impacted in turn later editions of the Greek *Life* that depended upon it. The three manuscripts that independently preserve copies of the *Vita prima* all appear to have contained this Pachomian collection. They include a tenth- or eleventh-century codex from the Biblioteca Medicea Laurenziana in Florence (MS XI, 9), an eleventh-century codex from the National Library in Athens (MS 1015), and an incomplete fourteenth-century paper manuscript from the Biblioteca Ambrosiana in Milan (MS D69 Suppl).[51] The Florence manuscript, which Halkin used for his edition, includes in its Pachomian collection the *Vita prima*, an excerpt from the *Rules*, the *Letter of Ammon*, and the *Ascetica*. The Athens codex includes the *Vita prima*, the *Ascetica*, an excerpt on Pachomius from Palladius's *Historia Lausiaca*, and the *Epistula Ammonis*. While the fragmentary Milan manuscript preserves only the *Vita prima* and the *Ascetica*, it appears to have included the *Letter of Ammon* in its lost pages.[52] What is clear is that the scribes who produced these manuscripts and the

50 See above, pages 39–40.
51 Halkin, *Sancti Pachomii vitae graecae*, 10–18, relied on the Florence and Milan manuscripts for his edition. A fourth manuscript, preserved in the Vatican (MS IV, 73 = Barberinianus 491), is a copy of the Florence text.
52 Goehring, *Letter of Ammon*, 40–59; the *Letter of Ammon* does not survive in Ambrosianus,

monks who read them came to know Pachomius and Pachomian monasticism through the collection of Greek texts rather than through the *vita* tradition alone. The doctrinal thrust evident in the *Letter of Ammon* and the *Ascetica*, for example, informed the reading of the *vita* tradition, and the inclusion of texts from the *Historia Lausiaca* and *Rules* underlined the role of the rule in the formation of the movement.

Later Greek editions of the *Life of Pachomius* pushed further in this direction by erasing the boundaries between various of the texts in the collection, incorporating them directly into the *Life*. The second Greek *Life*, or *Vita altera* (G²), for example, integrates the *Ascetica* into its text, and the third *Life* (G³) adds materials from the *Historia Lausiaca*, including the famous account of the angelic rule.[53] By incorporating the *Ascetica* into the *Life*, the editor of G² doubled Pachomius's negative reactions to Origenist teachings. While the *Vita prima* had already inserted an anti-Origenist account absent in the Coptic tradition, G² incorporates a second example of the saint's *bona fides* with the addition of the *Ascetica* account of the visiting Origenist anchorites.[54] The editor of the third Greek *Life* (G³), who retains the two references to Origen found in G², enhances the account still further by explicitly professing Athanasius's preeminence among the bishops, and hence Pachomius's allegiance to him.[55]

In a similar fashion, the inclusion of Palladius's account of the angelic rule in later versions of the *Life* informs the understanding of the *Rule*'s role in the formation of the Pachomian movement.[56] Presented to Pachomius on a tablet by an angel at the moment of his vision to found the first coenobitic monastic community, the *Rule* appears in Palladius's account as both divine and instrumental in the formation of Pachomius's first monastery. From here it is an easy step to assume that a written rule set the Pachomian movement apart from its inception, and over time in the West to understand the rule and its use through the later embodiment of monastic rules in the Benedictine movement. As I have suggested above, however, the evidence from the early Coptic and Greek

---

though it likely did in the original as the codex breaks off part way through the *Ascetica* (see ibid., chart on p. 41).
53 Halkin, *Sancti Pachomii vitae graecae*, 43–72.
54 G¹ 31 and *Ascetica* 7; the two episodes appear at G² 27 and 68, respectively. G² 88 adds an additional reference to Origen in a condemnation of heresies contending against Christ, which also mentions Melitius and Arius (Halkin, *Sancti Pachomii vitae graecae*, 268, lines 8–11).
55 Veilleux, *Pachomian Koinonia*, vol. 1, p. 411; Tim Vivian, *St. Peter of Alexandria: Bishop and Martyr* (Philadelphia: Fortress Press, 1988), 5–6.
56 Palladius, *Historia Lausiaca*, 32; François Halkin, "L' Histoire Lausiaque et les Vies grecques de S. Pachôme." *AnBoll* 48 (1930): 257–301.

Lives does not support that conclusion. While I do not have the space to make a full case here, I would suggest that collections of oral rules, borrowed, generated, and employed by monastic fathers, were part of individual, independent monastic communities, including the group of disciples that Pachomius joined under Palamon, from their inception. Pachomius's primary innovation was his decision to expand, creating an integrated federation of individual monasteries governed from the central monastery of Pbow. It was this move that necessitated the writing down of the rules. A written *Rule* became an essential feature of the new federation, designed to unify practice across the ever more geographically dispersed members of the movement. When there was only one monastery led by one father, his authority served as the only rule necessary. He clarified matters, corrected errors, and made decisions. In the federation's case, the written rule became a guideline to help unify the practice of authority by the leaders of the individual monasteries. I suspect the rules served, at least in the beginning, more as guidelines for the leaders than as a written code of conduct used to train new and continuing monks. How individual rules were applied or bent depended on the leader, whose authority remained the most powerful rule to shape the community in accordance with Pachomian goals.

In closing, let me assert once again that my efforts here should not be read as a license to interpret the early Pachomians as somehow less oriented towards Alexandria and more open to heretical influences. Their orientation towards Alexandria is clear from the very beginning of the movement's history. I would only suggest that the sources as they come down to us are much more complicated than they appear. Even when we get back to the earliest versions of the *Life*, assuming that we can, the influence of Lower Egyptian monastic ideas on the Pachomian movement and its literary portrayals has to be taken into account. Pachomian monasticism had close ties to Greek-speaking Alexandrian ascetics from very early in its existence, an association that connected it with the literature and political orientation of the episcopacy. What changes over time, I would argue, is not the alignment itself, but its degree and level of enforcement. This process was not, of course, limited to the Pachomian movement. More broadly speaking, it worked over time to reduce the diversity of perspectives and reading material allowed in Christian communities in general. That similar changes took place within the Pachomian federation comes as no surprise. At what point and in what ways the landscape changed for the Pachomian federation in general, let alone for specific monasteries within the federation, lies, however, clouded behind sources shaped over time by the very ideological concerns we seek to get behind.

Bibliography

Bacht, Heinrich. *Das Vermächtnis des Ursprungs: Studien zum frühen Mönchtum.* Studien zur Theologie des geistlichen Lebens 5. Würzburg: Echter, 1972.

Chadwick, Henry. "Pachomios and the Idea of Sanctity." In *The Byzantine Saint: University of Birmingham Fourteenth Symposium of Byzantine Studies*, ed. S. Hackel, 11–24. London: Fellowship of St. Alban and St. Sergius, 1981.

Chitty, Derwas. *The Desert a City: An Introduction to the Study of Egyptian and Palestinian Monasticism under the Christian Empire.* Oxford: Blackwell, 1966.

Crum, Walter E. *Der Papyruscodex saec. VI–VII der Phillippsbibliothek in Cheltenham: Koptische theologische Schriften.* Strasbourg: Trübner, 1915.

Cyril of Alexandria. *Letters.* English transl. John I. McEnerney, *St. Cyril of Alexandria, Letters 51–110.* FC 76–77. Washington, DC: Catholic University of America Press, 1987.

Festugière, A.-J. *Les moines d'Orient.* Vol. 4.2, *La première vie grecque de saint Pachôme.* Paris: Cerf, 1965.

Gascou, Jean. "Monastery of Metanoia." In *The Coptic Encyclopedia*, vol. 5 (1991), 1608–1611.

Goehring, James E. *Ascetics, Society, and the Desert: Studies in Early Egyptian Monasticism.* Harrisburg, PA: Trinity Press International, 1999.

Goehring, James E. *Chalcedonian Power Politics and Pachomian Monasticism.* Occasional Papers 15. Claremont: Institute for Antiquity and Christianity, 1989; reprinted in Goehring, *Ascetics*, 241–261.

Goehring, James E. "The First Sahidic *Life of Pachomius*." In *Religions of Late Antiquity in Practice*, ed. Richard Valantasis, 19–33. Princeton: Princeton University Press, 2000.

Goehring, James E. *The Letter of Ammon and Pachomian Monasticism.* PTS 27. Berlin: de Gruyter, 1986.

Goehring, James E. "New Frontiers in Pachomian Studies." In *The Roots of Egyptian Christianity*, ed. Birger A. Pearson and James E. Goehring, 236–240. Philadelphia: Fortress Press, 1986; reprinted with an addendum in Goehring, *Ascetics*, 162–186.

Goehring, James E. "The Pachomian Federation and Lower Egypt: The Ties that Bind." In *Christianity and Monasticism in Northern Egypt: Beni Suef, Giza, Cairo, and the Nile Delta*, ed. Gawdat Gabra and Hany N. Takla, 49–60. Cairo: The American University in Cairo Press, 2017.

Goehring, James E. "Pachomius and his Successors in the Library of Deir Anba Shenouda." In *From Gnostics to Monastics: Studies in Coptic and Early Christianity in Honor of Bentley Layton*, ed. David Brakke, Stephen J. Davis, and Stephen Emmel, 409–427. Leuven: Peeters, 2017.

Goehring, James E. "The Persistence of Crafted Memories: The Nag Hammadi Cartonnage, Upper Egyptian Monasticism, and the Literary Sources." In *Envisioning God* in the Humanities: Essays on Christianity, Judaism, and Ancient Religion in Honor of Melissa Harl Sellew, ed. Courtney J.P. Friesen, 153–172. Eugene, OR: Wipf and Stock, 2018.

Goehring, James E. *Politics, Monasticism, and Miracles in Sixth Century Upper Egypt: A Critical Edition and Translation of the Coptic Texts on Abraham of Farshut.* STAC 69. Tübingen: Mohr Siebeck, 2012.

Goehring, James E. "Remembering Abraham of Farshut: History, Hagiography, and the Fate of the Pachomian Tradition," *JECS* 14 (2006): 1–26.

Goehring, James E. "'Talking Back' in Pachomian Hagiography: Theodore's Catechesis and the *Letter of Ammon*." *StPatr* 96 (2017): 257–264.

Goehring, James E. "Withdrawing from the Desert: Pachomius and the Development of Village Asceticism in Upper Egypt." *HTR* 89 (1996): 267–285; reprinted in Goehring, *Ascetics*, 89–109.

Halkin, François. "L'Histoire Lausiaque et les Vies grecques de S. Pachôme." *AnBoll* 48 (1930): 257–301.

Halkin, François. *Sancti Pachomii vitae graecae*. SubsHag 19. Brussels: Société des Bollandistes, 1932.

Joest, Christoph. *Die Pachom-Briefe: Übersetzung und Deutung*. CSCO 655 / Subs. 155. Leuven: Peeters, 2014.

Joest, Christoph. *Die Mönchsregeln der Pachomianer*. CSCO 660 / Subs. 134. Leuven: Peeters, 2016.

Joest, Christoph. "Die *Praecepta* Pachoms: Untersuchung zu dem größten Abschnitt der Pachom-Regeln." *ZAC* 13 (2009): 430–451.

Joest, Christoph. *Über den geistlichen Kampf: Katechesen des Mönchsvaters Pachom*. Weisungen der Väter 9. Beuron: Beuroner Kunstverlag, 2010.

Joest, Christoph. "Ein Versuch zur Chronologie Pachoms und Theodoros'." *ZNW* 85 (1994): 132–144.

Kraatz, Wilhelm. *Koptische Akten zum Ephesinischen Konzil vom Jahre 431*. Leipzig: J.C. Hinrichs, 1904.

Layton, Bentley. *The Canons of Our Fathers: Monastic Rules of Shenoute*. Oxford: Oxford University Press, 2014.

Lefort, L.Th. *Oeuvres de S. Pachôme et de ses disciples*. CSCO 159–160 / Copt. 23–24. Louvain: Durbecq, 1956.

Lefort, L.Th. *S. Pachomii vitae sahidice scriptae*. CSCO 99–100 / Copt. 8. Paris: E typographeo reipublicae, 1933; reprint Louvain: Secrétariat du CorpusSCO, 1965.

Lefort, L.Th. *Les vies coptes de saint Pachôme et de ses premiers successeurs*. Bibliothèque du Muséon 16. Louvain: Bureaux du Muséon, 1943.

Lund University. "Monastica—a Dynamic Library and Research Tool." Accessed August 9, 2018. http://monastica.ht.lu.se/.

Lund University. "Early Monasticism and Classical Paideia." Accessed August 9, 2018.

http://portal.research.lu.se/portal/en/projects/early-monasticism-and-classical-pai deia(7439b4da-a030-4482-a7dd-5c08c4992977).html.

Orlandi, Tito. "Coptic Literature." In *The Roots of Egyptian Christianity*, ed. Birger A. Pearson and James E. Goehring, 60–63. Philadelphia: Fortress Press, 1986.

Remondon, Roger. "Le monastère alexandrin de la Metanoia etait-il beneficiaire du fisc ou a son service?" In *Studi in onore di Edoardo Volterra*. Vol. 5, 769–781. Milan: Giuffrè, 1971.

Rubenson, Samuel. "Christian Asceticism and the Emergence of the Monastic Tradition." In *Asceticism*, ed. Vincent L. Wimbush and Richard Valantasis, 49–57. New York: Oxford University Press, 1995.

Rubenson, Samuel. *The Letters of Antony: Origenist Theology, Monastic Tradition and the Making of a Saint*. Bibliotheca Historico-Ecclesiastica Lundensis 24. Lund: Lund University Press, 1990. Reprinted with a translation of the letters as *The Letters of Antony: Monasticism and the Making of a Saint*. Minneapolis: Fortress Press, 1995.

Schroeder, Caroline T. *Monastic Bodies: Discipline and Salvation in Shenoute of Atripe*. Philadelphia: University of Pennsylvania Press, 2007.

Van Lantschoot, Arn. "Allocution de Timothée d'Alexandrie prononcée a l'occasion de la dédicace de l'église de Pachôme a Pboou." *Le Muséon* 47 (1934): 13–56.

Veilleux, Armand. *La liturgie dans le cénobitisme pachômien au quatrième siècle*. StAns 57. Rome: Herder, 1968.

Veilleux, Armand. *Pachomian Koinonia*. Vol. 1, *The Life of Saint Pachomius and his Disciples*. Vol. 2, *Pachomian Chronicles and Rules*. Vol. 3, *Instructions, Letters, and Other Writings of Saint Pachomius and his Disciples*. CSS 45–47. Kalamazoo, MI: Cistercian Publications, 1980–1982.

Vivian, Tim. *St. Peter of Alexandria: Bishop and Martyr*. Philadelphia: Fortress Press, 1988.

CHAPTER 3

The Wisdom of the Fathers: The Use of the *Apophthegmata* in the Correspondence of Barsanuphius and John of Gaza

Lorenzo Perrone

1   A World of Elders, a Community of Fathers

The Correspondence of Barsanuphius and John (= C), the two recluses in the coenobium of Seridus near Gaza during the first decades of the 6th century, is among the most important witnesses for the spread of the *Apophthegmata Patrum* (= AP) in the early monastic literature of Palestine.[1] From a statistical point of view, as we shall see, only the writings of Dorotheus, a disciple of the two elders, offer a similar quantity of citations. Yet the presence of the AP is more pervasive than the explicit references or the allusions suggest, and the width and depth of their reception have yet to be fully investigated. This depends first of all on the process of transmission of the sayings of the Desert Fathers and the manifold ways through which they were collected in written form.[2] As a consequence of this well-known problem, it comes as no surprise that even an expert like Lucien Regnault was not always able to identify the references to the "Fathers" in the letters of Barsanuphius and John.[3]

---

1   See Lucien Regnault, "Les apophthegmes en Palestine aux Vᵉ–VIᵉ siècles," *Irénikon* 54 (1981): 320–330; reprinted in idem, *Les Pères du désert à travers leurs apophthegmes* (Solesmes: Abbaye Saint-Pierre de Solesmes, 1987), 65–72. Cf. also Graham Gould, *The Desert Fathers on Monastic Community* (Oxford: Clarendon Press, 1993), 9–17; Ugo Zanetti, "Les Apophthegmes et la Terre Sainte," *Connaissance des Pères de l'Église* 141 (2016): 22–28.

2   Chiara Faraggiana di Sarzana, "*Apophthegmata Patrum*: Some Crucial Points of Their Textual Transmission and the Problem of a Critical Edition," *StPatr* 30 (1997): 455–467; Samuel Rubenson, "Formation and Re-Formations of the Sayings of the Desert Fathers," *StPatr* 55 (2013): 5–22.

3   As evident already in his *Barsanuphe et Jean de Gaza: Correspondance*, transl. Lucien Regnault, Philippe Lemaire, and Bernard Outtier (Solesmes: Abbaye Saint-Pierre de Solesmes, 1971). For the critical edition, see *Barsanuphe et Jean de Gaza: Correspondance*, ed. François Neyt and Paula de Angelis-Noah, transl. Lucien Regnault, 5 vols., SChr 426–427, 450–451, 468 (Paris: Cerf, 1997–2002). I will quote the texts with the abbreviation C and the number of the letter (the Greek text of questions addressed to Barsanuphius and John will appear in italics). Regnault's translation (p. 523) signals unidentified references in C 250, 386, 453, 462, 503, 524,

On the other hand, the difficulty we meet when we try to appreciate the use of the AP in the Correspondence arises from one of its major features. The ascetic experiences and spiritual doctrines transmitted in this unique corpus of questions and responses mirror a world of "elders" (γέροντες)—starting with the two dominant figures of the Great Old Man (Barsanuphius) and the Other Old Man (John the Prophet)—who are interacting with their addressees within a community of "Fathers," in the past and in the present. No other word is more frequently attested than precisely the terms "father" or "fathers," whereas the plural "elders," used with an equivalent meaning, is far less common. Thus it is not misguided to consider the reception of the AP, in the first place, against the background represented by the idea of a spiritual paternity uniting in a continuous chain the actual "spiritual Fathers" (πνευματικοὶ πατέρες) to their "predecessors": the prophets, the apostles,[4] the martyrs,[5] the saint bishops and theologians of the Church,[6] and the first monastic generations (notably the monks of Scetis, but also some monks of Palestine) as reflected in the *Lives* and *Sayings* of the Desert Fathers.

It is not the nostalgic interest in a golden age of monasticism that primarily inspires the references to the ancient Fathers in the Correspondence,[7] notwithstanding the occasional complaint by the two elders about the supposedly more relaxed standards of contemporary monastic life; rather, appeals to the Fathers stem from concern to implement a "pneumatic paternity," understood as the charisma of monks spiritually mature and able to guide others, be they hesychasts, cenobites, clerics, or laymen. A paternity of this kind constitutes an essential resource for preventing the failures of monastic existence and for assuring the fulfillment of a monk's vocation. If the figures of the past emblematically embody this view, in the actual life "pneumatic paternity" is enacted through spiritual direction.[8]

546, 549 (see below, n. 23), 550 (in fact a reminiscence of *Poemen* 159), 587, 614, 691. The same list appears in the edition (SChr 450, p. 105).

4 In this sense C 778c juxtaposes the demands to God by the apostles and those made by the "ancient holy fathers."
5 See, e.g., C 706; and also C 74, 137b, 256, 513, and 752 (where John evokes Philemon's martyrdom from the story of the monk Apollonius in *Historia monachorum* 19).
6 C 604 (διαφωνοῦσί τινες τῶν Πατέρων), an interesting testimony at the time of the second Origenist controversy, deals with the diversity of opinions among the Fathers (of the Church), i.e., the great theologians such as Gregory of Nazianzus and Gregory of Nyssa. In its turn, C 58 mentions the "318 Fathers" of the Council of Nicaea (325).
7 Significantly, the Fathers are qualified as "the ancients" only twice in the whole correspondence, and both times the phrase occurs in a question (C 60: εἰς τοὺς ἀρχαίους πατέρας; C 778c: εἰς τοὺς ἀρχαίους ἁγίους Πατέρας).
8 I have dealt with this system of spiritual direction in "The Necessity of Advice: Spiritual Direc-

In the language of the Correspondence, then, the word "Fathers" means a living heritage of ascetic experience and doctrine, an essentially "practical wisdom" acting as spiritual authority and offering instructions for all those who are in need of orientation and support. Rather than referencing historical individuals by name and identifying their sayings or writings, the Correspondence evokes a collective and plastic tradition into which the present experience can merge, and in which the interpreter of that tradition even assumes a status similar to its previous exemplars. While Seridus' monastery may be designated simply as the place where "the holy fathers" dwell,[9] the ascetic teachings of Isaiah of Gaza (who antedates our two recluses by just two generations) are included as part of the pneumatic patrimony.[10] Moreover, the letters also show how the hesychast Euthymius considers the instruction of the Great Old Man as direct continuation of the apostolic witness as far back as Christ himself.[11] In his turn Barsanuphius, writing to a monk oppressed by "despondency" (ἀκηδία), does not refrain from pointing to Euthymius' paradigmatic endurance and glorious death, hence adding a new "hero" apt for imitation to the series of the virtuous elders.[12] Finally, Abba Zosimas, a contemporary of the two elders living in the region of Caesarea, is already reckoned among the "Fathers" by Dorotheus when he reminds some of his addressees of Zosimas' teachings.[13]

In this way, the tradition of spiritual paternity, originating in the experience of the Desert Fathers, further developed in the monasticism of Gaza and expanded by means of spiritual direction, best exemplified in the letters of the two Old Men. More than a code of rules, the wisdom of the Fathers constituted a creative pattern for spiritual guidance, to be remembered and implemented in any situation. Barsanuphius, for instance, when asked by a hesychast

---

tion as a School of Christianity in the Correspondence of Barsanuphius and John of Gaza," in *Christian Gaza in Late Antiquity*, ed. Brouria Bitton-Ashkelony and Aryeh Kofsky (Leiden: Brill, 2004), 131–149.

9   C 55 (ἐν τῷ Μοναστηρίῳ ἔνθα οἱ Πατέρες ἦσαν); 582 (τὸν τόπον ἐν ᾧ εἰσι οἱ Πατέρες ἅγιοι). For C 187, the spiritual guides are both the dead and the living Fathers (τῶν Πατέρων ἡμῶν, τῶν κοιμηθέντων καὶ τῶν νῦν ζώντων).

10 See the allusion to Abba Isaiah's *Asceticon* in C 163 (γράφουσιν οἱ Πατέρες); and François Neyt, "Citations 'isaïennes' chez Barsanuphe et Jean de Gaza," *Le Muséon* 84 (1971) 65–92. For the impact of Abba Isaiah on the daily life in Seridus' monastery, cf. Brouria Bitton-Ashkelony and Aryeh Kofsky, *The Monastic School of Gaza* (Leiden: Brill, 2016), 183–189.

11 Lorenzo Perrone, "Prayer as a Mirror of Monastic Culture in Byzantine Palestine: The Letters of the Hesychast Euthymius to Barsanuphius," *Proche-Orient Chrétien* 60 (2010): 277–278.

12 C 144 (Ἐὰν δὲ θλίβη σε ἡ ἀκηδία, μνήσθητι οἵαν στένωσιν ὑπέμεινεν ὁ ἀββᾶς Εὐθύμιος, καὶ ἀπῆλθεν ἐνδόξως πρὸς Κύριον).

13 Dorotheus, *Ep.* 7, 192 (p. 514): ὡς εἶπον οἱ Πατέρες (cf. Zosimas, *Adloquia* 3, PG 78, 1684C).

"whether he should visit an elder who lived nearby," elicited from the practice of the Desert Fathers the model which should govern such visits. His answer thus discloses precisely that "generative nucleus" which coalesced in creating the apophthegmatic traditions.

> Visit the neighbor; but guard yourself in order not to talk idly, instead imitating the encounters of the holy fathers, namely: 'How are you, Abba?' After this, say: 'Tell us a word of life, about how we may find the way of God. Pray for me; for I have many sins.'[14]

The legacy of spiritual paternity demanded a fidelity to the exemplary way of life of the ancient monks. At the same time, it permitted an adaptation to different conditions, provided that one did not go against the golden rule of Gaza monasticism, as set forth by the two elders (and their faithful disciple Dorotheus): "do nothing out of your own will." Responding to Dorotheus, who was thinking to seek advice from "secular people or spiritual fathers" during their visits to the monastery, John reminded him that "one who is truly a disciple of Christ does not have any authority over oneself to do anything whatsoever of one's own accord. For even if one believes that one will benefit from the company of the visitors, one is actually transgressing the commandment that says: 'Do everything with counsel' (Prov 24:72, 31:4 LXX)."[15] Before taking any initiative, Dorotheus should ask the abbot for permission. Through obedience, then, spiritual paternity established a firm bond between the spiritual "son" and his "father," at least until the disciple reached a spiritual maturity allowing him to exert personal discernment and so to instruct others in his own turn.[16]

2   Traditions on the Lives and Sayings of the Fathers: The AP in the Correspondence

The continuity between the present and the past, which permeates the literature of Gaza monasticism from Abba Isaiah to Dorotheus,[17] relies at its core on

---

14 C 189. Translation from John Chryssavgis, *Barsanuphius and John: Letters*, 2 vols., FC 113–114 (Washington DC: Catholic University of America Press, 2006), here: I, 198–199.
15 C 308; Chryssavgis, I, 292.
16 The first lot of letters (C 1–54) paradigmatically illustrates this spiritual itinerary. Cf. Lorenzo Perrone, "Εἰς τὸν τῆς ἡσυχίας λιμένα: Le lettere a Giovanni di Beersheva nella corrispondenza di Barsanufio e Giovanni di Gaza," in *Mémorial Dom Jean Gribomont (1920–1986)* (Rome: Institutum Patristicum Augustinianum, 1988), 463–486.
17 Whether or not we ought to consider it a "school" is discussed in Brouria Bitton-Ashkelony,

the permanent validity of the lives and sayings of the Desert Fathers as a source of inspiration. The *AP* exemplify the experiences of spiritual paternity; and the Correspondence of the two elders largely draws on them as an already existing literary corpus (rather than as an oral repository of shared memories), alongside other early monastic and theological literature cited to a lesser extent.[18] Only Scripture, obviously, surpasses the number of direct or implied references to the *AP*, although a process of "scripturalization" already attends citations of the sayings of the Desert Fathers by allotting to them, more or less, a sort of "canonical" status, as will be shown below.

Modern editors and translators of the Correspondence have long noticed that the letters include about eighty direct references to the *AP*, whereas Dorotheus has fifty-five.[19] Due to the large number of quotations and allusions, it is impossible to present a detailed analysis, in particular of those passages whose source has not yet been identified.[20] What first attracts our attention is the explicit mention of some figures whom we principally know through the *Alphabetic Collection* of the *AP*. In more than twenty passages, the names of the following Egyptian Fathers (and Mothers) appear: Antony (once),[21] Arsenius (four times),[22] John the Dwarf (twice),[23] Joseph of Panephysis (once),[24] Macarius (twice),[25] Nisteros the Cenobite (once),[26] Poemen (four times),[27] Sarah (once),[28] Sisoes (twice),[29] and Theodore of Pherme (three times).[30] In

---

"Monasticism in Late Antique Gaza: A School or an Epoch?" in *L'école de Gaza: Espace littéraire et identité culturelle dans l'antiquité tardive*, ed. Eugenio Amato, Aldo Corcella, and Delphine Lauritzen (Leuven: Peeters, 2017), 19–36.

18 With regard to the other monastic sources, apart from several allusions to the *Asceticon* of Abba Isaiah (see above, n. 10), we find references to Evagrius Ponticus (C 600), the *Historia Monachorum* (C 752), Palladius' *Historia Lausiaca* (C 42, 90, 143), and Jerome's *Vita Hilarionis* (C 618) and *Vita Malchi* (C 69). As regards the great theologians, the letters mention Origen (C 600), Athanasius (C 604), Basil (C 318–319, 604), Gregory of Nazianzus (C 604, 807), Gregory of Nyssa (C 604), Didymus the Blind (C 600), and John Chrysostom (C 464, 604).

19 See, e.g., SChr 450, pp. 69–105; Chryssavgis, *Barsanuphius and John*, 11.
20 Cf. above, n. 3.
21 C 599.
22 C 126, 191, 256 (twice).
23 C 311, 693.
24 C 432.
25 C 140 (Macarius the Egyptian) and 549 (this Macarius and his saying remain unidentified).
26 C 291.
27 C 604 (twice: οἱ Πατέρες ἡμῶν, οἱ περὶ τὸν ἀββᾶν Ποιμένα καὶ τοὺς καθ' ἑξῆς .... Ἐξιχνιάσατε τὰ ἴχνη τῶν Πατέρων ἡμῶν, Ποιμένος καὶ τῶν καθ' ἑξῆς); C 654 (twice).
28 C 237.
29 C 385.
30 C 123.

order properly to evaluate the significance of these numbers, one should compare them with the series of hidden or implied references. These contain sayings and stories of further monastic figures, and confirm the impression of a deep familiarity with the *AP*: Agathon,[31] Alonius,[32] Amoun,[33] Bessarion,[34] Daniel,[35] Euprepios,[36] Isaac of the Cells,[37] John the Persian,[38] Mios,[39] Moses,[40] Nisteros,[41] Peter the Pionite,[42] Silvanus.[43]

By comparing the list of explicit references in the Correspondence with the names mentioned by Dorotheus, we detect in his *Instructions* many other representatives of early monasticism and the "classic" patristic theology,[44] although such references are not completely ignored in the letters (see first and foremost, the important exchange on the doctrines of "Origenism").[45] One is especially struck by Dorotheus' frequent recourse to Evagrius, the ascetic teacher *par excellence*, and the two great Cappadocians Basil and Gregory of Nazianzus (whose hymns were even the subject of Dorotheus' commentaries,

---

31 C 261, 340, 342, 347, 410, 458.
32 C 346.
33 C 469.
34 C 207, 241.
35 C 605.
36 C 291.
37 C 123.
38 C 350.
39 C 144.
40 C 341.
41 C 291.
42 C 90.
43 C 204.
44 Antony (Dorotheus of Gaza, *Didaskaliai* 1,11; 2,30; 4,48; 7,86; *Epistulae* 1,181; 13,198), Agathon (*Didask.* 2,37; 4,52; 5,68; 9,102), Alonius (*Didask.* 9,102), Ammonas (*Didask.* 6,76), Arsenius (*Didask.* 10,104), Basil (*Didask.* 1,24; 2,31; 3,41; 4,48; 8,90; 10,106; 12,131.134.136; 14,157; 17,176–177), Evagrius Ponticus (*Didask.* 2,29.39; 8,89; 12,126.131; 14,153; 16,166; 17,176), Gregory of Nazianzus (*Didask.* 1,4; 2,31.39; 10,106; 16,166.168.170; 17,174.176), John Chrysostom (*Didask.* 12,128; 16,169), Macarius (*Didask.* 2,31), Pachomius (*Didask.* 1,11), Poemen (*Didask.* 5,63; 7,81.86; 10,109; 13,138; *Ep.* 6,191; 8,193; 14,199), Sisoes (*Didask.* 13,141); Zosimas (*Didask.* 1,14; 2,31.36; 6,77; 8,91–94). On Dorotheus' sources, see Judith Pauli, ed. and transl., *Dorotheus von Gaza, Doctrinae diversae*, Fontes Christiani 37, vol. 1, (Freiburg i. Br.: Herder, 2000), 35–43.
45 C 600–607. Cf. Lorenzo Perrone, "Palestinian Monasticism, the Bible, and Theology in the Wake of the Second Origenist Controversy," in *The Sabaite Heritage in the Orthodox Church from the Fifth Century to the Present*, ed. Josef Patrich (Leuven: Peeters, 2001), 245–259; Daniël Hombergen, "Barsanuphius and John of Gaza and the Origenist controversy," in *Christian Gaza in Late Antiquity*, 173–181.

written for his monastic community who used them in the liturgy).⁴⁶ Leaving aside the different emphasis on such spiritual and theological authorities, both the Correspondence and Dorotheus' *Instructions* are deeply immersed in the Fathers of the Desert. They eventually prefigure a behaviour not too different from that of a monk, whom Abba Zosimas described as "continually reading the *Sayings of the Fathers* and almost breathing in them, so as to extract from them the fruits of every virtue."⁴⁷

Unlike in Zosimas' *Adloquia*, the expression ἀποφθέγματα τῶν ἁγίων γερόντων occurs neither in the letters of Barsanuphius and John, nor in Dorotheus.⁴⁸ Yet these texts clearly indicate that the *Alphabetic* and the *Systematic Collections* were circulated as written collections of sayings and stories. Not incidentally, how the references are introduced often tends to obliterate the oral context that generated the sayings, so that we have "it is written in the Fathers" or "the Fathers write"⁴⁹ instead of the expected "the Fathers say." The same thing happens with the Correspondence itself: the responses go back to a "spoken word" (λόγος) addressed by the two recluses to the abbot, which Seridus (or other intermediaries) forwarded in turn as a written text.⁵⁰

Accordingly, the traditions of the AP must have already taken the form of a book which is referenced as: the Book(s) of the Elders,⁵¹ the Lives (or the Sayings and Lives) of the Elders,⁵² or the Lives of the Fathers (or the Life of the

---

46   Dorotheus, *Didask.* 16–17.
47   Zosimas, *Adloquia* 10 (PG 78, 1693C): ἠγάπα δὲ ὁ μακάριος πάντοτε διέρχεσθαι αὐτὰ (*scil.* τὰ ἀποφθέγματα τῶν ἁγίων γερόντων) καὶ σχεδὸν ἔπνεεν.
48   Not even the word ῥῆμα was more successful than ἀπόφθεγμα. Interestingly, it is used both for the verses taken from Scripture (C 16: πολλάκις ἔγραψά σοι, ἐξ ἐμοῦ τὰ τῆς Γραφῆς ῥήματα τοῦ Κυρίου; C 429: the ῥήματα of the Psalter) and for the divinely inspired words of the Fathers: see C 199 (φυλάξαι τὰ λαλούμενά σοι θεῖα ῥήματα, οὐκ ἐξ ἀνθρώπου ἀλλ' ἐκ Πνεύματος ἁγίου), C 229 (τὰ προσπαρέντα ῥήματα παρ' ἐμοῦ δι' ἐγγράφων ἀποκρίσεων), C 383 (Τὰ ῥήματα τῶν ἁγίων οὐκ ὀφείλομεν ἀργὰ νομίζειν, ἐνεργῆ γάρ εἰσι καὶ κατὰ Θεὸν εἰρημένα).
49   See, for instance, C 125 (Τί δὲ ὅτι καὶ περὶ τοῦ θεοῦ ἔγραψαν οἱ Πατέρες ἐρωτηθέντες), introducing a quotation of *Sisoes* 40. Cf. also C 128 (Γέγραπται εἰς τοὺς γέροντας), C 143 (ἐν τοῖς Βίοις τῶν Γερόντων γέγραπται), C 163 (γράφουσιν οἱ Πατέρες, a reference to the *Asceticon* of Abba Isaiah), C 350 (Γράφει γὰρ εἰς τοὺς Πατέρας), C 370 (ῥήματα τῶν Πατέρων ἐγγράφως κείμενα).
50   Thus C 32 compares Barsanuphius' letters to John of Beersheva (see above, n. 16) to "a whole library" (ὅλην γὰρ ἔχουσι τὴν βιβλιοθήκην), and, according to C 49, they recall both the Old and the New Testament, so that there is no need of another book (Μαρύκησον εἰς τὰς ἐπιστολὰς καὶ σώζῃ, ἔχεις γὰρ ἐν αὐταῖς, ἐὰν συνιῇς, τὴν Παλαιὰν καὶ τὴν Καινήν. Καὶ νοῶν αὐτάς, οὐ χρείαν ἔχεις ἄλλου βιβλίου).
51   C 185 (ἀνέγνω εἰς Γεροντικά), 605 (εἰς Βιβλία Γερόντων). See Dorotheus, *Didask.* 1,18 (Τὸ Γεροντικόν).
52   C 185 (ἐν τοῖς βίοις τῶν γερόντων), 600 (εἰς τὰ Ῥήματα αὐτῶν καὶ εἰς τοὺς Βίους). On C 143, see n. 53.

Fathers and their Responses).⁵³ The sayings as such were part of the monastic library, alongside other early ascetic literature such as the *Asceticon* of Abba Isaiah, the *Historia monachorum in Aegypto*, the *Lausiac History* of Palladius, and the monastic *Lives* of Jerome, and they were perhaps not always being clearly distinguished from them.⁵⁴ By contrast, the two elders and their correspondents differentiate them from the "dogmatic books," that is discourses dealing with theological matters, which were also available in the coenobium of Seridus.⁵⁵ At any rate, the establishment of the *AP* as a distinct literary corpus anticipated all the various performances and uses that a written text may convey, from reading, memorization and meditation to narration and interpretation.

3 Authoritative Words and Their Interpretation: Remarks on the Uses of the *AP* in the Correspondence

Many different aspects should be taken into consideration when dealing with the use of the *AP* in the Correspondence: what kind of references exactly do we have (quotations, reminiscences, allusions, generalizations and so on)? To what extent are the sayings endowed with an authority of their own? Are they viewed, for instance, as a sort of oracular statement or inspired words? Are they quoted literally or are they rewritten or adapted? Do they reflect in some way a practice of memorization concomitant with the habit of reading them? Have they gained, as a consequence, a proverbial status? How do they fit into the argument, given the essentially "paraenetic" nature of the letters in response to particular questions and needs of individuals? Is there, so to say, a rhetorical strategy for invoking the sayings? Does their insertion into the spiritual discourse of the two elders confer upon them a special weight? How do the sayings combine with the verses of Scripture? Do they normally appeal to a

---

53   C 150 (τοὺς Βίους τῶν Πατέρων), 689 (περὶ τοῦ Βίου τῶν Πατέρων καὶ τῶν Ἀποκρίσεων αὐτῶν).
54   In fact, C 143 (ἐν τοῖς Βίοις τῶν Γερόντων) is a reference to the *Historia Lausiaca*.
55   Concerning the possession and circulation of books, C 326 records Dorotheus' wish to put his books at the disposal of the coenobium so that everybody could read them (Ἐπειδὴ βιβλία ἔχω ἰδικά, καὶ ὁ λογισμός λέγει μοι δοῦναι αὐτὰ τῷ κοινοβίῳ καὶ ἀμεριμνῆσαι, ὁπότε κοινά ἐστι τὰ τοῦ κοινοβίου καὶ ἑκάστῳ δίδοται ἐν αὐτοῖς ἀναγινώσκειν). In C 547, a monk has "dogmatic books" among his personal belongings (Δογματικὰ βιβλία ἔχω καὶ ἀναγινώσκων εἰς αὐτά). For the reading of dogmatic books, see also C 606 (ἀνέγνων γὰρ εἰς βιβλίον δογματικὸν). C 600 mentions the books of Origen, Didymus, and Evagrius (ἐνέπεσα εἰς τὰ βιβλία Ὠριγένους καὶ Διδύμου, καὶ εἰς τὰ Γνωστικὰ Εὐαγρίου καὶ εἰς τὰ τῶν μαθητῶν αὐτοῦ). In C 228, most of the books are in Greek (Αἱ γὰρ πλεῖσται τῶν βίβλων ἑλληνικῇ διαλέκτῳ εὑρίσκονται).

shared spiritual heritage, or are they brought forth to establish that heritage more fully? Are the sayings mainly used for "pedagogical" purposes, that is for the instruction of younger monks or beginners in the monastic life, or do they support monasticism more generally? And in this case, do they also purport to be a presentation of Christianity valid in general for all the faithful?

A thoroughgoing analysis would require the address of all of these issues and others as well. But for the sake of this short investigation it will suffice to discuss some exemplary cases. Let us then analyze, as a paradigmatic selection, the references to Abba Poemen. He is indeed the Desert Father whom the Correspondence, according to the quantitative data of the *Alphabetic Collection*, most frequently cites or alludes to (with at least a dozen sayings and four explicit mentions of his name).[56] Besides, in the midst of the controversy on Origenism, Poemen is introduced as the one who, together with his disciples, personifies for Barsanuphius the goals and values of the monastic *praxis* as opposed to *gnôsis*.[57]

Poemen 38 (= *System*. IV, 34 bis) consists of a very short sentence, with a biblical imprint and devoid of any anecdotal context, that rejects "every bodily comfort" (σωματικὴ ἀνάπαυσις), since it "is an abomination to the Lord" (βδέλυγμά ἐστι Κυρίῳ).[58] Three letters echo this apophthegm: in C 96 we have a rephrasing of the *dictum* in a hortatory address, in order to avoid the estrangement from God coming from "the comfort of the flesh."[59] In C 186, an important "mystical" text of Barsanuphius, the Great Old Man closes the paraenetic section at the end of the letter with a nearly faithful quotation of Poemen's sentence.[60] Finally, the most literal quotation appears in C 191, as the *incipit* of a

---

[56]   Here is the list of the references to the *Alphabetic Collection* (with the corresponding letters): *Poemen* 38 (C 96, 186, 191), 45 (C 291), 48 (C 596), 55 (C 279), 58 (C 347bis), 86 (C 371), 120 (C 244), 123 (C 316), 125 (C 492), 129 (C 433, 541), 131 (C 654), 147 (C 205, 287), 149 (C 500, 613), 159 (C 550), 162 (C 237). See SChr 450, pp. 79–83.

[57]   Cf. C 604 (Περὶ τούτων ὀφείλομεν σπουδάσαι, περὶ ὧν καὶ οἱ Πατέρες ἡμῶν, οἱ περὶ τὸν ἀββᾶν Ποιμένα καὶ τοὺς καθ' ἑξῆς ἐσπούδασαν ... Ἐξιχνιάσατε τὰ ἴχνη τῶν Πατέρων ἡμῶν, Ποιμένος καὶ τῶν καθ' ἑξῆς). For the debate on the role of Poemen and its significance in early monasticism, see Daniël Hombergen, *The Second Origenist Controversy: A New Perspective on Cyril of Scythopolis' Monastic Biographies as Historical Sources for Sixth-Century Origenism*, StAns 132 (Rome: Centro studi S. Anselmo, 2001), 235. According to Zanetti, "Les Apophtegmes et la Terre Sainte," 26, "le noyau primitif [of the AP] a certainement pris naissance dans le cercle des disciples de Poemen."

[58]   *Poemen* 38 (Εἶπε πάλιν· βδέλυγμά ἐστι Κυρίῳ πᾶσα σωματικὴ ἀνάπαυσις).

[59]   C 96 (Μισήσωμεν τὴν ἀνάπαυσιν τῆς σαρκός, βδελυκτὴ γάρ ἐστι τῷ Θεῷ, ἵνα μὴ ἀλλοτριώσῃ ἡμᾶς τοῦ θεοῦ).

[60]   C 186 (βδελυκτὴ γάρ ἐνώπιον Κυρίου ἐστὶ πᾶσα ἀνάπαυσις σαρκός). For the "mystical" approach, cf. Giovanni Filoramo, "Mistica e politica: Il caso di Barsanufio di Gaza," in *L'Anti-*

long exhortation (here as elsewhere in relation to σάρξ and not to σῶμα, a preference probably dictated by the language of Scripture), followed by the image of the "narrow road" of Matt 7:14. Consequently, the insertion of the *dictum* at the beginning aims to sum up "the way of the good will,"[61] while Barsanuphius afterwards exemplifies the recommended "affliction of the flesh" by pointing to Arsenius, who was sleeping "on straw pillows" (*Arsenius* 36). In fact, by adding this detail, the Great Old Man modifies the sense of the story in the *Alphabetic Collection* (in *Arsenius* 36, the "pillow" was a reason for blaming, at first, the "comfort" of the elder) to reassert the ascetic standard of Arsenius.[62]

Another case in which we observe the mere quotation of a saying is *Poemen* 48 (= *System.* XI, 62). John cites it in C 596 as the axiomatic conclusion of a short answer to Elianus, Seridus' successor as abbot, regarding the observance of the commandments given by a spiritual father: "For it is said, even if you create a new heaven and a new earth, nevertheless you are unable to be carefree."[63] Dorotheus also uses the saying in one of the *Instructions*, though his reference appears in a different form: the *dictum* is part of an argument regarding whether or not one's heart may be worthy of receiving comfort from God, or whether such a comfort may harm him.[64] A second quotation likewise expands the apophthegm with a conditional clause on the possibility of receiving "comfort" (ἀνάπαυσις) for the sake of one's "education" (παιδεία).[65] One wonders whether such interpretive expansion might go back to Dorotheus or if he has received *Poemen* 48 in this form.

Elsewhere, with a recognizable allusion to *Poemen* 58 (= *System.* XIII, 5), Barsanuphius draws from the dialogue in the story personal advice for somebody "who had closed his cell door for a long time, but continued to be troubled by secret thoughts." In C 347b the Great Old Man recommends to him:

Babele. Sulla mistica degli antichi e dei moderni, ed. Isabella Adinolfi, Giancarlo Gaeta, and Andreina Lavagetto (Genoa: Melangolo, 2017), 217–229.

61   C 191 (πᾶσα ἀνάπαυσις σαρκός βδέλυγμα τῷ Θεῷ ἡμῶν ἐστιν).

62   "I should be ashamed … that some are sleeping on the ground, others on straw pillows (προσκεφαλαδίων ἀχύρων), such as Arsenius among the saints" (Chryssavgis, I, 200). But *Arsenius* 36 only speaks of a "pillow" (τὸ προσκεφάλαιον ὑποκάτω αὐτοῦ), and precisely this raised a scandal with a rustic brother.

63   C 596 (Ἐὰν γὰρ ποιήσῃς, φησίν, οὐρανὸν καινὸν καὶ γῆν καινήν, οὐ δύνασαι ἀμεριμνῆσαι); Chryssavgis, II, 173. Cf. *Poemen* 48 (Εἶπε πάλιν ὁ ἀββᾶς Ποιμήν, ὅτι Ἐὰν ποιήσῃ ἄνθρωπος καινὸν οὐρανὸν καὶ καινὴν γῆν, οὐ δύναται ἀμεριμνῆσαι).

64   Dorotheus, *Didask.* 7,84 (ἐὰν δὲ οὐκ ἔστιν ἄξιος τοῦ ἀναπαῆναι ἢ οὐ συμφέρει αὐτῷ, καινὸν οὐρανὸν καὶ καινὴν γῆν ἐὰν ποιήσῃ οὐχ εὑρίσκει ἀνάπαυσιν).

65   See *Ep.* 16, 201 (Ἐὰν δὲ οὐκ ἔστιν ἄξιος ἢ οὐ συμφέρει αὐτῷ ἐν τῇ παιδείᾳ αὐτοῦ παρακληθῆναι, καινὸν οὐρανὸν καὶ καινὴν γῆν ἐὰν ποιήσῃ, οὐχ εὑρίσκει ἀνάπαυσιν).

"Therefore, do not close your door but only your tongue."[66] A slight adaptation of a saying can also be found in C 244, where Barsanuphius inserts into a definition of "the repentance from sin" the interplay between question and answer in *Poemen* 120: "Repentance from sin … means no longer committing this sin."[67]

If the previous examples generally convey the idea of a basically faithful rendering of the sayings, this could depend primarily on the practice of reading the *AP*. Still, there are instances in the Correspondence where we might think that they reflect more directly the habit of memorization.[68] In such "performative" use the sayings would lead to the creation of proverbs or contribute to an "antirrhetic" stock of scriptural verses and sayings in conformity with Evagrius' method for responding to "thoughts."[69] One of these cases might be C 316, where John introduces *Poemen* 123 as a sentence of the Fathers: "As for being disturbed by other people, the Fathers have said: 'Is there a person in

---

[66] C 347b (Τὴν θύραν οὖν μὴ κλείσῃς, ἀλλὰ τὴν γλῶσσαν); Chryssavgis, I, 318. Cf. *Poemen* 58 (Λέγει αὐτῷ ὁ ἀββᾶς Ποιμήν· Ἡμεῖς οὐκ ἐμάθομεν κλείειν τὴν ξυλίνην θύραν, ἀλλὰ μᾶλλον τὴν τῆς γλώσσης θύραν).

[67] C 244 (Ἡ δὲ μετάνοια τῆς ἁμαρτίας, τὸ μηκέτι ποιῆσαι ταύτην ἐστί); Chryssavgis, I, 250. Cf. *Poemen* 120 (Ἠρώτησεν ἀδελφὸς τὸν ἀββᾶν Ποιμένα· Τί ἐστι μετάνοια τῆς ἁμαρτίας; Καὶ εἶπεν ὁ γέρων· Τὸ μὴ τοῦ λοιποῦ ποιεῖν αὐτήν).

[68] On the memorization of the sayings, see Dorotheus, *Didask.* 6 (Εἰ ἐμνημονεύομεν, ἀδελφοί, τῶν λόγων τῶν ἁγίων γερόντων, εἰ ἐμελετῶμεν αὐτοὺς πάντοτε δυσχερῶς εἴχομεν ἁμαρτάνειν, δυσχερῶς εἴχομεν ἀμελεῖν ἑαυτῶν). We may after all apply to the coenobium of Seridus the insight on Egyptian monasticism gained by Hugo Lundhaug, "Memory and Early Monastic Literary Practices," *Journal of Cognitive Historiography* 1 (2014): 109: "memory … was distributed both across the individual minds of the monks, who were each supposed to have memorized an impressive number of texts from which they were continually reciting, and from across a considerable collection of books, many of which were rehearsed by being read aloud to other members of the community at institutionally designated times."

[69] As for the performative use of the sayings, see C 256: "Say to yourself the words of the blessed Arsenius (εἰπὲ σεαυτῷ τὸν λόγον τοῦ μακαρίου Ἀρσενίου): 'Arsenius, why did you leave the world?'" (*Arsenius* 40; Chryssavgis, I, 261). Consider further the rich use of the imperative verb εἰπέ (or the expression εἰπὲ τῷ λογισμῷ, and similar phrases), also used for "spiritual exercises" and for recalling verses from Scripture for meditation and prayer as, for instance, in C 379 (Εἰ τοίνυν σωθῆναι θέλεις, μετανόησον καὶ κόψον ὅλα τὰ θανάσιμα ἐκεῖνα, καὶ εἰπὲ μετὰ τοῦ Δαβίδ· Νῦν ἠρξάμην (Ps 76:11)). Concerning the transformation into a proverb, perhaps the best example is the use of *Agathon* 1 (Οὐκ ἔστιν ἕτερον πάθος χαλεπώτερον τῆς παρρησίας· γεννήτρια γάρ ἐστι πάντων τῶν παθῶν) in C 261 (Ἡ δὲ παρρησία μήτηρ ἐστὶ πάντων τῶν παθῶν), C 340, C 342, C 347 (Οἱ Πατέρες γὰρ ἔλεγον περὶ αὐτῆς ὅτι ἀπολεῖ τοὺς καρποὺς τοῦ μοναχοῦ), C 458 (Ἔστι παρρησία ἀπὸ ἀναιδείας καὶ αὕτη ἐστὶ γεννήτρια πάντων τῶν κακῶν). See also Dorotheus, *Didask.* 4,52 (Οὐκ ἔστι πάθος χαλεπώτερον τῆς παρρησίας· γεννήτρια γάρ ἐστι πάντων τῶν παθῶν); Cyril of Scythopolis, *Vita Euthymii* 19 (τὴν παρρησίαν γὰρ χαλεπωτέραν εἶναι καὶ γεννήτριαν πάντων τῶν παθῶν οἱ πατέρες ὁρίζονται).

the throes of death and yet still involved in the friendships of this world?'"[70] In this case, as indicated by the use of a relatively rare verb (ῥέγχω [ῥέγκω]), we probably have a "proverbial" reception of the sentence, as happens with other sayings.[71]

A saying can be conveyed together with the story in which it originated, as is shown by the interesting reuse of *Poemen* 131 in C 654. John quotes it to contrast what happened to a faithful person (a master unable to endure his bad servant, who then went away) with the behaviour suggested by Poemen in a similar case.

> For indeed, some of the fathers used to say about Abba Poemen, regarding a certain elder, that he kept his disciple in spite of his laziness. And Abba Poemen said: "If I could, I would place a pillow under his head." And they said to him: "Then, what would you say to God?" And he replied: "I would say to God: 'You are the one who said, *Hypocrite, first remove the log from your own eye, and then you will see clearly to take the speck out of your brother's eye* (Matt 7:5).'"[72]

John suppresses the "historical" details concerning the other monastic figures around Poemen (Abba Nisteros and Abba Anub), but he "enriches" the story by accusing the disciple of an elder of "laziness" (ῥᾳθυμοῦντα), whereas Poemen's apophthegm only mentions Nisteros' patience. In this way, a basic fidelity

---

70   C 316 (Περὶ δὲ τῆς ὀχλήσεως τῶν ἀνθρώπων, εἶπον οἱ Πατέρες· "Ἔστιν ἄνθρωπος ῥέγχων εἰς τὸ ἀποθανεῖν, καὶ προσέχων φιλίαις τοῦ κόσμου τούτου"). I modify the translation of Chryssavgis, I, 297, following Regnault. Cf. *Poemen* 123 ("Ἔστιν ἄνθρωπος ῥέγχων εἰς τὸ ἀποθανεῖν, καὶ προσέχων φιλίαις τοῦ κόσμου τούτου).

71   We can perhaps point to the use of *Poemen* 129 (Εἶπε πάλιν, ὅτι Τὰ ὑπέρμετρα πάντα τῶν δαιμόνων εἰσίν) in C 433 (Ἠκούσαμεν γὰρ ὅτι τὰ μετὰ ταραχῆς καὶ λύπης καὶ τὰ περισσὰ ταῦτα ὅλα, τῶν δαιμόνων ἐστίν) and C 541 (Οἱ Πατέρες γὰρ λέγουσιν ὅτι τὰ περισσὰ τῶν δαιμόνων εἰσίν). For further examples, see the sentence "thanksgiving intercedes before God for one's human weakness" (Chryssavgis, I, 102) in C 77 (Ἐν παντὶ οὖν εὐχαρίστησον αὐτῷ, ὅτι ἡ εὐχαριστία πρεσβεύει ὑπὲρ τῆς ἀδυναμίας τοῦ ἀνθρώπου πρὸς τὸν Θεόν). Cf. *Systematic Collection* 21,48 (Εἶπε γέρων· Ἡ εὐχαριστία πρεσβεύει ὑπὲρ τῆς ἀδυναμίας ἔναντι Κυρίου). The same saying occurs three more times in the letters: C 92 (Τὴν εὐχαριστίαν εἰς πάντα κράτει, ὅτι αὕτη πρεσβεύει ὑπὲρ τῆς ἀδυναμίας ἐνώπιον τοῦ Θεοῦ), C 123 (Οὐκ ἀπαιτεῖ ὁ Θεὸς τὸν ἀσθενοῦντα, καθὼς πολλάκις ἤκουσεν, εἰ μὴ μόνον τὴν εὐχαριστίαν καὶ τὴν ὑπομονήν. Αὗται γὰρ πρεσβεύουσιν ὑπὲρ τῆς ἀδυναμίας ἐνώπιον τοῦ Θεοῦ), C 214 (Ἐπὶ πᾶσι δὲ εὐχαρίστησον τῷ Θεῷ, Ἡ γὰρ εὐχαριστία πρεσβεύει ὑπὲρ τῆς ἀδυναμίας πρὸς τὸν Θεόν). There are, as it seems, no other occurrences of this sentence, other than the AP and the Correspondence. Another example of a proverbial use is the quotation of a saying by *Peter the Pionite* 2 in C 90, "your little key opens my door" (τὸ κλειδίον σου ἀνοίγει μου τὴν θύραν); Chryssavgis, I, 111.

72   Chryssavgis, II, 227.

allows some room for an adaptation, reflecting, as it seems, more directly the language and the concerns of the Correspondence.[73]

Moreover, a saying can present itself as supporting a personal opinion or as a direct sentence of the Fathers. *Poemen* 147 addresses a major issue of the monastic way of life: "Is it better to talk or to be silent?" Poemen replies that both to talk and to be silent are good, provided that one does it according to God.[74] In C 205, John echoes Poemen's *dictum* in his response to a hesychast, who had asked his advice about encounters with other brethren. But he rephrases and adapts the apophthegm, presenting it as personal opinion: "What I think is the following: being in the company of others for the sake of God is a good thing; and not being in the company of others for the sake of God is also a good thing."[75] To the contrary, in C 287 John, addressing himself to Dorotheus, neatly distinguishes the *dictum* and his own interpretation:

> The fathers said that: 'One who speaks for God is doing a good thing; and one who is silent for God is also doing a good thing.' This saying of the fathers may be interpreted in the following way: as I have told you, one who speaks without passion is doing a good thing, for that person is speaking for the sake of God; and one who sees that one is about to speak with passion and therefore keeps silent, is also doing a good thing, for that person is keeping silent for God.[76]

As elsewhere in the Correspondence, the apophthegm is accompanied by an explanation that justifies the apparently paradoxical *dictum* and applies it to the particular situation of the addressee by considering the possible implication of the role of the passions. Returning to this same issue in C 291, in a response to Dorotheus, John explicitly states the necessity of interpreting the sayings of the Fathers. Dorotheus indeed was wondering why "he was allowed to speak, even before being asked," whereas "the fathers say that one should not speak without being asked." Dorotheus presumably thought also of *Euprepios* 7 and *Poemen* 45, but to exemplify such an attitude, he referred to

---

73   The group of words ῥᾳθυμέω, ῥᾳθυμία, ῥᾴθυμος is quite frequent in the Correspondence (30 occurrences), whereas in the AP it rarely occurs (4 times).
74   Poemen 147 (Ἀδελφὸς ἠρώτησε τὸν ἀββᾶν Ποιμένα, λέγων· Βέλτιόν ἐστι τὸ λαλῆσαι ἢ σιωπῆσαι; Λέγει αὐτῷ ὁ γέρων, ὅτι Ὁ λαλῶν διὰ τὸν θεὸν καλῶς ποιεῖ, καὶ ὁ σιωπῶν διὰ τὸν θεόν, ὁμοίως).
75   C 205 (Τοῦτο δὲ λογίζομαι ὅτι τὸ συντυγχάνειν διὰ τὸν θεὸν καλόν ἐστι, καὶ τὸ μὴ συντυγχάνειν διὰ τὸν θεὸν καλόν ἐστι); Chryssavgis, I, 213.
76   C 287 (Εἶπον οἱ Πατέρες ὅτι "Ὁ λαλῶν διὰ τὸν Θεὸν καλόν ἐστι, καὶ ὁ σιωπῶν διὰ τὸν Θεὸν καλόν ἐστιν." Ὁ λόγος δὲ τῶν Πατέρων τοῦτ' ἐστι ...); Chryssavgis, I, 282.

the *dictum* of Abba Nisteros, "The donkey and I are one" (*Nisteros the Cenobite* 2).[77] John replied that "the old men speak according to the measure of those who listen,"[78] thus pointing to the criterion of the ascetic "measure" (μέτρον)—a key notion in the spiritual discourse of the Correspondence—and stressing with it the necessity of spiritual discernment. He added also the notion of time and the circumstances (καιρός) to make the injunction of the elders more understandable and adaptable: "So there is a time and a measure when someone should serve others, and at that time one must display deeds of service. Moreover, there is also a time when the same person reaches the point of being served by others, and the measures of this are again different" (ἄλλα ἐστὶ τὰ μέτρα τούτου). Similar advice was delivered by John to Dorotheus in C 318 when he was "reading the *Ascetica* of St. Basil" and thought to apply an ascetic "chapter" (κεφάλαιον) to himself that in reality was meant for hermits able to exert "discernment" (διάκρισις). In this way, John implied again the diversity of "measures," in relation to the different conditions of the monastic life, while restating the primacy of obedience for a cenobite like Dorotheus.[79]

4 Words for a Perfect Life: The *Sayings of the Fathers* and Scripture

The need for interpretation and adaptation of the sayings, so as to be able to comply with them in different situations, while confirming their "canonical" status, did not of itself distinguish the *AP* from Scripture. As a matter of fact, the Bible too demanded a hermeneutical approach going beyond the mere adherence to it. The two Old Men were aware of this, as it seems, even in the wake of the Alexandrian tradition of allegorical exegesis.[80] In this sense it is possi-

---

77 C 291; Chryssavgis, I, 285.
78 C 291 (Ἀδελφέ, πρὸς τὸ μέτρον τοῦ ἀνθρώπου λέγουσιν οἱ Γέροντες).
79 C 318 (Τοῦτο τὸ κεφάλαιον τῷ κατὰ μόνας εἴρηται καὶ δυναμένῳ ἑαυτὸν κυβερνῆσαι μετὰ διακρίσεως); Chryssavgis, I, 298. For other examples, see C 123 with reference to *Isaac* 2 and the *dictum* of Theodore of Pherme: "For being ill, he should not apply to himself the word of Abba Theodore, who said about the brother: 'I am not the head of a monastic community (κοινοβιάρχης) in order to command him.'" (Chryssavgis, I, 141). Cf. also C 385 on *Sisoes* 12.
80 See, for instance, John's response in C 469, a quintessentially Alexandrian interpretation. Cf. also Barsanuphius' sentence in C 241 (Ἀδελφέ, ὅλα πνευματικῶς ἀλληγορεῖται καὶ σὺ σαρκικῶς ταῦτα νοεῖς). And in C 605, Barsanuphius appears to be familiar with the hermeneutical approach typical of Origen (Τί γὰρ καὶ εἰς τὴν Γραφὴν οὐκ ἔστι ῥήματα τοῖς ἀμαθέσι καὶ μὴ γινώσκουσι τὸ πνευματικὸν τῆς Γραφῆς πρόσκομμα; Ὀφείλομεν οὖν εἰπεῖν· Διὰ τί τὸ πνευματικὸν τῆς Γραφῆς φανερῶς οὐκ εἶπε ὁ Θεός, ἵνα μὴ βλάβωσιν ἄνθρωποι; Ἀλλ' ἀφῆκε τοῖς κατὰ καιρὸν ἁγίοις πόνον τοῦ ἑρμηνεῦσαι τὰ ζητούμενα).

ble to speak of convergent attitudes that were engaged towards the two bodies of writings. Besides, the juxtaposition of the Bible and the *AP* in the daily life of the monks, emerging in several passages of the Correspondence,[81] promoted to some extent their assimilation, while also creating a certain concurrence between them. Yet, although the *AP* are depicted as being accessible in principle to everyone—hesychasts, cenobites and even lay persons—the same is not true for Scripture. At least, to read Scripture and to search for its deeper meaning requires, according to the two Old Men, some caution and, most of all, spiritual maturity.

For Barsanuphius, writing in C 79 to the hesychast Andrew, Scripture and the Fathers are the two parallel authorities which, in the case of an illness, permit "condescension toward the body, when it is brought about not by sensual pleasure but with discernment."[82] There is an analogous parallelism in the way the letters articulate the message they wish to convey: in most cases, the sentences of the Fathers anticipate, echo or confirm the verses taken from Scripture, leading to a sort of "scripturalization" of the *AP* in the "highly biblical style" of the Correspondence.[83] To offer just one example: C 144, a letter of consolation and encouragement sent by the Great Old Man to a monk troubled by despondency, aligns the words of Scripture with those of the Fathers:

> In any case, it is written: "The measure that you measure out will be the measure you shall yourself receive in turn" (Luke 6:38). Furthermore, the fathers have said: "Obedience for obedience" (*Mios* 1). So offer a hand to your brother, who is beside you and is troubled; you will find that he shall in turn give you a hand in the time of your own affliction.[84]

---

[81] See especially the customs of praying with the Psalms, and meditating and reading the *Lives of the Fathers*, encouraged by John in C 143.

[82] C 79 (Οὐκ ἐκώλυσεν ἡ Γραφὴ οὐδὲ οἱ Πατέρες τὴν πρὸς τὸ σῶμα συγκατάβασιν, τὴν οὐ κατὰ ἡδονήν, ἀλλὰ μετὰ διακρίσεως γινομένην); Chryssavgis, I, 105. The combination of Fathers and Scripture appears also in Dorotheus, *Didask.* 9,117 (Ἰδοὺ πῶς καὶ οἱ γέροντες καὶ ἡ ἁγία Γραφὴ πάντες συμφωνοῦσι).

[83] I echo the judgment on Shenoute in Lundhaug, "Memory and Early Monastic Literary Practices," 110: "Not only are Shenoute's writings thoroughly permeated with scriptural quotations and allusions, but they are also written in a highly 'biblical' style."

[84] C 144 (Ἐπειδὴ γέγραπται· "Ὧι μέτρῳ μετρεῖς ἀντιμετρηθήσεταί σοι" καὶ οἱ Πατέρες εἶπον· Ὑπακοὴ ἀντὶ ὑπακοῆς, δὸς χεῖρα τῷ παρὰ σοὶ ἀδελφῷ χειμαζομένῳ, καὶ σὺ εὑρίσκεις τὸν διδόντα σοι χεῖρα ἐν καιρῷ θλίψεως); Chryssavgis, I, 168. *Mios* 1 (= *Systematic Collection* 14,9): Εἶπεν ὁ ἀββᾶς Μιὼς ὁ τοῦ Βελέου, ὅτι ἡ ὑπακοὴ ἀντὶ ὑπακοῆς ἐστιν. Εἴ τις ὑπακούει τῷ θεῷ, ὁ θεὸς ὑπακούει αὐτόν. I have dealt with the analogous interplay between Scripture and the sayings of Barsanuphius in "Prayer as a Mirror of Monastic Culture," 276–281.

THE WISDOM OF THE FATHERS

As stated by John in C 344, both Scripture and the Fathers provide us with the way to salvation, since together they enjoin the system of spiritual direction by asking the elders. It is revealing that the quotation of Deut 32:7 given here as the biblical proof text, otherwise appears in the AP only in *Antonius* 37.[85] In its turn the "way of the Fathers," once more according to John, is the way of Scripture, and in C 212 John tries to prove it by seamlessly weaving together scriptural verses and the practical wisdom of the elders.

> As for bodily diet, if the body cannot perform the liturgy when it receives sufficient food, and if you are afraid of illness when it receives insufficient food, then retain the middle way. Give it neither too much nor too little. Then the Scripture is fulfilled that says: "Deviate neither to the right hand nor to the left" (Num 20:17). But give the body just a little less than it requires. Indeed, this is the way of the fathers: neither to be extravagant nor to be crushed in one's discipline.[86]

Ultimately, the Correspondence proposes a message in which, as in the above passage, an overall continuity seems to exist between Scripture and the Fathers: both were indeed regarded as words leading to a perfect life.[87] In spite of that, the difference between them was not obliterated. The two elders encouraged a privileged access to the AP to the partial eclipse of Scripture. When John instructed the new abbot Elianus in C 584 on how to behave with the visitors, he stressed the fact that his "conversation should always be from the *Lives of the Fathers*, the Gospel, the Apostle, and the Prophets."[88] The successive order of the subjects suggested for the abbot's spiritual conversation is revealing:

---

85 C 344 (Ἀδελφέ, ἔδωκεν ἡμῖν ὁ Θεὸς διὰ τῶν θείων Γραφῶν, καὶ οἱ Πατέρες, τὴν ὁδὸν τῆς σωτηρίας, ἐν τῷ λέγειν· "Ἐπερώτησον τὸν Πατέρα σου καὶ ἀναγγελεῖ σοι, τοὺς πρεσβυτέρους σου καὶ ἐροῦσί σοι" (Deut 32:7)). Cf. *Antonius* 37 (= *Systematic Collection* 11,1). For another quotation of Deut 32:7 in the letters, see C 535.

86 C 212 (Περὶ δὲ τῆς διαίτης τοῦ σώματος, εἰ ὅταν λάβῃ τὴν ἱκανὴν τροφὴν οὐ δύναται λειτουργῆσαι, ἐὰν δὲ μὴ λάβῃ, φοβούμεθα τὴν ἀσθένειαν, κράτει τὴν μεσότητα μήτε ἄνω μήτε κάτω κάτω, καὶ πληροῦται ἡ γραφὴ λέγουσα· "Μὴ ἐκκλίνῃς εἰς τὰ δεξιὰ μηδὲ εἰς τὰ ἀριστερά." Ἀλλὰ δὸς τῷ σώματι τὴν χρείαν αὐτοῦ παρὰ μικρόν. Αὕτη γὰρ ἡ ὁδός ἐστι τῶν Πατέρων· τὸ μήτε σπαταλᾶν μήτε βαρηθῆναι ἐν τῇ πολιτείᾳ); Chryssavgis, I, 220–221. One should perhaps translate the biblical term σπαταλᾶν (Ezek 16:49, Sir 21:15, 1 Tim 5:6, Jas 5:5) not as "to be extravagant" but as "to give oneself to pleasure."

87 See Lorenzo Perrone, "Scripture for a Life of Perfection: The Bible in Late Antique Monasticism; The Case of Palestine," in *The Reception and Interpretation of the Bible in Late Antiquity: Proceedings of the Montréal Colloquium in Honour of Charles Kannengiesser*, ed. Lorenzo DiTommaso and Lucian Turcescu (Leiden: Brill, 2008), 393–417.

88 C 584; Chryssavgis, II, 167.

undoubtedly it bespeaks the interconnection between the *AP* and the Bible, but at the same time the priority of the *AP* in the list betrays an actual preference for them. Not incidentally, when the same Elianus, while still a pious layman, asked in C 469, "Is it always a good thing or not to tell others about good stories found in Scripture and in the *Lives of the Fathers*?," John responded, "Since we have not reached the point of walking the way of the perfect, on account of weakness, let us speak about those things which contribute to edification, namely, from the *Sayings of the Fathers*, rather than risking our souls by using accounts from Scripture."[89] The *AP* were expected to procure more easily and generally that "edification" (ὠφέλεια) that Origen had vindicated for the inspired Scripture as a whole. And yet they could do so only by reminding their readers how far they were from a perfect life.[90]

∴

Since the mid-nineties the work of Samuel Rubenson on Egyptian monasticism has been a reference point for me and my colleagues of the "Italian Research Group on Origen and the Alexandrian Tradition." My first acquaintance with him at that time soon became a warm friendship, extending to his family and the team he created in Lund. Later on, when we worked together for AIEP/IAPS, in addition to the brilliant scholar, I discovered in Samuel a person with much practical wisdom and generosity. I am happy now to contribute to the volume in his honour as a sign of my deep admiration and gratitude.

---

89   C 469; Chryssavgis, II, 81. As for the necessity of a spiritual interpretation of Scripture, C 241 has the same distinction and/or opposition σαρκικῶς—πνευματικῶς. Note also the same approach promoted by Jesus among his disciples according to C 93: Christ makes their fleshly hearts spiritual, so that they might be able to receive spiritually his teachings and precepts.

90   In C 689, Barsanuphius advised a secular person who was fond of talking about the *Lives of the Fathers* that he should always remember that he talked about the virtues of the Fathers without possessing any of them. With a similar concern in C 547, the Great Old Man exhorted a monk who appreciated "dogmatic books" to read instead the sayings of the Fathers, so as to humble himself.

Bibliography

Primary Sources

Apophthegmata Patrum. *Alphabetical Collection*. PG 65 (1858), 71–440.

Apophthegmata Patrum. *Systematic Collection*. Ed. Jean-Claude Guy, *Les apophthegmes des Pères. Collection systématique*. 3 vols. SChr 387, 474, 498. Paris: Cerf, 1993, 2003, 2005.

Barsanuphius and John. *Correspondence* (= C). Ed. with French transl. François Neyt and Paula de Angelis-Noah, *Barsanuphe et Jean de Gaza, Correspondance*. 5 vols. SChr 426–427, 450–451, 468. Paris: Cerf, 1997–2002. English transl. John Chryssavgis, *Barsanuphius and John: Letters*. 2 vols. FC 113–114. Washington, DC: Catholic University of America Press, 2006–2007. French transl. Lucien Regnault, Philippe Lemaire, and Bernard Outtier, *Barsanuphe et Jean de Gaza, Correspondance*. Solesmes: Abbaye Saint-Pierre de Solesmes, 1971.

Cyril of Scythopolis. *Vita Euthymii*. Ed. Eduard Schwartz, *Kyrillos von Skythopolis*, 3–85. TU 49. Leipzig: J.C. Hinrichs, 1939.

Dorotheus of Gaza. *Didaskaliai*. Ed. with German transl. Judith Pauli, *Dorotheus von Gaza, Doctrinae diversae = Die geistliche Lehre*. Fontes Christiani 37. Vol. 1. Freiburg i. Br.: Herder, 2000.

Dorotheus of Gaza. *Didaskaliai* and *Epistulae*. Ed. Lucien Regnault and Jean de Préville, *Dorothée de Gaza, Œuvres spirituelles*, 488–524. SChr 92. Paris: Cerf, 1963.

Historia monachorum. Ed. André Jean Festugière. Brussels: Société des Bollandistes, 1971.

Zosimas. *Adloquia*. PG 78, pp. 1680–1701.

Secondary Sources

Bitton-Ashkelony, Brouria. "Monasticism in Late Antique Gaza: A School or an Epoch?" In *L'école de Gaza: Espace littéraire et identité culturelle dans l'antiquité tardive*, ed. Eugenio Amato, Aldo Corcella, and Delphine Lauritzen, 19–36. Leuven: Peeters, 2017.

Bitton-Ashkelony, Brouria, and Aryeh Kofsky. *The Monastic School of Gaza*. Leiden: Brill, 2016.

Faraggiana di Sarzana, Chiara. "*Apophthegmata Patrum*: Some Crucial Points of Their Textual Transmission and the Problem of a Critical Edition." *StPatr* 30 (1997): 455–467.

Filoramo, Giovanni. "Mistica e politica. Il caso di Barsanufio di Gaza." In *L'Anti-Babele. Sulla mistica degli antichi e dei moderni*, ed. Isabella Adinolfi, Giancarmo Gaeta, and Andreina Lavagetto, 217–229. Genoa: Melangolo, 2017.

Gould, Graham. *The Desert Fathers on Monastic Community*. Oxford: Clarendon, 1993.

Hombergen, Daniël. "Barsanuphius and John of Gaza and the Origenist Controversy."

In *Christian Gaza in Late Antiquity*, ed. Brouria Bitton-Ashkelony and Aryeh Kofsky, 173–181. Leiden: Brill, 2004.

Hombergen, Daniël. *The Second Origenist Controversy: A New Perspective on Cyril of Scythopolis' Monastic Biographies as Historical Sources for Sixth-Century Origenism.* StAns 132. Rome: Centro studi S. Anselmo, 2001.

Lundhaug, Hugo. "Memory and Early Monastic Literary Practices." *Journal of Cognitive Historiography* 1 (2014): 98–120.

Neyt, François. "Citations 'isaïennes' chez Barsanuphe et Jean de Gaza." *Le Muséon* 84 (1971): 65–92.

Perrone, Lorenzo. "Εἰς τὸν τῆς ἡσυχίας λιμένα: Le lettere a Giovanni di Beersheva nella corrispondenza di Barsanufio e Giovanni di Gaza." In *Mémorial Dom Jean Gribomont (1920–1986)*, 463–486. Rome: Institutum Patristicum Augustinianum, 1988.

Perrone, Lorenzo. "The Necessity of Advice: Spiritual Direction as a School of Christianity in the Correspondence of Barsanuphius and John of Gaza." In *Christian Gaza in Late Antiquity*, ed. by Brouria Bitton-Ashkelony and Aryeh Kofsky, 131–149. Leiden: Brill, 2004.

Perrone, Lorenzo. "Palestinian Monasticism, the Bible, and Theology in the Wake of the Second Origenist Controversy." In *The Sabaite Heritage in the Orthodox Church From the Fifth Century to the Present*, ed. Josef Patrich, 245–259. Leuven: Peeters, 2001.

Perrone, Lorenzo. "Prayer as a Mirror of Monastic Culture in Byzantine Palestine: The Letters of the Hesychast Euthymius to Barsanuphius." *Proche-Orient Chrétien* 60 (2010): 257–290.

Perrone, Lorenzo. "Scripture for a Life of Perfection: The Bible in Late Antique Monasticism; The Case of Palestine." In *The Reception and Interpretation of the Bible in Late Antiquity: Proceedings of the Montréal Colloquium in Honour of Charles Kannengiesser*, ed. Lorenzo DiTommaso and Lucian Turcescu, 393–417. Leiden: Brill, 2008.

Regnault, Lucien. "Les apophthegmes en Palestine aux Ve–VIe siècles." *Irénikon* 54 (1981): 320–330; reprinted in idem, *Les Pères du désert à travers leurs apophthegmes*. Solesmes: Abbaye Saint-Pierre de Solesmes, 1987, 65–72.

Rubenson, Samuel. "Formation and Re-Formations of the Sayings of the Desert Fathers." *StPatr* 55 (2013): 5–22.

Zanetti, Ugo. "Les Apophthegmes et la Terre Sainte." *Connaissance des Pères de l'Église* 141 (2016): 22–28.

PART 2

Wisdom in Translation:
Apophthegmata in New Languages

∴

CHAPTER 4

The Unmentionable Apophthegm: An Overview of the Pagan Greek Tradition

Denis M. Searby

The great Christian tradition of the *Apophthegmata Patrum* had its counterpart and antecedent in the traditions of *apophthegmata* attributed to wise and witty Greeks, the collecting of which began probably in the classical period and no later than the early Hellenistic Age, continuing down through the Middle Ages and beyond.[1] I will approach the profane tradition first by looking at the early usage of the noun ἀπόφθεγμα and the corresponding verb; I turn then to evidence for early collections, briefly examine overlappings of apophthegm with *gnōmē*, *apomnēmoneuma*, *paroimia* and *chreia*, and conclude with another brief look at the continuity of the tradition, especially against the background of the Christian *apophthegmata*. I will use the English "apophthegm" as equivalent to its Greek original but usually prefer "maxim" to "gnome" or *gnōmē*,[2] anecdote to *apomnēmoneuma*, proverb to *paroimia*, but will simply use *chreia* for χρεία.

1   The Semantics of Apophthegm

The noun ἀπόφθεγμα (apophthegm) comes from the verb ἀποφθέγγομαι but is attested prior to it.[3] The unprefixed root verb is, of course, φθέγγομαι (*utter a*

---

1 I am delighted to offer this contribution to the volume celebrating the scholarship of Professor Rubenson.
2 "Maxim" derives from *propositio maxima*, the greater (greatest) premise in a syllogism, a sense not dissimilar to the technical use of *gnōmē*, although I use maxim in its more common sense of a "pithily expressed precept of morality or prudence." See the entry on maxim in the *Oxford English Dictionary*.
3 For special treatments of the concept of apophthegm, see W. Gemoll, *Das Apophthegma: Literarhistorische Studien* (Wien: Hölder-Pichler-Tempsky, 1924); J.F. Kindstrand, *Anacharsis: The Legend and the Apophthegmata* (Uppsala: Uppsala University, 1981), 99–100; T. Klauser and P. de Labriolle, "Apophthegma," *RAC* 1 (1950), 545–550; O. Gigon and K. Rupprecht, "Apophthegma," *Lexikon der alten Welt* (1965), 222–223. For treatments of apophthegm together with related terms such as *chreia* and maxim, see especially J.F. Kindstrand, "Dio-

sound), and that is documented about as early as can be, appearing frequently in Homer. The unprefixed noun φθέγμα (sound, utterance, saying) is attested first in Pindar (e.g., *Pythian* 8.31) and the tragedians (e.g., Sophocles, *Oedipus Colonnus* 1623; Euripides, *Hippolytus* 648). What does the prefix ἀπο- do to the meaning of the word?[4] If it is like ἀπο- (back, again) in words like ἀποδίδωμι, then ἀποφθέγγομαι and ἀπόφθεγμα may have indicated a "talking back," that is, a reply or retort.[5] I am quite sure, however, that ἀπο- only strengthens the root meaning, so ἀπόφθεγμα is a particularized form of φθέγμα.[6] It means a *sound-*

---

genes and the *Chreia* Tradition," *Elenchos* 7 (1986): 221–224; O. Overwien, *Die Sprüche des Kynikers Diogenes in der griechischen und arabischen Überlieferung* (Stuttgart: Steiner, 2005), 28–35; J. Russo, "Prose Genres for the Performance of Traditional Wisdom in Ancient Greece: Proverb, Maxim, Apothegm," in *Poet, Public, and Performance in Ancient Greece*, ed. L. Edmunds and R.W. Wallace (Baltimore: Johns Hopins University Press, 1997), 49–64; J. Stenger, "Apophthegma, Gnome und Chrie. Zum Verhältnis dreier literarischer Kleinformen," *Philologus* 150 (2006): 203–221. T. Morgan, *Popular Morality in the Early Roman Empire* (Cambridge: Cambridge University Press, 2007), deals with proverbs, maxims, and *chreiai* (*exempla*), primarily as evidence for popular morality, though she does analyze the terminology to some extent, and refers to much revelant literature. A recent example of a lengthy discussion of the Greek terminology within biblical studies (with some inaccuracies) is M.C. Moeser, *The Anecdote in Mark, the Classical World and the Rabbis* (London: Sheffield, 2002), 57–72. I have also dealt with the terminology in general in D.M. Searby, *Aristotle in the Greek Gnomological Tradition* (Uppsala: Uppsala University, 1998), 13–20 and D.M. Searby, *The Corpus Parisinum*, 2 vols. (Lewiston, NY: Mellon, 2007), 1–8, but some of my earlier statements have been modified in the present treatment.

4   P. Bortone, *Greek Prepositions: From Antiquity to the Present* (Oxford: Oxford University Press, 2010), 164, writes of the preposition: "Greek ἀπό indicated position or distancing movement from the outer surface of the reference object (*away from*, cf. German cognate *ab-*), while ἐκ/ἐξ expressed a distancing motion from the inside of a three-dimensional volume (*out of*)." However, the same author takes pains to distinguish prepositional meaning and usage from that of prefixes (also called preverbs) and agrees with those authors who see them as separate semantic categories; see pp. 119–121. Certainly, ἀπο- prefixed to verbs shows a semantic range distinct from ἀπό as a preposition.

5   Gemoll, *Apophthegma*, 1, first states unhesitatingly: "Nun ist ἀποφθέγγομαι offenbar mit ἀποκρίνομαι und ἀπαμείβομαι synonym." He then immediately qualifies this: "aber die drei Worte unterscheiden sich nicht wenig." He also states (correctly) that the prefix ἀπο- has a different sense in each. Gemoll emphasizes the sense of "retort," stating on p. 2 that the classic form of the apophthegm is ἐρωτηθεὶς εἶπε, and citing a few passages (out of many possible) to support this, but none of the many that contradict it.

6   There are several imprecisions concerning Greek in V.K. Robbins, "Picking Up the Fragments: From Crossan's Analysis to Rhetorical Analysis," *Foundations and Facets Forum* 1 (1985): 30–64, among which is the claim that the preverb in ἀπόφασις (ἀπόφανσις) simply means "from," i.e., "a statement from" some person (p. 36), this in order to define aphorism, of all words, as a saying attributed to a specific person. In a vague sense the preverb does mean *from* in ἀπόφασις, but in a direct sense it is like an apophthegm: a statement that a person speaks forth.

ing off or a *speaking out*, an *utterance*, an *enunciation*. The very consistent use of the verb brings this out clearly.

Having gone through most if not all the instances of the verb ἀποφθέγγομαι in the *Thesaurus Linguae Graecae* database, I conclude that the verb is consistently used to underline an authoritative speech act, calling attention to a particular individual's dramatic statement. Forms of the verb are not attested before Philo of Alexandria, who uses it several times, often in the context of prophetic utterances.[7] Greek authors also use it frequently to express the uttering of oracles.[8] Diogenes Laertius, possibly quoting from Sotion, uses the participle to describe how the gymnosophists and Druids expressed their philosophy in riddling apophthegms (αἰνιγματωδῶς ἀποφθεγγομένους φιλοσοφῆσαι, DL 1:6). He also uses the verb to express the utterance of distinctive apophthegms in the case of the seven sages: ἀπεφθέγξατο ... μηδὲν ἄγαν (1:63, Solon), ἀπεφθέγξατο ἐγγύα πάρα δ' ἄτα (1:73, Chilon), ἀπεφθέγξατο οἱ πλεῖστοι κακοί (1:88, Bias), ἀπεφθέγξατο μέτρον ἄριστον (1:93, Cleobulus). Luke introduces Peter's speech on the day of Pentecost in Acts 2:14 with ἀπεφθέγξατο; see also Acts 2:4 (καθὼς τὸ πνεῦμα ἐδίδου ἀποφθέγγεσθαι αὐτοῖς), 26:25 (ἀληθείας καὶ σωφροσύνης ῥήματα ἀποφθέγγομαι). Of course, the verb was not always used to denote oracular or proverbial speech. It was also used to introduce witty sayings or dramatic speech of a more ordinary variety, as when Athenaeus points out that the courtesan Gnathaena was very good at witty remarks (οὐκ ἀνάστειος ἀποφθέγξασθαι, 13:584F), or when Cassius Dio notes that Lucius Junius had said something very witty (ἀστειότατόν τι ἀπεφθέγξατο, *Hist. Rom.* epitome 61:35).

2 First Occurrence in Xenophon

The "unmentionable" in my chapter title refers to the earliest occurrence of the noun ἀπόφθεγμα. According to LSJ it is first attested in Xenophon's description of the unlucky Theramenes' last words and actions in *Hellenica* 2.3.56:

Λέγεται δ' ἓν ῥῆμα καὶ τοῦτο αὐτοῦ. ὡς εἶπεν ὁ Σάτυρος ὅτι οἰμώξοιτο, εἰ μὴ σιωπήσειεν, ἐπήρετο· Ἂν δὲ σιωπῶ, οὐκ ἄρ᾿, ἔφη, οἰμώξομαι; καὶ ἐπεί γε ἀποθνῄσκειν ἀναγκαζόμενος τὸ κώνειον ἔπιε, τὸ λειπόμενον ἔφασαν ἀποκοτταβίσαντα εἰπεῖν αὐτόν· Κριτίᾳ τοῦτ᾿ ἔστω τῷ καλῷ. καὶ τοῦτο μὲν οὐκ ἀγνοῶ, ὅτι

---

7 For example, *Vita Moysis* 2.263: ἀποφθέγγεται λόγιον τὸ περὶ τῆς ἱερᾶς ἑβδόμης.
8 Cf. Plutarch, *Aetia romana* 268F (ἀποφθέγγεσθαι λόγια); Lucian, *Alexander* 25:11 (χρησμὸν ἀπεφθέγξατο); Galen, *De naturalibus facultatibus* 2:70 (χρησμὸν ἀποφθεγγόμενος).

ταῦτα ἀποφθέγματα οὐκ ἀξιόλογα, ἐκεῖνο δὲ κρίνω τοῦ ἀνδρὸς ἀγαστόν, τὸ τοῦ θανάτου παρεστηκότος μήτε τὸ φρόνιμον μήτε τὸ παιγνιῶδες ἀπολιπεῖν ἐκ τῆς ψυχῆς.

One saying of his that is reported was this: when Satyrus told him that if he did not keep quiet, he would suffer for it, he asked: "Then if I do keep quiet, shall I not suffer?" And when, being compelled to die, he had drunk the hemlock, they said that he threw out the last drops, like a man playing kottabos, and exclaimed: "Here's to the health of my beloved Critias." Now I am not unaware of this, that these are not *sayings* worthy of record; still, I deem it admirable in the man that when death was close at hand, neither self-possession nor the spirit of playfulness departed from his soul.[9]

The translator has rendered two different Greek words by "saying," the second being our apophthegm, the first ῥῆμα (*rhēma*), something said (like Latin *dictum*). *Rhēma* is the most basic noun for "word" or "saying." Plato uses it in *Protagoras* 342e–343b when describing the Laconic custom of uttering (φθέγγεσθαι) short and memorable sayings (ῥήματα βραχέα ἀξιομνημόνευτα), and then likens these Spartan *rhēmata* to those of the traditional seven sages whom he lists by name, thus alluding to two important and durable traditions of pagan Greek apophthegms, the sayings of the seven sages and the sayings of Spartans. This first attested use of apophthegm is noteworthy in that it combines action, reaction and words, just like many later apophthegms. Xenophon describes Theramenes' apophthegms as not worthy of mention (οὐκ ἀξιόλογα), not, I think, because he thinks sayings have no place in serious history, but because he regards these two sayings as too undignified to record, though illustrative of Theramenes' character. He is probably being coy about their unmentionability; certainly later writers found them worthwhile, including Cicero who retells the anecdote in his own words (*Tusc. disp.* 1 96).

3   Apophthegms in Aristotle

Though it is not a frequent word in Aristotle's extant writings, his usage gives the impression that *apophthegma* had already become a common term. In *Metaphysics* 1009b26, he uses it when citing certain words of Anaxagoras to

---

9   Translation by Carleton L. Brownson in Loeb Classical Library.

some of his companions (πρὸς τῶν ἑταίρων τινάς) as being remembered or recorded (μνημονεύεται): τοιαῦτ' αὐτοῖς ἔσται τὰ ὄντα οἷα ἂν ὑπολάβωσιν (reality will be for them such as they suppose it to be). In *Economics* 1345a12, he cites apophthegms of "the Persian" and of "the Libyan" to prove his point that no one takes the same care of another's property as of his own. These apophthegms display both the question-and-answer form and the attribution to characters identified only by ethnicity, both of which features are typical of many of the apophthegms in later collections:

Καὶ τὸ τοῦ Πέρσου καὶ τὸ τοῦ Λίβυος ἀπόφθεγμα εὖ ἂν ἔχοι. Ὁ μὲν γὰρ ἐρωτηθεὶς τί μάλιστα ἵππον πιαίνει, ὁ τοῦ δεσπότου ὀφθαλμός ἔφη· ὁ δὲ Λίβυς ἐρωτηθεὶς ποία κόπρος ἀρίστη, τὰ τοῦ δεσπότου ἴχνη ἔφη.

We may commend also a pair of apophthegms, one attributed to a Persian and the other to a Libyan. The former on being asked what best conditions a horse, replied "His master's eye." The Libyan, when asked what kind of manure is best, answered "The master's footprints."[10]

Two instances of apophthegm in Aristotle's *Rhetoric* are of particular interest. Since the first occurs in his discussion of maxims or γνωμολογία, I will describe the context in detail. The essence of the art of persuasion, according to Aristotle, lies in proofs (πίστεις), and in *Rhetoric* Book II chapter 20, he begins his treatment of proofs common to all kinds of rhetoric, these being the example (παράδειγμα) and the argument or *enthymeme* (ἐνθύμημα), the maxim itself not being a proof but part of an *enthymeme* (ἡ γὰρ γνώμη μέρος ἐνθυμήματος ἐστίν, *Rhet*. 1393a25). He deals with the example—which may be historical or invented, such as fables—for the rest of chapter 20. In chapter 21 he turns to "speaking in maxims" (γνωμολογία). Aristotle's definition of maxim, which set the tone for later rhetoricians, is this:

ἔστι δὴ γνώμη ἀπόφανσις, οὐ μέντοι οὔτε περὶ τῶν καθ' ἕκαστον, οἷον ποῖός τις Ἰφικράτης, ἀλλὰ καθόλου, οὔτε περὶ πάντων, οἷον ὅτι τὸ εὐθὺ τῷ καμπύλῳ ἐναντίον, ἀλλὰ περὶ ὅσων αἱ πράξεις εἰσί, καὶ ⟨ἃ⟩ αἱρετὰ ἢ φευκτά ἐστι πρὸς τὸ πράττειν.

Rhet. 1394a22–26

---

10 Translation by Hugh Tredennick in Loeb Classical Library, but I substitute apophthegms for Tredennick's "sayings."

A maxim is a statement, not about particulars, such as what kind of a man Iphicrates is, but a general statement, though not about any matter, such as straight is opposed to bent, but about whatever concerns actions, that is, what should be chosen or avoided with respect to action.

He then discusses the use of the maxim as part of rhetorical argumentation, whereupon he classifies four kinds of maxims, beginning with a first division into those that need an epilogue and those that do not, an epilogue being simply a statement of the reason for the maxim (the αἴτιον or "the why," τὸ διότι). The four kinds of maxim would then be: 1) those that need an epilogue and are supplied with one; 2) those that need one but are left without it; 3) those that do not need one and therefore have no epilogue because the maxim is generally accepted; or 4) those that do not need one because the meaning is obvious as soon as stated. Thus the maxim is one thing, the epilogue another. In this context Aristotle mentions two kinds of apophthegms:

περὶ δὲ τῶν μὴ παραδόξων ἀδήλων δὲ προστιθέντα τὸ διότι στρογγυλώτατα. ἁρμόττει δ' ἐν τοῖς τοιούτοις καὶ τὰ Λακωνικὰ ἀποφθέγματα καὶ τὰ αἰνιγματώδη, οἷον εἴ τις λέγει ὅπερ Στησίχορος ἐν Λοκροῖς εἶπεν, ὅτι οὐ δεῖ ὑβριστὰς εἶναι, ὅπως μὴ οἱ τέττιγες χαμόθεν ᾄδωσιν.

Concerning obscure but not paradoxical matters one should add the reason why in the most compact way possible. Applicable in such cases are both the Laconic and the riddling apophthegms, such as saying as did Stesichorus to the Locrians that they should not be insolent lest their cicadas should sing from the ground.[11]

Although this occurs in the chapter on *gnōmologia*, Aristotle is not including these apophthegms in the category of maxim, but rather recommends appending a Laconic or a riddling apophthegm in order to make the maxim clearer (without implying that these are the only two classifications of apophthegms possible). This is meant to contrast with maxims in which the reason of what is stated is obvious. Many scholars do not grasp the point that these apophthegms are being distinguished from maxims here. Instead they see "Laconic and riddling apophthegms" in the chapter on maxims and assume that Aristotle understands these as maxims as well. Yet the preceding passage clarifies this (1394b20f.):

---

11   *Rhet.* 1394b35–1395a1, my translation.

> εἰσὶ δ' αὗται (sc. γνῶμαι) ἐν ὅσαις ἐμφαίνεται τοῦ λεγομένου τὸ αἴτιον, οἷον ἐν τῷ ἀθάνατον ὀργὴν μὴ φύλασσε θνητὸς ὤν· τὸ μὲν γὰρ φάναι μὴ δεῖν ἀεὶ φυλάττειν τὴν ὀργήν γνώμη, τὸ δὲ προσκείμενον θνητὸν ὄντα τὸ διὰ τί λέγει.
>
> These maxims are the ones in which the reason for the statement is obvious, as for example in "being mortal do no cherish immortal rage." For the maxim is that one should not cherish immortal rage, the addition "being mortal" tells the reason why.

This is meant to illustrate the most valuable kind of maxim, one that comes with the reason why. When that is not the case, Aristotle recommends adding a Laconic or riddling apophthegm to supply the lack.

In Aristotle's example, in which the maxim is "one should not be insolent," the reason why (τὸ διότι) is most compactly (στρογγυλώτατα) added by means of Stesichorus' riddling apophthegm. Stesichorus' saying also occurs in slightly different form in 1412a22, which is the second explicit use of the word *apophthegma* in the *Rhetoric*:

> Τῶν ἀποφθεγμάτων δὲ τὰ ἀστεῖά ἐστιν ἐκ τοῦ μὴ ὃ φησι λέγειν, οἷον τὸ Στησιχόρου, ὅτι οἱ τέττιγες ἑαυτοῖς χαμόθεν ᾄσονται.
>
> Urbane (witty) apophthegms come from not meaning what one says, as in the one by Stesichorus, that "the cicadas will sing to themselves from the ground."

What do the Laconic apophthegms have in common with Stesichorus' riddling or urbane apophthegms or those of "the Persian" and the "Libyan" or with the apophthegms of Theramenes in Xenophon or, in fact, with the later apophthegms in Plutarch, Diogenes Laertius, Stobaeus and other sources? I would say two things: brevity and the attribution to a specific person or character. They are all brief sayings of someone, either a historical person or an ethnic character, and not merely "proverbial" or anonymous. The word "apophthegm" itself invites attribution: an apophthegm is someone's pointed utterance, often, but not necessarily, in response to a question.

4   After Aristotle

After Aristotle, the word "apophthegm" occurs in fragments of Peripatetics like Theophrastus and Dicaearchus. It is noteworthy that Cicero identifies wittiness (*facete dicta*) as a distinguishing feature of Greek apophthegms.[12] The word occurs more frequently even later, not least in writers heavily reliant on Hellenistic sources, like Plutarch, Athenaeus and Diogenes Laertius. Not to be forgotten, of course, are its occurrences in titles (see below). Yet we never find a technical definition of the word "apophthegm" in our ancient writers. This is in complete contrast to *chreia*, which, in the sense of "saying," rarely occurs outside of technical discussions. It is truly remarkable that *apophthegma*, as far as I know, occurs only twice in the *progymnasmata*, both times in Theon. In the *thesis* exercise, Theon writes:

> Ληψόμεθα δὲ τὰ προοίμια τῶν θέσεων ἤτοι ἀπὸ γνώμης κατασκευαζούσης τὴν θέσιν ἢ ἀπὸ παροιμίας ἢ χρείας ἢ ἀποφθέγματος χρησίμου ἢ ἱστορίας ἢ ἀπὸ ἐγκωμίου ἢ ψόγου τοῦ πράγματος ὑπὲρ οὗ τὸ ζήτημα.

> We shall get the prooemia of theses either from a maxim supporting the thesis or from a proverb or a *chreia* or a useful saying (ἀποφθέγματος) or an historical report or from encomion or invective against the thing which is in question.[13]

Here it would seem that Theon makes a distinction between *chreia* and apophthegm, as well as between proverb and maxim. However, this is not the case earlier on in the preface:

> Καὶ μὴν ἡ διὰ τῆς χρείας γυμνασία οὐ μόνον τινὰ δύναμιν λόγων ἐργάζεται, ἀλλὰ καὶ χρηστόν τι ἦθος ἐγγυμναζομένων ἡμῶν τοῖς τῶν σοφῶν ἀποφθέγμασιν.

> Surely the exercise of the *chreia* not only creates a certain faculty of speech but also good character while we are being exercised in the moral sayings of the wise.

Theon here clearly equates apophthegms with *chreiai*, that is, with the sayings of the wise that are used in the *chreia* exercise. Certainly, in the apophthegms labeled as such in Xenophon, Aristotle, Plutarch, Diogenes Laertius, Stobaeus

---

[12] Cicero informs us that Cato made collections of Greek sayings: *multaque multorum facete dicta, ut ea, quae a sene Catone collecta sunt, quae vocantur* ἀποφθέγματα (*De officiis* 1.29.104; cf. *De oratore* 2.67.271). On this, cf. J.F. Kindstrand, "Two Romans in Late Greek Florilegia: Cato Maior and Romulus," *Classica et Mediaevalia* 38 (1987): 92.

[13] Translation by G.A. Kennedy, in *Progymnasmata: Greek Textbooks of Prose Composition and Rhetoric* (Atlanta: Society of Biblical Literature, 2003), 56.

and other sources, it is practically impossible to distinguish them from the category of *chreia*, but more on this below.

5 Collections of Apophthegms

Collections entitled "apophthegms" of various persons or groups may well have existed already in classical Greece, given that Aristotle mentions τὰ Λακωνικὰ ἀποφθέγματα (Laconic, or Spartan, apophthegms), which suggests that a collection was already in circulation. In any case, *apophthegmata* occurs as a title for collections or as a header introducing lists of sayings in biographies from Hellenistic to medieval times:

- Ἀποφθέγματα attributed to Aristotle's nephew Callisthenes according to Julius Pollux (*Onomasticon* 9.93 = *Fragmenta Historicorum Graecorum* 124 F4).[14]
- Ἀποφθέγματα compiled by the Hellenistic comic poet Lynceus (brother of Duris, the tyrant of Samos, ca. 340–260), involving parasites, musicians and courtesans, cited by Athenaeus.[15]
- Τῶν ἑπτὰ σοφῶν ἀποφθέγματα (*Apophthegms of the seven sages*) collected by the Peripatetic philosopher and Athenian statesman Demetrius of Phalerum and excerpted in Stobaeus.[16]
- The word ⟨ἀπο⟩φθεγμάτω⟨ν⟩ appears to be a heading in a papyrus contain-

---

14 See W. Kroll, "Kallisthenes," *RE* 10 (1919), 1674–1726, who deals with this title on col. 1685 and suggests that the ἀπομνημονεύματα of Stratonicus in Athenaeus 350D–352C are taken from this work. This work is also mentioned in A.F. Natoli, *The Letter of Speusippus to Philip II: Introduction, Text, Translation, and Commentary* (Stuttgart: Steiner, 2004), 62, to prove an association with Atarneus.

15 Different works by Lynceus are frequently cited by Athenaeus, including *Apophthegmata* and *Apomnēmoneumata*. For *apophthegmata* see Book 6.245a: Λυγκεὺς δ' ὁ Σάμιος ἐν τοῖς ἀποφθέγμασι Σιλανός, φησίν, ὁ Ἀθηναῖος Γρυλλίωνος παρασιτοῦντος Μενάνδρῳ τῷ σατράπῃ, [παρ'] εὐπαρύφου δὲ καὶ μετὰ θεραπείας περιπατοῦντος ἐρωτηθεὶς τίς ἐστιν οὗτος Μενάνδρου, ἔφησεν, ἀξία γνάθος. Olson translates: "Lynceus of Samos says in his *Memorable Sayings*: When Gryllion was sponging off the satrap Menander and was going around dressed in a splendid robe with a purple border, and accompanied by a retinue, someone asked Silanus the Athenian: 'Who's this?'; and he said: 'Menander's distinguished jaw.'"

16 Hense's edition of Stobaeus has not yet been superseded; it contains valuable annotations to Stobaeus 3.1.172. This corresponds to Demetrius frag. 87 (ed. Fortenbaugh and Schütrumpf). See also W. Brunco, "De dictis VII sapientum a Demetrio Phalereo collectis," *Acta Seminarii Philologici Erlangensis* 3 (1884): 299–397, and M. Tziatizi-Papagianni, *Die Sprüche der sieben Weisen. Zwei byzantinische Sammlungen. Einleitung, Text, Testimonien und Kommentar* (Stuttgart: Teubner, 1994), 2–5.

ing the "Life and Sayings of Socrates" dated to between 280 and 250 BC (Hibeh II 182 col. VII 90).[17]
- The heading Σωκράτους ἀποφθέγματα can also be made out in one of the Herculaneum Papyri.[18]
- Two large collections entitled *apophthegmata* are attributed to Plutarch: Βασιλέων ἀποφθέγματα καὶ στρατηγῶν (apophthegms of kings and commanders) and Ἀποφθέγματα Λακωνικά (Spartan apophthegms, including Spartan customs—νόμιμα—and apophthegms of Spartan women).[19]
- In Diogenes Laertius' *Lives of the Philosophers*, separate sections of apophthegms are introduced by formulas such as φέρεται δὲ καὶ ἀποφθέγματα αὐτοῦ τάδε (these apophthegms are also attributed to him; 1.35), ἀποφθέγματα χρειώδη ... οἷον (useful or chreia-like apophthegms ... such as; 4.47), ἀποφθέγματα κάλλιστα ταυτί (the following very fine apophthegms; 5.17), ἀποφθέγματα ταυτὶ χρειώδη (the following useful or chreia-like apophthegms; 5.39). However no book entitled ἀποφθέγματα is cited.
- "Apophthegms" appears in the title of the anthology of Stobaeus as described by Photios in *Bibliotheca* cod. 167: ἐκλογῶν ἀποφθεγμάτων ὑποθηκῶν βιβλία τέσσαρα (four books of excerpts, apophthegms, precepts).
- In *Bibliotheca* cod. 161, Photios says that he has read extracts made by the sophist Sopater (fourth century?) ἐκ τῶν Διογένους τοῦ κυνικοῦ ἀποφθεγμάτων (from the apophthegms of Diogenes the Cynic) in the second book of extracts, as well as an anonymous collection τῶν σπουδαίων ἀποφθέγματα (apophthegms of the virtuous) in the eighth book ("from an ancient untitled tome"), and extracts from Plutarch's *Apophthegms of famous men* (Ἀνδρῶν ἐνδόξων ἀποφθέγματα) in the ninth book.[20]

This last title is not, of course, included in the corpus of Plutarch's works that we know. It cannot be identified with the *Apophthegms of kings and commanders*, because Photios mentions the latter as a separate title in the same paragraph about Sopater's ninth book. In the catalogue of Lamprias, we find Ἀποφθέγματα ἡγεμονικά, στρατηγικά, τυραννικά (apophthegms related to commander-

---

17 Papyrus Hibeh 182, "Life and Apophthegms of Socrates," ed. E.G. Turner, *The Hibeh Papyri*, vol. 2 (London: Egypt Exploration Society, 1955), 26–40.
18 See W. Crönert, "Herkulanensische Bruchstücke einer Geschichte des Sokrates und seiner Schule," *Rheinisches Museum* N. F. 57 (1902): 297, 300.
19 The latest edition is François Fuhrmann, *Plutarque, Oeuvres morales*, vol. 3, *Apophtegmes de rois et de généraux; Apophtegmes laconiens* (Paris: Les Belles Lettres, 1988).
20 On Sopater, cf. Kindstrand, "Two Romans," 94; F. Focke, "Quaestiones Plutarcheae de vitarum parallelarum textus historia" (Diss. Münster, 1911), 57–69; E. Orth, *Photiana*, Rhetorische Forschungen 1 (Leipzig: Noske, 1928), 62–68; R. Henry, "Remarques à propos des «Codices» 161 et 239 de Photius," *L'Antiquité classique* 7 (1938): 291–293.

ship, generalship, kingship; title 108), which is most reasonably identified with the *Apophthegms of kings and commanders*. In the same catalogue we also find Ἀπομνημονεύματα (*Anecdotes*, no. 125) and Περὶ ἐνδόξων ἀνδρῶν (*About famous men*, no. 168), both of which may be candidates for Photios' *Apophthegms of famous men*.[21]

The word ἀποφθέγματα occurs frequently in titles of collections of pagan sayings in Byzantine manuscripts,[22] sometimes in combination with γνῶμαι. It appears that the school distinction between maxim (*gnōmē*) and *chreia* or apophthegm, these two being synonyms for our purposes, was maintained in a number of Byzantine compilations. The large, non-Christian collection in the *Corpus Parisinum*, for example, is careful to separate *gnōmai* and *apophthegmata* under different headings.[23] The same distinction is implicit in manuscript headings such as Ἀποφθέγματα καὶ γνῶμαι διαφόρων φιλοσόφων κατὰ στοιχεῖον (*Apophthegms and maxims of various philosophers in alphabetical order*) in cod. Vindob. gr. theol. 149 fol. 302ᵛ (13th century) and Ἀρχαίων φιλοσόφων γνῶμαι καὶ ἀποφθέγματα (*Ancient philosophers' maxims and apophthegms*) in cod. Patmos 263 fol. 236ʳ (10th century).[24] These titles are unremarkable but signal some awareness of maxim and apophthegm as separable categories.

I do not find *apophthegmata* and *gnōmai* combined in a single heading prior to these medieval sources. However, the word *gnōmologia* is a synonym for *gnōmē*,[25] and this we do find combined with apophthegms in the title-like phrase ἐν τοῖς ἀποφθέγμασι καὶ ταῖς γνωμολογίαις (in the apophthegms and the

---

21   In the dedicatory letter to the emperor Trajan, Plutarch (or pseudo-Plutarch) refers to the apophthegms of kings and commanders as *apomnēmoneumata*.
22   To take two out of any number of examples, cf. Ἀποφθέγματα τῶν ἔξω σοφῶν (*Apophthegms of the pagan sages*) in cod. Bar. gr. 111 fol. 58ʳ and cod. Vindob. gr. phil. 154 fol. 369ᵛ.
23   See Searby, *Corpus Parisinum*, 80–81.
24   Ed. A. Bertini Malgarini in "ΑΡΧΑΙΩΝ ΦΙΛΟΣΟΦΩΝ ΓΝΩΜΑΙ ΚΑΙ ΑΠΟΦΘΕΓΜΑΤΑ in un manoscritto di Patmos," *Elenchos* 5 (1984): 153–200.
25   Etymologically, the -λογία of γνωμολογία could refer either to discourse or selection, but *gnōmologia* is in fact consistently used in Greek for gnomic discourse. In the entry on γνωμολογία, LSJ claims that the word means not only "sententious style" (gnomic discourse) but also a collection of maxims, citing Plutarch's *Life of Cato* and the entry in the Suda under Theognis (ed. Adler θ 136). In the Supplement, this is corrected to "title of collection of aphorisms," this time citing only the Suda. The misunderstanding in the main body of LSJ is also found in *The Brill Dictionary of Ancient Greek* (ed. Montanari) and *Diccionario Griego-Español*. The earliest instance I find is in Stephanus, citing the Suda on Theognis. This Suda entry has: ἔγραψεν ... γνώμας δι' ἐλεγείας ... καὶ πρὸς Κῦρον, τὸν αὐτοῦ ἐρώμενον, γνωμολογίαν δι' ἐλεγείων καὶ ἑτέρας ὑποθήκας παραινετικάς (he composed ... elegiac maxims ... and to Cyrus, his beloved, an elegiac gnomology and other hortatory precepts). However, if γνωμολογία here means a collection of maxims, it is an unique occurrence. It should rather be understood broadly as a "a gnomic composition in elegiac verses," paral-

gnomologies) in Plutarch's *Cato* 2.6 as well as in the ἀποφθέγματα πλεῖστα καὶ γνωμολογίαι (many apophthegms and gnomologies) of Demosthenes in Photios, *Bibliotheca* cod. 265, found probably in the biography which Photios summarizes from the same codex.[26]

6   Distinguishing Kinds of Sayings

Distinguishing between words meaning "saying" is as difficult in Greek as it is in English, although we do receive considerable help from the technical distinctions made by teachers of rhetoric which remained fairly consistent over the centuries. As we have seen, the maxim (*gnōmē*) was regularly defined as a universal statement, not necessarily attached to a person, and the maxims as transmitted in collections match that definition: unlike apophthegms or anecdotes, there is no accompanying narrative; the personal attribution of these maxims is regularly only given in a title, such as Pythagorean maxims, or the maxims of Euripides.

Some scholars see little or no difference between παροιμία (*paroimia*, proverb) and maxim (γνώμη).[27] Yet the evidence in Greek points to a general awareness of some difference between the two categories, although, obviously, one must expect overlap. Aristotle points out that some—but not all—proverbs may be used as maxims when they involve a moral proposition. His example "Attic neighbor" typifies the way proverbs are generally cited: anonymously, with just a few words and in incomplete sentences, the assumption being that most people will catch the reference because it is a commonly known expression. Surviving collections of proverbs (Diogenianus, Zenobius, edited in *CPG*) show the same features (brevity, anonymity) and are quite different from collections of maxims from the same period. One difference is, of course, that the proverb collections come with explanations. Now why is that? Because proverbs are far more cryptic and inscrutable than, say, the maxims of Pythago-

lel, for example, to the Γνωμολογία τετράστιχος (a gnomic composition in four-line verses) attributed to Gregory of Nazianzus (PG 37, 927–928 *Carmina Moralia* 33).

26   One might also mention the phrase ἀποφθεγματικὸν ἡ βραχύτης καὶ γνωμολογικόν in pseudo-Demetrius, *De elocutione* 9 (Περὶ ἑρμηνείας).

27   N. Lazaridis, *Wisdom in Loose Form: The Language of Egyptian and Greek Proverbs in Collections of the Hellenistic and Roman Periods* (Leiden: Brill, 2007), sees no reason to separate them; Robbins, "Fragments," thinks γνώμη means proverb, cf. n. 6 above. On the concept of proverb, see Morgan, *Popular Morality*, 23–31; J.F. Kindstrand, "The Greek Concept of Proverbs," *Eranos* 76 (1978): 71–85; K. Rupprecht, entries "Paroimia" and "Paroimographoi" in *RE* 18 (1949), cols. 1707–1778; Russo, "Prose Genres," 52–55.

ras or Sextus or Menander or Euripides. After all, proverbs are normally cited in the most compressed fashion whereas both maxims and apophthegms or *chreiai* normally come in complete sentences, apophthegms and *chreiai* including even a modicum of narrative detail. Proverbs tend to be anonymous and are cited anonymously.

The word ἀπομνημόνευμα (*apomnēmoneuma*) derives from the strengthening prefix ἀπο- (cf. note 4 above), the verb μνημονεύω (remember) and the common ending -μα signifying the result of a process (etc.): a thing to be especially remembered. It may be rendered as memoir, mention, recollection, reminiscence; however I prefer to render it with the modern word anecdote as most appropriate for our purposes.[28] Remembrance or memory is the key concept; an *apomnēmoneuma* is a record of some words or some incident worth remembering. Late in its history it was used by the authors of the *progymnasmata* when defining the *chreia* as a concise *apomnēmoneuma*. Athenaeus refers to the *chreiai* of the Hellenistic writer Machon as *apomnēmoneumata*; Plutarch refers in similar fashion to his apophthegms of kings and commanders (172C). The *apomnēmoneuma* may thus be seen as an overarching category that includes, on the one hand, *chreiai* and apophthegms and, on the other hand, historical anecdotes of greater length. The key thing is that the *apomnēmoneuma* is presented as something remembered, something historical, even if, in fact, one may question its historicity; it need not be witty or pointed, just memorable. The *apomnēmoneuma* is longer than the apophthegm or *chreia*, even if the latter is defined as a short *apomnēmoneuma*. *Apomnēmoneumata* is a relatively common word in titles, occurring most famously as the title of Xenophon's recollections of Socrates. Both Athenaeus and Plutarch cite various works by this title, as does Diogenes Laertius; by far the most important for the latter is Favorinus' Ἀπομνημονεύματα. Unlike *apophthegmata*, it does not seem to occur, as far as I know, in the titles of anonymous collections of anecdotes in extant manuscripts.

I have equated apophthegm and *chreia* several times already in the preceding discussion. If any scholars are uncomfortable with this, I would ask them to look carefully at the apophthegms in the collections in Diogenes Laertius or Plutarch or in any of the medieval collections, such as *Gnomologium Vaticanum*, and contrast these with the *chreiai* found in the *progymnasmata*,

---

28 See E. Schwartz, "Apomnemoneumata," RE 2 (1896), 170–171; E. Köpke, *Ueber die Gattung der Ἀπομνημονεύματα in der griechischen Litteratur*, Programm der Ritter-Akademie zu Brandenburg (1957), 1–30. Köpke, p. 4, defines it as *eine durch Erinnerung überlieferte, in Erzählungsform mitgetheilte Rede oder Aussage*, and pp. 4–6 indicates several passages where it is used synonymously with *chreia* and apophthegm.

and then to try to distinguish apophthegm and *chreia*. It cannot be done, for the simple reason that they are not only cast in the same form but are very often exactly the same sayings. I deal with the semantics of *chreia* and the development of its sense as saying in a lengthy article recently published in *Mnemosyne*.[29] Hence I will not go into many details, but refer the interested reader to that discussion. Unlike ἀπόφθεγμα, there is nothing in the core senses of *chreia* (use, need) that naturally connects it to anecdote or saying. The usage thus begs an explanation, and already the late antique grammarians came up with one that is generally repeated today: it somehow or other derives from use or usefulness. In my article I argue that during the fourth century the word *chreia* underwent a development in one of its semantic fields, that of familiar usage. Put briefly, the *chreia* and apophthegm became synonyms for the same kind of brief anecdotal saying, *chreia* being the term of preference among school-teachers, apophthegm outside the classroom. This explains why the term *chreia* drops out of use in titles and makes ever more rare appearances as "brief anecdote" in extant literature, going out of fashion by the end of the Hellenistic Age, while *apophthegmata* remained the term of choice to describe the same kind of sayings—from the Hellenistic Age to Plutarch, from Plutarch to Diogenes Laertius and, generally, from Late Antiquity to the Middle Ages. In popular usage, *apophthegma*—with its narrow semantic sense of utterance—remained the natural choice for describing the anecdotal sayings that the schoolmasters placed under the category of *chreia*, although Greek handbooks of rhetoric retain the term *chreia* from imperial times down to and throughout the Middle Ages.

7   Biography

In some of the titles mentioned in "Collections of Apophthegms" above, *apophthegmata* occurs in connection with biographies. There is an obvious logical connection between the writing of βίοι of famous people and the collecting of anecdotes and apophthegms of famous people, and we also have palpable evidence that the two went hand in hand. The biographical work most relevant here is, of course, Diogenes Laertius' *Lives of the Philosophers* in which we find apophthegms both woven into the narrative of the lives and sectioned off in separate appendices to the narratives. Plutarch, too, offers examples of both

---

29   D.M. Searby, "The Fossilized Meaning of *Chreia* as Anecdote," *Mnemosyne* 72 (2019): 197–228.

techniques, the most relevant for our purposes being the *Lives* of Lycurgus, Themistocles, and Cato the Elder which contain series of apophthegms. Both Laertius and Plutarch exploited Hellenistic sources, so it is not surprising that we find similar techniques in Hellenistic biographical fragments, such as the already mentioned *Life* of Socrates in Papyrus Hibeh II 182, dated 280–250 BC, which even contains the word *apophthegmata*, possibly as a section heading.[30] Perhaps the sayings of Simonides in Hibeh I 17, dated to the same time period, derive from a similar combination of biographical narrative followed by sayings. The same could be said for the sayings of Diogenes in P. Vindob. inv. G 29946, whether or not this may be a fragment of Metrocles' *chreiai* known from Diogenes Laertius, as Guido Bastianini has argued.[31]

In his instructive study on late antique commentaries, Jaap Mansfeld includes a chapter on Diogenes Laertius in light of the following passage in Cicero's *De inventione*:

> Deinde, qua in sententia scriptor fuerit *ex ceteris eius scriptis et ex factis, dictis, animo atque vita eius* sumi oportebit, et eam ipsam scripturam, in qua inerit illud ambiguum de quo quaeretur totam *omnibus ex partibus* pertemptare, si quid aut ad id appositum sit, quod nos interpretemur, aut ei quod adversarius intellegat adversetur.[32]

> In the next place, one ought to estimate what the writer meant *from the rest of his writings and from his acts, words, character and life*, and to examine the whole document which contains the ambiguity in question *in all its parts*, to see if any thing agrees with our interpretation or is opposed to the sense in which our opponent interprets it.[33]

Mansfeld argues for the importance of biographical ingredients in the method of interpretation of Hellenistic and Greco-Roman exegetes. Applying this to

---

30   Cf. note 17 above.
31   G. Bastianini, "Edition of P. Vindob. G 29946," in *Corpus dei papiri filosofici greci e latini*, 1.1** (Florence: Olschki, 1992), 107, sees the early "collection" of anecdotes (the word *chreia* does not appear) in Pap. Vindob. 29946 as a possible testimony to the *Chreiai* of Metrocles, which, he suggests, is the same work as that which Sotion attributes to Diogenes, being *chreiai* of Diogenes collected by Metrocles.
32   *De inv.* II 117.
33   Jaap Mansfeld, "Ciceronian Light on the Aids to Interpretation, and on Diogenes Laertius," chapter 6 in idem, *Prolegomena: Questions to be Settled before the Study of an Author, or a Text* (Leiden: Brill, 1994), 177–191. I retain his emphasis and Hubbell's translation as modified by Mansfeld (p. 178).

Diogenes Laertius, he remarks: "Scholars have as a rule been dissatisfied with what seems to us an odd medley of biographical data, apophthegms (occasionally insipid), bibliographies and information about the doctrines to be found in Diogenes' sections devoted to individual philosophers." But he points out that the study of *facta* and *dicta* of a philosopher was seen as an indispensable preliminary to that of his writings. If biographical data were lacking, they could be "fabricated from what a person wrote." Collections of apophthegms circulated on a "massive scale," and these "gnomologia could serve as a source for the other genres, and conversely."[34]

The collecting of the orally circulating anecdotes and apophthegms of famous people was related to growing biographical interests in character studies as well as a reflection of an increasingly literate society, or at least of the literary habits of an educated elite with cosmopolitan tastes. On the analogy of fictitious dialogues, we can also assume that some apophthegms were first created in writing before passing into general circulation. This is demonstrably the case for apophthegms based on passages in the author to whom they are attributed. Thus we have originally oral sayings and recollections recorded in writing and also literary fabrications of sayings, both of which were feeding into a rapidly growing literary market. Like other forms of literature of the time, these written records, whether in the form of individual collections or as part of biographies or other extended prose narratives, became fitting objects for anthologizing. It is in the Hellenistic period, then, that we should place the original sources for later extant collections, allowing, of course, for a good deal of intervention and rearrangement by the later collectors.

8 Christian and Non-Christian *Apophthegmata*

Pagan Greek apophthegms attributed to Greek celebrities, usually making a moral point, sometimes only a witty one, were ubiquitous in Greek and Roman society by the time the Christians got around to compiling their own collections of the apophthegms of the desert fathers. Children were introduced to them in basic language instruction; more advanced students learned to manip-

---

34 Words in quotation marks from Mansfeld, *Prolegomena*, 179–181 (including notes 322, 325). I would add that his later book, *Prolegomena Mathematica: From Apollonius of Perga to Late Neoplatonism; With an Appendix on Pappus and the History of Platonism* (Leiden: Brill, 1998), outlines the same exegetical practices held (*mutatis mutandis*) within the field of mathematics and that can be demonstrably traced back at least to the times of Apollonius of Perga, 260–190 BC.

ulate them in rhetorical training; apophthegms turned up in moral essays and letters; collections of them circulated not only as tools of writing but also for their entertainment and formative value. Collections of apophthegms in late antiquity—which no doubt were based on earlier collections, in many cases going all the way back to Hellenistic times—survived into the Middle Ages as did collections of maxims. Such collections may be found transmitted in the same manuscripts containing handbooks on rhetoric or other school subjects or even side by side with philosophical or theological works or, simply, in the many miscellaneous manuscripts extant from the Byzantine Middle Ages. Eventually pagan apophthegms and maxims were incorporated into the Christian compilations known as the sacro-profane florilegia. Noteworthy, however, is the fact that the pagan apophthegms are almost never found in the same manuscripts as the *Apophthegmata Patrum*, these latter being normally found in the company of such works as *Scala paradisi* (John Climacus) or *Historia Lausiaca* or *Pratum spirituale* (John Moschos). It seems these monastic collections were generally, though not always, kept separate from the more secular collections of apophthegms.

Yet the two traditions of apophthegms do share similarities of origin; first of all, the interest in the lives of founders and seminal figures which led naturally to the collection of sayings and anecdotes about them; secondly, the active use of such sayings in both secular and monastic schooling in order to teach language and rhetoric.[35] School usage, if nothing else, ensured their long-lasting conservation. Stylistically, however, the two traditions of apophthegms do differ. The pagan apophthegms are always kept short and tend to a greater formal standardization, whereas the apophthegms of the Fathers are much more variable in length and style. Calling to mind our earlier distinctions, we might rather characterize them as *apomnēmoneumata*.

9 Apophthegms on the Move

Since this book is called *Wisdom on the Move*, I will close with a few remarks on the cross-cultural movements of non-Christian Greek apophthegms. Even

---

35 On the apophthegms of the fathers in schools, see Lillian I. Larsen, "Monastic Paideia: Textual Fluidity in the Classroom," in *Snapshots of Evolving Traditions: Jewish and Christian Manuscript Culture, Textual Fluidity, and New Philology*, TU 175, ed. Liv Ingeborg Lied and Hugo Lundhaug (Berlin: de Gruyter, 2017), 146–177. See also chapter 4 ("Rhetoric of the Fear of God") in Yury Arzhanov, *Syriac Sayings of Greek Philosophers: A Study in Syriac Gnomologia with Edition and Translation*, CSCO 669 / Subs. 138 (Leuven: Peeters, 2019).

after the Middle Ages, during which they were extant not only in Greek but also in translations to Arabic, Syriac, Latin, old Slavonic and other languages, the pagan apophthegms kept attracting interest. Early modern writers took a great interest in the apophthegms of old and made new collections. In his *Apophthegmes New and Old*, which, as the title implies, includes anecdotes of the recent past as well as of antiquity, Francis Bacon offers reflections on their effects:

> They are useful not only for pleasure and decoration but also for practical matters and social relations. They are (as Cicero used to say) like verbal hatchets or pointed blades that cut and penetrate the knots of affairs and negotiations. Occasions keep returning. What was once useful can be put to advantage again, whether you cite it as your own words or on ancient authority.[36]

Bacon's words display a theoretical appreciation of how apophthegms—pointed sayings—can be used to cut an opening in a conversation.[37] A similar observation is found in Benjamin Disraeli's "Dissertation on Anecdotes," where he points out that "facts are anecdotes, but anecdotes are not always facts," though they "may produce in an ingenious observer, those leading thoughts that throw the mind into an agreeable train of thought" (pp. 29–30). Ancient Greek apophthegms keep turning up in unexpected places, such as William H. Gass' use of an Anaxagoras saying at the start of his post-modern novel *The Tunnel* (1995) or, more recently, Eugene Vodolazkin's citation of a number of

---

36 This translation is found in the Preface to the Apophthegms, *The Works of Francis Bacon*, ed. James Spedding et al., vol. 13, p. 313 (Boston, 1890). The original Latin in Bacon's *De dignate et augmentis scientiarum*, Liber II Caput 12 (Spedding, vol. 1, p. 517) is: *Neque apophthegmata ipsa ad delectationem et ornatum tantum prosunt, sed ad res gerendas etiam et usus civiles. Sunt enim (ut aiebat ille) veluti secures aut mucrones verborum; qui rerum et negotiorum nodos acumine quodam secant et penetrant; occasiones autem redeunt in orbem, et quod olim erat commodum rursus adhiberi et prodesse potest, sive quis ea tanquam sua proferat, sive tanquam vetera.* Cf. Bacon's similar English formulation at the beginning of *Apophthegmes New and Old* (ed. Spedding, vol. 13, p. 327): "Certainly, they (sc. apophthegms) are of excellent use. They are *mucrones verborum, pointed speeches*. Cicero prettily calls them, *salinas, salt pits*; that you may extract out of, and sprinkle it, where you will. They serve to be interlaced in continued speech. They serve to be recited upon occasion of themselves. They serve if you take out the kernel of them, and make them your own."

37 See Sean R. Silver, "'Pale Fire' and Johnson's Cat: The Anecdote in Polite Conversation," *Criticism* 53 (2011): 252–254, for a recent discussion of Bacon's and other early modern authors' views and use of apophthegms and anecdotes.

apophthegms, as they might have survived in medieval Russian translations, in his prize-winning novel *Laurus* (2013). Our Greek apophthegms stem from the Hellenistic Age but have wandered many a weary way since then, passing through various literary and educational uses, crossing cultural and religious boundaries and entering multiple new language settings. Perhaps even our digital world of miscellaneous tweets is ready for a new wave of reception.

Bibliography

Primary Sources

Aristotle. *Metaphysica*. Ed. W. Jaeger. Oxford Classical Texts. Oxford, 1957.
Aristotle. *Ars rhetorica*. Ed. W.D. Ross. Oxford Classical Texts. Oxford, 1959.
Aristotle. *Oeconomica*. Ed. F. Susemihl. Bibliotheca Teubneriana. Leipzig, 1887.
Athenaeus. *The Learned Banqueters* (Deinosophistai). Ed. and transl. S. Douglas Olson. Loeb Classical Library. Cambridge, MA: Harvard University Press, 2007–2012.
Cassius Dio. *Historiarum Romanarum quae supersunt*. 3 vols. Ed. U.P. Boissevain. Berlin, 1896–1901.
Cicero. *De officiis*. Ed. M. Winterbottom. Oxford Classical Texts. Oxford, 1994.
Cicero. *De inventione*. Ed. E. Stroebel. Bibliotheca Teubneriana. Leipzig, 1915.
Cicero. *Tusculanae disputationes*. Ed. M. Pohlenz. Bibliotheca Teubneriana. Leipzig, 1918.
CPG = *Corpus Paroemiographorum Graecorum*. Ed. E.L. Leutsch and F.W. Schneidewin. 3 vols. Göttingen, 1839–1841; reprint Hildesheim, 1958–1961.
Crönert, W. "Herkulanensische Bruchstücke einer Geschichte des Sokrates und seiner Schule." *Rheinisches Museum* N. F. 57 (1902): 285–300.
Pseudo-Demetrius (of Phalerum). *On Style*. Ed. W. Rhys Roberts, *Demetrius On Style: The Greek Text of Demetrius De elocutione*. Cambridge: Cambridge University Press, 1902.
Diogenes Laertius. *Lives of the Eminent Philosophers*. Ed. T. Dorandi. Cambridge: Cambridge University Press, 2013.
Euripides. *Fabulae*. Ed. J. Diggle. Vol. 1. Oxford Classical Texts. Oxford, 1984.
Galen. *De naturalibus facultatibus*. Ed. K.G. Kühn, *Claudii Galeni omnia opera*. Vol. 2. Leipzig, 1821–1833; reprint Hildesheim: Olms, 1964–1965.
Gnomologium Vaticanum e codice Vaticano graeco 743. Ed. L. Sternbach, in *Wiener Studien* 9 (1887): 175–206; 10 (1888): 1–49, 211–260; 11 (1889): 43–64, 192–242. Reprinted with introduction by O. Luschnat, in *Texte und Kommentare* 2 (1963).
Hibeh papyri: see Turner below.
Lucian. *Opera*. Ed. M.D. Macleod. Oxford Classical Texts. Oxford, 1972–1987.

Philo of Alexandria. Ed. R. Arnaldez, J. Pouilloux, and P. Savinel, *Les oeuvres de Philon d'Alexandrie, De vita Mosis I–II*. Paris: Cerf, 1961.

Photios. *Bibliothèque*. Ed. R. Henry. 8 vols. Paris: Les Belles Lettres, 1959–1977.

Pindar. *Pindari Carmina cum fragmentis*. Ed. C.M. Bowra. Oxford Classical Texts. Oxford, 1935.

Plato. *Opera*. Vol. 3. Ed. J. Burnet. Oxford Classical Texts. Oxford, 1922.

Plutarch. *Apophtegmes de rois et de généraux; Apophtegmes laconiens*. Ed. F. Furhmann. *Plutarque, Oeuvres morales*. Vol. 3. Paris: Les Belles Lettres, 1988.

Plutarch. *Plutarchi Vitae Parallelae*. Ed. C. Lindskog and K. Ziegler. Leipzig: Teubner, 1914.

Plutarch. *Plutarchi Moralia*. Ed. W. Nachstädt et al. Leipzig: Teubner, 1925.

Pollux (Ἰούλιος Πολυδεύκης). *Onomasticon*. Ed. I. Bekker. Berlin, 1846.

Sophocles. *Sophoclis Fabulae*. Ed. H. Lloyd-Jones and N. Wilson. Oxford Classical Texts. Oxford, 1990.

Stobaeus. *Ioannis Stobaei Anthologium*. Ed. C. Wachsmuth and O. Hense. 5 vols. Berlin: Weidmann, 1884–1923; reprint Zürich, 1958.

Suda. *Suidae lexicon*. Ed. A. Adler. 4 vols. Leipzig: Teubner, 1928–1935; reprint Stuttgart, 1967–1971.

Theon. *Aelius Theon. Progymnasmata*. Ed. M. Patillon. Paris: Les Belles Lettres, 1997.

Turner, E. *The Hibeh Papyri. Part II. Edited with Translations and Notes*. London: Egypt Exploration Society, 1955.

Xenophon. *Xenophontis Opera*. Vol. 1. Ed. E.C. Marchant. Oxford Classical Texts. Oxford, 1900.

Secondary Sources

Arzhanov, Yury. *Syriac Sayings of Greek Philosophers: A Study in Syriac Gnomologia with Edition and Translation*. CSCO 669 / Subs. 138. Leuven: Peeters, 2019.

Bacon, Francis. *The Works of Francis Bacon*. 15 vols. Ed. J. Spedding, R.L. Ellis, and D. Denon Heath. Boston: Brown and Taggard, 1890.

Bastianini, G. "Edition of P. Vindob. G 29946." In *Corpus dei papiri filosofici greci e latini, 1.1**, ed. by l'Accademia Toscana di Scienze e Lettere "La Colombaria," pp. 99–143. Florence: Olschki, 1992.

Bertini Malgarini, A. "ΑΡΧΑΙΩΝ ΦΙΛΟΣΟΦΩΝ ΓΝΩΜΑΙ ΚΑΙ ΑΠΟΦΘΕΓΜΑΤΑ in un manoscritto di Patmos." *Elenchos* 5 (1984): 153–200.

Bortone, P. *Greek Prepositions: From Antiquity to the Present*. Oxford: Oxford University Press, 2010.

Brunco, W. "De dictis VII sapientum a Demetrio Phalereo collectis." *Acta Seminarii Philologici Erlangensis* 3 (1884): 299–397.

Disraeli, Benjamin. *Anecdotes*. London, 1793.

Focke, F. *Quaestiones Plutarcheae de vitarum parallelarum textus historia*. Diss. Münster, 1911.

Fortenbaugh, W.W., and E. Schütrumpf. *Demetrius of Phalerum. Text, Translation and Discussion.* New Brunswick, NJ: Transaction Publishers, 2000.

Gass, William H. *The Tunnel.* New York: Alfred A. Knopf, 1995.

Gemoll, W. *Das Apophthegma: Literarhistorische Studien.* Wien: Hölder-Pichler-Tempsky, 1924.

Gigon, O., and K. Rupprecht. "Apophthegma." *Lexikon der alten Welt* (1965), 222–223.

Henry, R. "Remarques à propos des «Codices» 161 et 239 de Photius." *L'Antiquité classique* 7 (1938): 291–293.

Kennedy, G.A., ed. and transl. *Progymnasmata: Greek Textbooks of Prose Composition and Rhetoric.* Atlanta: Society of Biblical Literature, 2003.

Kindstrand, J.F. "The Greek Concept of Proverbs." *Eranos* 76 (1978): 71–85.

Kindstrand, J.F. *Anacharsis: The Legend and the Apophthegmata.* Studia Graeca Upsaliensia 16. Uppsala: Uppsala University, 1981.

Kindstrand, J.F. "Diogenes and the *Chreia* Tradition." *Elenchos* 7 (1986): 219–243.

Kindstrand, J.F. "Two Romans in Late Greek Florilegia: Cato Maior and Romulus." *Classica et Mediaevalia* 38 (1987): 91–111.

Klauser, T., and P. de Labriolle. "Apophthegma." *RAC* 1 (1950), 545–550.

Köpke, E. *Ueber die Gattung der Ἀπομνημονεύματα in der griechischen Litteratur.* Programm der Ritter-Akademie zu Brandenburg. Berlin, 1957.

Kroll, W. "Kallisthenes." *RE* 10 (1919), 1674–1726.

Larsen, Lillian I. "Monastic Paideia: Textual Fluidity in the Classroom." In *Snapshots of Evolving Traditions: Jewish and Christian Manuscript Culture, Textual Fluidity, and New Philology,* ed. Liv Ingeborg Lied and Hugo Lundhaug, 146–177. TU 175. Berlin: de Gruyter, 2017.

Lazaridis, N. *Wisdom in Loose Form: The Language of Egyptian and Greek Proverbs in Collections of the Hellenistic and Roman Periods.* Leiden: Brill, 2007.

LSJ = *Greek-English Lexicon, Revised Supplement.* Ed. H. Liddell, R. Scott, H.S. Jones, and R. McKenzie. Oxford: Clarendon, 1996.

Mansfeld, J. *Prolegomena: Questions to be Settled before the Study of an Author, or a Text.* Leiden: Brill 1994.

Mansfeld, J. *Prolegomena Mathematica: From Apollonius of Perga to Late Neoplatonism; With an Appendix on Pappus and the History of Platonism.* Leiden: Brill, 1998.

Montanari, F. *The Brill Dictionary of Ancient Greek.* Digital edition 2015. https://dictionaries.brillonline.com/montanari.

Moeser, M.C. *The Anecdote in Mark, the Classical World and the Rabbis.* London: Sheffield, 2002.

Morgan, T. *Popular Morality in the Early Roman Empire.* Cambridge: Cambridge University Press, 2007.

Natoli, A.F. *The Letter of Speusippus to Philip II: Introduction, Text, Translation, and Commentary.* Stuttgart: Steiner, 2004.

Orth, E. *Photiana*. Rhetorische Forschungen 1. Leipzig: Noske, 1928.

Overwien, O. *Die Sprüche des Kynikers Diogenes in der griechischen und arabischen Überlieferung*. Stuttgart: Steiner, 2005.

Robbins, V.K. "Picking Up the Fragments: From Crossan's Analysis to Rhetorical Analysis." *Foundations and Facets Forum* 1 (1985): 30–64.

Rupprecht, K. "Paroimia" and "Paroimographoi," *RE* 18 (1949), 1707–1778.

Russo, J. "Prose Genres for the Performance of Traditional Wisdom in Ancient Greece: Proverb, Maxim, Apothegm." In *Poet, Public, and Performance in Ancient Greece*, ed. L. Edmunds and R.W. Wallace, 49–64. Baltimore: Johns Hopkins University Press, 1997.

Schwartz, E. "Apomnemoneumata." *RE* 2 (1896), 170–171.

Searby, D.M. *Aristotle in the Greek Gnomological Tradition*. Studia Graeca Upsaliensia 19. Uppsala: Uppsala University, 1998.

Searby, D.M. *The Corpus Parisinum*. 2 vols. Lewiston, NY: Mellen, 2007.

Searby, D.M. "The Fossilized Meaning of *Chreia* as Anecdote." *Mnemosyne* 72 (2019): 197–228.

Silver, Sean R. "'Pale Fire' and Johnson's Cat: The Anecdote in Polite Conversation." *Criticism* 53 (2011): 241–264.

Stenger, J. "Apophthegma, Gnome und Chrie. Zum Verhältnis dreier literarischer Kleinformen." *Philologus* 150 (2006): 203–221.

Stephanus = Henri Estienne (Étienne), *Thesaurus Graecae Linguae*. 5 vols. Geneva, 1572; reprint Paris, 1831–1865.

Tziatizi-Papagianni, M. *Die Sprüche der sieben Weisen. Zwei byzantinische Sammlungen. Einleitung, Text, Testimonien und Kommentar*. Stuttgart: Teubner, 1994.

Vodolazkin, Eugene. *Laurus* (Лаер). Transl. L.C. Hayden. London: Oneworld, 2015.

CHAPTER 5

Between East and West: Cassian the Roman in Greek and Latin

Britt Dahlman

1   Introduction

One of the most influential persons to transmit the Eastern spiritual tradition to the Latin West was Cassian the Roman (or John Cassian, as he is called in the West). Two of his works, the *Institutiones* and the *Collationes*, are preserved in both Latin and Greek. Yet almost all scholars have taken it for granted that Cassian wrote exclusively in Latin, and that the Latin version fully preserves his thought. Panayiotis Tzamalikos, however, author of two books on Cassian, including a new edition with English translation of the Greek text preserved in MS Meteora 573,[1] claims that the Latin versions of the *Institutiones* and the *Collationes* are highly interpolated, later translations of Greek works composed by a sixth-century monk, Cassian the Sabaite, who is mentioned by Cyril of Scythopolis in his *Life of Sabas* 56. Moreover, Tzamalikos asserts that the fifth-century Latin author called John Cassian likely never wrote anything. According to Tzamalikos, the Greek writings by Cassian the Sabaite were translated into Latin and falsely attributed to John Cassian, while the Sabaite was forgotten. The Latin Cassian is thus the product of a medieval forgery merging the two Cassian into one.[2]

---

1   Panayiotis Tzamalikos, *A Newly Discovered Greek Father: Cassian the Sabaite Eclipsed by John Cassian of Marseilles*, SVigChr 111 (Leiden: Brill, 2012); idem, *The Real Cassian Revisited: Monastic Life, Greek Paideia, and Origenism in the Sixth Century*, SVigChr 112 (Leiden: Brill, 2012). For earlier editions of the Greek Cassian, see Britt Dahlman, "Textual Fluidity and Authorial Revision: The Case of Cassian and Palladius," in *Monastic Education in Late Antiquity: The Transformation of Classical Paideia*, ed. Lillian I. Larsen and Samuel Rubenson (Cambridge: Cambridge University Press, 2018), 288, n. 31. Unfortunately, Tzamalikos' edition is highly insufficient, but since it is easily accessible it is quoted in this study.
2   Tzamalikos, *Real Cassian*, 210–212. Tzamalikos' views have received little approval. Critical review articles have been published by Roberto Alciati, "Il Cassiano greco di Panayiotis Tzamalikos," *Rivista di storia del Cristianesimo* 11 (2014): 451–477; Augustine Casiday, "Translation, Controversies, and Adaptations at St Sabas Monastery during the Sixth Century," *Journal of Medieval Monastic Studies* 2 (2013): 1–18, idem, review of *A Newly Discovered Greek Father:*

I have elsewhere questioned Tzamalikos' assertion that this monk, Cassian the Sabaite living in the sixth century, was the author of both the Greek and Latin versions of the Cassianic texts, by pointing out that several excerpts of Cassian's discourses were already included in the oldest Greek and Latin collections of the *Apophthegmata Patrum*.³ A close study of the Greek sayings shows that those excerpted from the *Institutiones* were translated from the Latin version, whereas those taken from the *Collationes* were taken directly from the Greek.⁴ This documents that several versions of Cassian's text, in both Greek and Latin, circulated at the end of the fifth century.⁵

Thus, concerning the question of language one cannot easily dismiss Tzamalikos' thesis. But based on philological observations, I have argued that the *Collationes* were originally written in Latin, but that the Greek version represents an earlier stage of the text than does the preserved Latin text. The Greek version takes the form of a letter, titled Πρὸς Λεόντιον ἡγούμενον περὶ τῶν κατὰ τὴν Σκῆτιν ἁγίων πατέρων (*To the Hegumen Leontius, on the Holy Fathers in Scetis*), and corresponds to the Latin *Collationes* I–II and VII–VIII. Concerning the *Institutiones*, however, I posited that Cassian originally wrote them in Greek, and as two separate works, namely letters addressed to Bishop Castor. I suggested that the Latin version is a translation that has been revised and expanded, largely by Cassian himself, but perhaps also by others.⁶ The first of these two letters, titled Πρὸς Κάστορα ἐπίσκοπον περὶ διατυπώσεως καὶ κανόνων τῶν κατὰ τὴν Ἀνατολὴν καὶ Αἴγυπτον κοινοβίων (*To Bishop Castor, on the Rules and Regulations of the Coenobia in the*

Cassian the Sabaite Eclipsed by John Cassian of Marseilles and *The Real Cassian Revealed: Monastic Life, Greek 'Paideia', and Origenism in the Sixth Century*, by Panayiotis Tzamalikos, *Journal of Medieval Monastic Studies* 3 (2014): 119–125; Columba Stewart, "Another Cassian?" *JEH* 66 (2015): 372–376. An exception is the positive review by Ioan I. Ică, Jr., "'Cassian Savaitul' 'adevăratul Cassian' grec al 'Filocaliei' din umbra latinului 'Ioan Cassian' Implicațiile revoluționare pentru patrologie ale unei recente ediții și interpretări," *Revista Teologica* 3 (2013): 164–178.

3 Dahlman, "Textual Fluidity," 288–295. Additional arguments are supplied by Alciati, "Il Cassiano greco"; Casiday, "Translation, Controversies"; and Stewart, "Another Cassian?"
4 An exception is AP/G Serapion 4 (AP/GS VIII.12), which is derived from *Collatio* XVIII.11, a text which is not preserved in the Greek Cassian. However, the text of the apophthegm is so different from the Latin Cassian that one may speculate that there once was a Greek version of this *Collatio* (or at least part of it) that did not survive. Wilhelm Bousset compared Cassian's Latin text with the apophthegm and concluded that Cassian's text is secondary (*Apophthegmata: Studien zur Geschichte des ältesten Mönchtums* (Tübingen: Mohr Siebeck, 1923), 72–73). For the abbreviations of the collections of *Apophthegmata Patrum*, AP/G and AP/GS, see the Bibliography.
5 Dahlman, "Textual Fluidity," 289–292.
6 Dahlman, "Textual Fluidity," 290–292, 294.

East and Egypt), corresponds to the Latin *Institutiones* I–IV, whereas the second epistle, Περὶ τῶν η' λογισμῶν (*On the Eight Thoughts*), corresponds to the Latin *Institutiones* V–XII.

The author of the Latin text was clearly bilingual, with excellent knowlege of Greek. Maxime Yévadian proposed that Cassian was of Oriental origin (more precisely, Armenian), with Greek as his cultural language. She demonstrated that in the Latin Cassian, Greek theology and concepts prevail, which indicates that the author was trained in a Greek-speaking milieu.[7] It would therefore not be strange to think that Cassian wrote in both Greek and Latin, and that he could have translated and revised his own works.

In the following, I will discuss two excerpts from Cassian's writings, one from the *Institutiones* and the other from the *Collationes*, that are preserved in both Latin and Greek. Analysis of the first passage (*Inst.* IV.39) will focus on philological aspects related to style and rhetoric, yielding new evidence in support of the hypothesis that Cassian originally composed the *Institutiones* in Greek. In the second passage (*Coll.* 11.13), the comparison of Greek and Latin versions will concentrate on the theological implications. These two detailed case studies will help us better understand the flexibility of Cassian's writings in both Greek and Latin, and highlight how attentively Cassian attuned his text to his recipients, sometimes by deliberately reorienting his theology.

2 An Evagrian Florilegium and the *Institutio* IV.39 in Latin and Greek

It is well known that Cassian depended on the great eastern theologian Evagrius of Pontus and used some of his material.[8] A text which has hitherto received little scholarly attention is a florilegium in MS Paris gr. 2748 (fols. 153ʳ–183ᵛ), which includes a chapter of excerpts from Evagrius titled Ἐκ τῶν Εὐαγρίου (*From the Writings of Evagrius*).[9]

---

7   Maxime Yévadian, "Le grec de Jean Cassien," in *Le livre scellé*, ed. Laurence Mellerin (Turnhout: Brepols, 2017), 179–203. See also Columba Stewart, "From λόγος to *verbum*: John Cassian's use of Greek in the Development of a Latin Monastic Vocabulary," in *The Joy of Learning and the Love of God: Studies in Honor of Jean Leclercq*, ed. Ellen Rozanne Elder, CSS 160 (Kalamazoo, MI: Cistercian Publications, 1995), 5–31.
8   See Salvatore Marsili, *Giovanni Cassiano ed Evagrio Pontico: Dottrina sulla carità e contemplazione*, StAns 5 (Rome: Editrice Anselmiana, 1936).
9   The whole florilegium consists of two series of excerpts from various authors, the second one consisting of seven chapters, each attributed to a specific author. The chapter attributed to Evagrius is the second one in this second series.

The sixty-nine excerpts attributed to Evagrius (fols. 162ʳ–165ʳ) were edited by J. Muyldermans.[10] He was able to identify fifty-one of the passages, of which forty-five originate from works by Evagrius (in some cases transmitted under the name of Nilus) and six from the *Sentences of Sextus*. C. Guillaumont identified seven further passages as originating from works by Evagrius.[11] The remaining eleven excerpts remain unidentified, except for the one which will be discussed here. It should not surprise to find passages from the *Sentences of Sextus* amongst Evagrian material, since portions of the *Sentences* were included in collections of aphorisms attributed to Evagrius, and it is likely that Evagrius revised and edited a collection of the *Sentences of Sextus*.[12]

One of the previously unidentified passages in the Evagrian florilegium (II.68) discusses humility and offers a description with ten characteristic features. Adalbert de Vogüé recognized it as an excerpt from Cassian, *Inst.* IV.39.[13] The text is also transmitted in the Greek version of the *Institutiones*. Table 5.1 presents the three parallel texts,[14] but for reasons of space, and since they are less important for the analysis, the second, third, seventh, and eighth features of humility are omitted. Table 5.2 presents the full English translation of the passages in the florilegium and the Greek Cassian.

As can be seen, both the Latin and Greek versions of Cassian are longer and more elaborate than the florilegium. In Cassian, for example, the signs of humility are numbered; they are written in bold in Table 5.1. Only one sentence of the florilegium is absent from both the Greek and Latin versions of Cassian: τὸ μὴ μετρεῖν ἑαυτόν (not measuring oneself), written in bold in Table 5.1.

---

10 Joseph Muyldermans, *À travers la tradition manuscrite d'Évagre le Pontique. Essai sur les manuscrits grecs conservés à la Bibliothèque Nationale de Paris*, Bibliothèque du Muséon 3 (Louvain: Bureaux du Muséon, 1932), 85–94.

11 Antoine Guillaumont and Claire Guillaumont, Introduction to *Évagre le Pontique, Traité pratique, ou, Le Moine*, vol. 1, SChr 170 (Paris: Cerf, 1971), 283–286.

12 Ed. Henry Chadwick, *The Sentences of Sextus: A Contribution to the History of Early Christian Ethics* (Cambridge: Cambridge University Press, 1959), 162; Augustine Casiday, *Evagrius Ponticus* (London: Routledge, 2006), 173. Cf. Daniele Pevarello, *The Sentences of Sextus and the Origins of Christian Asceticism*, STAC 78 (Tübingen: Mohr Siebeck, 2013), 26–29.

13 Adalbert de Vogüé, "Un morceau célèbre de Cassien parmi des extraits d'Évagre," *Studia Monastica* 27 (1985): 7–12.

14 The texts are taken from Muyldermans, *À travers la tradition manuscrite*, 93–94; Tzamalikos, *Newly Discovered Greek Father*, 56–61; John Cassian, *Institutiones*, ed. and transl. Jean-Claude Guy, *Jean Cassien, Institutions cénobitiques*, SChr 109 (Paris: Cerf, 1965), 178–180.

TABLE 5.1

Florileg. Evagr. 11.68	Cass. graec.	Cass. lat. *Inst.* IV.39
Ἀρχὴ τῆς σωτηρίας φόβος Θεοῦ·	Πρῶτος βαθμὸς τῆς ἀρετῆς καὶ ἀρχὴ τῆς ἡμετέρας σωτηρίας καὶ ἀσφάλεια ὁ φόβος ἐστὶν τοῦ Κυρίου·	Principium nostrae salutis eiusdemque custodia timor Domini est.
οὗτος τίκτει καταφρόνησιν πάντων τῶν τοῦ κόσμου τερπνῶν· αὕτη δὲ γεννᾷ τὴν ταπείνωσιν.	διὰ τούτου γὰρ καὶ τῶν ἁμαρτημάτων ἀποκάθαρσις καὶ τῶν ἀρετῶν φυλακὴ καὶ ὁδὸς ἐπὶ τὴν τελείωσιν γίνεται. Ὅταν γὰρ ὁ τοῦ Θεοῦ φόβος εἰσέλθῃ εἰς ψυχήν, καταφρονεῖν πείθει πάντων τῶν τοῦ κόσμου πραγμάτων καὶ λήθην τῶν κατὰ σάρκα συγγενῶν γεννᾷ καὶ αὐτοῦ ὅλου τοῦ κόσμου. Ἐκ δὲ τούτων ταπείνωσις τὸ κεφάλαιον καὶ πλήρωμα πάντων τῶν καλῶν κατορθοῦται· καταφρονήσει γὰρ καὶ στερήσει πάντων τῶν ⟨τοῦ κόσμου⟩ πραγμάτων ἡ ταπείνωσις προσγίνεται.	Per hunc enim et initium conversionis, et vitiorum purgatio et virtutum custodia his qui imbuuntur ad viam perfectionis acquiritur. Qui cum penetraverit hominis mentem, contemptum rerum omnium parit, oblivionem parentum mundique ipsius gignit horrorem: contemptu autem ac privatione omnium facultatum humilitas acquiritur.
Σημεῖα δὲ ταπεινώσεως,	Ἡ ταπείνωσις δὲ τούτοις τοῖς γνωρίσμασιν δοκιμάζεται καὶ δείκνυται.	Humilitas vero his indiciis comprobatur:
νέκρωσις ἰδίου θελήματος, [...]	Πρῶτον εἰ νεκρωθέντα τις ἔχει ἐν αὐτῷ τὰ ἴδια θελήματα· [...]	**primo** si mortificatas in sese omnes habeat voluntates, [...]
καὶ δουλεύειν τοῖς αὐτοῦ προστάγμασιν ἀνεπαισχύντως·	τέταρτον, εἰ ἐν πᾶσιν ἀνεπαισχύντως δουλεύει τοῖς τοῦ πατρὸς προστάγμασιν·	**quarto** si in omnibus servet oboedientiae mansuetudinem patientiaeque constantiam,
τὸ μὴ τολμᾶν ὑβρίσαι τινὰ τῶν ἁπάντων, ἀλλὰ καὶ μᾶλλον πᾶσαν ὕβριν ὑπομένειν παρὰ παντός· τὸ μὴ μετρεῖν ἑαυτόν·	πέμπτον, εἰ μὴ μόνον αὐτὸς οὐ τολμᾷ ὑβρίσαι τινά, ἀλλὰ καὶ τὰς ὑπὸ ἄλλων ἐπαγομένας αὐτῷ ὕβρεις μετὰ χαρᾶς προσδέχεται·	**quinto** si non solum iniuriam inferat nulli, sed ne ab alio quidem sibimet inrogatam doleat atque tristetur,
τὸ μὴ ἐπιχειρεῖν καινοτέρῳ πράγματι παρὰ τὸν κανόνα τῶν πατέρων· [...]	ἕκτον, εἰ μηδὲν ἐπιχειρήσῃ καινότερον πρᾶξαι, ὅπερ οὐχ ὁ κοινὸς κανὼν ἐπιτρέπει, οὐδὲ τῶν πατέρων τὰ παραδείγματα· [...]	**sexto** si nihil agat, nihil praesumat, quod non vel communis regula vel maiorum cohortantur exempla, [...]
τὸ γλώσσης κρατεῖν, καὶ μήτε ἐν λόγοις προπετεύεσθαι, μήτε τῇ φωνῇ τραχύνειν.	ἔνατον, εἰ γλώσσης κρατεῖ καὶ μὴ ἐστιν προπετὴς ἐν λόγοις καὶ τραχὺς ἐν φωνῇ·	**nono** si linguam cohibeat vel non sit clamosus in voce,

(cont.)

Florileg. Evagr. 11.68	Cass. graec.	Cass. lat. *Inst.* IV.39
τὸ μὴ προχείρως γελᾶν.	δέκατον, εἰ μή ἐστιν εὐχερὴς καὶ πρόχειρος ἐν γέλωτι.	**decimo** si non sit facilis ac promptus in risu.
Τούτοις καὶ τοῖς τοιούτοις ἡ ταπείνωσις κατορθουμένη πρὸς τὸ τῆς θείας ἀγάπης ὕψος ἀνάγει, τῆς μηκέτι φόβον κολάσεως ἐχούσης, ἀλλὰ πόθον τοῦ νυμφίου διαπυρώτατον.	Τούτοις γὰρ καὶ τοῖς ὁμοίοις τούτοις σημείοις ἡ ταπείνωσις γνωρίζεται, ἥτις, ὅταν ἐν ἀληθείᾳ κατορθωθῇ, ταχέως πρὸς τὸ ὕψος τῆς ἀγάπης ἀνάγει, ἐν ᾗ φόβος οὐκ ἔστιν κολάσεως καὶ δι' ἧς τὰ πάντα οὐκέτι μετὰ ἀνάγκης καὶ κόπου φυλάττεται, ἀλλὰ **πόθῳ διαπύρῳ** καὶ ἐπιθυμίᾳ τοῦ καλοῦ.	Talibus namque indiciis et his similibus humilitas vera dinoscitur. Quae cum fuerit in veritate possessa, confestim te ad charitatem, quae timorem non habet, gradu excelsiore perducet, per quam universa, quae prius non sine poena formidinis observabas, absque ullo labore velut naturaliter incipies custodire non iam contemplatione supplicii vel timoris ullius, sed amore ipsius boni et delectatione virtutum.

A. de Vogüé recognised that the passage in the florilegium bears greater resemblance to the Greek than to the Latin version of Cassian. The most conspicuous example is the words μήτε ἐν λόγοις προπετεύεσθαι (neither being premature with words) in the ninth sign of humility in the florilegium, which corresponds to μή ἐστιν προπετὴς ἐν λόγοις (is not presumptuous in his words) in the Greek version of Cassian.[15] The phrase is missing from the Latin. Other examples where the florilegium concurs with the Greek against the Latin are found in the fourth sign and in the epilogue. The words δουλεύειν τοῖς αὐτοῦ προστάγμασιν ἀνεπαισχύντως (unashamedly obeying his commands) in the fourth sign of humility in the florilegium correspond to ἀνεπαισχύντως δουλεύει τοῖς τοῦ πατρὸς προστάγμασιν (he carries out the commands of the father without feeling ashamed) in the Greek Cassian. The Latin Cassian differs and reads *servet obedientiam, mansuetudinem, et patientiae constantiam* (he maintains obedience, gentleness and constant patience). In the epilogue, the words meaning "the height of divine love" and "a most ardent desire" in the florilegium are found with only minor variation in the Greek Cassian, but are missing from the Latin. All these examples are written in bold in Table 5.1.[16] The word νυμφίου (bridegroom) will be discussed below.

15   de Vogüé, "Morceau célèbre de Cassien," 9, n. 10.
16   de Vogüé, "Morceau célèbre de Cassien," 10, n. 17.

There is clearly a relation between the two Greek texts. De Vogüé pointed out that the florilegium cannot depend upon the Latin Cassian, because it would be rather unlikely that both the Greek Cassian and the compiler of the florilegium independently added the same words. Since de Vogüé assumed that Cassian wrote in Latin, and that thus the Greek version must be a translation from the Latin, he concluded that Cassian could not have used this Evagrian text as a source. He therefore considered the text of the florilegium as an excerpt from the Greek Cassian that had been revised, and at some point included in this florilegium.[17]

A closer study of the florilegium reveals similarities to a collection of *progymnasmata*. Such collections were an important part of the ancient school curriculum. A pupil's first stage of training in grammar and rhetoric consisted of "elementary exercises" (*progymnasmata*) such as genre exercises on fable, narration, *chreia*, and maxim.[18] According to Theon, author of a handbook on rhetorical exercises, a *chreia* is defined as "a concise statement or action which is attributed with aptness to some specified character or to something analogous to a character. Closely related to the *chreia* are maxim and reminiscence. For every concise maxim, if it is attributed to a character, produces a *chreia*."[19] Thus Theon regards the maxim as a form of the *chreia*, namely one lacking the attribution to a character. Students of rhetoric were taught to elaborate the *chreia* by using a set of elements. Hermogenes describes this exercise, called *ergasia* (elaboration), as including the following eight features: 1) praise (ἐγκώμιον); 2) paraphrase (παράφρασις); 3) cause (αἰτία); 4) expansion through contrast (κατὰ τὸ ἐνάντιον); 5) expansion through analogy (ἐκ παραβολῆς); 6) expansion through example (ἐκ παραδείγματος); 7) expansion through authority (ἐκ κρίσεως); 8) exhortation (παράκλησις).[20] Aphthonius lists the same elements, except that he refers to the seventh as "testimony of the elders" (μαρτυρία παλαιῶν) and to the eighth as "short epilogue" (ἐπίλογος βραχύς).[21] Maxims too could be elaborated following the same *ergasia* pattern.[22]

---

17   de Vogüé, "Morceau célèbre de Cassien," 11.
18   Ronald F. Hock and Edward N. O'Neil, ed. and transl., *The Chreia in Ancient Rhetoric*, vol. 1, *The Progymnasmata* (Atlanta: Scholars Press, 1986), 20–22. For more on ancient education, see Raffaella Cribiore, *Gymnastics of the Mind: Greek Education in Hellenistic and Roman Egypt* (Princeton: Princeton University Press, 2001); Teresa Morgan, *Literate Education in the Hellenistic and Roman Worlds* (Cambridge: Cambridge University Press, 1998); Lillian I. Larsen, "'On Learning a New Alphabet': The Sayings of the Desert Fathers and the Monostichs of Menander," *StPatr* 55 (2013): 59–77.
19   Theon, *Progymnasmata* 96, transl. Hock and O'Neil, *Chreia*, vol. 1, pp. 82–83.
20   Hermogenes, *Progymnasmata* 7–8, transl. Hock and O'Neil, *Chreia*, vol. 1, pp. 176–177.
21   Aphthonius, *Progymnasmata* 4, transl. Hock and O'Neil, *Chreia*, vol. 1, pp. 224–245.
22   Hermogenes, *Progymnasmata* 9–10; Aphthonius, *Progymnasmata* 8.

In recent research, scholars have pointed out that monastic authors were influenced by this type of rhetorical training.[23] In particular, the *Apophthegmata Patrum* (AP) have been studied in light of the genre of sayings, and they have been described as collections of *chreiai*.[24]

Analysing the florilegium more closely, it could be described as a collection of maxims (γνῶμαι). The structure of our passage, no. 11.68, could be described as containing the following elements from the *ergasia*: a maxim, a cause (3), a set of maxims describing the signs of humility, and finally an epilogue (8). Those elements, including the maxims, are further expanded in the Greek and Latin Cassian. The first maxim is paraphrased, the cause and the epilogue are elaborated and expanded.[25] The set of maxims describing the signs of humility is paraphrased, and the grammar is changed in that the maxims are turned into conditional clauses. Table 5.2 presents the translations by Casiday and Tzamalikos, both slightly modified.[26]

---

23   The significance of monastic education and its alignment with ancient rhetorical methods has been demonstrated by Lillian Larsen in several works: "The Apophthegmata Patrum and the Classical Rhetorical Tradition," *StPatr* 39 (2006): 409–415; "The Apophthegmata Patrum: Rustic Rumination or Rhetorical Recitation," *MCPL* 23 (2008): 21–30; "Early Monasticism and the Rhetorical Tradition: Sayings and Stories as School Texts," in *Education and Religion in Late Antique Christianity: Reflections, Social Contexts and Genres*, ed. Peter Gemeinhardt, Lieve Van Hoof, and Peter Van Nuffelen (Farnham: Ashgate, 2016), 13–33. The subject was extensively treated in the research programme called "Early Monasticism and Classical Paideia" (MOPAI), directed by Samuel Rubenson at Lund University from 2009 to 2015. Important contributions from a conference arranged by the programme are published in Lillian I. Larsen and Samuel Rubenson, eds., *Monastic Education in Late Antiquity*.

24   Kathleen McVey, "The *Chreia* in the Desert: Rhetoric and the Bible in the *Apophthegmata Patrum*," in *The Early Church in its Context: Essays in Honor of Everett Ferguson*, ed. Abraham J. Malherbe, Frederick W. Norris, and James W. Thompson (Leiden: Brill, 1998), 245–255; Lillian I. Larsen, "Pedagogical Parallels: Re-reading the Apophthegmata Patrum" (PhD diss., Columbia University, 2006); Per Rönnegård, *Threads and Images: The Use of Scripture in Apophthegmata Patrum* (Winona Lake, Ind.: Eisenbrauns, 2010). See also the studies by Larsen mentioned in note 22, and her article "Ørkenfedrenes Apophthegmata og den klassiske retoriske tradisjon," *MCPL* 16 (2001): 26–35. For a general overview of the formation of the *Apophthegmata Patrum*, see Samuel Rubenson, "The Formation and Re-Formations of the Sayings of the Desert Fathers," *StPatr* 55 (2013): 3–22.

25   The exercises "paraphrase" and "elaboration" are described by Theon, *Progymnasmata*, pp. 107–111 in Patillon's edition.

26   Casiday, *Evagrius Ponticus*, 179; Tzamalikos, *Newly Discovered Greek Father*, 56–61.

TABLE 5.2

Flor. Evagr. 11.68	Cass. graec.
Maxim (γνώμη)	**Paraphrase of the maxim**
The beginning of salvation is the fear of God.	The first step towards virtue, and beginning of our salvation, and the safeguard of it, is the fear of the Lord.
Cause (αἰτία)	**Elaboration of the cause**
[The fear] begets disdain for all the delights of the world, which in turn produces humility.	For it is through this that purification from vices and preservation of virtues and the way of perfection can be accomplished. For when fear of the Lord has gained an entrance into the soul, it persuades it to contempt all things of this world, and begets a forgetfulness of kinsfolk, indeed of all the world itself. Consequently, humility is gained and completeness of all virtues is attained. For humility is acquired by means of contempt and deprivation of all the worldly things.
Maxims (γνῶμαι)	**Paraphrase of the maxims**
The signs of humility are:	Moreover, humility is tried out and attested by these signs:
the death of one's own will;	**First**, if a man has all his personal desires mortified.
heartfelt confession of both actions and words, as well as thoughts;	**Second**, if he conceals none of his actions, nor his thoughts, from his father.
not trusting in one's conscience, but laying everything before one's father in the spirit and depending upon his words	**Third**, if he puts no trust in his own judgment, but considers everything through the discretion of his own father, always thirsting for and listening dearly to his admonition.
and **unashamedly obeying his commands**;	**Fourth**, if **he carries out the commands of the father** in all cases, **without feeling ashamed of this**.
not daring to do anything at all spitefully, but rather enduring all spite from everyone; **not measuring oneself**;	**Fifth**, if he not only hurts nobody else, but also receives any harm inflicted upon him by others joyfully.
not setting one's hand to any new thing contrary to the rule of the fathers;	**Sixth**, if he ventures no innovation, which is not allowed by the Common Rule or by the example of the fathers.

(cont.)

Flor. Evagr. 11.68	Cass. graec.
being satisfied with thriftiness, even confessing oneself unworthy of it;	**Seventh**, if he is contented with the fewest goods possible, and is thankful for whatever is given to him, considering himself as unworthy of even those things.
making oneself last of all, in word and deed with full conviction;	**Eighth**, if he considers himself from the bottom of his heart as inferior to all others, and as being superior to none.
prevailing over the tongue, **neither being premature with words** nor using harsh tones;	**Ninth**, if he governs his tongue, and **is not presumptuous in his words** and harsh in the tone of his voice.
not laughing readily.	**Tenth**, if he is not prone to laughing or too ready to do so.
Epilogue (ἐπίλογος)	**Elaboration of the epilogue**
Accomplished in these and similar things, humility leads to **the height of divine love**, no longer having fear of correction but instead **a most ardent desire for the bridegroom**.	For by such signs and the like humility is recognised. And when this has been truly attained, then at once it leads on to **the heights of love**, in which there is no fear of hell, and through which everything is no longer observed with effort and because this is imposed by necessity, but because of **earnest ardour and desire for goodness**.

As mentioned above, de Vogüé claimed that the text of the florilegium is an excerpt from the Greek Cassian that has been revised, condensed, and at some point included in this florilegium.[27] But why would a compilor of excerpts from Evagrius incorporate a heavily revised text by Cassian? Or, even more unlikely, why would he himself rework it before including it? As demonstrated above, the passage in the florilegium seems to have been expanded in the manner of *ergasia*. As for Cassian's text, it is a further development of *ergasia*, and it also changes grammar and style. For example, the numbers in a list are more likely to have been added than omitted. Assuming that the passage in the florilegium was originally written by Evagrius, it is highly probable that

---

27 de Vogüé, "Morceau célèbre de Cassien," 11.

Cassian used and expanded it to suit his context. The correlation of the two Greek texts over against the Latin Cassian—particularly the shared expressions in the ninth sign and in the epilogue, which are entirely absent from the Latin—indicates that the florilegium is not dependent on the Latin. Since it is highly unlikely that both the florilegium and the Greek Cassian independently expanded the text with the very same phrases, the Latin appears to be secondary.

3   *Institutio* IV.39 and the Monastic Rules

The excerpt under consideration, Cassian's *Institutio* IV.39, was an influential text. The Latin version influenced the monastic rules in the sixth century, when it was revised and included in the chapter on humility in the *Regula magistri* (ch. 10), and soon thereafter in the *Regula Benedicti* (ch. 7). A textual comparison shows that these monastic rules draw upon the Latin Cassian, and that the *Regula magistri* follows the Latin more closely than does the *Regula Benedicti*.[28]

Susanna Elm has suggested that Evagrius wrote his *Sententiae ad virginem* as a primitive monastic rule for the community in Jerusalem, headed by Melania.[29] Her argument is based upon three criteria of what constitutes a rule, as articulated by de Vogüé: legislative nature, i.e., there must be a normative value; content, i.e., there must be regulations for the community's relations both within and outside the group; and finally, authority, i.e., it must be accepted also by other communities and in later times.[30]

The maxims constituting the ten signs of humility in the florilegium aim at spiritual guidance, and thus prescribe monastic conduct. As do the *Sententiae ad virginem*, they emphasise obedience to the monastic leader. In fact, the text references "the rule of the fathers" (τὸν κανόνα τῶν πατέρων, no. 6). In the Greek Cassian, this is rendered as "the common rule" (ὁ κοινὸς κανών), in Latin as *communis regula*. The fact that Cassian's text was integrated into the early monastic rules shows that its value for the governance of the communi-

---

28   Owen Chadwick, *John Cassian*, 2nd ed. (Cambridge: Cambridge University Press, 1968), 153.

29   Susanna Elm, "The *Sententiae ad Virginem* by Evagrius Ponticus and the Problem of Early Monastic Rules," *Augustinianum* 30 (1990): 393–404; eadem, "Evagrius Ponticus' *Sententiae ad Virginem*," *DOP* 45 (1991): 97–120.

30   Adalbert de Vogüé, *Les règles monastiques anciennes (400–700)*, Typologie des sources du moyen âge occidental, fasc. 46 (Turnhout: Brepols, 1985), 19–22, 37–40, 49–52.

ties was recognized. Thus one might describe the passage in the florilegium, if not as a complete rule, as a portion of a monastic rule in a preliminary stage.

Elm also directs attention to a specific concept used by Evagrius in his *Sententiae ad virginem*: the image of Christ as bridegroom. This nuptial metaphor, drawing upon the *Song of Songs*, became a common way to describe the church as the bride of Christ, as well as the union of the soul with Christ, the bridegroom. The idea of a future union with the bridegroom was applied to both male and female ascetics. However, in the fourth century this notion was more frequently applied of the female ascetic.[31] Evagrius addresses his *Sententiae ad virginem* to a virgin, probably Melania, and he here uses the image of Christ as bridegroom five times (11, 43, 52, twice in 55), whereas the metaphor is rare in his other works.[32]

In the epilogue of the florilegium, humility is said to lead to desire for the bridegroom (τοῦ νυμφίου). This may suggest that the recipient of this text was a woman or a group of women, but there is nothing more to corroborate this theory. In Cassian the idea is revised, for now the object of desire is no longer the bridegroom but goodness, in Greek πόθῳ διαπύρῳ καὶ ἐπιθυμίᾳ τοῦ καλοῦ (earnest ardour and desire for goodness), and in Latin *amore ipsius boni et delectatione virtutum* (love of goodness itself and desire in virtue). As Cassian addressed a male community, it is plausible that he adapted the text to suit his audience.

4   *Collatio* 11.13 in Latin and Greek

In order further to consider the implications of these textual analyses, I will now turn to my second example, a passage from the *Collationes*. As noted above, I have argued elsewhere that the *Collationes* were originally written in Latin, but that the Greek version of I–II and VII–VIII represents an earlier stage of the text than the extant Latin version. This earlier research included analysis of an apophthegm found in *Collatio* 11, which had previously been discussed by Hans-Oskar Weber.[33] I will return here to this example, since it has important theological implications.

---

31   Elm, "Evagrius Ponticus," 113.
32   "Themes in Evagrius: Christ the Bridegroom," webpage by Luke Dysinger, http://www.ldysinger.com/Evagrius/60_themes/00a_start.htm. In most of the other instances where Evagrius uses this image, he explicitly comments upon or refers to the *Song of Songs*.
33   Dahlman, "Textual Fluidity," 292; Hans-Oskar Weber, *Die Stellung des Johannes Cassianus zur ausserpachomianischen Mönchstradition* (Münster: Aschendorff, 1960), 32–35.

The text of *Collatio* 11.13.1–2, 4–10 is found in collections of the *Apophthegmata Patrum*.[34] Weber compared the Latin text of *Coll.* 11.13.4–10 with an apophthegm in the Latin systematic collection, AP/PJ V.4 (PL 73, 874B–875C) and reached the conclusion that Cassian must have known this saying, expanded and adapted it for his own purposes.[35] However, Weber had access neither to the text of the Greek systematic collection, AP/GS V.4b, nor to Cassian's Greek version.[36] The Greek and Latin *apophthegmata* are very similar, and there is no reason to doubt that the Latin is a translation of the Greek. Likewise, a comparison of the Greek apophthegm AP/GS V.4b with the Greek and Latin Cassian shows that the Greek texts agree almost word for word, whereas the Latin Cassian is a much more elaborate version. The situation thus is similar to that encountered previously in our analysis of the text of the florilegium and Cassian's *Collatio* IV.39.

Table 5.3 illustrates the relation between these texts, with relevant passages written in bold.[37] The expressions "by God's dispensation" and "due to his great despondency" are shared by AP/GS V.4b, PJ V.4, and the Greek Cassian, but absent from the Latin Cassian. Moreover, the direct question, "what is the reason for you to look so sad?" is an indirect question in the Latin Cassian. And the statement that Apollo was "the most skilful of the elders" occurs in both the Greek and Latin Cassian, but not in the *Apophthegmata*.

---

34 For a table of Cassian's *apophthegmata* in Greek and Latin collections, see Dahlman, "Textual Fluidity," 290. See also Philip Rousseau, "Cassian's Apophthegmata," *JAC* 48–49 (2005–2006): 19–34. Texts and more detailed tables are available in the "Apophthegmata Patrum Database" (APDB), created by IT architect Kenneth Berg for the MOPAI research programme. An online version will soon be available. For the abbreviations of the collections of *Apophthegmata Patrum* used below, AP/PJ and AP/GS, see the Bibliography.
35 Weber, *Johannes Cassianus*, 35.
36 The first volume of Guy's edition of the Greek systematic collection was published in 1993.
37 For a thorough comparison of the Latin texts AP/PJ V.4 and the Latin Cassian *Coll.* 11.13.4–10, see Weber, *Johannes Cassianus*, 32–35. The texts of Cassian in Table 5.3 are taken from Tzamalikos, *Newly Discovered Greek Father*, 200, lines 15–20; and John Cassian, *Collationes*, ed. Michael Petschenig, *Cassiani opera: Conlationes XXIII*, CSEL 13, 2nd rev. ed. by Gottfried Kreuz (Vienna: Austrian Academy of Sciences Press, 2004), 54.

TABLE 5.3

AP/GS-Dahlman v.4b[38]	AP/PJ v.4	Cass. graec.	Cass. lat. Coll. 11.13.5
[...] Ταῦτα ἀκούσας ὁ ἀδελφὸς ἀπογνοὺς ἑαυτοῦ καὶ καταλείψας τὸ ἴδιον κελλίον ἐπὶ τὸν κόσμον ἀπήρχετο. **Κατὰ δὲ Θεοῦ οἰκονομίαν** ὑπαντᾷ αὐτῷ ἀββᾶ Ἀπολλώς. Καὶ βλέπων αὐτὸν τεταραγμένον καὶ πάνυ σκυθρωπάζοντα ἠρώτα αὐτὸν λέγων· Τέκνον, τίς ἡ αἰτία τῆς τοιαύτης στυγνότητος; Ὁ δὲ τὴν μὲν ἀρχὴν ἐκ τῆς πολλῆς ἀθυμίας οὐκ ἀπεκρίθη οὐδέν. [...]	[...] Haec audiens frater, desperans seipsum, reliquit propriam cellam, et ad saeculum redibat. **Secundum vero Dei dispensationem** occurrit ei abbas Apollo; et videns eum perturbatum, et nimium tristem, interrogavit eum, dicens: Fili, **quae est causa tantae tristitiae tuae?** Ille autem prius **ex multa confusione animi** sui non respondit ei quidquam; [...]	ταῦτα οὖν ἀκούσας ὁ ἀδελφὸς ἀπογνοὺς ἑαυτὸν καὶ καταλείψας τὸν ἴδιον τόπον ἐπὶ τὸν κόσμον ἐπανήρχετο. **κατὰ δὲ Θεοῦ οἰκονομίαν** ἀπαντᾷ αὐτῷ ὁ ἀββᾶς Ἀπολλώς, τῶν γερόντων ὁ δοκιμώτατος, καὶ βλέπων αὐτὸν τεταραγμένον καὶ πάνυ σκυθρωπάζοντα ἠρώτα αὐτὸν λέγων· τέκνον, τίς ἡ αἰτία τῆς τοιαύτης στυγνότητος. ὁ δὲ τὴν μὲν ἀρχὴν ἐκ τῆς πολλῆς ἀθυμίας οὐδὲν ἀπεκρίθη.	cumque ei tali maerore depresso nec iam de remedio passionis, sed de expletione conceptae concupiscentiae profunda cogitatione tractanti abbas Apollo **seniorum probatissimus** occurrisset laboremque et obpugnationis vehementiam, quae in corde eius tacite volvebantur, de contemplatione vultus et deiectione coniectans causam tantae perturbationis inquireret, atque ille **molliter** se conpellanti seni ne responsum quidem ullum posset referre [...].
The brother despaired of his case when he heard those things; he left his own cell and went back to the world, but, **by the providence of God**, Abba Apollo encountered him. When [the elder] saw him trou-	When the brother heard this, he despaired of himself, and left his cell, and started on his way back to the world. But **by God's providence**, Abba Apollos met him. And seeing him disturbed and melancholy, he	When the brother heard this, he gave up all hope, then abandoned his place, and was on his way back to the world. However, **by God's dispensation**, Abba Apollos, **the most proficient among the**	And when he, oppressed with such a sorrow, was plunged in deep thought, no longer [knowing] how to cure his passion, but how to gratify his lust, the Abbot Apollos, **the most skilful of the Elders**, met

---

38 The Greek text is from the edition by Britt Dahlman in *Paradiset: Ökenfädernas tänkespråk, den systematiska samlingen*, vol. 5, *Olika berättelser till skydd när otukten ansätter oss*, ed. Britt Dahlman and Per Rönnegård (Sturefors: Silentium, 2014). The apophthegm is found in the old Greek systematic collection (stage a according to Guy) in MS Parisinus graecus 2474, which was not used by Guy for his edition (AP/GS-Guy), although he described its content in Jean-Claude Guy, *Recherches sur la tradition grecque des Apophthegmata Patrum*, 2nd ed., SubsHag 36 (Brussels: Société des Bollandistes, 1984), 188–190. In vol. 5 of the series *Paradiset*, this apophthegm and a few others are edited by Dahlman according to the Paris MS, but the majority of the apophthegms in this chapter are edited from another important MS (containing stage b[1] of the Greek systematic collection according to Guy): Athos, Protaton 86.

AP/GS-Dahlman v.4b	AP/PJ v.4	Cass. graec.	Cass. lat. Coll. 11.13.5
bled and looking so sad, he asked him, "**What is the reason for such gloom as this?**" At first he would not reply, **he was so despondent**. (tr. Wortley)	asked him: "Son, **why are you so sad?**" The brother, **much embarrassed**, at first said not a word. (tr. Chadwick)	**Fathers**, came upon him; and since he saw [the brother] embarrassed and utterly downhearted, he asked him this question: "Child, **what is the reason for you to look so sad?**" He initially did not respond, **due to his despondency**. (tr. Tzamalikos)	him, and seeing by his looks and gloominess his trouble and the violence of the assault which he was secretly revolving in his heart, asked him the reason of this upset; and when he could not possibly answer the old man's gentle inquiry […]. (tr. Gibson)

If Weber's conclusion is correct that the text of the apophthegm is primary, then the Greek Cassian must be prior to the Latin Cassian since it would be absurd to think that Cassian first revised and expanded the text in Latin, and that later someone translated this text into Greek, revising it so as to look almost exactly as the apophthegm. The simplest explanation is that Cassian wrote the Greek text (or a version very similar to it), and that an excerpt of the Greek *Collationes* was incorporated into the *Apophthegmata Patrum*.

However, as I have shown in a previous publication, the Greek version of the *Collationes* displays some signs of having had a Latin *Vorlage*.[39] This early Latin version must have been translated into Greek, after which the Latin text was further revised and expanded by Cassian, and probably by others as well, until it took the shape it has in the manuscripts. Since the early Latin version has not been preserved, the Greek one is important for studying Cassian's early views and theology. What are the implications for our understanding of Cassian's theology if we compare the Greek and Latin versions of *Collatio* 11?

Collatio 11 deals with discretion, and Abba Moses is the speaker. He describes the virtue of discretion as "no small virtue, nor one that can be gotten hold of by human effort in some way or other and without the assistance of divine generosity" (11.1.3). Then, after giving a definition of discretion in the words of Abba Antony, Moses recounts stories from the fathers to demonstrate the practice of this virtue. The monk can learn to discern what is right and how to avoid all kind of excess by submitting to the judgment of the elders. But not all elders can be trusted. An episode recounted in *Coll.* 11.13 illustrates that old age is not

---

39 Dahlman, "Textual Fluidity," 293–294.

enough to make a father suitable to pass judgments on younger monks: A young brother, who is described as "one of the most earnest" in the Greek text and as "not the laziest of young men" in the Latin, is troubled by the spirit of fornication and confesses to an elder, who dismisses him as no longer fit to be a monk. The Latin text states that he was "in a state of hopeless despair and deadly despondency" (11.13.4), an expression not found in the Greek. However, Abba Apollos meets him, and the Greek remarks that it happened "by God's dispensation" (κατὰ δὲ Θεοῦ οἰκονομίαν), an expression not found in the Latin. The young brother confesses his thoughts and shares with Abba Apollos what the elder had said. Here the Latin explicitly states that he intended to take a wife in the world, since he "could not be a monk." Apollos consoles him by telling him that he himself has had such thoughts daily. The Greek text omits "daily," instead noting that Apollos was "at this age and experience of the spiritual life."[40] Further he tells him that the violence of the attack "can be defeated not so much by zealous efforts, as by the mercy and grace of the Lord" (11.13.6).

Apollos goes to the elder and on his way he prays that the assault would be turned from the young man upon the old one. He prays, according to the Latin version: "O Lord, who alone are the righteous judge and unseen Physician of secret strength and human weakness, turn the assault from the young man upon the old one, that he may learn to condescend to the weakness of sufferers, and to sympathize even in old age with the frailties of youth." In the Greek text, the prayer has a different emphasis in that the image of God as a physician who heals human weakness, and the reference to "the frailties of youth" are missing.[41] The outcome is that the elder is hurt by darts from the devil and begins to act like a lunatic (in Greek, "a drunken man"). Seeing this, Apollos asks him what he is doing without receiving any answer. Here, the Latin text is longer, more elaborate and embellished than the Greek. Apollos exhorts him to return to his cell, and explains that he has been spared until now because he has been weak, and therefore was ignored or deemed unworthy of fight by the devil. The Latin version expands the narrative, adding that Apollos admonished the elder saying: "you have been wounded so that you at least may learn in your

---

40 Tzamalikos, *Newly Discovered Greek Father*, 202, line 1, has "at this age and grey hair," i.e., πολιᾷ (grey hair) instead of πολιτείᾳ (way of life). However, the textual tradition of the manuscripts for both Cassian and the apophthegm is divided. The majority of Greek manuscripts have πολιτείᾳ (way of life). The Latin apophthegm has an equivalent to *politeia*: *conversatione*.

41 Translation by Tzamalikos, *Newly Discovered Greek Father*, 203: "O Lord, you who send temptations to the benefit [of men], turn the assault from the young man upon this old man, that he may learn now, in his old age and by experience, what he has not been taught during so long a time, namely, to suffer together with those who are under attack."

old age to sympathize with infirmities to which you are a stranger, and may know from your own case and experience how to condescend to the frailties of the young." He also explains that the young monk was attacked so severely because he was stronger than the old monk, and therefore deemed a worthy contestant for the devil. Then in both the Latin and Greek Apollos quotes from Proverbs 24:11 and Isaiah 42:3 (Matt 12:20). A third quotation, from Isa 50:4, is given here in the Latin, but placed at the end of the story in the Greek. Apollos concludes his speech by referring to God's grace and saving dispensation: "for no one could bear the devices of the enemy, [...] unless God's grace assisted our weakness, or protected and supported it."[42] At the end he quotes Job 5:18 and 1 Kings (1 Sam) 2:6–7. The last part of the apophthegm describes how the abba is released from the attacks. In the Greek Cassian, this is followed by Moses' comments on the importance to confess all our thoughts to the elders and not to trust our own judgment. In the Latin Cassian, the information that the abba is delivered from his pain is incorporated in Moses' comments. Here too his teaching aims at the younger monk's confession of sins regardless of how severe they are, and encourages him not to deviate from the right course, even if the elder happens to be unexperienced, since "the clever enemy misuses their grey hairs to deceive the young" (a sentence not found in the Greek).

As Weber has pointed out, the emphasis differs in the apophthegm and the Latin Cassian. The apophthegm focuses on the spiritual guide: he must not reject confessions even if the sins are great. The Latin Cassian puts more stress on what the young monk must learn: to make a whole-hearted confession even if the abba seems to be unfit for the task, and not to judge himself. However, this shift is less perceptible when one compares not only the story as found in the apophthegm, but also the last part of Cassian, *Coll.* 11.13, in both Latin and Greek. In the parts of the Latin Cassian that are absent from the Greek, the stress is on the monk's own experience and his own responsibility, thus on human free will. The devil plays a larger role in the Latin as well. The Greek version puts greater emphasis on God's providence and divine grace. If Cassian wrote both versions, why is there in the Latin the greater stress on the monk's own responsibility and human free will, and less focus on God's providence and divine grace? Did Cassian revise his own discourse so that it would better fit into the ongoing theological discussion about divine grace and human will?

Cassian's theological position on grace and human will has frequently been discussed by scholars,[43] who often reference his views in *Collatio* XIII but to a

---

42   Translation from the Latin; the Greek has "for no one can endure the assaults of the enemy, [...] unless God's grace guarded human frailty."
43   See, e.g., Chadwick, *John Cassian*; Augustine Casiday, *Tradition and Theology in St John*

lesser extent address his other writings. However, as we have seen, *Collatio* 11 contains relevant information on the subject, which researchers have largely overlooked. Comparison of the Latin and Greek of other *Collationes* would certainly prove fruitful for our understanding of Cassian's theology.

5   Conclusion

In language and theology, Cassian was deeply rooted in the Greek Eastern tradition. He wrote in a monastic context in Gaul, introducing for a Western audience this Eastern tradition. When composing his well-known works, the *Institutiones* and the *Collationes*, Cassian used many sources, including wisdom literature such as the *Apophthegmata Patrum*. Comparison of Cassian's *Institutio* IV.39 with certain maxims attributed to Evagrius and preserved in a florilegium, shows that Cassian's text, in both the Latin and Greek versions, appears to be an expansion of the Evagrian passage according to ancient rhetorical models. However, Cassian's Greek version has greater resemblance to the florilegium than does the Latin, which supports the hypothesis that Cassian originally wrote the *Institutiones* in Greek. When Cassian used the Evagrian text, he transformed it, adapting grammar and vocabulary to suit a new context. Others, in turn, used and transformed Cassian's text and incorporated it into monastic rules.

Analysis of a passage from Cassian's *Collatio* 11, and comparison of its Latin and Greek versions, implies that Cassian most likely wrote the text originally in Latin, even though the Greek extant version constitutes an earlier stage than the preserved Latin. The Greek Cassian, although mentioning the monk's own responsibility, stresses God's providence and divine grace. In the Latin Cassian, on the other hand, the emphasis lies more explicitly on the monk's own responsibility and human free will. This difference is not simply the result of translation from one language to another, but marks a conscious reorientation in theology that may reflect the ongoing debates in Gaul, as well as differences between Eastern and Western tradition and thought.

Cassian (Oxford: Oxford University Press, 2007); Donato Ogliari, *Gratia et certamen: The Relationship between Grace and Free Will in the Discussion of Augustine with the So-called Semipelagians* (Leuven: Peeters, 2003).

Acknowledgements

The research presented in this paper was supported by funding from the Swedish Research Council (Vetenskapsrådet) for the project "Formative Wisdom. The Reception of Monastic Sayings in European Culture: Scholarly Collaboration on a Digital Platform" (FOWIS), headed by Samuel Rubenson, at Lund University. I am grateful to Lillian Larsen, University of Redlands, for sharing her insights into ancient practices of rhetoric and for directing my attention to early monastic rules. Her findings have influenced much of my thinking about monastic education. I also wish to thank Benjamin Ekman, Lund University, for providing me with material on Evagrius.

Bibliography

Primary Sources

Aphthonius. *Progymnasmata*. Ed. Hugo Rabe, *Aphthonii Progymnasmata*. Leipzig: Teubner, 1926. Partial English transl. in Hock and O'Neil, *Chreia* (see below).

AP/G = *Apophthegmata Patrum. Collectio Graeca Alphabetica*. Ed. Jean Baptiste Cotelier, *Ecclesiae Graecae monumenta*. Vol. 1. Paris, 1677, pp. 338–712. Reprinted in PG 65 (1858), 71–440.

AP/GS-Dahlman = *Apophthegmata Patrum. Collectio Graeca Systematica*. Chapter 5. Greek text ed. Britt Dahlman, Swedish translation publ. by Johannesakademin in *Paradiset: Ökenfädernas tänkespråk, den systematiska samlingen*. Vol. 5, *Olika berättelser till skydd när otukten ansätter oss*, ed. Britt Dahlman and Per Rönnegård. Silentium Apophthegmata 5. Sturefors: Silentium, 2014.

AP/GS-Guy = *Apophthegmata Patrum. Collectio Graeca Systematica*. Ed. and transl. Jean-Claude Guy, *Les Apophtegmes des Pères: Collection systématique*. 3 vols. SChr 387, 474, 498. Paris: Cerf, 1993–2005. English transl. in John Wortley, *The Book of the Elders: Sayings of the Desert Fathers. The Systematic Collection*. Collegeville, MN: Liturgical Press, 2012.

AP/PJ = *Apophthegmata Patrum. Collectio Latina Systematica interpretibus Pelagio, Iohanne et anonymo*. Ed. Heribert Rosweyde, *Vitae Patrum*. Vols. 5–6. Antwerp, 1615. Reprinted in PL 73 (1849) 851–1024, 1060–1062. English transl. Owen Chadwick, in *Western Asceticism*. LCC 12. London: SCM Press, 1958.

(Joannes) Cassianus. *Collationes*. Ed. Michael Petschenig, *Cassiani opera: Conlationes XXIII*. 2nd rev. ed. by Gottfried Kreuz. CSEL 13. Vienna: Austrian Academy of Sciences Press, 2004. English transl. Edgar C.S. Gibson, "The Conferences of John Cassian." NPNF, 2nd ser., 11 (1894).

(Joannes) Cassianus. *Institutiones*. Ed. and transl. Jean-Claude Guy, *Jean Cassien, Institutions cénobitiques*. SChr 109. Paris: Cerf, 1965.

Cassianus graecus. Ed. and transl. Panayiotis Tzamalikos, *A Newly Discovered Greek Father: Cassian the Sabaite Eclipsed by John Cassian of Marseilles*. SVigChr 111. Leiden: Brill, 2012.

Florilegium Evagrianum. Ed. in Joseph Muyldermans, *À travers la tradition manuscrite d'Évagre le Pontique: Essai sur les manuscrits grecs conservés à la Bibliothèque Nationale de Paris*, Appendix, pp. 79–94. Bibliothèque du Muséon 3. Louvain: Bureaux du Muséon, 1932. English transl. in Casiday, *Evagrius Ponticus* (see below).

Hermogenes. *Progymnasmata*. Ed. Hugo Rabe, *Hermogenes, Opera*. Leipzig: Teubner 1913. Partial English transl. in Hock and O'Neil, *Chreia* (see below).

Theon. *Progymnasmata*. Ed. and transl. Michel Patillon and Giancarlo Bolognesi, *Aelius Théon, Progymnasmata*. Paris: Les Belles Lettres, 1997. Partial English transl. in Hock and O'Neil, *Chreia* (see below).

Theon. *Progymnasmata*. Ed. James R. Butts, "The Progymnasmata of Theon: A New Text with Translation and Commentary." 2 vols. PhD diss., Claremont Graduate School, 1986. Partial English transl. in Hock and O'Neil, *Chreia* (see below).

Secondary Sources

Alciati, Roberto. "Il Cassiano greco di Panayiotis Tzamalikos." *Rivista di storia del Cristianesimo* 11 (2014): 451–477.

Bousset, Wilhelm. *Apophthegmata: Studien zur Geschichte des ältesten Mönchtums*. Tübingen: Mohr Siebeck, 1923.

Casiday, Augustine. *Evagrius Ponticus*. The Early Church Fathers. London: Routledge, 2006.

Casiday, Augustine. Review of *A Newly Discovered Greek Father: Cassian the Sabaite Eclipsed by John Cassian of Marseilles* and *The Real Cassian Revealed: Monastic Life, Greek 'Paideia', and Origenism in the Sixth Century*, by Panayiotis Tzamalikos. *Journal of Medieval Monastic Studies* 3 (2014): 119–125.

Casiday, Augustine. *Tradition and Theology in St John Cassian*. OECS. Oxford: Oxford University Press, 2007.

Casiday, Augustine. "Translation, Controversies, and Adaptations at St Sabas Monastery during the Sixth Century." *Journal of Medieval Monastic Studies* 2 (2013): 1–18.

Chadwick, Henry, ed. *The Sentences of Sextus: A Contribution to the History of Early Christian Ethics*. Cambridge: Cambridge University Press, 1959.

Chadwick, Owen. *John Cassian*. 2nd ed. Cambridge: Cambridge University Press, 1968.

Cribiore, Raffaella. *Gymnastics of the Mind: Greek Education in Hellenistic and Roman Egypt*. Princeton: Princeton University Press, 2001.

Dahlman, Britt. "Textual Fluidity and Authorial Revision: The Case of Cassian and Palladius." In *Monastic Education in Late Antiquity: The Transformation of Classical Paideia*, ed. Lillian I. Larsen and Samuel Rubenson, 281–305. Cambridge: Cambridge University Press, 2018.

Dysinger, Luke. "Themes in Evagrius: Christ the Bridegroom." http://www.ldysinger.com/Evagrius/60_themes/00a_start.htm.

Elm, Susanna. "Evagrius Ponticus' *Sententiae ad Virginem*." *DOP* 45 (1991): 97–120.

Elm, Susanna. "The *Sententiae ad Virginem* by Evagrius Ponticus and the Problem of Early Monastic Rules." *Augustinianum* 30:2 (1990): 393–404.

Guillaumont, Antoine, and Claire Guillaumont, ed. and transl. *Évagre le Pontique, Traité pratique, ou, Le Moine*. Vol. 1. SChr 170. Paris: Cerf, 1971.

Guy, Jean-Claude. *Recherches sur la tradition grecque des Apophthegmata Patrum*. 2nd ed. SubsHag 36. Brussels: Société des Bollandistes, 1984.

Hock, Ronald F., and Edward N. O'Neil. *The Chreia in Ancient Rhetoric*. Vol. 1, *The Progymnasmata*. Texts and Translations 27. Graeco-Roman Religion Series 9. Atlanta: Scholars Press, 1986.

Ică, Ioan I., Jr., "'Cassian Savaitul' 'adevăratul Cassian' grec al 'Filocaliei' din umbra latinului 'Ioan Cassian' Implicațiile revoluționare pentru patrologie ale unei recente ediții și interpretări." *Revista Teologica* 3 (2013): 164–178.

Larsen, Lillian I. "The Apophthegmata Patrum and the Classical Rhetorical Tradition." *StPatr* 39 (2006): 409–415.

Larsen, Lillian I. "The Apophthegmata Patrum: Rustic Rumination or Rhetorical Recitation." *MCPL* 23 (2008): 21–30.

Larsen, Lillian I. "Early Monasticism and the Rhetorical Tradition: Sayings and Stories as School Texts." In *Education and Religion in Late Antique Christianity: Reflections, Social Contexts and Genres*, ed. Peter Gemeinhardt, Lieve Van Hoof, and Peter Van Nuffelen, 13–33. Farnham: Ashgate, 2016.

Larsen, Lillian I. "'On Learning a New Alphabet': The Sayings of the Desert Fathers and the Monostichs of Menander." *StPatr* 55 (2013): 59–77.

Larsen, Lillian I. "Ørkenfedrenes Apophthegmata og den klassiske retoriske tradisjon." *MCPL* 16 (2001): 26–35.

Larsen, Lillian I. "Pedagogical Parallels: Re-reading the Apophthegmata Patrum." PhD diss., Columbia University, 2006.

Larsen, Lillian I., and Samuel Rubenson, eds. *Monastic Education in Late Antiquity: The Transformation of Classical Paideia*. Cambridge: Cambridge University Press, 2018.

Marsili, Salvatore. *Giovanni Cassiano ed Evagrio Pontico: Dottrina sulla carità e contemplazione*. StAns 5. Rome: Editrice Anselmiana, 1936.

McVey, Kathleen. "The *Chreia* in the Desert: Rhetoric and the Bible in the *Apophthegmata Patrum*." In *The Early Church in its Context: Essays in Honor of Everett Ferguson*, ed. Abraham J. Malherbe, Frederick W. Norris, and James W. Thompson, 245–255. Leiden: Brill, 1998.

Morgan, Teresa. *Literate Education in the Hellenistic and Roman Worlds*. Cambridge: Cambridge University Press, 1998.

Ogliari, Donato. *Gratia et certamen: The Relationship Between Grace and Free Will in the Discussion of Augustine with the So-called Semipelagians*. Leuven: Peeters, 2003.

Pevarello, Daniele. *The Sentences of Sextus and the Origins of Christian Asceticism*. STAC 78. Tübingen: Mohr Siebeck, 2013.

Rönnegård, Per. *Threads and Images: The Use of Scripture in Apophthegmata Patrum*. Winona Lake, IN: Eisenbrauns, 2010.

Rousseau, Philip. "Cassian's Apophthegmata." *JAC* 48–49 (2005–2006): 19–34.

Rubenson, Samuel. "The Formation and Re-Formations of the Sayings of the Desert Fathers." *StPatr* 55 (2013): 3–22.

Stewart, Columba. "Another Cassian?" *JEH* 66 (2015): 372–376.

Stewart, Columba. "From λόγος to *verbum*. John Cassian's Use of Greek in the Development of a Latin Monastic Vocabulary." In *The Joy of Learning and the Love of God. Studies in Honor of Jean Leclercq*, ed. Ellen Rozanne Elder, 5–31. CSS 160. Kalamazoo, MI: Cistercian Publications, 1995.

Tzamalikos, Panayiotis. *A Newly Discovered Greek Father: Cassian the Sabaite Eclipsed by John Cassian of Marseilles*. SVigChr 111. Leiden: Brill, 2012.

Tzamalikos, Panayiotis. *The Real Cassian Revisited: Monastic Life, Greek Paideia, and Origenism in the Sixth Century*. SVigChr 112. Leiden: Brill, 2012.

Vogüé, Adalbert de. *Les règles monastiques anciennes (400–700)*. Typologie des sources du moyen âge occidental, fasc. 46. Turnhout: Brepols, 1985.

Vogüé, Adalbert de. "Un morceau célèbre de Cassien parmi des extraits d'Évagre." *Studia Monastica* 27 (1985): 7–12.

Weber, Hans-Oskar. *Die Stellung des Johannes Cassianus zur ausserpachomianischen Mönchstradition*. Münster: Aschendorff, 1960.

Yévadian, Maxime. "Le grec de Jean Cassien." In *Le livre scellé*, ed. Laurence Mellerin, 179–203. Turnhout: Brepols, 2017.

CHAPTER 6

The *Apophthegmata Patrum* in the Slavonic Context: A Case Study of Textual Doublets

Karine Åkerman Sarkisian

1   Introduction

"Every telling is a retelling," the comparative literature scholar Maria Tymoczko points out.[1] This observation is just as valid for the monastic stories preserved in the collections of *Apophthegmata Patrum* (*AP*) as for the Irish myths to which she refers. It is very much also applicable to the Russian tradition, the Eastern inheritor of the textual reception by the Slavs, as this essay will highlight.

It is well known that translations from the Greek formed the initial nucleus of Russian literature and determined its development over several centuries to come. The corpus of Greek texts transmitted to the Slavs was painstakingly selected to align with the objectives of Christianization, an effort that started in 863 in Moravia, where two brothers from Thessalonica, Cyril and Methodius, were sent from Byzantium in response to a request from the Moravian Prince Rostislav. They introduced a script known today as Cyrillic (derived from the Glagolitic alphabet) in order to make available to the Slavs Scripture and other works indispensable for the Orthodox liturgy. The language of those writings is now called Old Church Slavonic. Although the missionary effort initially aimed at the West Slavs, the translation activity was redirected to the Bulgarians after the Latin mission had conquered the Moravian region. The subsequent advance of the Turks (after 1018) eventually resulted in the transmission of these South Slav translations (Bulgarian and Serbian) to Kievan Rus', i.e., the East Slavs. Thus, Christianity arrived in Rus' accompanied by a selection of central writings translated into Old Church Slavonic, the literary language which all Slavs at that time could understand.

The specific literary context in which the monastic sayings of the *AP* were conveyed to this new audience signals the ideological importance of these col-

---

1   Maria Tymoczko, *Translation in a Postcolonial Context: Early Irish Literature in English Translation* (Manchester: St. Jerome Publishing, 1999), 43.

lections. This becomes even more apparent when we bear in mind the suggestion that the AP may have been translated by Methodius himself.[2] An intriguing reference to translation of "books of the fathers" in the *Vita Methodii* has sparked the desire to identify those books. But as the *Vita* does not disclose any details, the challenge of attributing translations to Methodius has become a matter of debate.[3]

Nevertheless, this early reception of Greek texts, consisting overwhelmingly of monastic stories from the AP as well as Byzantine hagiography, came to serve as a powerful ferment for later canonical works, such as the works of Nikolaj Gogol, Nikolaj Leskov, Leo Tolstoy, and Fedor Dostoevsky, to mention but a few. Echoing the voices and the spirit of distant and dimly perceived times, these apophthegmatic and hagiographic stories continue to exert an influence upon more recent writers.[4]

The remarkable literary heritage of the AP, shared by all ancient Christian communities, was the result of indefatigable work of many generations of scribes, who selected from the abundant material of stories and filtered these sayings through their minds, hearts, and souls. This work of devotion reached the Slavs in the Middle Ages, and it continues down to the present time. The epistemic context of that monastic practice, and other formative factors such as book-making, that might have had an impact on the genesis of the AP and its further reproduction and transmission, are issues that have intrigued scholars and are still current today.[5] One of many challenges in this area is to discern the mechanisms and principles by which texts were selected centuries ago.

Previous research has focused on large-scale matters such as trying to identify the original core of the AP collections, or has compared compositional elements and content of the extant manuscripts. As for the Slavonic material,

---

2 As we will see, several AP collections have been attributed to Methodius. William Veder, for instance, argued in his edition of the *Scete Paterikon* that Methodius translated the AP collection known as *Skitskij Paterik* (the *Scete Paterikon*) (Amsterdam: Pegasus, 2012), vol. 1, p. 13.

3 For a survey of different interpretations of that expression, see Richard Pope, "Did Methodius Translate a Patericon?" in Nikolaas van Wijk, *The Old Church Slavonic Translation of* Ἀνδρῶν ἁγίων βίβλος, ed. Daniel Armstrong, Richard Pope, and C.H. van Schooneveld (The Hague: Mouton, 1975), 1–26.

4 See Anna Grodeckaja, *Otvety i predanija: žitija svjatyx v duxovnom poiske L'va Tolstogo* (St. Petersburg: Nauka, 2000); Per-Arne Bodin, *Language, Canonization and Holy Foolishness* (Stockholm: Stockholm University, 2009).

5 The latest findings are presented in Lillian I. Larsen and Samuel Rubenson, eds., *Monastic Education in Late Antiquity: The Transformation of Classical Paideia* (Cambridge: Cambridge University Press, 2018).

questions concerning the sources of the translations have also been of major importance. This research on provenance and on the relationships within the complex body of transmitted texts is indispensable for further research.

A study of the reception of the AP presents a number of difficulties, since we are dealing with a genre that is characterized by its fluid and complex nature, caused by the rich variability of its textual representations. Digital advances in the last decades, especially corpus linguistics, have been a game-changer for philology and linguistics, much as the microscope was for the natural sciences, to cite the comparison used by the esteemed linguist Professor Vladimir Plungjan.[6] One such tool, developed under the direction of Professor Samuel Rubenson at Lund University, is the relational database and web-based dynamic library "Monastica,"[7] accompanied by analytical tools in the "Apophthegmata Patrum Database" (APDB). As a growing dynamic library, it makes text witnesses available by gathering the AP material in all its linguistic representations: editions, manuscript transcripts, and translations, as well as scholarly literature on the AP. As an analytical tool, it enables the comparison of different linguistic traditions and facilitates the identification of textual relations. After having been furnished with digital analytical tools, the database will offer new possibilities for resolving questions on the intricacies of the AP landscape.

Already at present, however, the database can cluster data which proves useful for comparative studies and a deeper analysis across linguistic borders. For instance, a number of interesting observations have been made in AP material. This essay examines a puzzling phenomenon of repetitions within the Slavonic AP material. What is the reason for such repetitions, or doublets; why and how did they originate? Is it possible to establish whether they are unintentional? Might the analysis of phenomena such as this throw new light on how a new anthology would have been compiled? Perhaps answers to these questions convey a deeper understanding of the transmission of the AP in general, and of the reception in a specific linguistic milieu in particular. The analysis of a particular case—one and the same story presented twice in the same codex—will allow us to address questions of a more general nature.

---

6 The comment was made during a presentation at Uppsala University, May 14, 2018.
7 https://monastica.ht.lu.se.

2 The Slavonic *Paterikon* Tradition: A Brief Overview[8]

Due to their potential for edification and to inspire virtue,[9] the narratives of the AP were especially well suited to conveying the missionaries' purposes. "The legacy of the desert has been, perhaps, even stronger within Eastern Christianity than in West," Douglas Burton-Christie claimed.[10] It would seem that the East Slav community was particularly susceptible to the monastic spiritual wisdom condensed in the AP.[11] Once they reached the newly converted audience, the sayings and stories of Byzantine ascetics were received unconditionally and whole-heartedly. Collections of apophthegms and hagiography became immensely popular. They were copied, disseminated, and eventually rearranged into new narrative collages, and thus came to exist in multiple anthologies and miscellanea, representing an extraordinarily vital and fluid tradition.

In a specific medieval manner of text borrowing, these collections served as a sort of reservoir, providing native authors with passages, chapters, and even plots for their own storytelling.[12] There are many convincing testimonies of such borrowings in Old Russian literature, when scribes who compiled the life of a local saint reused not only the narrative structure, but also details and events from the earlier, translated accounts. Extensive excerpts from the AP were "borrowed" by Slavic hagiographers when writing lives of Russian saints.

---

8   The survey presented below aims to give a brief overview of the intricate AP landscape. For a more detailed discussion of each type of *paterikon*, see Svetlina Nikolova, *Pateričnite razkazi v b"lgarskata srednovekovna literatura* (Sofia: B"lgarskata akademija na naukite, 1980), and the relevant entries in N.I. Nikolaev, *Slovar' knižnikov i knižnosti Drevnej Rusi* ed. Dmitrij Lixačev (Leningrad: Nauka). http://lib.pushkinskijdom.ru/Default.aspx?tabid =2048.

9   For a reconsideration of monastic institutions as agents of Christian and secular formation, see Larsen and Rubenson, eds., *Monastic Education in Late Antiquity*.

10 Douglas Burton-Christie, *The Word in the Desert: Scripture and the Quest for Holiness in Early Christian Monasticism* (Oxford: Oxford University Press, 1993), 9.

11 Francis J. Thomson would dismiss such a thought, highlighting that until the fourteenth century "the monastic inheritance was primarily ascetic rather than spiritual and the monastic ideal was misinterpreted to be the Christian ideal" and that "as opposed to the situation in the West, the conversion of Russia brought literacy not learning, sciolism not education; what the Church offered Russia was: a translated, impoverished, vulgarized Hellenism, inferior to the original" ("The Nature of the Reception of Christian Byzantine Culture in Russia in the Tenth to the Thirteenth Centuries and its Implications for Russian Culture," in idem, *The Reception of Byzantine Culture in Medieval Russia*, no. 1 (Aldershot: Ashgate, 1999), 118–120).

12 See for example Karine Åkerman Sarkisian, "Žitie Onufrija Pustynnika v rukopisnoj tradicii srednevekovoj Rusi" (PhD diss., Uppsala University, 2007).

The AP collections, along with similar anthologies of stories and maxims, came to constitute a separate genre in Russian literature called *pateriki*—the plural form of *paterik* 'paterikon.' Within these collections, monastic sayings often were transmitted alongside hagiographic material, sometimes resulting in uncertainty about the classification of these literary compositions. That is why scholars, when discussing genres in early Russian literature, had to stress that *paterika* should not simply be considered hagiographic collections, since in addition to the lives of saints they include vignettes of influential ascetics. In fact, unlike hagiographic works which offer a *vita* (the saint's deeds, death, and miracles), *paterika* predominantly record isolated (albeit momentous and impactful) episodes from the lives of exemplary monks. Nevertheless, the singular and remarkable genre of *paterika* still escapes comprehensive definition.[13]

On account of their compositional inconsistency, Mixail Speranskij likened this kind of collection to a string of pearls in which every single pearl, being its own unit, is related to the adjacent one only by an external idea of selection, guided either by a resemblance, a certain moral conception, or simple alphabetical principle based on the name of the elder.[14] Therefore in a new string, the pearls could easily be replaced or omitted, and new ones could be inserted, borrowed from different anthologies. We are faced, then, with an overabundance, a vast variety of miscellanies, which were already preserved in multiple copies within the Byzantine tradition.[15] Unsurprisingly, the complexity increases with the transmission of translated texts, since their rearrangement in a new linguistic environment leads to further intricacy and variety of the compilations.

The study of *paterika* limited to the scope of one particular literary system makes it difficult to distinguish collections that originated in the source language from those which emerged within the receiving culture. The Italian Slavist Raffaele Caldarelli distinguished among the Slavonic reproductions of *paterika* those he termed *primaries*, that is collections that were shaped before they reached the Slavs, and *secondaries*, that is rearrangements based on already circulating primaries and other contemporaneously existing Slavonic

---

13   See Dmitrij Lixačev, *The Poetics of Early Russian Literature* (Moscow: Nauka, 1979), 61, quoting D. Chizhevsky, "On the Question of Genres in Early Russian Literature," *Harvard Slavic Studies* 2 (1954): 102. For an overview of various concepts of genre regarding the AP see Per Rönnegård, "Threads and Images: The Use of Scripture in Apophthegmata Patrum" (PhD diss., Lund University, 2007), 7–12.

14   Mixail Speranskij, *Perevodnye sborniki izrečenij v slavjano-russkoj pis'mennosti* (Moscow: Imperatorskoe obščestvo istorii i drevnostej rossijskix pri Moskovskom universitete, 1904), 9.

15   Speranskij, *Perevodnye sborniki izrečenij*, 9.

material[16] and which therefore represent the next generation of *AP* collections. This type of distinction is of a more theoretical significance, rather than an actual reconstruction, since the reality was inevitably much more intricate and is now much less discernible. Nevertheless, a schematization such as the one presented below can be a way to render a messy world depictable and in a certain sense susceptible to analysis.

Five translated collections are usually considered as primaries: *Azbučno-Ierusalimskij* (the Alphabetical Jerusalem), *Skitskij* (the Scete Paterikon), *Rimskij* (the Roman), *Sinajskij* (the Sinaitic) and *Egipetskij* (the Egyptian), since they are presumed to represent translations of preexisting Greek compilations. The first two reflect the two main types of the Greek *AP* tradition, known as the alphabetical-anonymous and the systematic collections. Interestingly, these two collections possibly represent two different stages in the Slavonic reception of the *AP* since the *Skitskij Paterik* is thought to have been translated during the first phase of the mission, i.e., in Moravia, whereas the *Azbučno-Ierusalimskij* was rendered during the subsequent Bulgarian phase of the mission at the beginning of the tenth century.[17] The remaining three collections represent anthologies based on translations, mainly from Greek works such as the *Pratum spirituale* of John Moschus (in *Sinajskij Paterik*, 10th cent., Bulgaria); the *Historia Lausiaca*, the *Historia monachorum in Aegypto* and *De gentibus Indiae et Bragmanibus* by Palladius of Helenopolis (in *Egipetskij Paterik*, 10th to 11th cent., Bulgaria); and Gregory the Great's *Dialogues* (in *Rimskij Paterik*, 9th cent., Moravia). Unfortunately, textual witnesses representing *AP* anthologies are often simply catalogued as *paterik* collections, or take their title from the first chapter of that particular collection, which complicates their mapping and identification.

The *Azbučno-Ierusalimskij Paterik* (*AIP*), following the Greek alphabetical-anonymous collection, is divided into two parts. The first part consists of a preface and an alphabetical series, the *Azbučnyj Paterik*, containing 467 stories and sayings attributed to 112 ascetics whose names are arranged according to the Greek alphabet.[18] The second part, the *Ierusalimskij Paterik*, opens with its own preface, followed by a list of contents for the subsequent seventeen chapters (forty in some manuscripts) on monastic virtues. The main body of text presents 473 anonymous accounts (in which the elders are not named), dis-

---

16 Raffaele Caldarelli, *Il Paterik Alfabetico-Anonimo in traduzione antico-slava* (Rome, 1996), 1–2.
17 Caldarelli, *Il Paterik Alfabetico-Anonimo*, 1–2. See also Richard Pope, "Did Methodius Translate," 1–24.
18 This part of the *AIP* is ed. Caldarelli, *Il Paterik Alfabetico-Anonimo*.

tributed thematically into the seventeen chapters. A few witnesses for the *AIP* have an additional part or a supplementary dossier, which includes 122 apophthegms (or, in abridged versions, 27, 23 or 19 episodes).

According to Caldarelli, the first two parts have a relatively stable tradition, in which the macrostructure especially persists. He concludes that the alphabetical-anonymous derived collection represents the "normal form," and that its structure results from the transformation of a systematic collection into an alphabetical-anonymous one.[19] His understanding of the *AIP* as derivative of the systematic collection is supported by William Veder, who posits that without the *Skitskij Paterik* the *AIP* remains incomplete in its coverage of the monastic experience.[20]

It has been suggested that the *Skitskij Paterik*, edited by Veder,[21] was the earliest collection to reach the Slavs, since several scholars have attributed its translation to Methodius himself.[22] The Slavonic designation *Skitskij* is a scholarly convention[23] that refers to Scetis, a monastic settlement in Lower Egypt whose organisation, practices, and beliefs are reflected in the *systematicon*, more so than those of other monastic communities.[24] In his encyclopaedic edition of the *Skitskij Paterik*, Veder constructed a hypothetical "hyparchetype" of the Slavonic *systematicon* as most representative of the original state of this type of *AP*. He considered its content and structure as close to the Latin translation

---

19   Raffaele Caldarelli, *Il Paterik Alfabetico-Anonimo*.
20   William R. Veder, "The Slavic *Paterika* on Mount Athos: Features of Text Transmission in Church Slavic," in *Monastic Traditions: Selected Proceedings of the Fourth International Hilandar Conference*, ed. C.E. Gribble and P. Matejic (Bloomington, IN: Slavica Publishers, 2003), 358–369.
21   William R. Veder, ed., *The Scete Paterikon*, 3 vols. (Amsterdam: Pegasus, 2012).
22   Veder is more specific: Methodius translated it during his mission to Moravia between 863 and 885, more precisely in 880 (*Scete Paterikon*, vol. 1, pp. 31–32). Indications within vocabulary and morphology of the *Skitskij Paterik* prompted Veniamin Preobraženskij in his 1909 dissertation to suggest that the *Skitskij Paterik* was translated into Bulgarian during the earliest, Methodian period of transmission of the *AP* (*Slavjano-russkij skitskij paterik: Opyt istoričeskogo i bibliografičeskogo issledovanija* (Kiev, 1909), 151–157; cited from Pope, "Did Methodius Translate," 21). This view was followed by Nikolaas van Wijk (see Pope, ibid., 24).
23   Yet in 1975, van Wijk, when working on his edition of the *Skiskij Paterik*, entitled the Slavonic collection Ἀνδρῶν ἁγίων βίβλος because he was convinced that an extant Greek anthology with the same name represents an abridged version of the collection *Mega Leimonaron*, described by Photius, patriarch of Constantinople, in his renowned work *Bibliotheca*. See Klementina Ivanova-Konstantinova, "Ob odnoj rukopisi XIV v. Pogodinskogo sobranija," *Trudy Otdela Drevnerusskoj Literatury*, 25 (1970): 297, and Svetlina Nikolova, *Paterični razkazi*, 12.
24   Veder refers to Bousset and Jean-Claude Guy in his *Scete Paterikon*, vol. 1, p. 17.

of Pelagius and John.[25] Veder's edition recreates the archetype of the *systematicon* in two representations: in Cyrillic (*textus receptus*) and in its Glagolitic transcription (*textus reconstructus*). This edition supplies also an English translation of the Slavonic *systematicon*, supplemented by variant readings documented in a number of extant manuscripts. Moreover, the Greek text is printed parallel with the Latin.

The collection as presented in Veder's edition has 1197 apophthegms divided into the twenty-one chapters of the *Scete Paterikon*, each corresponding to a Christian virtue. Within each thematic chapter, the accounts are organized alphabetically by name of the ascetic, followed by anonymous sayings. Thus, in its main part the *Skitskij Paterik* corresponds to the systematic collection of the AP. It also includes additional, partly non-apophthegmatic sections, most of which are identified by the editor; these are foreign to the *systematicon* and consequently absent from the PJ translation of the Greek systematic collection.[26] Further evidence of transcription errors, found in several manuscripts, allowed Veder to suggest that these were transcribed from Glagolitic protographs.

Comparing the archaic and particularly the ecclesiastical lexicon of the *Sinajskij Paterik* with the vocabulary of the *Nomocanon*, which is attributed to Methodius, Tat'jana A. Ivanova concluded that Methodius must have translated the *Sinajskij Paterik* in the ninth century.[27] The oldest surviving Slavonic witness is the manuscript GIM, Sinod. 551, dating from the 11th or 12th century, which contains a collection of apophthegms which the Slavs later (probably in the 14th or 15th cent.) designated as *Sinajskij*.[28] The first part of this Slavonic collection (episodes 1 to 301) represents the Greek *Pratum spirituale* of John Moschus. The remaining chapters (episodes 302 to 336) are extracts from the *Books of the Holy Men*, the *Alphabetical-Anonymous Collection*, and the *Historia monachorum in Aegypto* attributed to Rufinus of Aquileia (345–411).

The translation of the *Rimskij Paterik* has also been ascribed to Methodius. Aleksej I. Sobolevskij analysed the language of the Church Slavonic translation in relatively late manuscripts containing the *Rimskij Paterik*. Using manuscript

---

25   Veder, *Scete Paterikon*, vol. 1, p. 18. PJ refers to the Latin translation of *Collectio Latina Systematica interpretibus Pelagio, Iohanne et anonymo*, ed. Heribert Rosweyde, in *Vitae Patrum*, vols. 5–6 (Antwerp, 1615). Reprinted in PL 73 (1849), 851–1024, 1060–1062.
26   Veder, *Scete Paterikon*, vol. 1, pp. 18–21.
27   Tat'jana Ivanova, "Zametki o leksike Sinajskogo paterika (K voprosu o perevode Paterika Mefodiem)," in *Izbrannye Trudy*, ed. S.A. Averina (St. Petersburg: Filologičeskij fakul'tet, 2004), 46.
28   The reason for this name in Slavonic remains unclear, but it is known that the author of the Greek original spent ten years on Mount Sinai.

RNB, Pogodin 909 from the sixteenth century, he identified the *Rimskij Paterik* as the only collection that could have been translated by Methodius himself.[29] Sobolevskij observed that manuscript Sinod. 265 (15th or 16th cent.) best preserves the original translation of this collection, since he found that the 14th-century South Slav manuscripts RNB, Q.I.275 and Viln. Publ. Bibl. 3 showed signs of later reworking. He also noted that the Slavonic translation of the *Rimskij Paterik* was made from the Greek translation of the Latin original.[30]

As we have seen, in their attempts to identify the *Corpus Methodianum*, scholars have attributed different *paterika* to Methodius. These results of separate and independent studies corroborate the assumption that the term "books of the fathers" (Greek *paterika biblia*), in the plural, must refer to several works.[31] One may assume that at least three later *paterika*, namely the *Skitskij*, *Sinajskij*, and *Rimskij*, may have been part of that collection of books intended to convey Christian virtues to Slavic proselytes.

The *Egipetskij Paterik* covers almost the whole of the *Historia monachorum in Aegypto*, with the exception of two chapters, the *De gentibus Indiae et Bragmanibus*, excerpts from the *Historia Lausiaca* (also known as the *History of the Monks of Egypt and Palestine*) attributed to Palladius, and two excerpts from the *alphabeticon*.[32] Igor' Eremin established that the Slavonic translation was made from a Greek version of the *Historia monachorum in Aegypto*. Mario Capaldo likewise found strong indications of a Greek prototype containing the same elements, albeit in a different order.[33]

Once they reached a new environment, the primary types of AP collections gave rise to new generations of *paterika* by conflating and interpolating similar monastic texts conveyed from Byzantium. Among the secondaries, or derivative collections, which were probably assembled in Slavic lands using available *paterika*, hagiography, Synaxaria, and other works, the most pertinent from the

---

29 Aleksej Sobolevskij, *Rimskij Paterik v drevnem cerkovno-slavjanskom perevode* (Kiev, 1904), 4.
30 Sobolevskij, *Rimskij Paterik*, 2.
31 This position is summarized in Pope, "Did Methodius Translate," 3. There is no scholarly agreement what "books of fathers" could mean. Some scholars believe the term might have been inserted later, while others reject the *paterikon* theory, considering apophthegms and stories of Egyptian desert monks as less relevant to the Cyrillo-Methodian mission in Moravia (cf. Pope, 3).
32 Igor' Eremin, "K istorii drevnerusskoj perevodnoj povesti," *Trudy Otdela Drevnerusskoj literatury* 3 (1936): 46.
33 Mario Capaldo, "Caratteristiche strutturali e prototipi greci dell' Azbučno-Ierusalimskij e dell' Egipetskij paterik," *Cyrillomethodianum* 3 (1975): 17–18.

early period are the following anthologies: the *Scaliger Paterik* (10th cent., Bulgaria), a collection of succinct aphorisms based on the *Skitskij Paterik*, but also containing fragments from the *Scala paradisi* by John Climacus and the *Egipetskij Paterik*; a florilegium titled *Izbornik* (1076, Bulgaria);[34] the Slavonic Synaxarion *Prolog* (11th cent., Rus'),[35] compiled principally on the basis of the Synaxarion, the AIP, and the *systematicon*. The *Svodnyj Paterik* (14th cent., Bulgaria) is a digest of the five basic *paterika* "and *historiae animae utiles* without any discernible system of ordering, nor any semblance of completeness of coverage."[36] Another important secondary is the *Kievo-Pečerskij Paterik* (Kievan Cave *paterikon*, 13th cent., Rus'),[37] into which parts of the *Skitskij Paterik* are interpolated, but which also reflects the hagiographic *Historia religiosa* of Theodoret.[38] The *Menaion* of 1552 should be mentioned as well, since it contains sections from the AIP.

3   Some Observations on the Slavonic Material

At the time of this study, the Slavonic material documenting the AP reception available in the database was quite limited: the database included Veder's edited version of the *Scete Paterikon*, that is the systematic collection (henceforth OS, in accordance with the designation in the database); the index of the alphabetical part of the AIP, edited by R. Caldarelli; and transcriptions of several manuscripts kindly provided to Monastica/APDB by Veder. Manuscripts included in this study are:[39]

A¹   Belgrade, Public Library of Serbia, MS Dečany 93 (1150–1250, Rus')
W⁶   Belgrade, Museum of the Serbian Orthodox Church, MS Krka 4/1 (1346, Bulgaria)
S¹   Leiden, Universiteitsbibliotheek, MS Scaliger 74 (1200–1300, Bulgaria)

---

34   Ed. M.S. Mušinskaja, E.A. Mišina, and V.S. Golyšenko, *Izbornik 1076 goda* (St. Petersburg: Nestor-Istorija, 2009).
35   Ed. Larisa V. Prokopenko, Veselka Željazkova, Vadim B. Krys'ko, Ol'ga P. Ševčuk, and Igor' M. Ladyženskij, *Slavjano-russkij Prolog po drevnejšim spiskam. Sinaksar'* (Moscow: Azbukovnik, 2010).
36   Veder, "The Slavic *Paterika*," 368.
37   On Syriac and Palestinian ascetic traditions as ideological sources for Kievan cave monasticism, see Fedotov, *Russian Religious Mind*, 132–157.
38   Fedotov, *Russian Religious Mind*, 155.
39   Information on date and provenance of the manuscripts here follows Veder, *Scete Paterikon*, vol. 1, pp. 37–46.

C² Moscow, Russian State Library, MS F 304-703 (1350-1450, Rus')
A³ St. Petersburg, Russian National Library, MS Pogodin 267 (14th cent.)
W⁵ Vienna, Österreichische Nationalbibliothek, MS Slav. 152 (1200-1300, Serbia)

These text witnesses, selected with the *stemma codicum* established by Veder as a starting point, reflect different stages of the AP reception in terms of time and circumstance, namely both the primary stage and the derivative one. These manuscripts are particularly useful because they may have a more complete content, fewer lacunae, or reflect divergent branches of the Slavonic tradition, to judge from Veder's stemma.

Some of these text witnesses already attracted the attention of scholars. The St. Petersburg manuscript (RNB Pogodin 267) was described by the Bulgarian scholar Klementina Ivanova-Konstantinova.[40] Nikolaas van Wijk based his edition of the *Skitskij Paterik* on the Vienna manuscript, which he abbreviated as *Mih* (Mihanović codex) and considered as the main witness amongst three key sources. He used the manuscript from the Serbian monastery Krka,[41] albeit only to clarify blurred passages.[42] Van Wijk took into account also the manuscripts of Bulgarian provenance, Leiden UB Scal. 74 and Paris 10. To judge by the selection of manuscripts for his edition, van Wijk did not use (or perhaps did not have access to) manuscripts in Russian depositories.

The complexity intrinsic to a tradition characterized by fluid transmission and continuous adaptation is well known. Apart from the resulting difficulties for text-critical studies, our case also has to take into consideration that Monastica/APDB is designed as a dynamic library with continuous improvements and additions, and thus will provide constantly changing figures and charts. The observations and figures presented here are based on the data and digital tools of Monastica/APDB accessible in autumn 2018. Even if perhaps not definitive, the results indicate critical issues to explore in further research.

A simple chart shows the number of segments[43] found in each Slavonic manuscript in relation to the whole database:

---

40 Ivanova-Konstantinova, "Ob odnoj rukopisi."
41 In van Wijk's edition, the manuscript has the number 264/62.
42 van Wijk, *The Old Church Slavonic Translation*, 41, 92, 94.
43 In order to enable correlation within the vast amount of data, the apophthegms of the database are segmented into small units. A segment is a text entity often smaller in size than the apophthegm. Furnishing every segment with a unique ID-number makes it possible to conduct quantitative analysis of large data, which can reveal interesting phenomena of the practices of reception.

Siglum	Manuscript	Date	No. of segments	Percentage	Content
A¹	Belgrade NBS Dec. 93	1150–1250	1736	26%	Systematicon
A³	St. Petersburg RNB Pog. 267	14th c.	1638	25%	Systematicon
C²	Moscow RGB F 304–703	1350–1450	1389	21%	Kievo-Pečerskij Paterik
W⁶	Belgrade MSPC Krka 4–1	1346	1088	16,4%	Miscellanea: Svodnyj, AIP, vitae, etc.
S¹	Leiden UB Scal. 74	1200–1300	618	10%	Scaliger Paterik
W⁵	Vienna ÖNB Slav. 152	1200–1300	532	8%	Miscellanea: Scala paradisi (John Climacus), Quod semper mente versare debemus diem exitus de vita (Symeon Mesopotamites), De morte et iudicio (Theophilus of Alexandria)

Within this sample, the oldest manuscript A¹ leads the chart with its 1736 segments that represent more than a quarter (26%) of the all segments in the database (6630), including all linguistic traditions hitherto entered. Second in "completeness" in terms of the number of apophthegms is A³, with 1638 segments representing 25% of the total. A preliminary textual analysis of this group of manuscripts reveals manifest errors, omissions, and other readings of significance, indicating the closeness of these two manuscripts, revealing the dependence of A³ upon A¹, which is in line with Veder's classification. According to his *stemma codicum*, A¹ and A³ descend from the same archetype α. A¹ is proposed to be a direct copy of α, whereas A³ is thought to derive from an intermediary a′.[44] It is evident that both A¹ and A³ might derive from the same defective antigraph, on account of an abrupt break that occurs both in apophthegm 11.28 of A¹ and apophthegm 9.28 of A³ (see Figure 6.1).[45]

The same disruption, referred to as "a defect in the antigraph" occurs in manuscript A²—Moscow GIM Sinod. 3, which is not included in the group studied here (see Figure 6.2). The manuscript in question is a later copy from the 15th or 16th century, and it belongs to group A according to the stemma of Veder.

---

44 Veder, *Scete Paterikon*, vol. 1, p. 46.
45 It is important to point out that the designation of the apophthegms used here has been changed in the database Monastica/APDB to A.11.28 (A¹) and to A.9.28 (A³), respectively (30 September 2019).

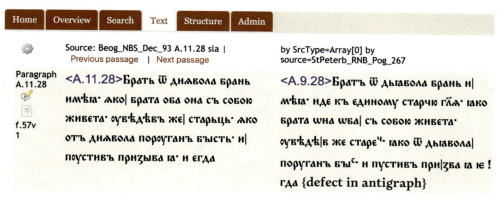

FIGURE 6.1 The apophthegm is interrupted at the same spot in A[1] and A[3].

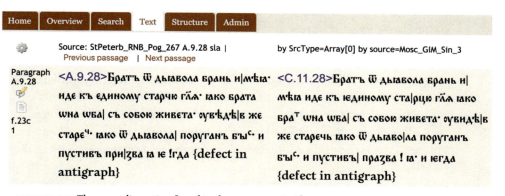

FIGURE 6.2 The same disruption found in the same spot in A[2].

As visible in both figures, manuscript A[1] has another omission in the beginning of the apophthegm, which can be reconstructed with the help of A[2] and A[3]: иде къ ѥдиному старцю гла (went to an old man saying). This instance seems to support further the idea of Veder of an intermediary between A[2] and A[3].

Moreover, as might have been expected, manuscript W[6] appears very different from the remaining ones in this group, which presumably indicates either that it presents an independent translation, or more likely that it is translated from a different Greek source. The analysis presented in the subsequent section will reveal details of its composition that contribute to understanding the textual peculiarities of W[6].

4 Textual Doublets within Slavonic Manuscripts: A Case Study

The most unexpected result of the database search was to find double occurrences of sayings within the same manuscript. Such doublets represent a retelling with recognizably identical components, such as structure, plot line, and other narrative features. Though usually modified by abridgement or change of certain details, the doublet retains the sense and message of the narrative.

The obvious explanation for duplicate apophthegms is to presume an accidental insertion of folia into the manuscript. This is the case with the A[1], the most comprehensive collection studied here, into which three folia were inserted.[46] But the explanation cannot be that simple in the case of the doublet found in manuscript W[6], because the duplication does not occur on the accidentally inserted folia. The duplicate saying, which will be analysed below, occurs in different chapters of the compilation. Neither can this doublet be caused by the involvement of several scribes in the compilation of the collection.[47]

Interestingly, although the doublet in question (apophthegm number 2248 in APDB) reflects a type of narrative that normally belongs to the chapter dealing with challenges of fleshly temptations faced by monks, in W[6] it is found in two different chapters quite far from each other. The first occurs in chapter 9, entitled *Pronouncements of the Aged Ascetics*, the second one appears in the untitled chapter 22.

After having ascertained that this is indeed the same story told twice in manuscript W[6], one can easily verify that it is not a case of identical copies. It is clear that the two passages are two narrations of the same story. The question arises whether these are different redactions of a single translation, or whether they reflect two independent translations of the same source text, or whether they reflect various source texts.

A close comparison of these two apophthegms 9.9 and 22.14[48] shows that they undoubtedly represent two separate translations. The following chart illustrates different renderings, lexical as well as syntactical.

---

46 Veder, *Scete Paterikon*, vol. 1, pp. 37, 41.
47 According to Veder, it is the work of a "single scribe, at the outset daunted by his task, [who] acquired a secure hand towards the end" (*Scete Paterikon*, vol. 1, p. 37).
48 The designation of chapters and apophthegms used here has been changed in the database Monastica/APDB to C.7.1 and to G.1.14, respectively (30 September 2019).

	W⁶, 9.9	W⁶, 22.14
1	Гл҃аше нѣкто старець д҃івеанинь⁴⁹ (*An old **Theban** used to say*)	Гл҃аше етерꙿ ѿ дива҇тскыхꙿ старецꙿ (*One of the **Theban** elders used to say*)
2	вънидохъ въ слѣдь его (*I went in after him*)	единожꙿ ѿтаи въниджхъ въ слѣдъ его (*and once **I secretly** went in after him*)
3	и ѡкрс҇ть воиньство его въсе прѣд҇стоѧще (*and his whole host was **standing round-about***)	и въса воа его прѣстоѧщаѧ емоу (*And his whole host **standing before him***)
4	и многы ч҃лкы поразихъ (*and I murdered many **humans***)	и многы мѫжѫ избихъ (*and I slaughtered many **men***)
5	ѿкѫдоу ты градеши (*Whence are you **coming**?*)	ѿкѫдꙋ ты пришелꙿ еси (*Whence **have you come**?*)
6	и въ нощь сіѫ низложихъ его въ блѫдь (*and in this night, **I led him down into adultery***)	и въ сиѫ нощь едва низложихъ его въ любодѣаніе (*and in this night, **I almost led him down into fornication***)
7	ꙗко велико ес҇ дѣлѡ иноучьское (*so great is the **monastic cause***)	толико ли ес҇ великь чинꙿ мнишꙿскыи (*is the **monastic rank** that great?*)

Not all these differences are the result of a mere replacement of one word with more desirable vocabulary. This is true in some instances, such as the interchangeable designations мѫжъ (man) and ч҃лкъ (abbreviation of человѣкъ, human being) in example (4); or describing the narrator's provenance in example (1) either by the ethnonym д҃івеанинь (Theban) in нѣкто старець д҃івеанинь (an old Theban) or by a genitive construction with an adjective derived from the toponym 'Thebe'—етерꙿ ѿ дива҇тскыхъ старецъ (one of the Theban elders). Moreover, the indefinite pronouns of both versions, нѣкто and етеръ (cf. the Greek ἕτερος) are synonymous and stand alongside many other word

---

49   The compared textual elements are shown in boldface.

pairs representing different lexical preferences, such as the following: воиньство and воѧ (host) in (3); aorist forms in the first person singular поразихъ of поразити (to strike, slay) and избихъ of избити (to slay, kill); present tense градеши—second person singular of the infinitive грѧсти (to go, come to, approach) and пришелъ еси, the perfect of прити (to come, arrive) in the second person singular of (4); or the nouns блѫдь (promiscuity, whoring) and любодѣанїе (fornication) in (5). The variation of syntactical wording—in particular the last example (7) which shows different interpretations of the final conclusive statement, expressed as an affirmation in 9.9 but as a rhetorical question in 22.14—suggests that we are dealing with two independent translations.

Consultation of other Greek parallels available in our database reveals textual features which indicate that this is not only a case of two different translations, but more likely of two different Greek source texts yielding independent Slavonic versions. These two Greek sources might reflect different types of the AP collections. The two versions of our saying are found in the edition of John Wortley[50] (henceforth GN-Wortley) and in manuscript Athos Protaton 86, 5.39 (henceforth Athos Prot. 86) respectively.[51] Both appear in the database:

---

8   W⁶, 9.9   W⁶, 22.14
ꙗко азь ѧадѡ быⁿ ереа еллиньска·   ꙗко азъ бѣⁿ ѧадо иереа идолъскаго·
(*that I was the child of a Hellenic priest*)   (*I was the child of a priest of idols*)

GN-Wortley   Athos Prot. 86
ὅτι ἐγὼ ἤμην τέκνον ἱερέως τῶν Ἑλλήνων.   Ἐγὼ ἤμην τέκνον ἱερέως τῶν εἰδώλων.
(*that I was the child of a priest of the Hellenes*)   (*I was the child of a priest of idols*)

9   W⁶, 9.9   W⁶, 22.14
дѣтищь сыи· единоѫ   сѣдѣⁿ въ црькви малъ еще сы·
(*Once, when I was little*)   (*When I was little, I sat in the temple*)

---

50   John Wortley, ed. and transl., *The Anonymous Sayings of the Desert Fathers: A Select Edition and Complete English Translation* (Cambridge: Cambridge University Press, 2013).

51   For the Greek source text of this apophthegm, Athos Prot. 86 v.39 (= AP/GS v.44), see Monastica/APDB. The Greek text of this manuscript has also been edited by Britt Dahlman in *Paradiset: Ökenfädernas tänkespråk, den systematiska samlingen*, vol. 5, *Olika berättelser till skydd när otukten ansätter oss*, ed. Britt Dahlman and Per Rönnegård, Silentium Apophthegmata 5 (Sturefors: Silentium, 2014).

GN-Wortley
Μικρὸς οὖν ἐκαθήμην
(when I (was) little, I sat)

Athos Prot. 86
Μικρὸς οὖν ὢν ἐκαθήμην ἐν τῷ ἱερῷ
(When I was little, I sat in the temple)

10 W⁶, 9.9
ꙗко видѣх ѡца своего вышедша въ коумирице·
(I saw my father coming into the temple)

W⁶, 22.14
и видѣхͧ ѡца своего · множицежѫ въходаща·
(and I saw my father many times going in)

Athos Prot. 86
καὶ ἐθεώρουν τὸν πατέρα μου εἰσερχόμενον
(I saw my father going in)

GN-Wortley
καὶ εἶδον τὸν πατέρα μου πολλάκις εἰσερχόμενον
(and I saw my father many times going in)

11 W⁶, 9.9
и ѿвѣща ѡнь· въ нѣкоеи веси бых
(and he answered, I was in a certain village)

W⁶, 22.14
ѡн же ѿвѣщавъ рʳⁱе емоу· на сеи странѣ бѣхъ
(and he said to him answering, I was in that land)

Athos Prot. 86
Ὁ δὲ εἶπεν·
Εἰς τήνδε τὴν κώμην ἤμην
(I was in such and such a village)

GN-Wortley
Ὁ δὲ εἶπεν·
Εἰς τήνδε τὴν χώραν ἤμην
(I was in such and such a land)

12 W⁶, 9.9
и възᵈвигох брани·
and I raised contention

W⁶, 22.14
възᵈвигох брани· и многы матежѫ
and I raised contention and much rebellion

GN-Wortley
καὶ ἐξήγειρα πολέμους
and I raised contention

Atos Prot. 86
καὶ ἐξήγειρα πολέμους
and I raised contention

13 W⁶, 9.9
ѡн же рʳⁱе· въ л̃· дни·
(and he said, In thirty days)

W⁶, 22.14
ѡн же рʳⁱе· за л̃· днеи·
(and he said, For/during thirty days)

GN-Wortley
Ὁ δὲ εἶπεν· Ἐν τριάκοντα ἡμέραις.
(and he said, In thirty days)

Athos Prot. 86
Ὁ δὲ εἶπεν· Ἐπὶ τριάκοντα ἡμέρας.
(and he said, For/during thirty days)

14 W⁶, 9.9
и въƷᴬвигоˣ вѣтры·
(and I raised **winds**)

GN-Wortley
καὶ ἐξήγειρα ἀνέμους
(and I raised **winds**)

W⁶, 22.14
и въƷᴬвигоˣ боура· и трѫсъ
(and I raised **storm and earthquake**)

Athos Prot. 86
καὶ ἐξήγειρα σεισμοὺς
(and I raised **earthquakes**)

15 W⁶, 9.9
и много крѫвопролитїе съдѣлавъ и самого невѣстника· и невѣстѫ· Ʒаклати сътвори
(and having made much bloodshed **I have killed the groom himself and the bride**)

GN-Wortley
καὶ πολλὴν ἔκχυσιν αἱμάτων ἐποίησα, ἀποκτείνας τὸν νυμφίον καὶ τὴν νύμφην
(and I made much bloodshed **having killed the groom and the bride**)

W⁶, 22.14
и множьство пролитїе крᵘве сътвориˣ съ женихомь и съ невѣстоѫ
(and I caused much bloodshed **with [to] the groom and the bride**)

Athos Prot. 86
καὶ πολλὴν ἔκχυσιν ποιήσας μετὰ καὶ τοῦ νυμφίου καὶ τῆς νύμφης
(and having caused much [blood]shed dealing **with both the groom and the bride**)

16 W⁶, 9.9
и приносимоу прѣстолоу· ...·сѣсти томоу повелѣ· блгодᴬрѧ его· и глᴬ·
(and when the throne was brought ..., he ordered him to sit down thanking him and saying ...)

W⁶, 22.14
и посади его съ собоѫ на прѣстолѣ· глᴬ емоу·
(and seated him **with [beside]** himself on the throne, saying ...)

GN-Wortley
καὶ ἐκάθισεν αὐτὸν ἐν τῷ θρόνῳ αὐτοῦ λέγων·
(and he seated him on his throne, saying ...)

Athos Prot. 86
καὶ ἐκάθισεν αὐτὸν μεθ' ἑαυτοῦ λέγων ὅτι·
(and he seated him **with [beside]** himself saying ...)

The synonymous adjectives in example (8), еллиньскъ (Hellene) in 9.9 and идолъскъ (idolatrous, of idols) in 22.14, terms which normally mean "pagan," could in all likelihood have emerged as translation variants on Slavonic soil, but it appears that these two lexemes have their origin in different Greek sources: one in the edition of GN-Wortley, ὅτι ἐγὼ ἤμην τέκνον ἱερέως τῶν Ἑλλήνων, and the second in Athos Prot. 86, ὅτι· Ἐγὼ ἤμην τέκνον ἱερέως τῶν εἰδώλων. Likewise, in example (13) two synonymous types of temporal prepositional phrases expressing a limited period of time are found in the Greek sources. Ἐν τριάκοντα ἡμέραις and Ἐπὶ τριάκοντα ἡμέρας gave rise to two prepositional constructions in the Slavonic translations, with properly corresponding prepositions Ἐν—въ and Ἐπὶ—za, resulting in: въ· л̄· днн· (in thirty days) and za· л̄· днен (in thirty days). Despite being different prepositions, these pairs are semantically synonymous constructions in their respective languages, denoting the time taken to complete an action. In this subtle difference, too, the Slavonic translation follows the Greek source text, although the English translation unfortunately does not reflect it.

Not only lexical equivalents, but also omissions and additions of phrases and constructions of the Greek source, such as in examples (12), (14) and (16), are reflected in the Slavonic parallels. At the same time, these examples suggest the existence of a Greek version with the extended readings of 22.14: καὶ ἐξήγειρα πολέμους καὶ πολλὴν ταραχήν, found in MS Paris gr. 2474, the early representative of the Greek systematic collection, which gave rise to възᴧвигох брани и многы матежѫ (and I raised contention and many rebellions) in example (12), or καὶ ἐξήγειρα ἀνέμους καὶ σεισμοὺς resulting in боура· и трѫсъ (and I raised storm and earthquake) in example (14).

In addition, in examples (9) and (10), the author of the Greek version represented in GN-Wortley introduces in passing the place where the reported incident occurred: "Once when I was little, I sat and saw my father coming into the temple" (9.9). Athos Prot. 86, on the other hand, expresses it more explicitly, since here the narrator while a child observed the depicted scene, sitting in the temple where the reported course of events was taking place during one of his father's visits: "When I was little, I sat in the temple and I saw my father many times going in" (22.14).

The approximate correlation between the Greek and Slavonic variants is challenged significantly by two examples, which disrupt the parallelism that we find elsewhere between 9.9. and GN-Wortley on the one hand, and 22.14 and Athos Prot. 86 on the other hand. The first dissimilarity appears in (10), where the words "many times" are added; and the second, in (11) with the use of the synonyms вьсь (village, country) in 9.9 and страна (country, village, place) in 22.14—here in locative веси or вьси, and странѣ, respectively. The Greek versions also offer a synonymous pair: τὴν κώμην (from ἡ κώμη; 'village, country town') parallels τὴν χώραν (from ἡ χώρα; 'land, country,' as opposed to 'town') of GN-Wortley, a detail which runs contrary to our other examples. Nevertheless, the comparison of lexical features noted above allows one to conclude that different Greek originals might have been used as source texts for the two Slavonic translations in this doublet. The variance in the Greek seems to rely on different types of *AP* collections—the systematic and the alphabetic-anonymous. Having been translated independently of each other, they could give birth to Slavonic translations such as those recorded in our doublet.

Moreover, compared with 22.14, the narrative in 9.9 seems rather abridged, reflecting a consistent revision of the dialogues by omitting discourse markers and by replacing the sequences of direct speech with reported speech, as illustrated in the two dialogues below.

W⁶, 9.9
Подбно же и дроугыи пришедъ рʸе
(*Likewise, another one having come, said,*)

W⁶, 22.14
и се дроугыи прїиде и тъ кланѣаше са емоу рече же и томоу
(*and lo, having come, another one bowed to him and said to him,*)

а ты ѿкѫдоу прїиде
(*Whence do you come?*)

ѡн же рʸе
(*He then said,*)

азь въ мори быхъ
(*I was at sea.*)

въ мори бѣхъ
(*I was at sea.*)

Таче и дроугыи прїиде
(*Then came another one*)

и се третїи прїиде кланѣѫ са емоу
(*and lo, a third one came and having bowed to him,*)

рече же емоу
(*said to him,*)

ты ѿкѫдоу пришелъ еси
(*Whence have you come?*)

ѡн же рʸе емȣ
(*he then said to him*)

ꙗко въ градѣ коемъ бракȣ бывшоу
(*that in such a city there was a wedding*)

въ нѣкоемъ градѣ бракъ быс
(*in such a city there was a wedding*)

It is evident that in 9.9 the conversation is creatively rewritten, resulting in fewer replies and references to the speaker, as is common in reported speech. The exchange of interlocutors here is presented without repetitions like "he asked," "he said to him," or "he then said" as in 22.14. Such expressions are absent from 9.9.

In addition, we should comment on the position of the doublets in question. This specific apophthegm normally belongs to the chapter on how to resist the demon of fleshly temptations, often entitled *On Wars against Fornication*. This is chapter 5 in GS-Guy[52] and PJ. This thematic section is represented by the hypothetical reconstruction of chapter 5, according to Veder's edition (here and in the database the chapter is designated as OS.5). As shown in the Chart 6.1,[53] the reconstructed OS.5 is almost perfectly reproduced in chapter 11 of collection A[1], represented in the early manuscript Belgrade NBS Dec. 93.

Chart 6.1 shows how the apophthegms of the hypothetic archetype of the Slavonic *systematicon* are distributed into the systematic collection, as reflected in A[1] and in the compilation of W[6].

Manuscript W[6] by contrast adopts only two thirds of the content of the chapter on fornication. The chart above clearly shows that W[6] takes the first third (1–16) and the last third of sayings in OS.5 (1–16 and 30–46) and omits the middle section (17–28). Furthermore, these two strings of sayings are arranged in two separate sections a significant distance apart, namely in chapters 6 and 22, respectively.[54] Chapter 6 is accurately entitled *Various Accounts for Strengthening those who Resist Wars of Fornication*, whereas chapter 12 lacks any heading. At present, it is difficult to discern with certainty why the middle part of OS.5 was omitted and why the last third was moved to an isolated and unnamed section within W[6]. In any case, such a division of the chapter probably emerged by chance, possibly as a consequence of equally distributing the copying assignment amongst three scribes. We cannot exclude such a possibility, in view of the fact that three hands have been identified in the production of this manuscript.[55]

Returning to the duplicate apophthegm analysed above, we find it in the penultimate position in OS.5, more exactly in 5.44. As we have already seen, in W[6] one of the repeated accounts is certainly located in its proper position, i.e.,

---

52   GS-Guy refers to Jean-Claude Guy, ed. and transl., *Les Apophtegmes des Pères: Collection systématique*, 3 vols., SChr 387, 474, 498 (Paris: Cerf, 1993–2005).
53   The Alluvial Diagram is created with web tool RAWGraphs.
54   The designation of chapters has been changed in the database Monastica/APDB to A.6 and to G.7, respectively (accessed 30 September 2019).
55   See Veder, *Scete Paterikon*, vol. 1, p. 44.

in the second third of the untitled chapter 22. One would have expected to find the other one in chapter 6 of W⁶, to which it belongs thematically. But unexpectedly it is located in chapter 9, on fols. 49ʳ–49ᵛ of the manuscript, which constitutes the saying's first occurrence in this collection. Chapter 9 bears the heading *Maxims of the Holy Fathers, also Very Useful and Lovely Accounts and Talks*. Thus, the first time our apophthegm occurs in this codex, it is embedded in a jumble of sayings assembled here for no apparent reason. Chapter 9 comprises 42 excerpts from identified as well as unidentified sources, and belongs to a large section between fols. 40ᵛ and 73ʳ, comprising miscellaneous texts such as homilies, maxims, and questions and answers. The paratext reads, "Sayings of the holy fathers, stories, and conversations, very beloved and useful, from which we picked out and copied a small number for the sake of love and for the soul's benefit …" Veder identifies the components of this section as excerpts from the *Compiled Paterikon* (the *Svodnyj Paterik*), the alphabetical-anonymous collection, a few saints' lives, and what we might call *ascetica varia*.[56]

Chart 6.2 makes clear the flow of the sayings of chapter os.5 into the Slavonic collections A¹ and W⁶. The chart also shows how our specific apophthegm os.5.44 is borrowed by 11.37 of A¹ and further by W⁶, taking two positions in W⁶ (in 9.09 and 22.24) and representing two versions of the same story, as argued above.

Chart 6.2 illustrates how the apophthegms of chapter os.5 are regrouped in collections A¹ (*systematicon*) and W⁶ (*miscellanea*).[57]

From the unmethodical and in some way *ad hoc* compilation of chapters, sayings, lives of saints, and other compositional elements in this collection, it appears that its scribes did not have an organizational concept in mind when shaping this anthology. We have every reason to surmise that manuscript W⁶ represents an attempt to compile, rather than make a copy of a fixed collection. The contrary assumption is less plausible, as there are no signs that the copyist rearranged a poorly organized *Vorlage*. Instead, it seems that the compiler made use of several sources. Since at least three individuals were involved in assembling this Bulgarian codex in 1345/6, one might imagine that each of the copyists of W⁶ had contributed his own section, resulting in a splitting up of the chapter on fornication. It may have remained incomplete in the first attempt and may have been re-copied later in an attempt to finish it. But this apparently completed chapter is missing its middle section, and the first and third sections

---

56   Veder, *Scete Paterikon*, vol. 1, p. 44.
57   The Cluster Dendrogram was created with the web tool RAWGraphs. See "How to Make an Alluvial Diagram," by RAWGraphs Team. Licensed under CC BY-NC-SA 4.0, accessed 26 July 2019, https://rawgraphs.io/learning/how-to-make-an-alluvial-diagram/.

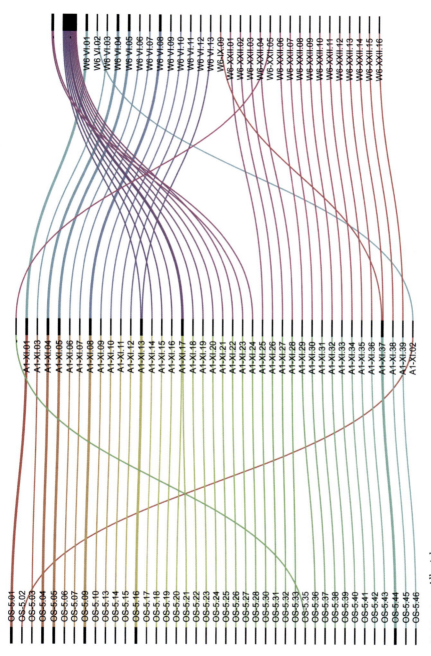

CHART 6.1 Alluvial

find themselves in different parts of the codex. However, all three chapters that contain stories associated with issues of fornication, 6, 9, and 22, are thought to have been written by the same hand. Thus, the reasons behind such an irregular organization of the codex seem even more elusive.

A consultation of the Monastica/APDB database shows that our doublets reflect two main types of AP collections: saying 22.14, which is parallel to Athos Prot. 86, corresponds to the systematic collection, whereas apophthegm 9.9 reflects the anonymous collection as presented in the edition by Wortley. The database does not include any collection with a similar structure, nor is there in the database such a doublet in the witnesses of other linguistic AP traditions. Hence we can conclude that W[6] probably represents a second generation of AP, most likely expanded without any clear concept or influence by other models.

5 Conclusions

A single case of "twin" apophthegms can reveal processes by which a collection was assembled, giving a glimpse of the compilation practices of medieval scribes who used AP material in the composition of new anthologies. It is important in its own right that two versions of an apophthegm, reflecting different AP traditions (the *systematicon* and the *alphabeticon*), were included in one particular Slavonic collection. It is obvious that conflation, interpolation, and contamination are features not alien to the Slavonic AP tradition which, as a relatively late one, shows no restraint in merging elements from diverse sources. The composition of W[6] therefore illustrates how collections of the second generation could come into existence. Since W[6] represents a distinct group, according to Veder's classification, it is justifiable to argue that at the time of the formation of the secondaries, the compilers may well have disregarded or simply lost the distinction between the different types of anthologies within the apophthegmatic genre. Further studies may shed new light on this issue and deepen our understanding of how the fluid AP tradition was passed down through time and generations.

The study has also prompted the idea of an evolutionary diversity of the narratives distributed between different AP types. Perhaps a typology of variants (primarily in Greek, but also contrasted to the Slavonic) based on the correlation between distinctive readings and collection types (systematic and alphabetical-anonymous) might be discerned. Such a classification, if it is feasible, could facilitate the understanding of processes by which AP collections developed and diversified. It could also make possible the tracing of stages of text evolution by studying instances of excerpting, revising and retelling.

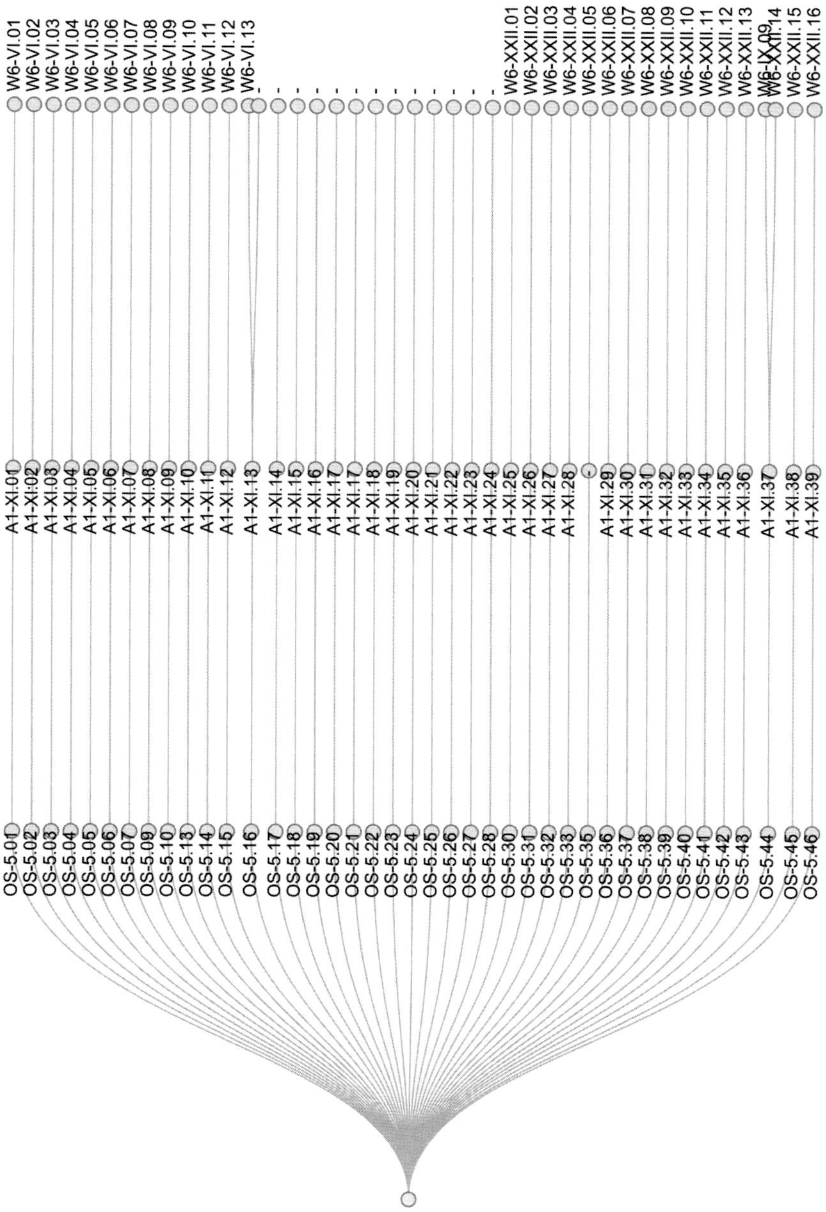

THE APOPHTHEGMATA PATRUM IN THE SLAVONIC CONTEXT 143

CHART 6.2 Dendrogram

This study raises general questions about the cultural transmission, on the one hand, and the stages in the evolution of a text, on the other. For instance, which processes guided the changes that our collections underwent, the diversification of variants and the correlation of these readings with a particular collection type. Is it possible to trace the evolution of this process of excerpting, revising and retelling? Further research on the peculiarities of the reception in various linguistic and cultural milieux will contribute to a deeper understanding of medieval textual networking.

Acknowledgements

I am most grateful to W. Veder for contributing numerous transcriptions of manuscripts, which constitute the main material of the database under construction. I also would like to extend my special gratitude to my colleagues Anthony John Lappin, Britt Dahlman, and Julie Hansen for the readiness to share their competence and support, and Kenneth Berg on whose technical assistance I always could count.

Bibliography

Primary Sources
  Manuscripts
Belgrade, Museum of the Serbian Orthodox Church, MS Krka 4/1 (1346)
Belgrade, Public Library of Serbia, MS Dečany 93 (1150–1250)
Leiden, Universiteitsbibliotheek, MS Scaliger 74 (1200–1300)
Moscow, Russian State Library, MS F 304–703 (1350–1450)
Moscow, State Historical Museum, MS Sinod. 3, (1400–1500)
St. Petersburg, Russian National Library, MS Pogodin 267 (14th cent.)
Vienna, Österreichische Nationalbibliothek, MS Slav. 152 (1200–1300)

  Editions
Apophthegmata Patrum. Collectio Graeca Systematica. Chapter 5. Ed. Britt Dahlman and
  Per Rönnegård, in *Paradiset: Ökenfädernas tänkespråk, den systematiska samlingen*.
  Vol. 5, *Olika berättelser till skydd när otukten ansätter oss*. Silentium Apophthegmata
  5. Sturefors: Silentium, 2014.
*Apophthegmata Patrum. Collectio Latina Systematica interpretibus Pelagio, Iohanne et
  anonymo*. Ed. Heribert Rosweyde, in *Vitae Patrum*. Vols. 5–6. Antwerp, 1615.
  Reprinted in PL 73 (1849), 851–1024, 1060–1062.

Caldarelli, Raffaele, ed. *Il Paterik Alfabetico-Anonimo in traduzione antico-slava: Parte alfabetica; Edizione del testo slavo e dell' originale Greco.* Rome, 1996.
Guy, Jean-Claude, ed. and transl. *Les Apophtegmes des Pères: Collection systématique.* 3 vols. SChr 387, 474, 498. Paris: Cerf, 1993–2005.
Veder, William R., ed. *The Scete Paterikon.* 3 vols. Amsterdam: Pegasus, 2012.
Wortley, John, ed. and transl. *The Anonymous Sayings of the Desert Fathers: A Select Edition and Complete English Translation.* Cambridge: Cambridge University Press, 2013.

Internet Sources

"Monastica—A Dynamic Library and Research Tool." http://monastica.ht.lu.se.

Secondary Sources

Åkerman Sarkisian, Karine. "Žitie Onufrija Pustynnika v rukopisnoj tradicii srednevekovoj Rusi." PhD diss., Uppsala University, 2007.
Bodin, Per-Arne. *Language, Canonization and Holy Foolishness.* Stockholm: Stockholm University, 2009.
Burton-Christie, Douglas. *The Word in the Desert: Scripture and the Quest for Holiness in Early Christian Monasticism.* Oxford: Oxford University Press, 1993.
Caldarelli, Raffaele. *Il Paterik Alfabetico-Anonimo* (see above).
Capaldo, Mario. "Caratteristiche strutturali e prototipi dell' Azbučno-Ierusalimskij e dell' Egipetskij Paterik." *Cyrillomethodianum* 3 (1975): 13–27.
Chizhevsky, Dmitry. "On the Question of Genres in Early Russian Literature." *Harvard Slavic Studies* 2 (1954): 11–112.
Fedotov, George P. *The Russian Religious Mind.* Cambridge, MA: Harvard University Press, 1946.
Grodeckaja, Anna. *Otvety i predanija: žitija svjatyx v duxovnom poiske L'va Tolstogo.* St. Petersburg: Nauka, 2000.
Eremin, Igor' P. "K istorii drevnerusskoj perevodnoj povesti." *Trudy Otdela Drevnerusskoj literatury* 3 (1936): 37–57.
Ivanova, Tat'jana A. "Zametki o leksike Sinajskogo Paterika (K voprosu o perevode Paterika Mefodiem)." In *Izbrannye Trudy*, ed. S.A. Averina, 46–51. St. Petersburg: Filologičeskij fakul'tet, 2004.
Ivanova-Konstantinova, Klementina. "Ob odnoj rukopisi XIV v. Pogodinskogo sobranija." *Trudy Otdela Drevnerusskoj Literatury* 25 (1970): 293–308.
Larsen, Lillian I., and Samuel Rubenson, eds. *Monastic Education in Late Antiquity: The Transformation of Classical Paideia.* Cambridge: Cambridge University Press, 2018.
Lixačev, Dmitrij. *The Poetics of Early Russian Literature.* Moscow: Nauka, 1979.
Mušinskaia, Marija S. *Izbornik 1076 goda: tekstologija i jazyk.* St. Petersburg: Nestor-Istorija, 2015.

Mušinskaja, Marija S., Elena A. Mišina, and Vera S. Golyšenko. *Izbornik 1076 goda*, ed. Aleksandr M. Moldovan. Moscow: Rukopisnye pamjatniki Drevnej Rusi, 2009.

Nikolaev, N.I. "Paterik." In *Slovar' knižnikov i knižnosti Drevnej Rusi*. Vypusk 2 (vtoraja polovina XIV–XVI vv.), čast' 2: L-JA. Ed. Dmitrij Lixačev. Leningrad: Nauka, 1989.

Nikolova, Svetlina. *Pateričnite razkazi v b"lgarskata srednovekovna literatura*. Sofia: B"lgarskata akademija na naukite, 1980.

Pope, Richard. "Did Methodius Translate a Patericon?" In Nikolaas van Wijk, *The Old Church Slavonic Translation of the Ἀνδρῶν ἁγίων βίβλος*, ed. Daniel Armstrong, Richard Pope, and C.H. van Schooneveld, 1–26. The Hague: Mouton, 1975.

Preobraženskij, Veniamin S. *Slavjano-russkij skitskij paterik: Opyt istoričeskogo i bibliografičeskogo issledovanija*, Kiev, 1909.

Prokopenko, Larisa V., Veselka Željazkova, Vadim B. Krys'ko, Ol'ga P. Ševčuk, and Igor' M. Ladyženskij, eds. *Slavjano-russkij Prolog po drevnejšim spiskam. Sinaksar'*, ed. Vadim B. Krys'ko. Moscow: Azbukovnik, 2010.

Rönnegård, Per. "Threads and Images. The Use of Scripture in Apophthegmata Patrum." PhD diss., Lund University, 2007.

Sobolevskij, Aleksej I. *Rimskij Paterik v drevnem cerkovno-slavjanskom perevode*. Kiev: Lito-Tipografija T.G. Mejnandera, 1904.

Speranskij, Mixail. *Perevodnye sborniki izrečenij v slavjano-russkoj pis'mennosti*. Moscow: Imperatorskoe obščestvo istorii i drevnostej rossijskix pri Moskovskom universitete, 1904.

Thomson, Francis J. "The Nature of the Reception of Christian Byzantine Culture in Russia in the Tenth to the Thirteenth Centuries and its Implications for Russian Culture." In idem, *The Reception of Byzantine Culture in Medieval Russia*, no. 1, pp. 107–139. Variorum. Aldershot: Ashgate, 1999. First published in *Slavica Gandensia* 5, Ghent, 1978.

Tymoczko, Maria. *Translation in a Postcolonial Context: Early Irish Literature in English Translation*. Manchester: St. Jerome Publishing, 1999.

Van Wijk, Nikolaas. *The Old Church Slavonic Translation of the Ἀνδρῶν ἁγίων βίβλος*, ed. Daniel Armstrong, Richard Pope, and C.H. van Schooneveld. The Hague: Mouton, 1975.

Veder, William R. "Old Russia's 'Intellectual Silence' Reconsidered." In *Medieval Russian Culture*, ed. Michael S. Flier and Daniel Rowland, 18–28. Berkeley: University of California Press, 1994.

Veder, William R. "The Slavic *Paterika* on Mount Athos: Features of Text Transmission in Church Slavic." In *Monastic Traditions: Selected Proceedings of the Fourth International Hilandar Conference*, ed. C.E. Gribble and P. Matejic, 358–369. Bloomington, IN: Slavica Publishers, 2003.

CHAPTER 7

The Armenian Transmission of the *Apophthegmata Patrum*

Anahit Avagyan

1   Introduction

According to tradition, the apostolic mission to Armenia was carried out by the apostles Thaddeus and Bartholomew. Christianity was declared state religion in 301 AD by King Tiridates, following the historical events connected with St. Gregory the Illuminator who subsequently became the first catholicos of the Armenian Church. The monastic tradition, which in different ways is characteristic of both Eastern and Western Christianity, has played a significant role in the Armenian Church. The remains of hundreds of monasteries—spread throughout present-day Armenia, its historical territory, and beyond—serve as witnesses for a once rich monastic life. Dietmar Winkler observes:

> By the 5th century, a basic pattern of monasticism developed, which included a common life and worship, apostolic works, study and preaching the Gospel. Armenian monasticism became predominant to link personal spiritual perfection to an active pastoral care. More than one thousand monasteries covered the area of greater Armenia of which about 900 are very well documented … In the 11th and 12th centuries, in the monasteries religious studies and education got more into the focus of Armenian monastic life. There was interest in Greek classical philosophy, science and medicine, manuscript culture and illumination, rhetoric, poetry, music etc.[1]

The rise of Armenian medieval literature, both translated and indigenous, is connected with the creation of the Armenian alphabet at the beginning of the fifth century. While the origin of the Armenian monastic tradition remains

---

1   Dietmar W. Winkler, "Monasticism in Oriental Christianity Today: A Brief Survey," in *Monastic Life in the Armenian Church: Glorious Past—Ecumenical Reconsideration*, ed. Jasmine Dum-Tragut and Dietmar W. Winkler (Zurich: LIT, 2018), 12.

controversial among scholars, the educational objectives of monasteries are no longer questioned: education took place in monastic schools and, later, in monastic academies.[2]

This article is an attempt to study the rich Armenian transmission of the *apophthegmata*, the *Sayings of the Desert Fathers*. These sayings have been translated into many ancient and modern languages, including Classical Armenian. A great number of manuscripts preserve Armenian *apophthegmata*, but only a few scholars have studied them. This paper will present a list of manuscripts that contain *apophthegmata*, *vitae*, or the like; this includes manuscripts with only one folio of monastic material as well as entire codices, sometimes with colophons. Such a list has value for our understanding of the emergence and development of the Armenian collections of *Vitae Patrum*.

The best known edition of Armenian monastic collections are the two volumes of *Vitae Patrum* published by the Mekhitarist Father Nerses Sarkissian in Venice in 1855. He depicts the rendering of monastic material from Greek and Syriac into Armenian as an extremely complex process, lasting for several centuries. He argues that when new material became available, it was simply added to the existing collections in the same order. During the late Cilician period (14th cent.), however, old and new pieces were assembled into a larger, new collection. But according to Sarkissian, some of the older pieces were omitted, so that the newer Armenian compilation is still less comprehensive than the equivalent collections in other languages. Due to translations at various times, two types of Armenian collections arose, the "old," and the "new" or "second" types.[3] The names of some of the translators, compilers, and redactors of these monastic lives and sayings have reached us by way of manuscript colophons and superscriptions, and they will be mentioned in the list below.[4]

Sarkissian's two volumes contain three parts, namely *Lives of the Fathers*, *Sayings of the Fathers* (in 19 chapters), and *Councils of the Fathers*. Louis Leloir translated the second, apophthegmatic part, into Latin and furnished every apophthegm with parallels in Greek, Latin, Syriac, and Ethiophic.[5] Sarkissian's

---

2　See Jasmine Dum-Tragut, "The Cultural Impact of Armenian Monasticism: A Brief Note on the Role of Armenian Monasteries in Medieval Armenian Society," in *Monastic Life in the Armenian Church*, ed. Dum-Tragut and Winkler, 30–32.

3　See P. Nerses Sarkissian, ed., *Lives of the Holy Fathers and their Politeia According to the Double Translation of the Ancestors* [Վարք սրբոց Հարանց եւ քաղաքավարութիւնք նոցին ըստ կրկին թարգմանութեան նախնեաց], vol. 1 (Venice: San Lazzaro, 1855), iii.

4　Sarkissian, *Lives of the Holy Fathers*, vol. 1, vi.

5　Louis Leloir, *Paterica armeniaca a P. P. Mechitaristis edita (1855) nunc latine reddita*, 4 vols., CSCO 353, 361, 371, 371 / Subs. 42, 43, 47, 51 (Louvain: Imprimerie Orientaliste, 1974–1976).

editorial method has been criticized by Wilhelm Bousset, who commented as follows, refering as Recensions A and B to the "old" and "new" translations, respectively:

> Die Herausgeber haben sich eines etwas sonderbaren Verfahrens bedient. Sie haben die eine der beiden Uebersetzungen (A) zugrunde gelegt, haben dann zu jedem Stück von A die Parallele der ganz anders geordneten Rezension B unten auf der Seite beigegeben, und endlich zu jedem der 19 Kapitel des Werkes den überschüssigen Text von B uno tenore als Paralipomena angefügt. So ist leider die ursprüngliche Anordnung aller der Stücke von B, die als Parallele zu A erscheinen aus der Ausgabe selbst nicht zu erkennen. Und was wir als Rezension B (Paralipomena) haben, ist nur ein Fragment.[6]

An edition published in Constantinople in 1720 contained the above-mentioned Recension B in its original sequence.[7] Recension B represents a systematic-alphabetic-anonymous collection in 26 chapters. Earlier still, in 1641, another edition of Recension B was published in New Julfa (Isfahan, Iran).[8]

2 Manuscript Heritage and the Collections of *Vitae Patrum* in Armenian Manuscripts

The following inventory of Armenian *Vitae Patrum* (*Haranc'vark'*) results from a study of catalogue records[9] and manuscripts in the main Armenian manuscript depositories: The Matenadaran, or Mesrop Mashtots Institute of Ancient Manuscripts of Yerevan (M), the libraries of the Mekhitarist Congregations in Venice (V) and in Vienna (W), and the library of the Armenian St. James Monastery in Jerusalem (J). In the following list, if a codex consists of several manuscripts, these are designated as A, B, C, etc.

---

6 Wilhelm Bousset, *Apophthegmata: Studien zur Geschichte des ältesten Mönchtums* (Tübingen: Mohr, 1923), 18.
7 *Book that is Called Lives of the Fathers* [Գիրք որ կոչի Շարանց վարք] (Constantinople, 1720).
8 *Lives of the Fathers* [Շարանց վարք] (New Julfa, 1641).
9 The manuscript data in the list below are normally given without explicit reference to the catalogues.

2.1 Matenadaran/Yerevan

1. M 11 Miscellany.[10] 1736, Van. Fols. 22ʳ, 36ᵛ, 37ʳ, 41ᵛ, 42ʳ, 109ʳ, 110ᵛ: new recension. The sayings were added later in the 19th cent.
2. M 20 Miscellany. 1497, Suceava (?); 1614, Lviv (?). Fols. 32ʳ–34ʳ: new recension.
3. M 39 Miscellany consisting of two different manuscripts. A. 17th cent., *Anapat*. B. 17th cent. Fols. 1ʳ–7ʳ, 8ᵛ–13ᵛ.
4. M 40 Miscellany. 14th cent., *Akancʻ anapat*. Fols. 25ᵛ–27ᵛ, 38ʳ–43ᵛ, 69ᵛ–74ᵛ *Corpus Nili*.
5. M 41 Miscellany consisting of three different manuscripts. A and B, 17th cent. C, 18th cent. Fols. 145ᵛ–148ᵛ: new recension.
6. M 57 Miscellany. 15th cent., monastery *Awag* (?). Fols. 160ʳ–171ᵛ: old recension.
7. M 84 Miscellany. 1614. Fols. 182ᵛ–185ʳ, 235ʳ–243ᵛ: old recension.
8. M 96 Miscellany consisting of six different manuscripts. 17th cent. Fol. 130ᵛ: new recension.
9. M 108 Miscellany. 1322, Jerusalem. Fols. 243ᵛ–246ᵛ. The unit is entitled "From the writing *Vitae Patrum* excerpted by *Vardan Vardapet Arewelcʻi*"[11] [Ի Շարանց վարուց զորց քաղուած Վարդան վարդապետի Արեւելցւոյ]. Cf. M 657, M 686, M 693, and M 848 below.
10. M 229 Miscellany. 17th cent. Fols. 182ᵛ–253ᵛ, 253ᵛ–267ʳ *Corpus Nili*, new recension. 19 chapters. The *Corpus Nili* follows upon chapter 19; Nil's counsel on dullness is included in chapter 12.
11. M 265 Gospels. 13th cent. Fol. 204ᵛ.
12. M 452 Miscellany. 18th cent. (before 1797). Fols. 33ᵛ–40ᵛ. Turkish in Armenian letters;[12] the manuscript is of interest because of the milieu for which it was intended.
13. M 557 Miscellany. 1386, *Eznkay*. Fols. 63ᵛ, 97ᵛ–101ᵛ, 133ʳ–167ʳ: old recension.
14. M 605 Miscellany. 17th cent. Fol. 31ʳ: an addition from the 18th cent.
15. M 625 Miscellany. 17th cent. Fols. 94ᵛ–102ᵛ, 1ᵛ: addition from the 18th or 19th cent.

---

10 "Miscellany" renders the term *ժողովածու* [collection] of the catalogues.
11 Ca. 1198–1271.
12 See also Hasmik Stepanyan, ed., *Catalogue of Turkish Materials Written in Armenian Letters of Armenian Manuscripts and Turkish Manuscripts in Armenian Letters: Manuscripts from "Matenadaran" in Yerevan and Mother See Holy St. Echmiadzin* (Yerevan: printed by the author, 2008), 43.

16.	M 640	Miscellany. 1297, village *Hayeli*. Fols. 4rv, 46ᵛ–58ᵛ, 138ᵛ–206ᵛ, 206ᵛ–210ᵛ, 210ᵛ–224ᵛ etc.

One of the colophons (fol. 314ᵛ) identifies the content (*Vitae Patrum*) and date of copying (1297).[13] This manuscript has lost many leaves (see the pinax, fols. 1ᵛ–3ʳ), which should also be of interest as units of *Vitae Patrum* collections, e.g., 29, *Life of the Blessed Mary the Egyptian* [ԻԹ. Վարք երանելոյն Մարիամու եգիպտուհւոյն].[14]

17.	M 657	Miscellany. 1614, New Julfa. Fols. 230ᵛ–243ʳ.

Fols. 233ᵛ–143ʳ, under the title "By the holy *Vardan Vardapet*, who wrote from the *Lives* of the Fathers for the sake of the monks" [Սուրբ վարդապետին Վարդանա գրեալ ի Հարանց վարուց. յաղագս այգտի կրաևատորաց] present the Preface or first chapter of the "new" recension (see also M 686).

18.	M 682	Miscellany. 1679. Fols. 12ʳ–13ʳ, 15ᵛ–21ᵛ: new recension.
19.	M 683	Miscellany consisting of two different manuscripts. 1707. A. Fols. 1–188: *Vitae Patrum*. Fols. 1ʳ–185ᵛ: new recension.
20.	M 684	*Vitae Patrum*.[15] 1650, *Arinj*. Fols. 3ʳ–583ʳ: new recension.
21.	M 685	*Vitae Patrum*. 1632, Jerusalem. Fols. 1ʳ–361ᵛ: new recension.
22.	M 686	Miscellany. 17th cent. Fols. 79ʳ–148ʳ: old recension.

The apophthegmic part[16] is entitled "By the holy *Vardan Vardapet*, who wrote from the *Lives* of the Fathers for the sake of the monks" [Սուրբ վարդապետին Վարդանայ գրեալ ի Հարանց վարուց Յաղագս այգտի կրաևատորաց]. The statement that *Vardan Vardapet* is the writer of the following text units means that he is the compiler of the material. Cf. above M 657 and M 108.

23.	M 687	Miscellany consisting of four different manuscripts. A. 1689, Yerevan. Fols. 5ʳ–132ʳ: *Mirror of Lives* transl. by *Step'anos Lehac'i*.[17] B. 1635. Fols. 139ʳ–363ᵛ: *Vitae Patrum*, new recension. C. 17th cent. Fols. 366ʳ–377ᵛ: two chapters of a collection of *Vitae Patrum*.

---

13 Onik Yeganyan, ed., *General Catalogue of Armenian Manuscripts of the Mashtots Matenadaran*, vol. 3 (Yerevan: Magałat Publishing House, 2007), 166; see also Artashes Matevosyan, ed., *Colophons of the Armenian Manuscripts: 13th c.* [Հայերեն ձեռագրերի Հիշատակարաններ. ԺԳ դար] (Yerevan: Publishing House of the Academy of Sciences of the Armenian Soviet Socialist Republic, 1984), 811.
14 Sarkissian, *Lives of the Holy Fathers*, vol. 1, pp. 287–291, 291–317.
15 "*Vitae Patrum*" renders the term Վարք Հարանց or Հարանց վարք [*Lives* of the Fathers] given in the manuscripts and catalogues.
16 Contains also the *Ladder of Divine Ascent* by John Climacus (Fols. 9ʳ–78ʳ).
17 See Knarik Ter-Davtyan, ed., *Mirror of Lives* [Հայելի վարուց] (Yerevan: Publishing House of the Academy of Sciences of the Republic of Armenia, 1994).

24.	M 689	*Vitae Patrum*. 1681, Urfa (Edessa). Fols. 1ᵛ–135ʳ: new recension.
25.	M 690	*Vitae Patrum*. 17th cent. Fols. 2ʳ–440ʳ: new recension.
26.	M 693	*Vitae Patrum*. 17th cent. Fols. 2ᵛ–156ᵛ, 196ʳ–298ʳ: new recension.
		On fol. 2ᵛ, the title indicates the authorship of *Vardan Vardapet*, as in M 657 and M 686.
27.	M 708	Miscellany. 1695–1703. Fols. 85ʳ–97ʳ, 101ʳ–107ʳ: new recension.
28.	M 723	Miscellany. 1731, Jerusalem; 1734. Fols. 341rv, 344ʳ–352ʳ.
29.	M 737	Miscellany. 1680–1730, monasteries of *Amrdolu, Glakay, Hnjucʿ, Kaffa* and *Atkʿerman*. Fols. 117ᵛ, 210ʳ.
30.	M 740	Miscellany. 1697, Rome. Fols. 99ʳ–155ᵛ.
31.	M 770	Miscellany. 14th cent. Fols. 18ᵛ–88ᵛ, 147ᵛ–173ᵛ: old recension.
32.	M 784	*Vitae Patrum*. 1641. Fols. 2ʳ–362ʳ: new recension.
		A later colophon dated 1675 (fol. 385ʳ) states, "Remember the last repairer of this book, the priest *Yohan, vardapet* of theology, in your pure prayers, o children of the Holy *Ejmiacin*, when you read this and benefit from it" [Զվերջին նորոգողի գրոյս՝ զտէր յոհան աստուածաբանութեան վարդապետն յ[իշեսջ]իք ի մաքրափայլ յաղօթս ձեր, ով մանկունք սուրբ էջմիածնի, յորժամ կարդայք զսա եւ օգտիք ի սմանէ]. This statement demonstrates that the book was meant be read and studied by the children[18] of the Holy *Ejmiacin*. This suggests that the apophthegmic stories were used in the instruction of novices. This hypothesis is supported by an abecedarius by *Karapet Vardapet* found in some manuscripts of the new recension (see below, M 789).
33.	M 785	*Vitae Patrum*. 1615, *Etingean (Tatʿew)*. Fols. 3ʳ–398ʳ: new recension.
34.	M 786	*Vitae Patrum*. 12th cent. Fols. 5ʳ–209ʳ: old recension.
		To date this is the oldest manuscript of the Armenian *Vitae Patrum* heritage.
35.	M 787	*Vitae Patrum*. 13th cent. Fols. 1ε–126ʳ: old recension.
36.	M 788	*Vitae Patrum*. 1688–1691, Bakhchysaray and Kaffa (Theodosia). Fols. 12ʳ–253ʳ: new recension.
		In addition to the translated texts, this codex contains the counsels by *Anania Narekacʿi*. Inclusion of these counsels in the *Vitae Patrum* collections is not rare and needs further investigation.

---

18 On the term "children" [*մանկունք*], see Manea Erna Shirinian, "Reflections on the 'Sons and Daughters of the Covenant' in the Armenian Sources," *Revue des Études Arméniennes* 28 (2001–2002): 261–285.

37. M 789   *Vitae Patrum*. Two different manuscripts. A. *Vitae Patrum*. 1633, Constantinople. Fols. 2ʳ–534ʳ: new recension. B. *Mirror of Lives* transl. by Step'anos Lehac'i. 1667. Copied on the free leaves (lacunae) of the first manuscript.[19]

Fols. 52ᵛ–55ʳ and 55ʳ–56ʳ represent two acrostics (both abecedaries), entitled "Useful counsels for the children of the church spoken by the great *vardapet* Karapet: poem with letters" [Կարապետի մեծի վարդապետի ասացեալ Խրատ պիտանիս մանկանց եկեղեցոյ ոտանաւոր տաղիս], and "For the teaching of young children, spoken by *vardapet* Aŕak'el" [Առաքել վարդապետի ասացեալ Վասն ուսման նորահաս մանկանց], respectively. Inclusion of these two poems within the collection could point to the milieu, for which the *Vitae Patrum* might have been intended. The poem of Karapet *Vardapet* together with acrostics on the author's name Karapet [Կարապետէ] are included also in M 1 (fols. 100ʳ–103ᵛ), M 33 (fols. 233ʳ–241ʳ; fols. 211ʳ–214ʳ contains the poem by Aŕak'el together with acrostics on his name), M 682 (fols. 13ʳ–14ᵛ), M 687 (fols. 141ʳ–143ᵛ), and others.

38. M 790   *Vitae Patrum*. 1611, Jerusalem. Fols. 3ᵛ–276ᵛ: new recension.
39. M 791   *Vitae Patrum*. 1644. Fols. 2ᵛ–450ᵛ: new recension.
40. M 792   *Vitae Patrum*. 1619. Fols. 1ᵛ–436ᵛ: new recension.
41. M 793   *Vitae Patrum*. 17th cent. Fols. 2ʳ–431ᵛ: new recension. Illuminated with 571 images.
42. M 794   *Vitae Patrum*. 17th cent. Fols. 1ʳ–213ᵛ: new recension.
43. M 845   *Vitae Patrum*. 1431, Ereran. Fols. 1ʳ–196ʳ, 212ʳ–222ʳ *Corpus Nili*, 222ᵛ–233ᵛ.
44. M 847   *Vitae Patrum*. 1419, Paŕvargak. Fols. 1ʳ–272ʳ: new recension.
45. M 848   Miscellany consisting of four different manuscripts. A. 14th cent. Fols. 1ʳ–12ᵛ, 14ʳ–36ᵛ, 178ʳ–202ᵛ.

On Fol. 1ʳ, the title on the authorship of *Vardan Vardapet* repeats the one of M 657, M 686 and M 693.

46. M 850   Miscellany consisting of three diffferent manuscripts. A. 17th cent. Fols. 1ʳ–12ʳ.
47. M 851   Miscellany. 14th cent. Fols. 1ʳ–106ʳ, 186ᵛ–215ʳ *Corpus Nili*, 232ʳ–236ʳ.
48. M 914   *Vitae Patrum*. 17th cent. Fols. 1ʳ–130ʳ: new recension.
49. M 1633   Miscellany. 1664, Łōnia. Fols. 2ʳ–96ʳ, 160ᵛ–190ᵛ: new recension.

---

19   See Yeganyan, *General Catalogue*, vol. 3, pp. 747–753.

50.	M 1661	Tałaran. 1594. Fols. 199^v–206^v: new recension.
51.	M 1667	Miscellany consisting of three different manuscripts. A. and B. 14th cent., C. 17th cent. Fols. 167^v–226^r, 240^r–244^r: new recension.
52.	M 1887	Miscellany. 17th cent. Fol. 400^v.
53.	M 1915	Miscellany consisting of two different manuscripts. A. 1750, B. 15th–16th cent. Fols. 136^r–155^v: new recension.
54.	M 1925	Miscellany. 1401, palace Tašk'awbru (Crimea). Fols. 221^r–232^v.
55.	M 1976	Miscellany. 17th cent. Fol. 99^v.
56.	M 1982	Miscellany consisting of three different manuscripts. A. 1702, Edirne (Adrianople); B. 1699, Adrianople; and C. 18th cent., Adrianople. Fols. 191^r–199^v, 203^v–214^r, 216^r–240^v. Fol. 214^r has the same colophon, after the same *vita*, as do J 228 (fol. 393^v) and J 268 (fol. 574).
57.	M 1983	Miscellany. 1687, 1712, Hamatan. Fols. 123^v–126^v, 130^v, 138^v, 189^v–224^r, 236^r–367^v: new recension.
58.	M 1999	Miscellany consisting of three different manuscripts. A. and B. 12th cent.; C. 13th cent. Fols. 135^r–139^v, 159^v–165^v, 165^v–167^r *Corpus Nili*.
59.	M 2002	Miscellany consisting of three different manuscripts. A. 1663; B. before 1696; and C. 17th cent. Fols. 66^r–82^r, 84^v–91^r, 108^v–121^v, 187^v, 226^v–229^r.
60.	M 2029	Miscellany. 1696, Holy Savior (Vank) Cathedral (New Julfa). Fols. 323rv (addition from the 18th cent.).
61.	M 2080	Miscellany. 18th cent. Fols. 236^r–238^v, 243^r–254^r.
62.	M 2106	Miscellany. 1715, Theodosiopolis (Erzurum / Karin). Fols. 430^r–431^r.
63.	M 2109	*Book of Sermons*. 1669–1686. Fols. 1rv, 4^v–5^r.
64.	M 2175	Gregory of Tatev, *Book of Sermons*. 1659, Ernjak. Fols. 3^v–6^r (addition from the 18th cent.).
65.	M 2177	Miscellany consisting of two different manuscripts. A. 1411, monastery *Mecop'ay*; B. 1609, *Varag* (?), 1675. Fols. 395^r–417^v, 423^r–429^v: new recension.
66.	M 2188	Miscellany. 15th cent. Fols. 201^v, 247^v–263^r.
67.	M 2196	Miscellany. 1683. Fols. 276^v–332^v.
68.	M 2224	Miscellany. 1771, Etchmiadzin. Fols. 269^r–284^v: new recension.
69.	M 2236	Miscellany. 17th cent. Fols. 85^r–186^v, 201^r–210^v: new recension.
70.	M 2244	Miscellany consisting of three different manuscripts. A. 12th cent.; B. 1708–1709, *Maraš* (*Germanik*); C. 17th cent. Fol. 57^r.
71.	M 2246	Miscellany. 1692–1693, Jerusalem. Fols. 15^r–61^v.
72.	M 2248	Miscellany. 1695, 1739. Fols. 244^r–294^v: new recension.
73.	M 2249	Miscellany. 17th cent. Fols. 155^v–165^r.

74.	M 2266	Miscellany. 1693, Julfa. Fols. 267ʳ–279ᵛ.
75.	M 2335	Miscellany. 1476, 15th cent., Jerusalem. Fols. 95ʳ–163ʳ.
		Fol. 155ᵛ has the same colophon as J 228 (fol. 299ᵛ) and J 285 (fol. 591).[20]
76.	M 2474	Miscellany. 17th cent. Fols. 1ᵛ–80ᵛ: new recension.
77.	M 2532	Miscellany. 13th cent. Fols. 7ʳ–35ᵛ, 138ʳ–159ᵛ *Corpus Nili*; 160ʳ–191ʳ (?): old recension.
78.	M 2556	Miscellany. 18th cent. Fols. 5ʳ–246ᵛ: new recension.
79.	M 2557	Miscellany consisting of three different manuscripts. A. 1333; B. 14th cent.; and C. 1554, Malazgirt, Holy Mother of God Church. Fols. 133ᵛ–156ᵛ *Corpus Nili*; 157ʳ–159ʳ, 175ʳ–178ᵛ, 181ʳ–202ᵛ: old recension.
80.	M 2575	Miscellany. 17th cent. Fols. 261ʳ–282ʳ, 283ᵛ–298ᵛ, 306ʳ–316ᵛ, 324ʳ–325ʳ, 329ᵛ–331ᵛ, 333ʳ–336ᵛ: new recension.
81.	M 2578	Miscellany. 1585–1589, Jerusalem. Fols. 3ʳ–14ʳ, 174ʳ–187ʳ: new recension.
82.	M 2608	Miscellany. 1635, Šinahayr (Orotn). Fols. 253ᵛ–254ᵛ.
83.	M 2642	Miscellany. 1663–1664, New Julfa. Fols. 491ʳ–514ᵛ, 515ʳ–519ʳ *Corpus Nili*; 519ʳ–526ᵛ: new recension.
84.	M 2680	Miscellany. 1371–1378, Ankełakoyt. Fols. 2ᵛ–149ʳ, 149ʳ–247ᵛ, 259ʳ–260ᵛ and 420ʳ–441ᵛ *Corpus Nili*; 277ʳ–286ʳ, 286ʳ–368ᵛ etc.
		The manuscript is a collection of lives and counsels, both translated and of Armenian origin. Only a few sayings could be identified. The manuscript is remarkable because colophons provide the translation data (date, place, and name of the translator). Athanasius' *Live of Antony* and the *Life of St. Parsam*[21] by Šmuēl were translated by Grigor.[22]
85.	M 2681	*Vitae Patrum*. 17th cent. Fols. 1ʳ–502ʳ: new recension.
86.	M 3208	*Vitae Patrum*. 17th th cent. Fols. 1γ–151ʳ: new recension.

---

20   See Gevorg Ter-Vardanean, ed., *General Catalogue of Armenian Manuscripts of the Mashtots Matenadaran*, vol. 7 (Yerevan: Nairi Publishing House, 2012), 987.

21   For the *Life and History of St. Parsam*, cf. also M 1952, fols. 163ʳ–172ʳ.

22   See Catholicos Karekin I (Hovsepian), ed., *Colophons of Manuscripts*, vol. 1, *From the Fifth Century to 1250* [Յիշատակարանք ձեռագրաց, Հատոր Ա. (Ե. դարից մինչեւ 1250 թ.)] (Antelias: Printing House of the Armenian Catholicosate of Cilicia, 1951), 333–334; Artashes Matevosyan, ed., *Colophons of the Armenian Manuscripts: 5th to 12th Centuries* [Հայերեն ձեռագրերի հիշատակարաններ Ե-ԺԲ դդ.] (Yerevan: Publishing House of the Academy of Sciences of Armenian Soviet Socialist Republic, 1988), 3 and 156; Gevorg Ter-Vardanean, ed., *General Catalogue of Armenian Manuscripts of the Mashtots Matenadaran*, vol. 8 (Yerevan: Nairi Publishing House, 2013), 1133, 1135–1136.

87.	M 3874	*Vitae Patrum*. 1422, *Trapēz*. Fols. 1^r–421^r: new recension.
88.	M 4739a and M 4739	*Vitae Patrum*. 1549, Jerusalem. Fols. 1^r–19^v and 1^r–296^v: new recension.
89.	M 4921	*Vitae Patrum*. 1416, Monastery of Holy Cross (Crimea). Fols. 1^r–248^v: new recension.
90.	M 5229	Miscellany. 14th cent. Fols. 1^r–119^r.
91.	M 5324	*Vitae Patrum*. 1627, *Varag*. Fols. 1^r–406^r: new recension. Illuminated.
92.	M 5453	*Čaṙəntir*. 13th cent. Fols. 66^r–84^v, 86^v–96^r, 100^v–120^r, 147^v–150^v, 153^r–158^r, 186^v–189^r.
93.	M 5608	Fragments from the Bible. 1363, Jerusalem. Fol. 148^v.
94.	M 5626	*Vitae Patrum*. 1696, Monastery *Amirdōlu*. Fols. 212^r–295^r.
95.	M 5631	Miscellany. 1620, Monastery of the Holy Archangel (Sebastia). Fols. 164^r–165^v.
96.	M 5707	Miscellany. 1386, *Ernǰak*. Fols. 287^r–336^v.
97.	M 5758	Miscellany. 18th cent. Fols. 1δ–19^r: new recension.
98.	M 5806	*Maštoc'jeṙac'*. 1677, village *Halmalawa*. Fol. 1^v.
99.	M 5827	*Vitae Patrum*. 16th cent. Fols. 2^v–286^v: new recension.
100.	M 5851	Miscellany. 17th cent. Fols. 52^r–68^v.
101.	M 5952	Miscellany. 17th cent. Fols. 6^v–137^v.
102.	M 5958	Miscellany. 1680, Rome (?). Fols. 132^r–133^r.
103.	M 5971	Miscellany. 1692–1693. Fols. 285^r–305^r.
104.	M 5992	Miscellany. 1645, town *Axalgōr*. Fols. 1^r–6^v.
105.	M 6014	Miscellany. 19th cent. Fols. 2^r–24^r. In modern Armenian.
106.	M 6031	Miscellany. 1404. Fols. 184^v–186^v, 285^v–288^v.
107.	M 6074	Miscellany. 1624–1625, 1626, Jerusalem. Fols. 56^r–98^r.
108.	M 6444	*Vitae Patrum*. 1716. Fols. 2^r–480^v: new recension.
109.	M 6464	*Oskep'orik*. 18th cent. (ca. 1729), Monastery St. *Gēorg*. Fol. 5^v. Compiled by the monk Andon.
110.	M 6522	Miscellany. 19th cent. Fols. 117^r–119^v.
111.	M 6643	Miscellany. 17th cent. Fols. 74^v–139^r, 183^v–199^r, 224^r–324^v: new recension.
112.	M 6703	Miscellany. 1816, *Bałēš*. Fol. 82^v.
113.	M 6708	Miscellany. 1635. Fols. 5^r–128^r.
114.	M 6751	*Vitae Patrum*. 1693, Izmir, 1701. Fols. 114^r–257^r: new recension.
115.	M 6898	Miscellany. 19th cent. (before 1855). Fols. 8^v–100^v.
116.	M 6919	Miscellany. 17th cent. Fols. 96^v–139^v.
117.	M 6957	Miscellany. 18th cent. Fols. 2^r–133^v: new recension.
118.	M 6961	Miscellany. 17th cent. Fols. 51^v–61^v.
119.	M 6976	*Vitae Patrum*. 1604, *Hamit'*. Fols. 2^r–339^r.

120.	M 7024	Miscellany. 1696, *Tigranakert*. Fols. 14ʳ–208ᵛ: new recension.
121.	M 7041	Miscellany. 17th cent. Fols. 178ᵛ–192ʳ.
122.	M 7115	Miscellany. 17th cent. Fols. 228ʳ–348ᵛ: new recension.
123.	M 7183	Miscellany. 1717, Lim. Fols. 140ʳ–147ʳ: new recension.
124.	M 7205	Miscellany. 17th cent. Fol. 66ᵛ.
125.	M 7290	*Vitae Patrum*. 1634. Fols. 1ʳ–558ᵛ: new recension.
126.	M 7324	Miscellany. 17th cent. Fols. 159ʳ–171ᵛ.
127.	M 7377	*Yaysmawurkʻ* (red. *Grigor Cerencʻ*). 1594–1610, Kaffa. Fols. 646ʳ–650ᵛ.
128.	M 7898	Miscellany. 17th cent., 1719, Erzurum (Karin). Fols. 129ᵛ–254ᵛ: new recension.
129.	M 7993	Miscellany. 1672, 18th cent. Fols. 1ʳ–81ᵛ.
130.	M 8029	Miscellany. 14th cent. (before 1376), *Kawksu* (Crimea). Fols. 164ʳ–178ʳ.
131.	M 8030	Miscellany. 1341, *Azax*. Fols. 1rv.
132.	M 8033	*Vitae Patrum*. 17th cent. Fols. 2ʳ–144ᵛ.
133.	M 8043	Miscellany. 1731, *Ernjak* (*Naxijevan*). Fols. 223ʳ–241ʳ.
134.	M 8046	*Vitae Patrum*. 17th cent. Fols. 1ʳ–204ᵛ: new recension.
135.	M 8068	Miscellany. 18th cent., 1829, monastery *Muturku*. Fol. 92ᵛ.
136.	M 8076	Miscellany. 17th cent. Fols. 58ʳ–59ᵛ.
137.	M 8100	Miscellany. 1784, Kars. Fols. 154ʳ–162ʳ, 163ᵛ–184ᵛ.
138.	M 8179	Miscellany. 14th cent. Fols. 315ʳ–327ᵛ, 336ᵛ–338ᵛ, 352ᵛ–362ᵛ.
139.	M 8223	Miscellany. 1842–1893, Karin (?). Fols. 4ᵛ–5ʳ.
140.	M 8502	Miscellany. 1619. Fols. 2ʳ–11ʳ, 104ʳ–116ᵛ.
141.	M 8674	Miscellany. 1617, 1622, 17th cent. Fols. 87ᵛ–89ʳ.
142.	M 8708	Miscellany. 17th cent. Fols. 86ᵛ–89ʳ.
143.	M 8727	Miscellany. 17th cent. Fols. 242ʳ–252ʳ, 265ʳ–300ᵛ, 437ʳ–438ᵛ.
144.	M 8756	Miscellany. 16th cent. Fols. 29ʳ–43ᵛ.
145.	M 9303	Miscellany. 17th cent. (after 1621), 1767. Fols. 28ʳ–29ʳ.
146.	M 9309	Miscellany. 1397, Jerusalem. Fols. 149ᵛ–263ᵛ.
147.	M 9436	*Vitae Patrum*. 1617, *Kamenicʻ*. Fols. 4ʳ–576ʳ: new recension.
148.	M 9832	Miscellany. 15th, 17th cent. Fols. 27ᵛ–38ᵛ.
149.	M 10062	Miscellany. 1271, St. Nicholas (?). Fols. 2ʳ–241ʳ.
150.	M 10210	Miscellany. 1649–1652, Jerusalem. Fols. 253ᵛ–277ᵛ.
151.	M 10236	Miscellany. 1700–1701, Van. Fols. 218ʳ–223ᵛ.
152.	M 10485	Miscellany. 19th cent. Fols. 145ʳ–151ᵛ.
153.	M 10609	Miscellany. 1758, Sebastia, 1778, Karin. Fols. 49ʳ–51ʳ, 63rv, 95rv.
154.	M 10725	Miscellany. 17th cent. Fols. 247ᵛ–301ᵛ.
155.	M 10882	Miscellany. 1644, *Šatax* (*Ganjak*). Fols. 158ʳ–168ʳ.
156.	M 10905	Miscellany. 1686, *Karmir vankʻ anapat*. Fols. 172ᵛ–187ʳ etc.

157. M 10945 Miscellany. 1709–1711, 1705–1711, 1712, *K'ilis*. Fol. 115ʳ.
158. M 10986 Miscellany. 17th cent. Fols. 80ʳ–83ᵛ.

2.2 Venice

159. V 1108   *Oskep'orik* XXVI. 1317–1318, monastery *Glajor*. Fols. 131ᵛ–171ᵛ: old
     (265)   recension. Basis of Sarkissian's edition.[23]
             The apophthegmic part is entitled "From the lives of the holy Fathers, collected out of many into one [volume] by holy *Vardan Vardapet* for the sake of everyone who wants to read it inwardly" [Ի վարուց սուրբ Հարանց. Զոր Հաւաքեալ ի բազմաց ի մի՛ սուրբ վարդապետին Վարդանա(յ) յաղութ ամենեցուն որք կամին սրտի մտաւք ընթեռնուլ].[24] Cf. also M 657, M 686, M 693, M 848 and M 108.
160. V 612   *Vitae Patrum* I. 1336, St. James Monastery (Jerusalem). Pp. 1–619:
     (1676) old recension. Basis of Sarkissian's edition.
161. V 806   *Vitae Patrum* II. 14th cent. Pp. 1–262, 508–558 *Corpus Nili*; pp. 559–
     (1677) 698: old recension. Basis of Sarkissian's edition.
162. V 1329   *Vitae Patrum* III. 14th cent., *Erznka* (?). Pp. 137–206: old recension.
     (1678) Possibly basis of Sarkissian's edition.
163. V 1324   *Vitae Patrum* IV. 14th–15th cent., 1608, *Amit'*. Pp. 1–689: old recen-
     (1679) sion. Possibly basis of Sarkissian's edition.
164. V 1922   *Vitae Patrum* V. 14th–15th cent. Fols. 1ʳ–5ᵛ. Illuminated.
     (1680)
165. V 536   *Vitae Patrum* VI. 1418, monastery *Awag*. Pp. 1–312: old recension.
     (1681) Basis of Sarkissian's edition.
166. V 133   *Vitae Patrum* VII. 1587, *Paṙagrkus anapat*, 1598. Pp. 222–270, 317–
     (1682) 412 *Corpus Nili*; new recension.
167. V 941   *Vitae Patrum* VIII. 1614, *K'ēōt'ahia*. Fols. 1ʳ–383ʳ: new recension.
     (1683) Basis of Sarkissian's edition.
168. V 844   *Vitae Patrum* IX. 1621, *Hizan*. Fols. 1ʳ–310ʳ: new recension. Basis of
     (1684) Sarkissian's edition. Iluminated.
             The colophon following the *Vita Onophrii* (fols. 233ʳ–239ᵛ) is the same as in J 228 and J 285 (see below).[25]

---

[23] For identification of the manuscripts used by Sarkissian in his edition, see Leloir, *Paterica armeniaca*, vol. 1, p. vii.

[24] See Barsegh Sargissian, ed., *Grand Catalogue of the Armenian Manuscripts in the Library of the Mekhitarist Brotherhood in Venice*, vol. 2 (Venice: San Lazzaro, 1924), 850.

[25] See Sahak Djemdjemian, ed., *Grand Catalogue of the Armenian Manuscripts in the Library of the Mekhitarist Congregation in Venice*, vol. 8 (Venice: San Lazzaro, 1998), 686.

169.	V 877 (1685)	*Vitae Patrum* X. 1651, Crimea and Sebastia. Pp. 1–243, 262–274: new recension.
170.	V 19 (1686)	*Vitae Patrum* XI. 1671, *Ant'ap'*. Fols. 1ʳ–382ʳ: new recension.
171.	V 594 (1687)	*Vitae Patrum* XII. 17th cent., *Xasgiwł* (?). Fols. 3ʳ–390ʳ: new recension.
172.	V 1154 (1688)	*Vitae Patrum* XIII. 17th–18th cent. Fols. 1ʳ–240ʳ: new recension.

2.3 Vienna

173.	W 66	*Vitae Patrum*. 1644, *Bałēš*. Fols. 1ʳ–431ᵛ: new recension.
174.	W 88 (68)	Miscellany. 1638–1657, Trebisond. Fols. 153ᵛ–179ᵛ: old recension.
175.	W 128 (103)	*Vitae Patrum*. 15th–16th cent. (?). Fols. 1ʳ–128ʳ: old recension.
176.	W 279	*Vitae Patrum*. 1640, Constantinople. Fols. 6ʳ–374ᵛ: new recension.
177.	W 522	Miscellany of counsels profitable for the soul, part I. 19th cent.
178.	W 523	Miscellany of counsels profitable for the soul, part II. 19th cent.
179.	W 527	Counsels to the monks. 1834.
180.	W 622	*Vitae Patrum*. 1714. Fols. 253ʳ–312ʳ: old recension.
181.	W 705	*Oskep'orik*. 1403, monastery of *Mec Anjnanapat*. Fols. 264ʳ–439ʳ: old recension.

2.4 Jerusalem

182.	J 23	*Vitae Patrum* I. 1625, Aleppo. Fols. 1–641ʳ: new recension. Illuminated with ca. 500 images.
183.	J 175	*Vitae Patrum* II. 1610, Jerusalem. Pp. 3–915: new recension.
184.	J 228	*Vitae Patrum* III. 1651, Jerusalem. Fols. 1ʳ–393ᵛ: new recension. Illiminated. Copy of J 285.

A colophon (fol. 299ᵛ) following the *Vita Onophrii* by Paphnutius states that the Armenian catholicos Gregory was the repairer (կրկնողող that is, redactor) and translator of the lives of saints, and that these were translated in Egypt in the year ՇԾԹ´ (559) of the Armenian era, thus in 1110 AD (559+551).[26] This note is important for

---

26 See Norair Bogharian, ed., *Grand Catalogue of St. James Manuscripts*, vols. 1–6 and 9 (Jerusalem: Armenian Convent Printing Press, 1966–1979), here vol. 1, p. 615.

the information it provides about the redactor and the date of the Armenian translations of monastic lives. As J 228 is a copy of J 285, the colophon will be further discussed below.

Another colophon (fol. 393^v) by the translator Father *Gagik* follows the *Life of the Son of the Greek King* (fols. 390^r–393^v) stating that this *vita* was translated from Syriac.[27] The colophon of the scribe *Yovanēs Mokac'I* (fols. 402 f.) repeats in the beginning almost literally the colophon of J 285 (see below).[28]

185. J 268   *Vitae Patrum* IV. 1710 (?), Jerusalem (?). Pp. 9–586: new recension. Illuminated with ca. 500 images.

The colophon on p. 574 is the same as in J 228, fol. 393^v and J 1686, fol. 390.[29]

186. J 285   *Vitae Patrum* V. 1430, Kaffa, Armenian monastery of St. Antony. Pp. 6, 9–754, 760–783, 793–823: new recension.

The monograph of the well-known Armenologist and art historian Nira Stone, entitled *The Kaffa Lives of the Desert Fathers: A Study in Armenian Manuscript Illumination*, discusses this codex.[30] The codex contains a collection of *Vitae Patrum* that is uniquely illuminated. Stone observes:

> There are a number of earlier manuscripts which contain *The Lives of the Desert Fathers* in Greek and Latin as well as in Armenian, Coptic and Syriac. However, the present manuscript, Jerusalem 285, dated to 1430 C.E., is the first one in any language which was extensively illustrated. The motives which brought about this surprising and innovative Armenian creation in Crimea are fascinating. They are to be sought in the Christian theological thought of the period, in the emergence of Hesychasm and in the revival of monasticism …
>
> This particular manuscript, together with its illustrations, was especially important in the period in which it was created and afterwards.

---

27   See Bogharian, *Grand Catalogue*, vol. 1, p. 616.

28   Cf. Levon Khachikyan, ed., *Colophons of the Armenian Manuscripts of the 15th Century: First Part (1401–1450)* [ԺԵ դարի հայերեն ձեռագրերի հիշատակարաններ. Մասն առաջին (1401–1450 թթ.)] (Yerevan: Publishing House of the Academy of Sciences of the Armenian Soviet Socialist Republic, 1955), 399–401; Bogharian, *Grand Catalogue*, vol. 1, p. 617; Nira Stone, *The Kaffa Lives of the Desert Fathers: A Study in Armenian Manuscript Illumination*, CSCO 566 / Subs. 94 (Louvain: Peeters, 1997), 30–32.

29   See Bogharian, *Grand Catalogue*, vol. 2, p. 73.

30   See n. 28 above.

A large number of apographs both of its text and its illuminations were made in the following three centuries.[31]

Stone investigated not only the illuminations, but also undertook an extensive study of other aspects of the manuscript including the colophons, which provide many interesting details regarding the compilation of this *paterikon* miscellany. She notes:

> In the main colophon he [the scribe and illuminator Thaddeus Avramenc'—A.A.] says that in order to create Jerusalem 285, the *Lives of the Desert Fathers*, he consulted numerous Armenian manuscripts, chose and selected those readings which seemed best to him, collected them together and created the manuscript which is made up of all [of] them. When the differences between the Armenian manuscripts were too great, as in the *Life of St. Alexius*, he also consulted a Greek copy.[32]

Since the colophon claims that *Thaddeus Avramenc'* not only copied from a now lost exemplar,[33] but also compiled and redacted the text, occasionally on the basis of Greek original(s), an in-depth textual analysis must be undertaken in order to come to more far-reaching conclusions. The study carried out by Stone will be of great assistance, since she traced the transmission of a subgroup of the Armenian *Vitae Patrum* in her study of J 285 and its apographs (J 23, J 228, J 971, J 410, J 293, J 268, J 1409, V 1922, BL Add. 27.301, M 789).[34] J 285 is the oldest extant manuscript of the "new recension."

With regard to the colophon which follows Paphnutius' *Life of Onophrius* (cf. above on J 228), Stone discusses the identity of the translator, Catholicos Gregory:

> Some scholars try to change the date in order to attribute the translation to St. Gregory Martyrophile, a famous translator and editor of hagiographical texts (hence, his cognomen "Martyrophile"—*Vkayasēr*). He was so fascinated by the ascetics of Christian antiquity that he travelled in their footsteps to Egypt. St. Gregory Martyrophile died in 1105. The colophon of the text, however, dates the translation of the Paphnutius material to the year 1110. This supposition is logical because the visit of St. Gregory Martyrophile was too early, having taken place in 1076–1077.

---

31 Stone, *Kaffa Lives*, VII–VIII.
32 Stone, *Kaffa Lives*, 30.
33 Stone, *Kaffa Lives*, 34–35.
34 Stone, *Kaffa Lives*, 36–37.

The nephew of St. Gregory Martyrophile was also called Gregory, and was appointed by his uncle to be Primate of the Armenians of Egypt and also received the title "Catholicos". The nephew continued his uncle's work of translation of hagiographic texts. So it is most reasonable to conclude that the translator of the Paphnutius material was the nephew, Catholicos Gregory, Primate of Egypt and not the uncle, Catholicos St. Gregory Martyrophile, Catholicos of All the Armenians.[35]

187.	J 293	*Vitae Patrum* VI. 1652, Constantinople. Fols. 5^r–785^v: new recension. Illuminated.
188.	J 300	*Vitae Patrum* VII; Writings of Evagrius II. Pp. 1–639: old recension.
189.	J 301	*Vitae Patrum* VIII. 1627, *Tełi*. Fols. 1^r–455^v: new recension.
190.	J 336	Questions of Basil of Caesarea I; *Vitae Patrum* IX. 1298, monastery *Gayl*. Fols. 155^v–285^r.
191.	J 410	*Vitae Patrum* X. 1631, *Tełi*. Fols. 3^r–756, 805–830: new recension. Illuminated. Fol. 830 has the same colophon after the *Vita Onophrii* as does J 228, fol. 393^v, following this *vita*.[36]
192.	J 547	*Vitae Patrum* XI. 1630, St. James Monastery (Jerusalem). Fols. 3–763^r, 765^r–794^r, 796^v–800^r: new recension.
193.	J 725	*Vitae Patrum* XII. 17th cent. Fols. 5^r–589^r, 601^r–764: new recension.
194.	J 726	Mirror of Lives III; *Vitae Patrum* XIII. 1678, Jerusalem. Pp. 311–857: new recension.
195.	J 728	*Vitae Patrum* XIV; Commentary on the Eight Thoughts of Evagrius IV. 15th cent. Pp. 3–310: new recension.
196.	J 756	*Vitae Patrum* XV. 17th cent. Pp. 4–800: new recension.
197.	J 906	Miscellany unit VII, *Vitae Patrum* XVI. Pp. 708–791: new recension.
198.	J 939	Miscellany unit XI, *Vitae Patrum* XVII. 1621, Monastery of the Apostles (Muš). Pp. 455–636: new recension.
199.	J 961	*Vitae Patrum* XVIII. 1624, *T'agirtał*. Pp. 5–788: new recension.
200.	J 971	*Vitae Patrum* XIX. 1623, *Tełi*. Pp. 9–777: new recension. Illuminated.
201.	J 991	*Vitae Patrum* XX. 17th cent. Fols. 3^r–498^v: new recension.
202.	J 1089	*Vitae Patrum* XXI; Miscellany. 1681, Izmir. Pp. iii, ix, 1–326: new recension.
203.	J 1173	Miscellany unit VIII, *Vitae Patrum* XXII. 17th cent. Pp. 400–528: new recension.

---

35 Stone, *The Kaffa Lives*, 59.
36 See Bogharian, *Grand Catalogue*, vol. 2, p. 348.

204.	J 1409	*Vitae Patrum* XXIII. Pp. 5–483: new recension. Illuminated.
205.	J 1602	*Vitae Patrum* XXIV. 1625, monastery Tat'ew. Pp. 119–465: new recension.
206.	J 1686	*Vitae Patrum* XXV. 1660, Tełi. Pp. 12–492: new recension.
		The *Vita Onophrii* is followed by the identical colophon discussed above (J 228 and J 285). On p. 390 there is a colophon following the *Life of the Son of the Greek King, Whose Name was Nersēh* identical to that in J 228, fol. 393ᵛ and J 268, fol. 574.[37]
207.	J 1819	Miscellany unit III, *Vitae Patrum* XXVI. Fols. 635ʳ–818ᵛ: new recension.
208.	J 2873	*Vitae Patrum* XXVII. 17th cent. Fols. 1ᵛ–103ᵛ. Illuminated.

3   Conclusion

The alphabetic and systematic collections of Greek *apophthegmata* found their way also into the Armenian tradition, where they developed into the very last redaction of systematic-alphabetic-anonymous collection(s) embedded in the *Vitae Patrum* miscellanies. Examination of the manuscript catalogues offers some preliminary conclusions. In the Armenian tradition, there are no manuscripts which contain only the apophthegms. Rather, we observe many fascinating and curious constellations of monastic lives, sayings, and counsels that could help us find clues about the probable milieu of the *Vitae Patrum*, including their intended audience. Hopefully over time further research on this ancient and important heritage will be published and inspire new readers, as I once was inspired and encouraged at the sight of this material.

Bibliography

Primary Sources

Book that is Called Lives of the Fathers [Գիրք որ կոչի Հարանց վարք]. Constantinople, 1720.

Lives of the Fathers [Հարանց վարք]. New Julfa, 1641.

Sarkissian, P. Nerses, ed. *Lives of the Holy Fathers and their Politeia According to the Double Translation of the Ancestors* [Վարք սրբոց Հարանց եւ քաղաքավարութիւնք նոցին ըստ կրկին թարգմանութեան նախնեաց]. 2 vols. Venice: San Lazzaro, 1855.

---

37 See Bogharian, *Grand Catalogue*, vol. 5, p. 549.

Secondary Sources

Bogharian, Norair, ed. *Grand Catalogue of St. James Manuscripts.* Vol. 1–6 and 9. Jerusalem: Armenian Convent Printing Press, 1966–1979.

Bousset, Wilhelm. *Apophthegmata: Studien zur Geschichte des ältesten Mönchtums.* Tübingen: Mohr, 1923.

Dashian, Jacobus, ed. *Catalog der armenischen Handschriften in der Mechitharisten-Bibliothek zu Wien.* Vol. 1. Vienna: Mechitharisten-Buchdruckerei, 1895.

Djemdjemian, Sahak, ed. *Grand Catalogue of the Armenian Manuscripts in the Library of the Mekhitarist Congregation in Venice.* Vol. 8. Venice: San Lazzaro, 1998.

Dum-Tragut, Jasmine, and Dietmar W. Winkler, eds. *Monastic Life in the Armenian Church: Glorious Past—Ecumenical Reconsideration.* Zurich: LIT, 2018.

Dum-Tragut, Jasmine. "The Cultural Impact of Armenian Monasticism: A Brief Note on the Role of Armenian Monasteries in Medieval Armenian Society." In *Monastic Life in the Armenian Church,* ed. Dum-Tragut and Winkler (see above), 25–44.

Hovsepian, Catholicos Karekin I, ed. *Colophons of Manuscripts.* Vol. 1, *From the Fifth Century to 1250* [Յիշատակարանք ձեռագրաց, Հատոր Ա. (Ե. դարից մինչեւ 1250 թ.)]. Antelias: Printing House of the Armenian Catholicosate of Cilicia, 1951.

Khachikyan, Levon, ed. *Colophons of the Armenian Manuscripts of the Fifteenth Century: First Part (1401–1450)* [ԺԵ դարի Հայերեն ձեռագրերի հիշատակարաններ. Մասն առաջին (1401–1450 թթ.)]. Yerevan: Publishing House of the Academy of Sciences of the Armenian Soviet Socialist Republic, 1955.

Leloir, Louis. *Paterica armeniaca a P. P. Mechitaristis edita (1855) nunc latine reddita.* 4 vols. CSCO 353, 361, 371, 371 / Subs. 42, 43, 47, 51. Louvain: Imprimerie Orientaliste, 1974–1976.

Malkhasyan, Armen, ed. *Catalogue of Manuscripts of the Mashtots Matenadaran.* Vol. 3. Yerevan: Yerevan University Publishing House, 2007.

Matevosyan, Artashes, ed. *Colophons of the Armenian Manuscripts: 13th Century.* [Հայերեն ձեռագրերի հիշատակարաններ. ԺԳ դար]. Yerevan: Publishing House of the Academy of Sciences of the Armenian Soviet Socialist Republic, 1984.

Matevosyan, Artashes, ed., *Colophons of the Armenian Manuscripts: 5th–12th Century* [Հայերեն ձեռագրերի հիշատակարաններ Ե-ԺԲ դդ.]. Yerevan: Publishing House of the Academy of Sciences of the Armenian Soviet Socialist Republic, 1988.

Oskian, Hamazasp, ed. *Katalog der armenischen Handschriften in der Mechitharisten-Bibliothek zu Wien.* Vol. 2. Vienna: Mechitharisten-Buchdruckerei, 1963.

Sargissian, Barsegh, ed. *Grand Catalogue of the Armenian Manuscripts in the Library of the Mekhitarist Brotherhood in Venice.* Vol. 2. Venice: San Lazzaro, 1924.

Shirinian, Manea Erna. "Reflections on the 'Sons and Daughters of the Covenant' in the Armenian Sources." *Revue des Études Arméniennes* 28 (2001–2002): 261–285.

Stepanyan, Hasmik, ed. *Catalogue of Turkish Materials Written in Armenian Letters of Armenian Manuscripts and Turkish Manuscripts in Armenian Letters: Manuscripts from the "Matenadaran" in Yerevan and Mother See Holy St. Echmiadzin.* Yerevan: printed by the author, 2008.

Stone, Nira. *The Kaffa Lives of the Desert Fathers: A Study in Armenian Manuscript Illumination.* CSCO 566 / Subs. 94. Louvain: Peeters, 1997.

Ter-Davtyan, Knarik, ed. *Mirror of Lives* [Հայելի վարուց]. Yerevan: Publishing House of the Academy of Sciences of the Republic of Armenia, 1994.

Ter-Vardanean, Gevorg, ed. *General Catalogue of Armenian Manuscripts of the Mashtots Matenadaran.* Vols. 6–8. Yerevan: Nairi Publishing House, 2012–2013.

Winkler, Dietmar W. "Monasticism in Oriental Christianity Today: A Brief Survey." In *Monastic Life in the Armenian Church*, ed. Dum-Tragut and Winkler (see above), 7–16.

Yeganyan, Onik, Andranik Zeytunyan, and Paylak Antabyan, eds. *Catalogue of Manuscripts of the Mashtots Matenadaran.* Vols. 1–2. Yerevan: Publishing House of the Academy of Sciences of the Armenian Soviet Socialist Republic, 1965–1970.

Yeganyan, Onik, Andranik Zeytunyan, and Paylak Antabyan, eds. *General Catalogue of Armenian Manuscripts of the Mashtots Matenadaran.* Vol. 1. Yerevan: Publishing House of the Academy of Sciences of the Armenian Soviet Socialist Republic, 1984.

Yeganian, Onik, Andranik Zeytunian, and Armine Keoshkerian, eds. *General Catalogue of Armenian Manuscripts of the Mashtots Matenadaran.* Vol. 2. Yerevan: Nairi Publishing House, 2004.

Yeganyan, Onik, ed. *General Catalogue of Armenian Manuscripts of the Mashtots Matenadaran.* Vol. 3. Yerevan: Magałat Publishing House, 2007.

Yeganyan, Onik, ed. *General Catalogue of Armenian Manuscripts of the Mashtots Matenadaran.* Vol. 5. Yerevan: Nairi Publishing House, 2009.

CHAPTER 8

The Monk as Storyteller? On the Transmission of the *Apophthegmata Patrum* among Muslim Ascetics in Basra

Ute Pietruschka

The textual transmission of the *Apophthegmata Patrum* (AP) is very complex, not only in Greek, Latin or Coptic, but also in Arabic where various collections of *apophthegmata* were often combined with other monastic texts.[1] Alongside the Bible, material from the Arabic version of the AP has served as one of the guidelines for monks and nuns in Coptic monasteries, and it remains a popular reading and source of inspiration for modern people, both monastic and lay. Sayings of the Desert Fathers (and Mothers) still form an integral part of the process of spiritual guidance in monastic circles.[2] Today, pious readers can use a printed version of the *apophthegmata*, the *Bustān al-Ruhbān* (*The Garden of the Monks*), published by the Coptic Orthodox Church,[3] that deals with different themes of monastic and spiritual life based on the lives and teachings of the Desert Fathers. The preface to this book states that since the spirit of strong faith is lacking in the present, one has to turn to the Desert Fathers who showed exemplary strength of asceticism and faith.

The manuscript tradition shows that already in the oldest Arabic collections stories and sayings of the Desert fathers were combined with other texts of an educational nature. We can assume that these miscellanies (multiple-text manuscripts)[4] were compiled for pedagogical purposes. One of the oldest Arabic manuscripts containing material from the AP dates from the end of the 9th

---

1 For an overview of the transmission in Arabic, see Samuel Rubenson, "The Apophthegmata Patrum in Syriac, Arabic and Ethiopic: Status Questionis," *ParOr* 36 (2011): 309–312.
2 Pieternella van Doorn-Harder, *Contemporary Coptic Nuns* (Columbia: University of South Carolina Press, 1995), 130.
3 *Bustān al-Ruhbān li-Ābā al-kanīsa al-qibṭiyya*, ed. by the Metropolitanate of Beni Suef (Cairo, 1968, 2nd ed. 1976).
4 Paola Buzi, "From Single-Text to Multiple-Text Manuscripts: Transmission Changes in the Coptic Literary Tradition; Some Case-Studies from the White Monastery Library," in *One-Volume Libraries: Composite and Multiple-Text Manuscripts*, ed. Michael Friedrich and Cosima Schwarke (Berlin: de Gruyter, 2016), 94.

century CE.[5] But very likely, stories and sayings from the AP circulated already orally in Arabic in the first decades of the 8th century CE, at a time when Arabic had developed into the *lingua franca* for the Christian population in an Islamicate world. Material from the AP was apparently also popular in Muslim circles, especially among ascetics, who disseminated educational and edifying sayings and stories of monks as exemplars of pious life.

In the following, we will discuss the transmission of this material during the first three Islamic centuries and the adaptation of the AP to a Muslim audience.

1 Ascetics in Basra

Under Umayyad rule, Basra developed into a metropolis that attracted traders from as far away as Persia, India and East Africa. The town reached its zenith in the 8th and early 9th century CE. The city provided fertile ground for the development of Arabic grammar and prose, and for the emergence of influential intellectual currents such as the Muʿtazila.[6] The Christians had a strong position in the city, and this situation influenced the intellectual climate of the city. The East Syriac patriarch Timothy I (727–823 CE) addressed a pastoral letter to his parish in Basra at the beginning of the 9th century CE, in which he discussed if Christ may be called "servant" (ʿabdā).[7] This was a subject often raised in debates between Christians and Muslims. The New Testament authors, as well as the church fathers, had used this appellation as an acceptable title for Jesus.[8] With the coming of Islam, however, and the Qurʾānic understanding of Jesus as mere creature,[9] Christians felt obliged to explain this christological title. Timothy's letter vividly illustrates the intellectual interaction between different religious communities in Basra.

Basra became the cradle of Muslim asceticism,[10] where influential ascetics such as al-Ḥasan al-Baṣrī (624–728 CE) preached. His moral exhortations and his views on renunciation (*zuhd*) made him a paragon of piety and spiritu-

---

5   Jean Mansour, "Un florilège arabe chrétien du Xᵉ s. (Ms. Strasbourg 4225): Introduction et édition critique par Jean Mansour" (PhD diss., Strasbourg, 1972), xx–xxi.
6   Charles Pellat and Katherine H. Lang, "Basra until the Mongol Conquest," in *EI³* online (Leiden: Brill, 2007–2019), accessed September 30, 2019.
7   Martin Heimgartner, transl., *Die Briefe 30–39 des ostsyrischen Patriarchen Timotheos I*, CSCO 662 / Syr. 257 (Leuven: Peeters, 2016), 11.
8   Matt 12:18, Phil 2:7, Acts 3:13.26, 4:27.30.
9   E.g., Q 43:59 ("He is only a servant we blessed"), Q 19:30.
10 As already stated by Ibn Taymiyya (d. 1328 CE) in his *Risāla al-Ṣūfiyya*; see Th. Emil Homerin, "Ibn Taimīyā's al-Ṣūfīyah wa-al-Fuqarāʾ," *Arabica* 32 (1985): 222–223.

ality whose ideas enjoyed further development among his disciples and later Sufis. Suleiman A. Mourad has published an in-depth study of the different literary representations of al-Ḥasan al-Baṣrī's life and his teaching.[11] Concerning the literary corpus transmitted under al-Ḥasan al-Baṣrī's name, Mourad concludes that several works were attributed to him only after his death. This posthumously created legacy, he posits, contributed more to medieval Islamic scholarship than did the historical person.[12] Mourad points out that "the intellectual and religious life in the Umayyad period and its presentation in the sources ... are necessarily incomplete at this time and therefore unsatisfactory. To reach more valid conclusions we must go on to examine other figures of similar symbolic importance."[13] A closer examination of the life and teachings of early Muslim ascetics is therefore an important desideratum.

The pioneers of Islamic asceticism (Arab. *zuhhād, nussāk, ʿubbād,* or *bakkāʾūn*) were sometimes accused by their contemporaries of being crypto-Christians or at least of being heavily influenced by Christian ideas. These Muslim ascetics valued renunciation, occasional solitude, silence; and in general they embraced an otherworldly orientation and thus appreciated monks and their lifestyle, although celibacy and monastic eating and fasting habits remained subjects of debate. It appears that the *zuhhād* knew and respected the practices and customs of Christian ascetics and monks.

Already some of the early traditionists suspected that the early Muslim ascetics (the "renunciants," as Christopher Melchert calls them)[14] uttered Christian sayings; and there are accounts of Basran ascetics that give the impression that in debates they drew upon (apocryphal) sayings of Jesus and quotations from the Old and New Testament.[15] The above-mentioned al-Ḥasan al-Baṣrī attracted, as Mourad has shown,[16] many accounts describing him as

11 Suleiman A. Mourad, *Early Islam between Myth and History: Al-Ḥasan al-Baṣrī (d. 110 H/ 728 CE) and the Formation of his Legacy in Classical Islamic Scholarship* (Leiden: Brill, 2006).
12 Hellmut Ritter, "Studien zur Geschichte der islamischen Frömmigkeit," *Islam* 21 (1933): 64–65.
13 Mourad, *Early Islam*, 243.
14 Christopher Melchert, "Quotations of Extra-Qurʾanic Scripture in Early Renunciant Literature," in *Islam and Globalisation: Historical and Contemporary Perspectives; Proceedings of the 25th Congress of L'Union Européenne des Arabisants et Islamisants*, ed. Agostino Cilardo (Leuven: Peeters, 2013), 97–107.
15 References to Jesus or the *"tawrāt"* of the Israelites in Abū Nuʿaym al-Isfahānī, *Ḥilyat al-awliyāʾ wa-ṭabaqāt al-aṣfiyāʾ*, vol. 3 (Beirut: Dār al-kutub al-ʿilmiyya, 1987), 45:2 ff.; 46:1 ff., 46:8 ff. Still valid and useful for our purposes is Joachim Jeremias, *Unbekannte Jesusworte*, 4th ed. (Gütersloh: Mohn, 1965), *passim*; see also Tarif Khalidi, *The Muslim Jesus: Sayings and Stories in Islamic Literature* (Cambridge, MA: Harvard University Press, 2001), 32–43.
16 Mourad, *Early Islam*, 63–94.

an ascetic and mystic. Of similar importance as exemplars of piety were his younger contemporaries Mālik ibn Dīnār (d. 748 CE)[17] and Abū Ḥāzim Salama b. Dīnār al-Makhzūmī (d. ca. 757 CE).[18] Both were appreciated for their ascetic lifestyle but also as gifted *quṣṣāṣ* (storytellers).[19] Other early ascetics, Farqad al-Sabākhī (d. 749 CE),[20] Thābit al-Bunānī (d. 744/45? CE)[21] or Ṭāwūs b. Kaysān (d. 725 CE),[22] to name but a few, were also well known as *quṣṣāṣ*. To all of them were attributed ascetic stories or sayings that were acceptable to both Christian and Muslim audiences. The older *tābiʿūn* (followers of the Prophet) also mentioned some of the early renunciants as transmitters of *ḥadīth*, but often harshly criticized them, because critics of the *muḥaddithūn* (transmitters of *ḥadīth*) accused the renunciants of carelessly handling *ḥadīth*s. The *zuhhād* consequently acquired a poor reputation and often were classified as *ḥadīth* "falsifiers," for instance by Ibn al-Jawzī (1126–1200 CE) in his *K. al-Quṣṣāṣ wa-l-mudhakkirūn*. Here Ibn al-Jawzī attributes the forgeries of the *quṣṣāṣ* to their laziness and selfishness. He was convinced that the *zuhhād*, by narrating particularly exciting traditions and accounts, aimed to secure listeners, gain influence and solicit donations.[23] On the other hand, the poor reputation of the early ascetics (*zuhhād*) as *ḥadīth* transmitters, resulting from their (alleged) familiarity with Christian circles, eventually led to a disregard of their accounts in canonical collections of *ḥadīth* in later times.

This familiarity with Christian traditions can be explained through contacts with Christians who still represented the majority of the population in the caliphate, or through the growing number of converts to the new religion (as

---

17   Fuat Sezgin, *Geschichte des arabischen Schrifttums*, vol. 1 (Leiden: Brill, 1967), 634; *Ḥilya*, vol. 2, 358–359, 369–370, 376–377, 381–382.
18   Sezgin, *Geschichte*, vol. 1, 634; Lyall R. Armstrong, *The Quṣṣāṣ of Early Islam* (Leiden: Brill, 2017), 307.
19   The translation of *quṣṣāṣ* as "storyteller" does not reflect the broad meaning of this term. A clear definition of *quṣṣāṣ* (and their role in early Islam) is still under discussion: a *qāṣṣ* was involved in a number of religious matters "from interpretation of the Qurʾān; through traditions of the Prophet (*ḥadīth*), stories of ancient prophets, and moral preaching; to admonition against the evil of sin and transgression." (Khalil Athamina, "Al-Qaṣaṣ: Its Emergence, Religious Origin and Its Socio-Political Impact on Early Muslim Society," *Studia Islamica* 76 (1992): 54). For a more detailed discussion of the term see Armstrong, *Quṣṣāṣ*, 1–13.
20   *Ḥilya*, vol. 3, 45–46; Josef van Ess, *Theologie und Gesellschaft im 2. und 3. Jahrhundert Hidschra*, vol. 2 (Berlin: de Gruyter, 1992), 94.
21   Armstrong, *Quṣṣāṣ*, 306.
22   Van Ess, *Theologie und Gesellschaft*, vol. 1 (1991), 78, 198.
23   Albrecht Noth, "Common Features of Muslim and Western Ḥadīth Criticism: Ibn al-Jawzī's Categories of Ḥadīth Forgers," in *Ḥadīth: Origins and Developments*, ed. Harald Motzki (Aldershot: Ashgate, 2004), 6.

was the case with Farqad al-Sabakhī, born into a Christian family in Armenia) that certainly had an impact on religious ideas and beliefs within Islam.[24] In order to legitimise these teachings and views, many were later attributed to Muslim personalities, to biblical figures and to renowned pre-Islamic sages or saints. In this process, Christian monasticism also played a role. The veneration of Christian monks is well attested already in the pre-Islamic literature of the Arabs, and it is reflected in some Qur'ānic passages.[25] The perception of Christian monks as holy figures survived into early Islamic times, and their sayings and anecdotes, especially with regard to ascetical and mystical practices and ideals, provided a blueprint for the Islamic ascetic movement in the 7th and 8th centuries CE. Beside these influences, monotheistic (but not necessarily Christian) tendencies on the Arabian Peninsula should be taken into consideration as possible roots of an ascetic movement.[26] Christopher Melchert proposed that quotations from biblical literature found in collections of renunciant sayings "are a vestige of an Old Testament stage of Islamic history. Perhaps the spread of ancient Jewish, Christian, Hellenistic, and Persian lore to Arabia was a sort of seventh-century cultural globalization."[27] While it should not be denied that some of these influences were rooted in pre-Islamic religious developments, most of the Christian material was incorporated and assimilated into Muslim thought during the first three centuries of Islam.

---

24 Ḥilya, vol. 3, 45–46.
25 Q 5:82 ("thou wilt surely find the nearest of them in love to the believers are those who say 'We are Christians'"). Other passages in the Qur'ān, however, have a negative connotation: Q 9:31, 34. On the perception of monks in early Islam, see Edmund Beck, "Das christliche Mönchtum im Koran," Studia Orientalia 13 (1946): 3–29; Raimund Köbert, "Zur Ansicht des frühen Islam über das Mönchtum (rahbānīya)," Orientalia, n. s. 42 (1973): 520–524; Jane D. McAuliffe, Qur'ānic Christians: An Analysis of Classical and Modern Exegesis (Cambridge: University Press, 1991), 260–284.
26 Elizabeth Key Fowden, "The Lamp and the Wine Flask: Early Muslim Interest in Christian Monasticism," in Islamic Crosspollinations: Interactions in the Medieval Middle East, ed. Anna Akasoy, J.E. Montgomery, and P.E. Pormann (Cambridge: Gibb Memorial Trust, 2007), 1–28; Ute Pietruschka, "Der Mönch mit der Öllampe: Zu einem Motiv in der vorislamischen Poesie," in Der Christliche Orient und seine Umwelt: Gesammelte Studien zu Ehren Jürgen Tubachs anläßlich seines 60. Geburtstages, ed. Sophia G. Vashalomidze and Lutz Greisiger (Wiesbaden: Harrassowitz, 2007), 303–308.
27 Melchert, "Quotations of Extra-Qur'ānic Scriptures," 97.

2 The Problem of Authorship: Methodological Considerations

Our knowledge of the early protagonists of asceticism, in Basra and beyond, is often limited to anecdotes or sayings attributed to them and transmitted in collections of traditions (*ḥadīths*) or biographical collections. None of these collections, however, is contemporary with the persons or events they describe. Often an interval of one or more centuries separates the time when the accounts about the early renunciants first appear and the time when they were definitively written down. The question arises if we can rely on these early reports, as transmitted in later collections. The answer is that we can use them critically, as Gregor Schoeler points out.

> To be sure, we cannot expect that these sources will provide information that is as accurate and as precise as the information we might glean from sources contemporary with the events they describe. But, if we examine them judiciously, always keeping in mind their individual specificities, we will find that they can often provide us with evidence or strong indications about matters that would otherwise remain nothing more than postulations or mere speculation.[28]

Collections of sayings, compiled by early ḥadīth transmitters, were already at the very beginning sources of gathered information about the Muslim renunciants. The oldest *ḥadīth* collections which have come down to us contain chapters on asceticism pertaining to the pre-Islamic prophets, Muḥammad and his companions, and his followers in the next generation. The oldest extant monograph on the subject is the *K. al-Zuhd wa-l-raqāʾiq* by the traditionist Ibn al-Mubārak (d. 797 CE). The work belongs to a genre that promotes specific forms of piety and asceticism, and prescribes by means of sayings and anecdotes those practices to which the believer should adhere.[29] The sayings and anecdotes attributed to these pioneers of asceticism were collected from *mawāʿiẓ* (exhortations), *khuṭab* (sermons), *waṣāyā* (advice), *qiṣaṣ* (stories) and *masāʾil* (questions). Other collections of renunciant sayings that were popular from the 9th century CE onwards and peaked in the 10th and 11th centuries, follow this pattern. One example is the collection on *zuhd* (renunciation) by Aḥmad b. Ḥanbal (780–855 CE) who was especially interested in the first generation of Muslim ascetics. The names of the first renunciants are also mentioned in

---

28   Gregor Schoeler, *The Genesis of Literature in Islam: From the Aural to the Read* (Edinburgh: University Press, 2002), 12.
29   Sezgin, *Geschichte*, vol. 1, 95, 636.

a collection from the early 10th century CE, entitled *Zuhd al-thamāniyya min al-tābiʿīn* by the traditionist Ḥātim al-Rāzī (d. 938).[30]

There is, however, little biographical information included in the traditions of early renunciants composed in the 8th or the 9th century CE. Neither Ibn al-Mubārak nor Aḥmad b. Ḥanbal provides such information. Details on the lives of the early *zuhhād* had to be reconstructed from sayings, sermons or anecdotes.

One of the most important collections of biographical information on ascetics and mystics is the *Ḥilyat al-awliyāʾ wa-ṭabaqāt al-aṣfiyāʾ* by Abū Nuʿaym al-Iṣfahānī (d. 1038 CE), comprising a total of 650 biographies of pious men and women. This work offers much longer biographies of the *zuhhād* than do comparable contemporary dictionaries, and it preserves material not transmitted elsewhere. The biographies of Muslim ascetics are organized in roughly chronological order from the Rightly Guided Caliphs to the famous Sufis of the 10th century.[31] The arrangement of the material shows the compilers' effort (and eagerness) to present the early renunciants in a "genealogical" perspective, namely as successors and true heirs of the pre-Islamic prophets, the Prophet Muḥammad himself, and the companions of the prophet, all of whom are described as having striven for a God-fearing and ascetic life.[32] The material transmitted in the *Ḥilyat al-awliyāʾ* is interesting because it often includes accounts that have been discarded in canonical collections due to concerns about their pro-Christian character.

Information about early ascetics can also be found in *adab* anthologies, a genre that flourished from the 9th century CE onwards, and that intended to instruct and advise the general public or bureaucratic elites. These anthologies contain micro-units[33] in various genres: *ḥadīth*, stories, anecdotes, proverbs, verses of poetry, and Qurʾān verses form the core of these collections. Both the

---

30   Sezgin, *Geschichte*, vol. 1, 632. To this group belong Uways b. ʿĀmir al-Qaranī (d. 657 CE), ʿĀmir b. ʿAbdallāh b. ʿAbdqays (d. before 680), Harim b. Ḥaiyān (d. after 647), al-Rabīʿ b. Khuthaym (d. 682), Masrūq b. al-Ajdaʿ (d. 683), al-Aswad b. Yazīd al-Nakhāʿī (d. 694), Abū Muslim ʿAbdallāh b. Thawb al-Khawlānī (d. 682), and al-Ḥasan al-Baṣrī (d. 728). See *Ḥilya*, vol. 2, 79–98, 102–161.

31   Christopher Melchert, "Abū Nuʿaym's Sources for Ḥilyat al-awliyāʾ, Sufi and Traditionist," in *Les maîtres soufis et leurs disciples: IIIe-Ve siècles de l'hégire (IXe-XIe s.); Enseignement, formation et transmission*, ed. Geneviève Gobillot and Jean-Jacques Thibon (Beirut: Presses de l'Ifpo, 2012), 145–160; Jawid A. Mojaddedi, "Abu Nuʿaym al-Isfahani," in *Medieval Islamic Civilization: An Encyclopedia*, vol. 1, ed. Josef W. Meri (New York: Routledge, 2006), 401–402.

32   Raif Georges Khoury, "Importance et authenticité des textes de Ḥilyat al-awliyā," *Studia Islamica* 46 (1977): 73–113.

33   Jaakko Hämeen-Anttila, "Adab, a) Arabic, early developments," in *EI*[3] online, accessed September 30, 2019.

compilers of *ḥadīth* collections and the compilers of *adab* anthologies found themselves in the same position with respect to their material—they were faced with large numbers of sayings and short narratives (*akhbār*, little snippets of text), which they felt called upon to collect, sift, select, and arrange according to particular headings. The original context of these texts, however, is for the most part lost to us: they are fragments. One often encounters the same quotations in different works, and their meaning changes according to the context. When a quotation is taken out of its context, it generates its own discourse which can be interpreted in various ways. The compiler can easily eliminate names, or attribute a saying to another person, and thus is able to give fresh insight into familiar material.[34] This feature is especially characteristic of *adab* literature and collections of sayings.[35]

Transfer of authorship is a common phenomenon that can be observed already in Greek pagan collections of sayings (gnomologia). After the rise of Christianity, sacro-profane gnomologia mingle sayings of Greek philosophers and Christian authorities: pagan material was re-used in Christian collections, a process that would continue when Muslims drew upon Christian collections. It is therefore hardly surprising that Muslim works on asceticism quote wise sayings that go back to Christian *Vorlagen*.[36] The content of such gnomic wisdom aligns perfectly with the ideals of the Muslim ascetics: the sayings advocate a humble life agreeable to God, abstinence and silence, and at the same time they also emphasise the significance of education and wisdom for pious people. The ethical universality of these sayings allowed them easily to be integrated into Muslim collections, in the process of which they underwent a certain degree of Islamisation. The content of a saying can be taken out of its Christian environment by eliminating Christian terms and replacing them with Muslim ones. The attribution of sayings to famous persons is a rhetorical device, for the effectiveness of a sermon, a wise saying or an anecdote largely depends on the person to whom it is ascribed. But how to convey the impression that the attribution to a certain well-known personality is correct? Because collections of sayings or *adab* collections rarely have extensive *isnāds* (chains of transmitters) that could attest to the veracity of a story, compilers chose to provide evidence of authenticity by "name-dropping." *Quṣṣāṣ* (storytellers) in early Islamic

---

34   Hilary Kilpatrick, "Adab," in Encyclopedia of Arabic Literature, vol. 1 (London: Routledge, 1998), 55.
35   For an overview of Arabic gnomologia, see Ute Pietruschka, "Gnomologia: Syriac and Arabic Traditions," in *Encyclopedia of Mediterranean Humanism*, ed. H. Touati (2014), accessed September 30, 2019, http://www.encyclopedie-humanisme.com/?Gnomologia.
36   Pietruschka, "Gnomologia."

times often employed this device: *onomatomania*, the obsession with providing names, had the important function of enhancing the credibility of a story.[37] This *onomatomania* is connected with one of the most striking phenomena in classical Arabic literature, namely the gradual development of large bodies of narrative material attributed to specific individuals. Well-known examples of this phenomenon, pertaining to different types of narrative, are Wahb ibn Munabbih (d. ca. 110/728 CE)[38] as a standard transmitter of stories or sayings of allegedly Jewish origin (*isrāʾīliyyāt*),[39] and al-Aṣmaʿī (d. 828 or 831 CE)[40] as storyteller (*qāṣṣ*) of encounters with the Bedouins. The figures concerned with this phenomenon are labelled in narrative research "Kristallisationsgestalten" or "focusees," i.e., individuals that serve as a focus for the attribution of narratives.[41] This basic concept, namely that certain kinds of narratives develop around certain personalities, was described already in the 9th century CE by al-Jāḥiẓ in his book *al-Bukhalāʾ*: "Anecdotes are only truly interesting when one knows the characters and can trace them back to their sources by establishing a kind of contact with their protagonists."[42]

The reports we have about the life and religious views of the early renunciants are overall inconsistent and even contradictory. The same sayings are attributed to different persons; or contradictory information is given for the same person. Any attempt to reconstruct the life and teachings of early ascetics from these accounts faces the problem whether one can trust the sources that convey information about them. A selective and partial use of the sources by scholars of early Islamic history, connected with a rather undifferentiated jux-

---

37 Albrecht Noth, *The Early Arabic Historical Tradition: A Source-Critical Study*, 2nd ed. (Princeton: Darwin Press, 1994), 123–129.

38 Raif Georges Khoury, *Wahb b. Munabbih*, vol. 1, *Der Heidelberger Papyrus PSR Heid Arab 23* (Wiesbaden: Harrassowitz, 1970), 247–157.

39 For this term (first evidence in the 10th century CE) see Roberto Tottoli, "Origin and Use of the Term *Isrāʾīliyyāt* in Muslim Literature," *Arabica* 46 (1999): 193–194.

40 Reinhard Weipert, "Al-Aṣmāʿī," in *EI³* online, accessed September 30, 2019. Adab literature presents a very large number of anecdotes that relate to al-Aṣmāʿī, who appears as the intellectual companion of Hārūn al-Rashīd; the original collections, however, seem to be lost.

41 Ulrich Marzolph, "'Focusees' of Jocular Fiction in Classical Arabic Literature," in *Story-Telling in the Framework of Non-Fictional Arabic Literature*, ed. Stefan Leder (Wiesbaden: Harrassowitz, 1998), 118–129; Ines Köhler-Zülch, "Kristallisationsgestalten," in *Enzyklopädie des Märchens: Handwörterbuch zur historischen und vergleichenden Erzählforschung*, ed. Rolf W. Brednich et al., vol. 8 (Berlin: de Gruyter, 1996), 459–466.

42 Ulrich Marzolph, *Arabia ridens: Die humoristische Kurzprosa der frühen adab-Literatur im internationalen Traditionsgeflecht* (Frankfurt am Main: Klostermann, 1992), 237.

taposition of the respective accounts, cannot solve this problem.[43] The mere indication of correspondences between sayings that are scattered in sundry collections provides no real clue as to which specific sources the compiler used. The same saying can be used in different contexts and can therefore easily change its meaning. A far more fruitful approach to the historical classification of a collection of sayings and anecdotes is to detect the motivation behind the compilation, and the particular religious or political interests reflected in them.[44]

3   The Transmission of Apophthegmata Patrum (AP) among Early Renunciants

A closer look at the sayings ascribed to early ascetics in many cases reveals parallels with and allusions to biblical material. The deep interest during early Islamic times in tracing earlier scriptures in the Qurʾān is documented in the early classical exegetical genre of the *isrāʾīliyyāt*. Beside the Torah (*al-tawrāt*) and the Gospel (*al-injīl*), pertaining to Moses and Jesus, respectively, the Psalms (*zabūr*), ascribed to David, exist as an independent scripture, and all of them could serve as some sort of *tafsīr*, a commentary or interpretation of Qurʾānic passages.[45] Already in pre-Islamic poetry, the term *zabūr* is used in its later Qurʾānic meaning to designate a scriptural corpus that played an important role in monastic life.[46] The recitation of the Psalms was an important element of monastic piety, and Angelika Neuwirth has observed that among Muslims a particular type of piety relying on the Psalms emerged at the end of the Meccan period of the genesis of the Qurʾān.[47] No Arabic translations of the

---

43   Richard Gramlich, *Alte Vorbilder des Sufitums. Erster Teil: Scheiche des Westens* (Wiesbaden: Harrassowitz, 1995), provides an impressive collection of pieces of information about early ascetics. However, he compares the accounts about and sayings of the various ascetics mostly within an Islamic context and rarely gives parallels to non-Muslim sources. Nevertheless, his editions and translations can serve as a useful starting point for a deeper analysis of the material.
44   Bernd Radtke, *Materialien zur alten islamischen Frömmigkeit* (Leiden: Brill, 2009).
45   Melchert, "Quotations of Extra-Qurʾānic Scripture"; Khalidi, *Muslim Jesus*; Khoury, *Wahb*.
46   Imruʾ l-Qays, *Dīwān* 88.1–2: "Years have come upon it since last I was there, and in the morning it was like the writing of a *zabūr*, contained in the codices of monks." (See Ḥasan al-Sandūbī, *Sharḥ Dīwān Imriʾ l-Qays* (Beirut: al-Maktaba al-thaqāfiyya, 1982), 208, no. 88.) For a discussion of the text, see Juan Monferrer-Sala, " 'Varietas preislamica': Kaḥaṭṭi zabūrin fī maṣāḥifa ruhbānī (Imruʾ al-Qays, Diwan 88/1–2)," *Collectanea Christiana Orientalia* 3 (2006): 143–169.
47   Angelika Neuwirth, "Qurʾānic Readings of the Psalms," in *The Qurʾān in Context: Historical*

Psalms are attested for pre-Islamic times, and one must assume that passages from the Psalms circulated orally among an Arabic-speaking audience, maybe as *ad hoc* translations into Arabic.

Already the authors of the earliest Arabic accounts on Muslim renunciants seem well acquainted with biblical stories and motifs. Often they explicitly marked these as texts from the Hebrew Bible, that is from the *tawrāt* or *zabūr*, by using expressions such as *qara'tu fī l-zabūr* (I read in the Psalms), *maktūb fī l-tawrāt* (it is written in the Torah), or *qara'tu fī l-kutub* (I read in the Scriptures).[48] Sometimes, however, the stories are traced back to the ancestors (*awā'il*) or the *Banū Isrā'īl*, the Israelites. Yet a closer reading of these passages shows that some of them are, in fact, adaptations of narratives taken from the *Apophthegmata Patrum* and from pious collections that were, together with the Psalms, a popular reading in monastic circles.[49]

In 2004, Suleiman A. Mourad published a paper on the sayings of Christian monks in Islamic literature.[50] As Mourad has pointed out, it is remarkable that the sources he examined draw a consistently positive picture of the monk, who serves the Muslim ascetic as counsellor and model.[51] The title of his paper, "Christian Monks in Islamic Literature: A Preliminary Report on Some Arabic *Apophthegmata Patrum*," however, is somewhat misleading. Mourad focuses on encounters between Christian monks and Muslim ascetics who used and adapted Christian textual material, and he refers to them in general as *apophthegmata*, without being able to indicate specific parallel passages in the AP. The compilation of this material is nevertheless a good starting point for further comparative studies of the use of the AP in Islamic sources. This brings us to a problem that is particularly relevant for the Arabic versions of the AP. Until now, there is no critical edition of the Arabic AP as a whole, and it is doubtful whether such an edition can ever be provided, since hardly any manuscript of the Arabic AP resembles another, and apparently local traditions played an

---

and *Literary Investigations into the Qur'ānic Milieu*, ed. Angelika Neuwirth, Nicolai Sinai, and Michael Marx (Leiden: Brill, 2011), 736–737.

48 The latter term, however, is not only to be understood with regard to religious texts, it can also refer to written material in general, see Schoeler, *Genesis of Literature*, 16–29.

49 Ute Pietruschka, "Apophthegmata Patrum in muslimischem Gewand: Das Beispiel Mālik ibn Dīnār," in *Begegnungen in Vergangenheit und Gegenwart*, ed. Claudia Rammelt, C. Schlarb, and E. Schlarb (Berlin: LIT, 2015), 164–168, with examples from Ḥilya.

50 Suleiman A. Mourad, "Christian Monks in Islamic Literature: A Preliminary Report on Some Arabic *Apophthegmata Patrum*," *Bulletin of the Royal Institute for Inter-Faith Studies* 6 (2004): 81–98.

51 Ibid., 83.

important role in the compilation process.[52] It is therefore not possible to determine which *apophthegmata* circulated in which form and in which wording at the beginning of the 8th century CE, the time when Muslim ascetics familiarised themselves with Christian narrative material. This problem can perhaps be partially resolved by examining the Christian material as it has been handed down in Islamic sources. However, one must not assume that the early Muslim ascetics drew upon written sources containing the *AP*, although the above-mentioned phrases such as "I have read in the books" might suggest this. It is questionable whether Muslim ascetics knew the *AP* in written form at all.[53] An anecdote describing an ascetic who throws his books—as dispensable goods—into the water shows that the possession of books was viewed rather negatively in early Islamic times.[54] To be sure, this negative attitude towards books might be a *topos* that indicates a preference for oral transmission. But one might rather assume that renunciants cited and transformed stories from the *AP* that circulated orally at the beginning of the 8th century in Basra and found an interested audience among Muslims. The stories are relatively short, just like the *ḥadīth*s, ranging from just one line to half a page, and address similar topics that fit well into the religious climate in Basra, such as weeping, *memento mori*, constant prayer and recitation, fasting, abstinence in general, seclusion, and so on.

An interesting example of the transformation of material from the *AP* is a story attributed to the renowned Basran ascetic Mālik b. Dīnār, who was known as an eloquent *qāṣṣ* (storyteller).[55] It is said that Mālik caught a thief who was searching for something useful in Mālik's home.

> Mālik said: "You did not get worldly goods. Do you want something otherworldly?" "Yes!" he replied. He (Mālik) said: "Do the ritual washing from the tub there and perform two prayers." He did. Then he said: "O master, I will stay here until morning prayer." When Mālik entered the mosque, his companions asked him: "Who is that with you?" He replied: "He came to rob us, then we robbed him."[56]

---

52   Rubenson, "Status Questionis," 309.
53   On the term *kutub* as designating any kind of written document, see Nabia Abbott, *Studies in Arabic Literary Papyri*, vol. 1, *Historical Texts* (Chicago: University of Chicago Press, 1957), 23.
54   Richard Gramlich, *Weltverzicht: Grundlagen und Weisen islamischer Askese* (Wiesbaden: Harrassowitz, 1997), 279–280.
55   Charles Pellat, "Mālik b. Dīnār," in *EI²*, vol. 6 (1991), 266b; van Ess, *Theologie und Gesellschaft*, vol. 2, 91–93.
56   Al-Dhahabī, *Ta'rīkh al-islām wa-wafayāt al-mashāhīr wa-l-a'lām*, ed. ʿUmar ʿAbd al-Salām

This narrative has a parallel in a story attributed to Abba John the Persian:

> It was said of Abba John the Persian that when some evildoers came to him, he took a basin and wanted to wash their feet. But they were filled with confusion, and began to do penance.[57]

The Arabic narrative transformed the story so that its Christian origin is no longer recognisable. Such an approach is not unknown in folk narrative research. Even small changes—above all the attribution to different personalities, changes of place names or terms that indicate a certain religious or cultural environment—facilitate the embedding into another cultural context. In our example, the motif of the tub is found in both the Christian and Muslim versions. In the Muslim version, it serves to perform the ritual washing in order to be ready for prayer, whereas in the Christian version, the foot washing in the tub is to be interpreted as a sign of hospitality and humility. Both narratives are identical in their message to force the evil-doer to repent.[58]

This is an excellent example of how a quick-witted storyteller reshaped the apophthegm from the *AP* into a gripping story. He transformed the rather short narrative into a dialogue—and one can imagine that the story was presented with appropriate gestures and facial expressions—and finished it with a clever pun. These rhetorical devices make the story not only educational, but also entertaining for the audience.

The story also serves to illustrate the modesty of Mālik, for just as with a monk's cell, there is nothing valuable to fetch from Mālik's house. Later authors derived from this anecdote biographical information about Malik. Abu Nuʿaym in his *Ḥilya* describes Mālik's belongings: "In his house there was only one copy of the Qurʾān, one water vessel and one prayer mat."[59] This example shows how carefully one has to approach information on the so-called "focusees" such as Mālik that is derived from anecdotes. These stories attributed to them fit their "profile", so to speak, but they are not authentic; and because there was none or only little biographical information about these figures, such details were taken from sayings or accounts in order to fill the gap. The "historical

---

Tadmūrī (Beirut: Dār al-kitāb al-ʿarabī, 1987), Year 121–140, 216–217. German translation in Gramlich, *Alte Vorbilder*, 113.

57   Greek alphabetical collection: *AP* Gr 418 (John the Persian 3); translation in Benedicta Ward, *The Sayings of the Desert Fathers: The Alphabetical Collection* (London: Mowbrays, 1975), 108.

58   Viktor Warnach, *Agape: Die Liebe als Grundmotiv der neutestamentlichen Theologie* (Düsseldorf: Patmos-Verlag, 1951), 156–157.

59   *Ḥilya*, vol. 2, 373:12–13.

nucleus" of these accounts seems to be rather doubtful, and a reconstruction of the life of a renunciant based on them remains problematic.[60]

However, these accounts convey valuable information about the religious atmosphere of the time. The early ascetics obviously liked to use non-Muslim narratives that were well known or seemed familiar to their listeners, and they transformed them according to their own ideals. Many of these stories belong to the edifying genre of *isrāʾīliyyāt*,[61] popular traditions about biblical history and cosmogony. In general, the term *isrāʾīliyyāt* functioned as a synonym for Jewish (and thus unreliable) reports. These probably became popular already under the *tābiʿūn*, the generation of Muslims after the companions of Muḥammad, and were further cultivated as parenetic literature by the early ascetics.[62] But not only biblical stories were subsumed under this term, non-biblical material also found its way into the corpus of *isrāʾīliyyāt*.

In the *Ḥilyat al-awliyāʾ* we find several stories originating from the AP that were transformed into *isrāʾīliyyāt*. A good example is a story about a worshipper (*ʿābid*) who enjoyed the hospitality of another *ʿābid* and who impregnates the daughter of his host. She gives birth to a boy, but is afraid to accuse the man. Finally the child's father accepts his responsibility and requests from the young woman's father: "Leave this boy to me! I accept him as my son." Then he carried the child around with all the "servants of the Israelites" and said: "Brothers, I warn you against anything similar to what has happened to me. My sin—I carry it on my neck."[63] This story strikingly resembles an apophthegm from the AP in which an old man (γέρων), a monk or hermit, impregnates a girl. In this story, too, the girl hands over the child to the old man, who puts his son on his shoulders and presents him to his brothers in the church with the words: "Look at this child, he is the son of disobedience (υἱὸς τῆς παρακοῆς)."[64]

---

60   For example, Gramlich, *Alte Vorbilder*, 59–121, tries to reconstruct Mālik's life based on his sayings and anecdotes about him.
61   George Vajda, "Isrāʾīliyyāt," in *EI*², vol. 4 (1978), 211b.
62   Tottoli, "Origin and Use," 202.
63   *Ḥilya*, vol. 2, 372:24–373:5. Gramlich, *Weltverzicht*, 254.
64   Greek systematic / anonymous collection: Guy v, 40 = N 187. Cf. the Syriac tradition: English transl. in E.A. Wallis Budge, *The Book of Paradise, Being the Histories and Sayings of the Monks and Ascetics of the Egyptian Desert by Palladius, Hieronymus, and Others, According to the Recension of ʿAnan-ishoʿ of Beth ʿAbhe*, vol. 1 (London: Chatto & Windus, 1907), 123.

4   Conclusion

Accounts about early Muslim ascetics that take up material from the AP are not uncommon in the biographical handbooks on ascetics and mystics, such as the previously mentioned *Ḥilyat al-awliyā'* and the *Qūt al-qulūb* by Abū Ṭālib al-Makkī (d. 996 CE).[65] The *isnād*s (chains of transmission) of these accounts largely rely upon an oral transmission that was mainly Basran. Key figures of transmission were Abū Salama Sayyār b. Ḥātim al-ʿAnazī (d. 814 or 816 CE) and ʿAbdallāh b. Aḥmad (d. 903 CE), the son of Aḥmad b. Ḥanbal.[66] The latter is said to have been in Basra several times; and in this regard the chain of transmission seems plausible.[67] Apparently, these literary pieces were disseminated and transmitted by early renunciants in Basra and were available in written form at the beginning of the 9th century CE.

From this literature, we gain an impression of the narratives that were transmitted orally in Basra, and the role which the early renunciants played in this process. The renunciants were appreciated for both their moral conduct and their rhetorical skills as storytellers. In this regard (and also sometimes in their behavior), they resembled Christian monks or Cynic philosophers, so that it is not surprising that even sayings of the latter ones were attributed to them.[68]

Later, in 11th-century Sufi hagiographies such as the *Ḥilyat al-awliyā'*, the compilers sometimes tried to revitalise the early protagonists of *zuhd* by adding miracles and saintly qualities to their biographies. Apparently several stories in the *Ḥilyat* were modeled upon biographical anecdotes about the Desert Fathers, which portray the pious men as almost saintly figures.

In the canonical *ḥadīth* collections compiled in the 9th century CE, such accounts originating from the AP or influenced by them are hard to find. This is due to the reservations that later *ḥadīth* scholars held towards the early ascetics and *quṣṣāṣ*, whose material they sometimes considered as unreliable. *Ḥadīth* scholars increasingly viewed critically the transmission of obviously Christian material, and in consequence they eliminated this narrative mate-

---

65   For more examples, see Pietruschka, "Apophthegmata Patrum." Thus far, I have been able to detect more than 30 stories in the *Ḥilyat al-awliyā'* and the *Qūt al-qulūb* that go back to AP material. Currently, I am preparing an in-depth study of the re-use of this material in Muslim collections.

66   Gramlich, *Alte Vorbilder*, 66, refers to a *K.al-Zuhd* that Malik had collected (as an *aide-mémoire*?) and which was apparently transmitted via Sayyār to Aḥmad b. Ḥanbal.

67   Christopher Melchert, *Ahmad ibn Hanbal* (Oxford: Oneworld Publications, 2006), 34.

68   On Cynic sayings in Arabic gnomologia and Sufi collections, see Oliver Overwien, *Die Sprüche des Kynikers Diogenes in der griechischen und arabischen Überlieferung* (Stuttgart: Steiner, 2005), 204–206.

rial from the canonical collections. The Sufis, who tried to align their lineage with the early ascetics, had less reservations concerning sayings of an allegedly Christian origin. Since Christian monks enjoyed wide acceptance among the Muslims, even in comparison with Muslim ascetics and mystics of the 9th and subsequent centuries, there was no obstacle for the *zuhhād* to rework texts of Christian origin for their own purposes and to disseminate them in sermons and through storytelling. Therefore we find more such Christian material in Sufi literature than in canonical *ḥadīth* collections, a subject which should be investigated further with regard to the tradition of the AP in Arabic. It becomes clear that narratives and motifs from the AP, now in a distinctly Islamic garb, had the same function as they did in their Christian context: to offer moral and religious instruction, and to strengthen faith and piety through edifying stories about holy men and women that remain popular to the present day.

Bibliography

Primary Sources

AP (PG) = *Apophthegmata Patrum*. PG 65 (1864), 71–440.

Budge, E.A. Wallis, ed. and transl. *The Book of Paradise, Being the Histories and Sayings of the Monks and Ascetics of the Egyptian Desert by Palladius, Hieronymus, and Others, According to the Recension of ʿAnan-ishoʿ of Beth ʿAbhe*. 2 Vols. London: Chatto & Windus, 1907.

Bustān al-Ruhbān li-Ābā al-kanīsa al-qibṭiyya. Ed. by the Metropolitanate of Beni Suef. Cairo, 1968, 2nd ed. 1976.

Dhahabī, al-. *Tāʾrīḫ al-Islām wa-wafayāt al-mashāhīr wa-l-aʿlām*. Ed. ʿUmar ʿAbd al-Salām Tadmurī. Beirut: Dār al-kitāb al-ʿarabī, 1987–2000.

Guy = *Les Apophtegmes des Pères: Collection systematique*. Vol. 1, *Chapitres I–IX*. Ed. and transl. Jean-Claude Guy. SChr 387. Paris: Cerf, 1993.

Heimgartner, Martin, ed. and transl. *Die Briefe 30–39 des ostsyrischen Patriarchen Timotheos I*. CSCO 661–662 / Syr. 256–257. Leuven: Peeters, 2016.

Ḥilya = Abū Nuʿaym al-Isfahānī. *Ḥilyat al-awliyāʾ wa-ṭabaqāt al-aṣfiyāʾ*. Vols. 2–3. Beirut: Dār al-kutub al-ʿilmiyya, 1987–1988.

Khoury, Raif Georges, ed. *Wahb b. Munabbih*. Vol. 1, *Der Heidelberger Papyrus PSR Heid Arab 23*. Wiesbaden: Harrassowitz, 1970.

Mansour, Jean. *Un florilège arabe chrétien du Xᵉ s. (Ms. Strasbourg 4225): Introduction et édition critique*. PhD diss., University of Strasbourg, 1972.

N = Nau, François. "Histoires des solitaires égyptiens (Ms. Coislin 126 fol. 158sqq.): Apophthègmes des saints vieillards." *Revue de l'Orient Chrétien* 12 (1907): 43–69, 171–

189, 393–413; 13 (1908) 47–66, 266–297; 14 (1909) 357–379; 17 (1912) 204–211, 294–301; 18 (1913) 137–146.

Sandūbī, Ḥasan al-. *Sharḥ Dīwān Imriʾ l-Qays*. Beirut: al-Maktaba al-thaqāfiyya, 1982.

Secondary Sources

Abbott, Nabia. *Studies in Arabic Literary Papyri*. Vol. 1, *Historical Texts*. Chicago: University of Chicago Press, 1957.

Armstrong, Lyall R. *The Quṣṣāṣ of Early Islam*. Leiden: Brill, 2017.

Athamina, Khalil. "Al-Qaṣaṣ: Its Emergence, Religious Origin and Its Socio-Political Impact on Early Muslim Society." *Studia Islamica* 76 (1992): 53–74.

Beck, Edmund. "Das christliche Mönchtum im Koran." *Studia Orientalia* 13 (1946): 3–29.

Buzi, Paola. "From Single-Text to Multiple-Text Manuscripts: Transmission Changes in the Coptic Literary Tradition: Some Case-Studies from the White Monastery Library." In *One-Volume Libraries: Composite and Multiple-Text Manuscripts*, ed. Michael Friedrich and Cosima Schwarke, 93–109. Berlin: de Gruyter, 2016.

Ess, Josef van. *Theologie und Gesellschaft im 2. und 3. Jahrhundert Hidschra*. 6 vols. Berlin: de Gruyter, 1991–1997.

Fowden, Elizabeth Key. "The Lamp and the Wine Flask: Early Muslim Interest in Christian Monasticism." In *Islamic Crosspollinations: Interactions in the Medieval Middle East*, ed. Anna Akasoy, J.E. Montgomery, and P.E. Pormann, 1–28. Cambridge: Gibb Memorial Trust, 2007.

Gramlich, Richard. *Alte Vorbilder des Sufitums. Erster Teil: Scheiche des Westens*. Wiesbaden: Harrassowitz, 1995.

Gramlich, Richard. *Weltverzicht: Grundlagen und Weisen islamischer Askese*. Wiesbaden: Harrassowitz, 1997.

Hämeen-Anttila, Jaakko. "Adab, a) Arabic, early developments." In *EI*[3] online (2007–2019). Accessed September 30, 2019.

Harmless, William. *Desert Christians: An Introduction to the Literature of Early Monasticism*. Oxford: Oxford University Press, 2004.

Holtzman, Livnat. "Aḥmad b. Hanbal." In *EI*[3] online (2007–2019). Accessed September 30, 2019.

Homerin, Th. Emil. "Ibn Taimīyā's al-Ṣūfiyah wa-al-Fuqarāʾ." *Arabica* 32 (1985): 219–244.

Jeremias, Joachim. *Unbekannte Jesusworte*. 4th ed. Gütersloh: Mohn, 1965.

Khalidi, Tarif. *The Muslim Jesus: Sayings and Stories in Islamic Literature*. Cambridge, MA: Harvard University Press, 2001.

Khoury, Raif Georges. "Importance et authenticité des textes de Ḥilyat al-awliyāʾ." *Studia Islamica* 46 (1977): 73–113.

Khoury, Raif Georges. "Wahb b. Munabbih." In *EI*[2], vol. 11 (2002), 34–36.

Kilpatrick, Hilary. "Adab." In *Encyclopedia of Arabic Literature*. Vol. 1. Ed. Julie Scott Meisami, 54–56. London: Routledge, 1998.

Köbert, Raimund. "Zur Ansicht des frühen Islam über das Mönchtum (*rahbānīya*)." *Orientalia*, N.S. 42 (1973): 520–524.

Köhler-Zülch, Ines. "Kristallisationsgestalten." In *Enzyklopädie des Märchens: Handwörterbuch zur historischen und vergleichenden Erzählforschung*. Vol. 8. Ed. Rolf W. Brednich et al., 459–466. Berlin: de Gruyter, 1996.

Livne-Kafri, Ofer. "Early Muslim Ascetics and the World of Christian Monasticism." *Jerusalem Studies in Arabic and Islam* 20 (1996): 105–129.

Marzolph, Ulrich. "Die Quelle der Ergötzlichen Erzählungen des Bar Hebräus." *OrChr* 69 (1985): 81–125.

Marzolph, Ulrich. *Arabia ridens: Die humoristische Kurzprosa der frühen adab-Literatur im internationalen Traditionsgeflecht*. Frankfurt am Main: Klostermann, 1992.

Marzolph, Ulrich. "'Focusees' of Jocular Fiction in Classical Arabic Literature." In *Story-Telling in the Framework of Non-Fictional Arabic Literature*, ed. Stefan Leder, 118–129. Wiesbaden: Harrassowitz, 1998.

McAuliffe, Jane D. *Qur'ānic Christians: An Analysis of Classical and Modern Exegesis*. Cambridge: University Press, 1991.

Melchert, Christopher. *Ahmad ibn Hanbal*. Oxford: Oneworld Publications, 2006.

Melchert, Christopher. "Abū Nuʿaym's Sources for *Ḥilyat al-awliyāʾ*, Sufi and Traditionist." In *Les maîtres soufis et leurs disciples: IIIe–Ve siècles de l'hégire (IXe–XIe s.); Enseignement, formation et transmission*, ed. Geneviève Gobillot and Jean-Jacques Thibon, 145–160. Beirut: Presses de l'Ifpo, 2012.

Melchert, Christopher. "Quotations of Extra-Qur'anic Scripture in Early Renunciant Literature." In *Islam and Globalisation: Historical and Contemporary Perspectives; Proceedings of the 25th Congress of L'Union Européenne des Arabisants et Islamisants*, ed. Agostino Cilardo, 97–107. Leuven: Peeters, 2013.

Mojaddedi, Jawid A. "Abu Nuʿaym al-Isfahani." In *Medieval Islamic Civilization: An Encyclopedia*. Vol. 1. Ed. Josef W. Meri, 401–402. New York: Routledge, 2006.

Monferrer-Sala, Juan. "'Varietas preislamica': Ka-ḥaṭṭi zabūrin fī maṣāḥifa ruhbāni (Imru' al-Qays, Diwan 88/1–2)." *Collectanea Christiana Orientalia* 3 (2006): 143–169.

Mourad, Suleiman A. "Christian Monks in Islamic Literature: A Preliminary Report on Some Arabic *Apophthegmata Patrum*." *Bulletin of the Royal Institute for Inter-Faith Studies* 6 (2004): 81–98.

Mourad, Suleiman A. *Early Islam between Myth and History: Al-Ḥasan al-Baṣrī (d. 110 H/ 728 CE) and the Formation of his Legacy in Classical Islamic Scholarship*. Leiden: Brill, 2006.

Neuwirth, Angelika. "Qur'ānic Readings of the Psalms." In *The Qur'ān in Context: Historical and Literary Investigations into the Qur'ānic Milieu*, ed. Angelika Neuwirth, Nicolai Sinai, and Michael Marx, 733–775. Leiden: Brill, 2011.

Noth, Albrecht. *The Early Arabic Historical Tradition: A Source-Critical Study*. 2nd ed. Princeton, NJ: Darwin Press, 1994.

Noth, Albrecht. "Common Features of Muslim and Western Ḥadīth Criticism: Ibn al-Jawzī's Categories of Ḥadīth Forgers," In *Ḥadīth: Origins and Developments*, ed. Harald Motzki, 309–316. Aldershot: Ashgate, 2004.

Overwien, Oliver. *Die Sprüche des Kynikers Diogenes in der griechischen und arabischen Überlieferung*. Stuttgart: Steiner, 2005.

Pellat, Charles. *Le milieu basrien et la formation de Ǧāḥiẓ*. Paris: Adrien-Maisonneuve, 1953.

Pellat, Charles. "Mālik b. Dīnār." In *EI*², vol. 6 (1991), 266b–267a.

Pellat, Charles, and Katherine H. Lang. "Basra until the Mongol Conquest." In *EI*³ online (2007–2019). Accessed September 30, 2019.

Pietruschka, Ute. "Der Mönch mit der Öllampe. Zu einem Motiv in der vorislamischen Poesie." In *Der Christliche Orient und seine Umwelt: Gesammelte Studien zu Ehren Jürgen Tubachs anläßlich seines 60. Geburtstages*, ed. Sophia G. Vashalomidze and Lutz Greisiger, 303–308. Wiesbaden: Harrassowitz, 2007.

Pietruschka, Ute. "Gnomologia: Syriac and Arabic Traditions." In *Encyclopedia of Mediterranean Humanism*, ed. H. Touati. 2014. Accessed September 30, 2019. http://www.encyclopedie-humanisme.com/?Gnomologia.

Pietruschka, Ute. "Apophthegmata Patrum in muslimischem Gewand: Das Beispiel Mālik ibn Dīnār." In *Begegnungen in Vergangenheit und Gegenwart: Beiträge dialogischer Existenz. Eine freundschaftliche Festgabe zum 60. Geburtstag von Martin Tamcke*, ed. Claudia Rammelt, C. Schlarb, and E. Schlarb, 160–171. Berlin: LIT, 2015.

Radtke, Bernd. *Materialien zur alten islamischen Frömmigkeit*. Leiden: Brill, 2009.

Ritter, Hellmut. "Studien zur Geschichte der islamischen Frömmigkeit." *Islam* 21 (1933): 1–83.

Rubenson, Samuel. "The Apophthegmata Patrum in Syriac, Arabic and Ethiopic: Status Questionis." *ParOr* 36 (2011): 305–313.

Schoeler, Gregor. *The Genesis of Literature in Islam: From the Aural to the Read*. Edinburgh: University Press, 2002.

Sezgin, Fuat. *Geschichte des arabischen Schrifttums*. Leiden: Brill, 1967–.

Tottoli, Roberto. "Origin and Use of the Term *Isrā'īliyyāt* in Muslim Literature." *Arabica* 46 (1999): 193–210.

Vajda, George. "Isrā'īliyyāt." In *EI*², vol. 4 (1978), 211b–212b.

Van Doorn-Harder, Pieternella. *Contemporary Coptic Nuns*. Columbia: University of South Carolina Press, 1995.

Ward, Benedicta, transl. *The Sayings of the Desert Fathers: The Alphabetical Collection*. London: Mowbrays, 1975.

Warnach, Viktor. *Agape: Die Liebe als Grundmotiv der neutestamentlichen Theologie*. Düsseldorf: Patmos-Verlag, 1951.

Weipert, Reinhard. "Al-Aṣmāʿī." In *EI*³ online (2007–2019). Accessed September 30, 2019.

PART 3

Wisdom in Transition: Hellenic, Jewish, Christian and Islamic Worlds

∴

CHAPTER 9

"Wise Elders" and "Nursing Infants": Wisdom Extended to the Gentiles in the Pseudo-Clementine *Homilies*

Karin Hedner Zetterholm

This study explores how the early fourth-century Pseudo-Clementine *Homilies* see wisdom, once considered a prerogative of Jews only, as being extended to gentiles who adhere to the teachings of Jesus. This idea is in line with the *Homilies*' notion that there are two parallel paths to salvation, one through Moses and another through Jesus, and that worshippers of the one God are made up of two distinct, yet united groups of people, Jews and Jesus-oriented gentiles.[1] Wisdom as understood by the *Homilies* is the knowledge to correctly interpret Scripture, which in the view of the author(s) or redactor(s)[2] is a necessary prerequisite for obtaining salvation.

Traditionally considered to contain "Jewish Christian" traditions, the *Homilies* advocate worship of the one God alone, trust in the Prophet of truth, and baptism for the remission of sins. In addition, these homilies attributed to Peter prescribe the observance of a number of ritual laws, such as abstinence from food offered to idols (εἰδωλοθύτων), the prohibition to consume blood and meat from animals not properly slaughtered, the requirement to wash after intercourse, and abstinence from sexual relations during a woman's menses (*Hom.* 7.8.1–2). While earlier scholarship understood these commandments as constituting a common practice of a separate group of "Jewish Christians," whether Jewish or gentile in origin, some scholars have recently recognized that the *Homilies* address these admonitions exclusively to non-Jews,[3] and accordingly

---

1 The *Homilies* do not use the word "Christian," and in this essay I will use the terms "Jesus-oriented" in order to avoid the implication that adherence to Jesus and Jewishness were mutually exclusive.
2 For the sake of simplicity, I will henceforth refer to the author(s)/redactor(s) as "the author," although the text is made up of many different sources and may have undergone several redactions.
3 Annette Yoshiko Reed, "'Jewish Christianity' after the 'Parting of the Ways': Approaches to Historiography and Self-Definition in the Pseudo-Clementines," in *The Ways That Never Parted: Jews and Christians in Late Antiquity and the Early Middle Ages*, ed. Adam H. Becker and Annette Yoshiko Reed (Minneapolis: Fortress Press, 2007), 213–217; Holger M. Zellentin, *The*

the text should probably be understood not as prescriptions for a uniform "Christian" group, but rather as requirements for gentile adherents of Jesus specifically.[4]

The *Homilies* were probably written in Antioch, or possibly in Edessa, and are considered a reworking of a no longer extant third-century source, commonly known as the *Grundschrift*.[5] Composed in the form of a Hellenistic novel, the text tells the story of the early mission to the gentiles (ἔθνη), with the Jewish Peter and the gentile Clement of Rome as the main characters.[6] Together they travel from Caesarea to Antioch, and on the way Peter gives sermons to the gentile inhabitants of the cities along the coast. A major concern of his homilies is to make the *ethnē* abandon their worship of many gods and instead embrace *theosebeia* or *thrēskeia*, defined as worship of the one God and observance of his law (*Hom.* 7.8; 13.4). Jesus, portrayed as "the Prophet of truth" (ἀληθείας προφήτῃ) and at times as a teacher (διδάσκαλος), appears in a few homilies[7] and is presented primarily as the teacher for non-Jews. Integral to the plot are numerous disputations between Peter and Simon Magus (cf. Acts 8:9–24), a character who represents a range of ideas that the *Homilies* find objectionable, such as Marcionite beliefs, Samaritan anti-Judaism, Alexandrian philosophy, and Egyptian magic (e.g., *Hom.* 2.22–26). Overall, the *Homilies* promote adherence to the one God, prophecy as opposed to philosophy as the

---

Qur'an's Legal Culture: The Didascalia Apostolorum as a Point of Departure (Tübingen: Mohr Siebeck, 2013), 95.

4   Karin Hedner Zetterholm, "Jewish Teachings for Gentiles in the Pseudo-Clementine *Homilies*: A Jewish Reception of Ideas in Paul and Acts Shaped by a Jewish Milieu?" *Journal of the Jesus Movement in Its Jewish Setting* 6 (2019): 68–87.

5   The *Homilies* together with the *Recognitions*, dated to the mid-fourth century, make up the two main texts of the Pseudo-Clementine literature. They share a considerable amount of material and are considered to be independent reworkings of the *Grundschrift*. For their complex literary history, see the survey in F. Stanley Jones, *Pseudoclementina Elchasaiticaque inter Judaeochristiana: Collected Studies* (Leuven: Peeters, 2012), 50–113, originally published in *Second Century* 2 (1982): 1–33, 63–96. For provenance, translations, sources and ancient witnesses, see Jan N. Bremmer, "Pseudo-Clementines: Texts, Dates, Places, Authors and Magic," in *The Pseudo-Clementines*, ed. Jan N. Bremmer (Leuven: Peeters, 2010), 1–23; Jones, *Pseudoclementina*, 8–49; Graham Stanton, "Jewish Christian Elements in the Pseudo-Clementine Writings," in *Jewish Believers in Jesus: The Early Centuries*, ed. Oskar Skarsaune and Reidar Hvalvik (Peabody, MA: Hendrickson, 2007), 305–315. The *Homilies* are also known as the *Klementia*; see Patricia A. Duncan, *Novel Hermeneutics in the Greek Pseudo-Clementine Romance* (Tübingen: Mohr Siebeck, 2017), 2–6, who favors this name over *Homilies*.

6   A convenient summary of the complicated plot is found in Duncan, *Novel Hermeneutics*, 19–23.

7   The discussions of the Prophet of truth appear mainly in *Hom.* 2–3 and 8. Brief references to Jesus as teacher are scattered throughout the work.

source of reliable knowledge, and the law of God over against polytheism and Hellenistic philosophy.[8]

In the worldview of the *Homilies*, the worshippers of the one God, called *theosebeis* by the author, are made up of Jews and of gentiles who adhere to Jesus. Those from the *ethnē* who abandon worship of many gods are included among the *theosebeis* through immersion (baptism), an initiation rite that cleanses them from the pollution of idolatry and gives them a new nature that enables them to keep the law of God (*Hom.* 7.8.1; 9.23.2; 13.4.3). They do not become Jews, however, as indicated by the fact that male converts are not circumcised and that they are bound only by the commandments that the Hebrew Bible prescribes for non-Israelites living among Israelites, as outlined in Leviticus 17–18 and summarized in the Decree of the Apostles (Acts 15:21.29; *Hom.* 7.8.1–2). Provided they keep these commandments, they achieve the same status in the eyes of God as Torah-observant Jews and become "heirs of eternal blessings" (*Hom.* 9.23), "sons of God," and "heirs of the eternal kingdom" (*Hom.* 10.25). Jews and baptized gentiles are united in their belief in the one God, but the two groups remain distinct.[9]

Interestingly, the *Homilies* do not use the word "Christian" (Χριστιανός). The term used to refer to worshippers of the one God (Jews, whether Jesus-oriented or not, and baptized gentiles) is *theosebeis*, indicating that adherence to the one God is the author's main focus, rather than adherence to Jesus. As suggested by Patricia Duncan, this terminological choice may reflect a deliberate protest against the separation of Jesus-followers from Jews and Judaism, as promoted within some more mainstream Christian groups.[10] The term *theosebēs* seems to have signalled a Jewish identity or connection, as evidenced in gravestones and inscriptions from the second century,[11] and it is possible that in choosing this term the author of the *Homilies* indicates his view that gentile *theosebeis* are

---

8   See Annette Yoshiko Reed, "'Jewish Christianity' as Counter-History? The Apostolic Past in Eusebius' *Ecclesiastical History* and the Pseudo-Clementine *Homilies*," in *Antiquity in Antiquity: Jewish and Christian Pasts in the Greco-Roman World*, ed. Gregg Gardner and Kevin L. Osterloh (Tübingen: Mohr Siebeck, 2008), 203; Annette Yoshiko Reed, "When Did Rabbis Become Pharisees? Reflections on Christian Evidence for Post-70 Judaism," in *Envisioning Judaism: Studies in Honor of Peter Schäfer on the Occasion of his Seventieth Birthday*, ed. Ra'anan S. Boustan et al. (Tübingen: Mohr Siebeck, 2013), 892.
9   On these ideas, see Zetterholm, "Jewish Teachings for Gentiles," 72–79.
10 Duncan, *Novel Hermeneutics*, 18.
11 Jones, *Pseudoclementina*, 151; Judith M. Lieu, "The Race of the God-Fearers," *JTS* 46 (1995): 483–501. Lieu writes: "Whereas pagan inscriptions are apt to celebrate their honorand as 'pious' (εὐσεβής), the claim that he or she was θεοσεβής seems to have been monopolized by the Jews" (p. 493).

united with Jews and Judaism.[12] Adherence to the one God and his law, alongside the teachings of Jesus, constitutes in the mind of the *Homilies'* author a kind of Judaism for gentiles.

1   Wise Jews and Infant Gentiles

This idea is most explicitly expressed in the claim that there are two parallel paths to salvation, one for Jews through Moses and another one for gentiles through Jesus. This is a rather exceptional stance and the *Homilies* deviate from most contemporaneous Christian texts in seeing Jesus as supplementing rather than superseding Moses. It is in this context that the author develops his idea of wisdom as being revealed to gentiles:

> For on this account Jesus is concealed from the Hebrews, who have taken Moses as their teacher, and Moses is hidden from those who have put their trust in Jesus. For, there being one teaching by both, God accepts him who has believed either of these. But believing a teacher is for the sake of doing the things spoken by God. And that this is so our Lord Himself says, "I thank you, Father of heaven and earth, because you have concealed these things from the wise elders [σοφῶν πρεσβυτέρων], and have revealed them to nursing infants [νηπίοις θηλάζουσιν]."[13] Thus, God himself has concealed a teacher [διδάσκαλον] from some because they know what it is necessary to do, and has revealed him to others, who are ignorant what they ought to do.
>
> *Hom.* 8.6.1–4[14]

This passage identifies "the wise elders" as the Hebrews/Jews who have Moses as their teacher, and a few lines further on, "the nursing infants" are defined as

---

12   For the *Homilies'* view that Jesus' teachings for gentiles stand in continuity with Judaism, see Annette Yoshiko Reed, "From Judaism and Hellenism to Christianity and Paganism," in *Nouvelles intrigues pseudo-clémentines. Plots in the Pseudo-Clementine Romance: Actes du deuxième colloque international sur la littérature apocryphe chrétienne, Lausanne-Genève, 30 aout–2 septembre 2006*, ed. Frédéric Amsler et al. (Prahins: Éditions du Zèbre, 2008), 425–435.

13   Matt 11:25, Luke 10:21.

14   Citations are from Bernhard Rehm's critical edition, updated by Georg Strecker, *Die Pseudoklementinen*, vol. 1, *Homilien*, 3rd ed. (Berlin: Akademie Verlag, 1992); translations are adapted from Thomas Smith, Peter Peterson, and James Donaldson, transl., *The Clementine Homilies and the Apostolic Constitutions*, ANF 17 (Edinburgh, 1870).

the nations/gentiles (ἐθνῶν) who are lacking a teacher (see below).[15] The Jesus saying, "I thank you, Father, Lord of heaven and earth, because you have hidden these things from the wise (σοφῶν) and the intelligent (συνετῶν) and have revealed them to infants" from Matt 11:25/Luke 10:21 draws on motifs within Jewish wisdom tradition according to which wisdom opens "the mouths of the mute" and makes "the tongues of infants [γλώσσας νηπίων] speak clearly" (Wis 10:21). More specifically, it echoes Isaiah 29:14 in the LXX, where the words *sofos* (wise) and *synetos* (intelligent) likewise appear together. Here, God complains that prophecy has been to his people "like the words of a sealed document," and because they have honoured him with their lips only and not with their hearts he threatens to "destroy the wisdom of the wise" and "hide the understanding of the intelligent." In the *Homilies*, by contrast, there is no punitive aspect in God's hiding of wisdom from the wise, and unlike some of the sayings from the wisdom tradition, which imply that the wise are wise only in their own eyes (e.g., Isa 5:21), or pride themselves of being the custodians of God's law while failing to live in accordance with it (e.g., Jer 8:8–9), the *Homilies* do not criticize the wise.[16] On the contrary, God has concealed a teacher (Jesus) from "the wise elders" (the Jews/Hebrews) precisely because they already know "what it is necessary to do" since they have Moses as their teacher, and instead revealed Jesus to "nursing infants" (the gentiles) who do not know what to do and hence need a teacher.[17] Since this is an act of divine concealment, the Hebrews are not to be faulted for it. Similarly, the gentiles are not condemned for not having accepted Moses as their teacher:

> Neither, therefore, are the Hebrews condemned on account of their ignorance of Jesus, by reason of him who has concealed him, if, doing the things [commanded] by Moses, they do not hate him whom they do not know. Neither are those from among the gentiles [ἐθνῶν] condemned, who know not Moses on account of him who has concealed him, pro-

---

15 The word συνετῶν (intelligent) in Matt 11:25 and Luke 10:21 has been replaced by πρεσβυτέρων (elders), and the conjunction "and" removed, so that "the wise and intelligent" have become a single group of "wise elders." Similarly, the contrasting group of νήπιοι (infants) has been made to match the first group by the addition of the attributive participle θηλάζουσιν (nursing); see Duncan, *Novel Hermeneutics*, 108.
16 By contrast, there is a hint of criticism of "the people of the Hebrews" in the parallel version in *Recognitions* 4.5. Although "instructed out of the law," they failed to recognize God's revelation in Jesus, whereas "the people of the gentiles," having none of the learning of the Hebrews, embraced Jesus, "on which account they too will be saved."
17 Cf. Duncan, *Novel Hermeneutics*, 109.

vided that these also, doing the things spoken by Jesus, do not hate him whom they do not know.
>
> *Hom.* 8.7.1–2

Each group has its own teacher, and as long as Moses' followers respect Jesus' followers and vice versa, there is no need for either group to adopt the teacher of the other, even though the ideal is to recognize both teachers (*Hom.* 8.7.6).[18]

2   The Nature of the Wisdom Extended to the Gentiles

As the instruction of Peter unfolds, it becomes clear that the Jews are wise because they possess the hermeneutical key to Scripture, defined as the oral tradition transmitted from Moses. The significance of such a key becomes evident when we consider the *Homilies*' view of Scripture. The problem with the written version of God's revelation, according to the author of the *Homilies*, is that it contains false pericopes that were never meant to be part of God's law. These spurious passages were not part of the original revelation given orally to Moses (*Hom.* 3.47.1) but crept in later when the law was written down.[19] As a result, Scripture contains "certain falsehoods contrary to the law of God" (*Hom.* 2.38.2).[20] To these false interpolations belong scriptural passages that seem to imply that there are many gods, that God is not perfect, omniscient and good, as well as verses that ascribe imperfections to key biblical figures such as Adam,

---

18 On this passage, see Reed, "Jewish Christianity," 213–217; Duncan, *Novel Hermeneutics*, 108–109; Kelley Coblentz Bautch, "Obscured by the Scriptures, Revealed by the Prophets: God in the Pseudo-Clementine *Homilies*," in *Histories of the Hidden God: Concealment and Revelation in Western Gnostic, Esoteric, and Mystical Traditions*, ed. April D. DeConick and Grant Adamson (Durham: Acumen, 2013), 128.

19 According to the *Homilies*, the Pentateuch was written down after the time of Moses by people who were not prophets (*Hom.* 3.47). The *Homilies*' reservation toward writing and their preference for orally transmitted teachings was shared by many contemporary Christians as well as by rabbinic Jews; see Bautch, "Obscured," 125. Cf. *y. Pe'ah* 2:6 that states explicitly that "[T]hings derived from what is oral are preferred over things derived from what is written."

20 On this idea, known as the theory of the false pericopes, see Donald H. Carlson, *Jewish-Christian Interpretation of the Pentateuch in the Pseudo-Clementine Homilies* (Minneapolis: Fortress Press, 2013), 51–75; Karl E. Shuve, "The Doctrine of the False Pericopes and Other Late Antique Approaches to the Problem of Scripture's Unity," in *Nouvelles intrigues*, ed. Amsler et al., 437–445. Strecker considered the idea of the false pericopes to be part of the *Grundschrift*, but much recent scholarship attributes it to the *Homilies*; see Jones, *Pseudoclementina*, 168–169.

Abraham, Jacob and Moses (e.g., *Hom.* 2.38–48; 16.6–14; 18.19). Such passages easily mislead people who are not familiar with "the mystery of scriptures" [τὸ μυστήριον τῶν γραφῶν], as Peter explains (*Hom.* 2.40.4). Pagans, for instance, who believe in many gods are particularly predisposed to misunderstanding it (*Hom.* 3.4.1). Thus, Scripture is a source of divine truth but only if it is interpreted by someone who has access to its original form, as it was given "with the explanations" [σὺν ταῖς ἐπιλύσεσιν] to Moses and transmitted by his followers (*Hom.* 2.38.1).[21] This means that until the coming of Jesus, the only ones possessing the knowledge to properly interpret Scripture were the Jews who, as Peter explains, received from their forefathers "the worship of the God who made all things, and the mystery [μυστήριον] of the books which are able to deceive" (*Hom.* 3.4.1).[22] The immense importance of proper interpretation of Scripture is clear from Peter's statement that "every man who wishes to be saved must become, as the Teacher [Jesus] said, a judge of the books written to try us" (*Hom.* 18.20.4).

In a private conversation with his followers, Peter explains that Scripture itself indicates that a prophetic source outside of it must be consulted in order to properly understand it, and then goes on to outline the two ways in which one may gain access to prophetic teachings. One is through the Prophet of truth, of whom Jesus is the most recent incarnation, and the other is through the scribes and Pharisees and their rabbinic successors. Expounding the verse, "Ask your father, and he will inform you; your elders, and they will tell you" (Deut 32:7), he says:

> This father and these elders ought to be inquired of. But you have not inquired whose is the time of the kingdom and whose is the seat of prophecy [προφητείας καθέδρα], even though he himself [Jesus] points this out, saying "The scribes and the Pharisees sit in the seat of Moses [καθέδρας Μωϋσέως]; all things that they say to you, hear them" [cf. Matt 23:2–3]. "Hear them," he said, as entrusted with the key to the kingdom [τὴν κλεῖδα τῆς βασιλείας], which is knowledge [γνῶσις], which alone can open the gate of life, through which alone is the entrance to eternal

---

21   Shuve, "Doctrine," 439–440.
22   Cf. *Hom.* 16.14.4–5: "Moreover, being furnished by our ancestors with the truths of the scriptures, we [Jews] know that there is only one who has made the heavens and the earth, the God of the Jews and of all those who worship him. Our fathers, with pious thought, setting down a fixed belief in him as the true God, handed down this belief to us, that we may know that if anything is said against God, it is a falsehood." On the importance of oral tradition as a hermeneutical key to Scripture and the similarity with rabbinic Judaism, see Carlson, *Jewish-Christian Interpretation*, 111–115.

life. "But truly," he says, "they possess the key, but those wishing to enter they do not let them do so." On this account, I say, he himself, rising from his seat as a father for his children, proclaiming the things which from the beginning were transmitted in secret to the worthy, extending mercy even to the gentiles, and having compassion for the souls of all, neglected his own blood.[23]

> Hom. 3.18.2–19.1

Peter urges his audience to turn to their "father," namely to the Prophet of truth who appears in various guises throughout the ages, and of whom Jesus is the most recent incarnation,[24] or to inquire of their "elders," the scribes and Pharisees who are entrusted with "the key to the kingdom" and whose authority the Prophet of truth himself affirmed. These two sources both provide access to the prophetic teachings necessary to secure a correct understanding of Scripture. As argued by Annette Yoshiko Reed, the author of the *Homilies* seems to have seen the scribes and Pharisees of the Gospels as rabbinic Jews of his own time, as suggested by the distinctly rabbinic traits that the *Homilies* associate with Pharisaic oral tradition.[25] According to Peter's exposition of Deut 32:7, then, both Jesus (the Prophet of truth) and the Pharisees and their rabbinic successors (the elders) are repositories of prophecy; Jesus as the most recent incarnation of the Prophet of truth, and the rabbinic heirs of the scribes and Pharisees by virtue of being connected to "the seat of Prophecy" through an unbroken line of succession from Moses, an earlier incarnation of the Prophet of truth. In line with the two equivalent ways to salvation

---

23   This is the *Homilies*' only reference to Jesus' blood and it seems to be used in a genealogical sense to affirm his place within the Jewish people rather than denoting his suffering and death; see Annette Yoshiko Reed and Ra'anan S. Boustan, "Blood and Atonement in the Pseudo-Clementines and the Story of the Ten Martyrs: The Problem of Selectivity in the Study of 'Judaism' and 'Christianity,'" *Henoch* 30 (2008): 344; Duncan, *Novel Hermeneutics*, 9.

24   On the idea in the *Homilies* that the Prophet of truth appears in various guises throughout the ages, and that Adam, Moses and Jesus are all incarnations, see Han J.W. Drijvers, "Adam and the True Prophet in the Pseudo-Clementines," in *History and Religion in Late Antique Syria*, ed. Han J.W. Drijvers (Aldershot: Variorum, 1994), 314–323.

25   For instance, the *Homilies* describe the explanations of the Torah as having been revealed orally alongside Scripture and as having been transmitted to seventy wise men (*Hom.* 2.38.1; 3.47.1) in a way that closely resembles *m. Avot* 1–5 (cf. *Sifre* Deut § 351; *y. Meg.* 4:1; *y. Pe'ah* 2:6); see Reed, "When Did Rabbis," 888–891. Overall, the *Homilies*' portrait of the Pharisees is much more positive than Matthew's, emphasizing among other things that Jesus' critique was directed only at some of them (11.29.1) and that they knew "the true things of the law" (3.51.1).

outlined in *Hom.* 8:5–7, one through Moses and another through Jesus, the author of the *Homilies* sees prophetic teachings emanating from "the seat of prophecy" (3.18.1) as being transmitted through two parallel lines, one through the Pharisees and rabbinic Jews sitting in "the seat of Moses" [καθέδρας Μωϋσέως], and one through Peter's bishops on "the throne of Christ" [θρόνον οὖν Χριστοῦ] (*Hom.* 3.70.2, cf. 3.60.1).[26] Because some individual scribes and Pharisees/Jews did not share their knowledge of the kingdom with those seeking it, and because people did not seek their advice, God deemed it necessary to send another teacher and prophet—Jesus—who would extend to the gentiles the teachings that were previously reserved for Jews. The "seat of Moses" remains a source of prophetic knowledge in spite of the shortcomings of some of its individual occupants.

The teachings of Jesus, the Prophet of truth, are now added as another source of prophetic truth, providing baptized gentiles with a hermeneutical key to Scripture equal to the teachings passed on from Moses. As Peter explains: "[B]elieving his teaching, you will know what of the Scriptures are true and what are false" (*Hom.* 3.49.2).[27] Jesus did not come to abolish the law, Peter emphasizes quoting Matt 5:17–18, but to disclose and excise the false passages (*Hom.* 3.51.2–3), thus restoring God's revelation to its original uncorrupted form. As proof, he invokes Jesus' saying in Matt 15:13: "Every plant which the heavenly father has not planted will be rooted up" (*Hom.* 3.52.1–2), thus transforming its meaning. The phrase with which the Matthean Jesus rejects the *oral* "tradition of the elders" is now applied to passages of the *written* Torah to demonstrate that the false passages found there will not endure. Peter then goes on to demonstrate how Jesus' teachings function as a corrective to Scripture (*Hom.* 3.55–57). For instance, the impression that God is not omniscient, which one might get from reading certain passages of Scripture, is refuted by Jesus' words: "[F]or your heavenly father knows what you need before you ask him" (Matt 6:8), and "Pray in secret, and your father, who sees all things, will reward you" (Matt 6:6). Similarly, any doubts as to the goodness of God, the creator of heaven and earth, is dispelled by Jesus' words: "If you then, who are evil, know how to give good gifts to your children, how much more will your Father in heaven give good things to those who ask him!" (Matt 7:11).[28] Thus, Jesus' teachings about God restore the Torah to its original

---

26 On the two parallel lines emanating from "the seat of prophecy" and the two chairs of teaching, see Reed, "Counter-History," 191–193; Reed, "When Did Rabbis," 887–888; Duncan, *Novel Hermeneutics*, 72–73, 82–83.
27 Cf. *Hom.* 16.14.3: "Obeying Christ, we learn to know what is false from the scriptures."
28 For more detailed analyses of the teachings of Jesus as a guide to a correct understanding

uncorrupted form, and accordingly reading Scripture in light of his teachings will expose the false pericopes and guide the reader to its true meaning. For the author of the *Homilies*, it is Jesus' role as a teacher that is important. He shows very little interest in Jesus' life and attributes no soteriological significance to his death and resurrection.[29] It is his teachings that save, and they do so because they lead to a correct understanding of Scripture and hence of God.

Admittedly, the *Homilies* do voice some criticism of non-Jesus-oriented Jews in a second passage where the quote about God concealing from "the wise elders" what he has revealed to "nursing infants" appears. It stands somewhat in tension with the passage in *Hom.* 8.6, but even so the portrait of the scribes and Pharisees is considerably less negative than in the gospels. Here also, the wise are implicitly identified as the scribes and Pharisees through the statement that they possess "the key of the kingdom of heaven" (κλεὶς τῆς βασιλείας τῶν οὐρανῶν), defined as "the knowledge of the secrets" (γνῶσις τῶν ἀπορρήτων), but are accused of keeping it to themselves (cf. Matt 23:13, Luke 11:52).[30] Because they did not share their knowledge of the kingdom, God now conceals from them "the things that belong to the kingdom" in a measure-for-measure punishment (*Hom.* 18.15.7–16.3). However, in line with the *Homilies*' general tendency to accommodate non-Jesus-oriented Jews, the author hastens to add some mitigating circumstances. Although "the things that belong to the kingdom" are hidden from the Pharisees and their present-day rabbinic successors, they are said to be "wise in other matters" (18.16.4), and above all they are still in possession of "the way that leads to the kingdom." A more precise description of the things of the kingdom that God conceals from them is not given, but the way that leads to the kingdom is defined as "a way of life" (πολιτεία) governed by the law prescribed by Moses (Deut 30:15–16) and which Jesus affirmed, saying, "If you wish to enter into life, keep the commandments" (*Hom.* 18.17.1–4; cf. Matt 19:17, Luke 18:18).[31] Thus, although the author of the *Homilies* criticizes contemporary non-Jesus-oriented Jews for not sharing their knowledge of the

---

of Scripture, see Carlson, *Jewish-Christian Interpretation*, 88–105; Duncan, *Novel Hermeneutics*, 90–92.

29 Cf. Reed and Boustan, "Blood and Atonement," 344.
30 The next passage (*Hom.* 18.17.1) implies that "the wise" are to be understood as "the sons of Israel" more broadly, and thus conforms to the understanding of the wise as Jews in *Hom.* 8.6. The fact that the *Homilies* here use "the sons of Israel" as a synonym for "the scribes and Pharisees" provides further support for Reed's claim that the author identified the Pharisees with the rabbinic Jews of his own time.
31 Duncan, *Novel Hermeneutics*, 168–170.

kingdom of heaven with others (presumably including gentiles), and states that as a result they are punished by not being able to recognize "the things of the kingdom" (whatever this may mean precisely), he is also careful to say that the path to the kingdom remains open to them.

In sum, the two equivalent paths to salvation laid out in *Hom.* 8.5–7 are matched by two parallel hermeneutical keys to Scripture, the teachings of Jesus as transmitted via Peter and his followers on the one hand, and the oral interpretive tradition transmitted from Moses to (rabbinic) Jews via the biblical elders and Pharisees, on the other. Thus, what is extended to the gentiles through Jesus' teachings is the ability to understand Scripture, enabling them to be saved. Being in possession of God's law is necessary but not sufficient. One must also have the hermeneutical key to properly interpret it. The wise are those who possess such a key, and accordingly the Jews who are in possession of the interpretive tradition handed down from Moses remain wise, while wisdom is extended also to the gentiles who receive their own hermeneutical key through the teachings of Jesus. Thus, in the end, both Jews and gentiles are granted the tools necessary to acquire knowledge of God. Wisdom is not taken away from the wise (the Jews) but simply extended to the infants (the Jesus-oriented gentiles), making them also wise.

3   A Shared Space for Jews and Jesus-Oriented Gentiles?

An intriguing question is what kind of social milieu could have prompted the emergence of an ideology according to which the key to salvation is extended to gentiles who adhere to Jesus, but not taken away from Jews who do not accept Jesus as their teacher or Messiah. As noted above, this position is quite different from most contemporary Christian authorities.[32] A theology inclusive of non-Jesus-oriented Jews seems, as Joel Marcus has remarked, likely "to arise in situations in which there is a substantial presence of non-Christian Jews and/or Jewish Christians."[33] Indeed, the Homilies' familiarity with specific rabbinic ideas and his sympathy for contemporary non-Jesus-oriented Jews have

---

32   Cf., e.g., Ignatius, Tertullian, Eusebius, and Chrysostom.
33   Joel Marcus, "Israel and the Church in the Exegetical Writings of Hippolytus," *Journal of Biblical Literature* 130 (2011): 389. See also Timothy J. Horner, who says of the Protoevangelium of James that it "would have been understood—perhaps only fully understood—within a community that was familiar with concerns and images of contemporary Judaism" ("Jewish Aspects of the Protoevangelium of James," *JECS* 12 (2004): 317).

led scholars to posit close contacts with rabbinic Jews. In the words of Albert Baumgarten: "There can be no doubt that we are dealing with two groups in close proximity that maintained intellectual contact with each other."[34]

While we tend to envision groups and communities through the lens of our own time and thus imagine them as separate entities with clearly defined religious identities, we should perhaps not rule out the possibility that Jewish and gentile followers of Jesus, of the kind we encounter in the *Homilies*, had remained a subgroup within the Jewish community even as other Jesus-believing groups had left it.[35] For instance, inscriptions from Aphrodisias and Sardis show that as late as the fourth century there were groups of people called *theosebeis* who were associated with the synagogue. Although we cannot know for certain, some of these *theosebeis* may have been Jesus-believers, as some scholars have suggested.[36] Moreover, objects found in an excavation of a row of shops, located next to the synagogue in ancient Sardis, may point to a close relationship between Jesus-believers and the synagogue. One of the shops, identified as Christian because a bronze lamp decorated with a cross was found there, shared a wall with the synagogue and was surrounded by shops and residences identified as Jewish. In another shop, excavators found two marble fragments incised with menorahs and a weighing device decorated with a cross. Although the owners of these shops could have been Jesus-oriented Jews, it has been argued that a more plausible scenario is that they were Jesus-oriented gentiles. If so, it would seem to point to a significant integration of

---

34 Albert I. Baumgarten, "Literary Evidence for Jewish Christianity in the Galilee," in *The Galilee in Late Antiquity*, ed. Lee I. Levine (New York: Jewish Theological Seminary of America, 1992), 47. See also Reed, "From Judaism and Hellenism," 432.

35 Although one should be wary of automatically assuming the existence of a group behind a text, we may note that the author of the third-century *Didascalia Apostolorum* polemicizes precisely against those ritual practices that the *Homilies* prescribe for gentiles, a fact that increases the likelihood that such rituals were actually practiced; see Zellentin, *Qur'an's Legal Culture*, 95–96.

36 The Aphrodisias inscriptions have recently been re-dated to the fourth or even fifth century and are considered by Lee I. Levine as "conclusive evidence of a group of pagan (or possibly, in part, Christian) God-fearers of high rank and significant number who were publicly and actively associated with the local Jewish community" (*Visual Judaism in Late Antiquity: Historical Contexts of Jewish Art* (New Haven: Yale University Press, 2012), 195). Paula Fredriksen likewise suggests that some of these *theosebeis* may have been Christian; see her *Paul: the Pagans' Apostle* (New Haven: Yale University Press, 2017), 205. On the Sardis inscriptions, see Richard Last, "The Other Synagogues," *Journal for the Study of Judaism* 47 (2016): 353. He does not suggest that some of these *theosebeis* may have been Jesus-believers, but it remains a possibility.

Jesus-oriented gentiles with the Jewish residents of Sardis, and could possibly indicate involvement in the synagogue right next to their shops.[37]

In light of this evidence, we should not rule out the possibility that the *Homilies*' "*ekklēsia* of Christ," if it represented any kind of historical reality, had remained a subgroup within the Jewish community, or closely associated with it. Although "the assemblies of Christ" that Peter is said to have founded are portrayed as having a leadership of their own, consisting of bishops, presbyters/elders and deacons (3.67.1), indicating a level of institutional independence, the call to honour "the seat of Moses" along with "the throne of Christ" (3.70.2; cf. 3.60.1) at the same time seems to indicate deference to a (non-Jesus-oriented) Jewish leadership.[38] Thus, it appears that the author of the *Homilies* at least envisioned his assembly of Christ as closely attached to the broader community of Jews.

Another kind of space where Jesus-oriented Jews and gentiles could have co-existed closely with non-Jesus-oriented Jews were neighbourhood associations and trade guilds. Life in Greco-Roman society was organized around voluntary associations of different types, of which synagogues devoted to the cult of the God of Israel were only one kind. Voluntary associations drew membership from a variety of networks based on household connections, a common trade or profession (trade guilds), residence in the same neighbourhood (neighbourhood associations), ethnic identity or origin from the same geographical area, or the cult of a certain deity.[39] People were often members of multiple associations,[40] creating a wide network of contacts across ethnic and cultic boundaries. Thus, Jewish neighbourhood associations and professional guilds may have been additional spaces where Jesus-oriented Jews (and possibly gentiles) interacted with non-Jesus-oriented Jews within the same institution. This means that even if the *Homilies*' assemblies of Christ were independent associations with their own leadership, their members may at the same

---

37 See Keir E. Hammer and Michele Murray, "Acquaintances, Supporters, and Competitors: Evidence of Inter-Connectedness and Rivalry among the Religious Groups in Sardis," in *Religious Rivalries and the Struggle for Success in Sardis and Smyrna*, ed. Richard S. Ascough (Waterloo: Wilfrid Laurier University Press, 2005), 175–194.

38 Anders Runesson, "Jewish and Christian Interaction from the First to the Fifth Centuries," in *The Early Christian World*, ed. P.F. Esler (London: Routledge, 2017), 259, notes that institutional separation, "although a 'parting' of sorts, is not an indicator of the creation of separate 'religious' identities ('Jews' and 'Christians')."

39 See Philip A. Harland, *Associations, Synagogues, and Congregations: Claiming a Place in Ancient Mediterranean Society* (Minneapolis: Fortress Press, 2003), 28–52.

40 Harland, *Associations*, 38. Jews and Christians would have been no different; see pp. 184 and 206.

time have been affiliates of associations with a strong presence of non-Jesus-oriented Jews, such as synagogues and Jewish neighbourhood associations or trade guilds.

As pointed out by Annette Reed, the concern of the *Homilies*' author to portray Jesus' teachings for gentiles as being in continuity with Moses' teachings for Jews could be understood as part of an effort to counteract the separation of Jesus-adherents from Jews and Judaism that was increasingly becoming the norm in many contemporary Christian groups;[41] and his respect for the leadership of non-Jesus-oriented Jews, including acceptance of rabbinic claims to authority, may reflect a wish to convince non-Jesus-oriented Jews that, contrary to the supersessionist claims of other Christian groups, his gentile *theosebeis* were loyal admirers and allies of Jews and Judaism. The concern to establish that non-Jesus-oriented Jews were still in possession of the wisdom that saves, even as wisdom was being extended to gentile adherents of Jesus, would make sense in a milieu in which these two groups shared a common space.

Bibliography

Primary Sources

Die Pseudoklementinen. Vol. 1, *Homilien*. Ed. Bernhard Rhem, updated by Georg Strecker. 3rd ed. Berlin: Akademie Verlag, 1992. English transl. Thomas Smith, Peter Peterson, and James Donaldson, *The Clementine Homilies and the Apostolic Constitutions*. ANF 17 (Edinburgh, 1870).

Secondary Sources

Baumgarten, Albert I. "Literary Evidence for Jewish Christianity in the Galilee." In *The Galilee in Late Antiquity*, ed. Lee I. Levine, 39–50. New York: Jewish Theological Seminary of America, 1992.

Bautch, Kelley Coblentz, "Obscured by the Scriptures, Revealed by the Prophets: God in the Pseudo-Clementine *Homilies*." In *Histories of the Hidden God: Concealment and Revelation in Western Gnostic, Esoteric, and Mystical Traditions*, ed. April D. DeConick and Grant Adamson, 120–136. Durham: Acumen, 2013.

Bremmer, Jan N. "Pseudo-Clementines: Texts, Dates, Places, Authors and Magic." In *The Pseudo-Clementines*, ed. Jan N. Bremmer, 1–23. Leuven: Peeters, 2010.

Carlson, Donald H. *Jewish-Christian Interpretation of the Pentateuch in the Pseudo-Clementine Homilies*. Minneapolis: Fortress Press, 2013.

---

41 Reed, "From Judaism and Hellenism," 431–435.

Drijvers, Han J.W. "Adam and the True Prophet in the Pseudo-Clementines." In *History and Religion in Late Antique Syria*, ed. Han J.W. Drijvers, 314–323. Aldershot: Variorum, 1994.

Duncan, Patricia A. *Novel Hermeneutics in the Greek Pseudo-Clementine Romance*. Tübingen: Mohr Siebeck, 2017.

Fredriksen, Paula. *Paul: the Pagans' Apostle*. New Haven: Yale University Press, 2017.

Hammer, Keir E., and Michele Murray. "Acquaintances, Supporters, and Competitors: Evidence of Inter-Connectedness and Rivalry among the Religious Groups in Sardis." In *Religious Rivalries and the Struggle for Success in Sardis and Smyrna*, ed. Richard S. Ascough, 175–194. Waterloo: Wilfrid Laurier University Press, 2005.

Harland, Philip A. *Associations, Synagogues, and Congregations: Claiming a Place in Ancient Mediterranean Society*. Minneapolis: Fortress Press, 2003.

Horner, Timothy J. "Jewish Aspects of the Protoevangelium of James." *JECS* 12 (2004): 313–335.

Jones, F. Stanley. *Pseudoclementina Elchasaiticaque inter Judaeochristiana: Collected Studies*. Leuven: Peeters, 2012.

Last, Richard. "The Other Synagogues." *Journal for the Study of Judaism* 47 (2016): 330–363.

Levine, Lee I. *Visual Judaism in Late Antiquity: Historical Contexts of Jewish Art*. New Haven: Yale University Press, 2012.

Lieu, Judith M. "The Race of the God-Fearers." *JTS* 46 (1995): 483–501.

Marcus, Joel. "Israel and the Church in the Exegetical Writings of Hippolytus." *Journal of Biblical Literature* 130 (2011): 385–406.

Reed, Annette Yoshiko. "'Jewish Christianity' after the 'Parting of the Ways': Approaches to Historiography and Self-Definition in the Pseudo-Clementines." In *The Ways That Never Parted: Jews and Christians in Late Antiquity and the Early Middle Ages*, ed. Adam H. Becker and Annette Yoshiko Reed, 189–231. Minneapolis: Fortress Press, 2007.

Reed, Annette Yoshiko. "From Judaism and Hellenism to Christianity and Paganism." In *Nouvelles intrigues pseudo-clémentines. Plots in the Pseudo-Clementine Romance: Actes du deuxième colloque international sur la littérature apocryphe chrétienne, Lausanne-Genève, 30 aout–2 septembre 2006*, ed. Frédéric Amsler, Albert Frey, Charlotte Touati, and Renée Girardet, 425–435. Prahins: Éditions du Zèbre, 2008.

Reed, Annette Yoshiko. "'Jewish Christianity' as Counter-History? The Apostolic Past in Eusebius' *Ecclesiastical History* and the Pseudo-Clementine *Homilies*." In *Antiquity in Antiquity: Jewish and Christian Pasts in the Greco-Roman World*, ed. Gregg Gardner and Kevin L. Osterloh, 172–216. Tübingen: Mohr Siebeck, 2008.

Reed, Annette Yoshiko. "When Did Rabbis Become Pharisees? Reflections on Christian Evidence for Post-70 Judaism." In *Envisioning Judaism: Studies in Honor of Peter Schäfer on the Occasion of his Seventieth Birthday*, ed. Ra'anan S. Boustan, Klaus

Herrmann, Remund Leicht, Annette Yoshiko Reed, and Guiseppe Veltri, 860–895. Tübingen: Mohr Siebeck, 2013.

Reed, Annette Yoshiko, and Ra'anan S. Boustan. "Blood and Atonement in the Pseudo-Clementines and the Story of the Ten Martyrs: The Problem of Selectivity in the Study of 'Judaism' and 'Christianity.'" *Henoch* 30 (2008): 333–364.

Runesson, Anders. "Jewish and Christian Interaction from the First to the Fifth Centuries." In *The Early Christian World*, ed. Philip F. Esler, 244–264. London: Routledge, 2017.

Shuve, Karl E. "The Doctrine of the False Pericopes and Other Late Antique Approaches to the Problem of Scripture's Unity." In *Nouvelles intrigues pseudo-clémentines. Plots in the Pseudo-Clementine Romance: Actes du deuxième colloque international sur la littérature apocryphe chrétienne, Lausanne-Genève, 30 aout–2 septembre 2006*, ed. Frédéric Amsler, Albert Frey, Charlotte Touati, and Renée Girardet, 437–445. Prahins: Éditions du Zèbre, 2008.

Stanton, Graham. "Jewish Christian Elements in the Pseudo-Clementine Writings." In *Jewish Believers in Jesus: The Early Centuries*, ed. Oskar Skarsaune and Reidar Hvalvik, 305–324. Peabody, MA: Hendrickson, 2007.

Zellentin, Holger M. *The Qur'an's Legal Culture: The Didascalia Apostolorum as a Point of Departure.* Tübingen: Mohr Siebeck, 2013.

Zetterholm, Karin Hedner. "Jewish Teachings for Gentiles in the Pseudo-Clementine *Homilies*: A Jewish Reception of Ideas in Paul and Acts Shaped by a Jewish Milieu?" *Journal of the Jesus Movement in Its Jewish Setting* 6 (2019): 68–87.

CHAPTER 10

Training the Women's Choir: Ascetic Practice and Liturgical Education in Late Antique Syriac Christianity

Susan Ashbrook Harvey

The transmission of holy wisdom, or religious knowledge, in late antique Christianity took place in a variety of social locations and through diverse methods of pedagogy.[1] Among the most important contexts for such transmission was liturgical celebration in all its different modes.[2] In recent scholarship, the work of liturgy as a pedagogical setting larger than that of the bishop's sermon has offered fruitful material.[3] Increasingly, scholars look to the role of hymns as a source of instruction for the congregation.[4] Consideration of hymns

---

1 The scholarship here is vast. Samuel Rubenson has been at the frontier of exploring monastic literature from precisely this perspective: see, for example, Samuel Rubenson, *The Letters of Saint Antony: Monasticism and the Making of a Saint* (Minneapolis: Fortress Press, 1995); idem, "Wisdom, Paraenesis, and the Roots of Monasticism," in *Early Christian Paraenesis in Context*, ed. James Starr and Troels Engberg-Pedersen (Berlin: de Gruyter, 2004), 521–534; idem, "Monasticism and the Philosophical Heritage," in *The Oxford Handbook of Late Antiquity*, ed. Scott Fitzgerald Johnson (New York: Oxford University Press, 2012), 487–512. See also, e.g., Arthur Urbano, *The Philosophical Life: Biography and the Crafting of Intellectual Identity in Late Antiquity* (Washington, DC: The Catholic University of America Press, 2013); Edward Watts, *City and School in Late Antique Athens and Alexandria* (Berkeley: University of California Press, 2006).

2 For example, Mary Cunningham and Pauline Allen, eds., *Preacher and Audience: Studies in Early Christian and Byzantine Homiletics* (Leiden: Brill, 1998); Jaclyn Maxwell, *Christianization and Communication in Late Antiquity: John Chrysostom and his Congregation in Antioch* (Cambridge: Cambridge University Press, 2006); S.A. Harvey, "Liturgy and Ethics in Ancient Syriac Christianity: Two Paradigms," *Studies in Christian Ethics* 26 (2013): 300–316.

3 E.g., Derek Krueger, *Liturgical Subjects: Christian Ritual, Biblical Narrative, and the Formation of the Self in Byzantium* (Philadelphia: University of Pennsylvania Press, 2014); S.A. Harvey, *Scenting Salvation: Ancient Christianity and the Olfactory Imagination* (Berkeley: University of California Press, 2006).

4 E.g., Thomas Arentzen, *The Virgin in Song: Mary and the Poetry of Romanos the Melodist* (Philadelphia: University of Pennsylvania Press, 2017); Sarah Gador-Whyte, *Theology and Poetry in Early Byzantium: The Kontakia of Romanos the Melodist* (Cambridge: Cambridge University Press, 2017); Georgia Frank, "Romanos and the Night Vigil in the Sixth Century," in *A People's History of Christianity*, vol. 3, *Byzantine Christianity*, ed. Derek Krueger (Minneapolis: Augsburg Fortress Publishers, 2006), 59–78; Georgia Frank, "Dialogue and Deliberation: The

from this perspective, however, also requires attention to the choirs and chanters who performed them.

In the exchange between chanter, choir, and congregation, sacred knowledge was transmitted and received. Singers adorned the liturgy with beautiful music, but more importantly functioned as teachers whose verses provided essential instruction.[5] The congregation as students participated in a dialogue of verses and refrains, through which to learn, master, and demonstrate Christian truth. For this basic yet crucial pedagogical interaction, we must ask: How were the "teachers" trained to transmit their knowledge? In the ritual context of liturgy, a "classroom" defined by and through a complex sequence of agents, words, movements, exchanges, articulated spaces, and patterned times, what did the choir need to know? How were they trained to be effective? Here, the example of Syriac women's choirs offers intriguing material.

Late antiquity was an era of expansion for Christian liturgical life across the Mediterranean. A major feature of this development was the emergence during the fourth century of trained choirs for liturgical service, along with new forms of hymnography crafted to highlight their participation.[6] In Syriac churches, these changes included the distinctive establishment of women's liturgical choirs. Generally comprised of consecrated virgins known as daughters of the covenant, Syriac women's choirs performed hymns that engaged and instructed the congregation on Bible, theology, and the life of the Christian community.[7] Attested across a variety of late ancient sources, both West and

---

Making of the Sensory Self in the Hymns of Romanos the Melodist," in *Religion and the Self in Antiquity*, ed. David Brakke, Steve Weitzman, and Michael Satlow (Bloomington, IN: Indiana University Press, 2005), 163–179.

5   This view of the role and function of liturgical choirs is deeply embedded still in Christians of the Middle East. See, e.g., Renee Hanna Hattar, "Sacred Oriental Music: Preserving the Identity of Middle Eastern Christians," *ParOr* 44 (2018): 301–310; Tala Jarjour, *Sense and Sadness: Syriac Chant in Aleppo* (Oxford: Oxford University Press, 2018).

6   See above all Christopher Page, *The Christian West and Its Singers: The First Thousand Years* (New Haven: Yale University Press, 2010). The account in Eusebius, *Ecclesiastical History* 7.27–30, regarding the heterodoxy and excommunication of Paul of Samosata in 268, has often been presumed to indicate that women's choirs were disallowed in ancient Christianity. One of the reasons Paul was condemned was his use of women's choirs to sing hymns in his honor. However, the story could well indicate the opposite: that women's choirs were not a problem. The real issue was the hymns themselves, which according to the report were composed to honor Paul rather than Christ.

7   See S.A. Harvey, "Performance as Exegesis: Women's Liturgical Choirs in Syriac Tradition," in *Inquiries into Eastern Christian Worship: Acts of the Second International Congress of the Society of Oriental Liturgy*, ed. Basilius J. Groen, Stephanos Alexopoulos, and Steven Hawkes-Teeples, Eastern Christian Studies 12 (Leuven: Peeters, 2012), 47–64; Johannes Quasten, "The Liturgical Singing of Women in Christian Antiquity," *Catholic Historical Review* 27 (1941): 149–165.

East Syriac, these choirs exercised a significant teaching ministry over some centuries. Explicit evidence for their liturgical role can be found through at least the ninth century.[8] Women's choirs remain a living tradition in the Syriac-speaking churches of the present day.[9]

Late antique Syriac sources mention these women's choirs with brief yet vivid references. Jacob of Sarug (d. 521), for example, refers to the women's choirs as "[female] teachers" (*malphanyatha*, in the feminine plural), whose singing declared the "proclamation" (*karuzutha*, corresponding to the Greek *kerygma*) in the liturgy.[10] He describes them as singing "songs of praise," "with a serene sound."[11] According to Jacob, the "pure" voices of these "pious" women[12] sang "instructive melodies,"[13] with "soft tones" and "wonderful tunes" by which heresies were defeated and the truth gloriously performed.[14]

Both Ephrem the Syrian (d. 373) and Jacob of Sarug urged their congregations to pay close heed to the women's choirs, which, Jacob admonished, were nothing less than a gift from God for the church's benefit.[15] The more one heard these choirs, Jacob assured his listeners, the more one would become oneself "pure, modest, and full of hope and discernment."[16] In one homily, he extolled the women's choir in a prayer, "By the sweet voices of the young women who sing Your praise, [O Christ], / You have captured the world."[17]

---

8   The major primary sources are discussed in Harvey, "Performance as Exegesis." While there appears a long silence in the sources after the ninth century, in the late thirteenth century Gregory Bar Hebraeus offered the comment: "As far as women are concerned the Daughters of the Covenant are only ordered by the Canons to sing responsories and doctrinal hymns [*madrashe*] among themselves in the church." Bar Hebraeus, *Ethicon*, Memra 1.3 (ed. Teule, CSCO 534–535 / Syr. 218–219, p. 72 (text), p. 61 (transl.)).
9   See Sarah Bakker Kellogg, "Ritual Sounds, Political Echoes: Vocal Agency and the Sensory Cultures of Secularism in the Dutch Syriac Diaspora," *American Ethnologist* 42 (2015): 431–445; eadem, "Perforating Kinship: Syriac Christianity, Ethnicity, and Secular Legibility," *Current Anthropology* 60 (2019):475–498; Sarah Aaltje Bakker, "Fragments of a Liturgical World: Syriac Christianity and the Dutch Multiculturalism Debates" (PhD diss., University of California, Santa Cruz, 2013).
10 Jacob of Sarug, *Homily on Ephrem*, v. 42 (ed. Amar, 34–35).
11 Jacob of Sarug, *Homily on Ephrem*, v. 99 (ed. Amar, 48–49).
12 Jacob of Sarug, *Homily on Ephrem*, v. 101 (ed. Amar, 48–49).
13 Jacob of Sarug, *Homily on Ephrem*, v. 114 (ed. Amar, 52–53).
14 Jacob of Sarug, *Homily on Ephrem*, vv. 152, 154 (ed. Amar, 64–65).
15 Ephrem, *Hymns on the Resurrection* 2.6, 8 (transl. Brock and Kiraz, *Ephrem the Syrian: Select Poems*, 174–175); Jacob of Sarug, *On the Partaking of the Holy Mysteries*, vv. 131–132 (ed. Harrak, 18).
16 Jacob of Sarug, *On the Partaking of the Holy Mysteries*, v. 175 (transl. Harrak, 22, Syriac on p. 23).
17 Jacob of Sarug, *Homily 4 on Elisha*, v. 25 (transl. Kaufman, 176, Syriac on p. 177).

From ecclesiastical canons in both the East Syriac (dyophysite) and West Syriac (miaphysite) traditions and from other attestations, we know that these women's choirs sang in civic churches in villages, towns, and cities.[18] According to the anonymous sixth-century *Life of Ephrem*, these choirs sang at the daily morning and evening services, at Sunday liturgies, on feast days, and at funerals.[19] Where Greek churches of the same era sometimes included choirs of nuns or consecrated virgins who sang the Psalms,[20] Syriac churches—according to ecclesiastical canons as well as the anonymous *Life of Ephrem* and Jacob of Sarug—assigned the choirs of daughters of the covenant to sing the *madrashe*. These were doctrinal hymns which, as the anonymous *Life of Ephrem* describes, contained "words of subtle meaning and spiritual knowledge about the birth and baptism and fasting and the entire economy of Christ; the passion and resurrection and ascension; and about the martyrs and repentance and about the deceased."[21]

References such as these give the strong impression that Syriac women's choirs were, in fact, trained choirs, having received some education beyond the melodies and tunes they sang (all of which have been lost to us). The so-called Maruta Canons, for example, which appear to date to the early fifth century, mandate that both sons and daughters of the covenant should "be educated in doctrine and in instruction" and then assigned to assist in churches and monasteries (canon 26); further, that daughters of the covenant should be assigned to civic churches and "instructed in the Scripture lessons, and particularly in the service of the Psalms" (canon 41).[22] These canons, at least, indicate that choirs

---

18 The sources are collected and discussed in Harvey, "Performance as Exegesis."
19 *Life of Ephrem* 31 (ed. and transl. Amar, CSCO 629–630 / Syr. 242–243, pp. 71–73 (text) and 77–80 (transl.)).
20 As described in Egeria, *Diary* 24 (transl. Gingras, 89–93). Key passages are included in James McKinnon, *Music in Early Christian Literature* (Cambridge: Cambridge University Press, 1987), nos. 242–254, pp. 112–117, with helpful commentary.
21 *Life of Ephrem* 31 (transl. Amar, 79–80). Further references that specify women's choirs singing *madrashe* include, e.g., Ephrem, *Hymns on the Resurrection* 2.6, 8 (transl. in Brock and Kiraz, *Ephrem the Syrian*, 174–175); Rabbula, *Canons for Priests and Covenanters* 20 (ed. and transl. in Phenix and Horn, *The Rabbula Corpus*, 106–107); Jacob of Sarug, *Homily Against the Jews* 7.538 (ed. and transl. Albert, PO 38.1 (1976), 271); Jacob of Sarug, *Homily on Ephrem*, vv. 96–116 (ed. and transl. Amar, 48–53). East Syriac sources of a later date (seventh through ninth centuries) continue to mention the *madrashe* assigned to the women's choirs: for example, an anonymous liturgical commentary ascribed to George of Arbela, and Canon 9 of the Synod of Catholicos George I in 676. These are discussed in Juan Mateos, *Lelya-Ṣapra: Essai d'interprétation des matines chaldéennes*, OCA 146 (Rome: Pontificium Institutum Orientalium Studiorum, 1959), 408–410.
22 *Canons of Maruta* 26, 41 (ed. and transl. Vööbus, CSCO 439–440 / Syr. 191–192, pp. 76, 85 (text), 65, 72 (transl.)).

as liturgical agents required knowledge of doctrine, scripture, and various services. What was their training, and how did it happen?

Most of the sources that might help address these questions date between the fourth and sixth centuries, with the clearest evidence falling in the sixth century. While it is difficult to argue that the evidence might be broadly applied throughout Syriac churches of the late antique period (or beyond), I suggest that these sources present a plausible account for understanding Syriac women's choirs as both educated and educating in their work.

Three Syriac sources, all apparently from the sixth century, provide glimpses: Jacob of Sarug's *Homily on Ephrem the Syrian* (which may be from the late fifth century, but in any event predates Jacob's death in 521), the anonymous *Life of Ephrem*, and John of Ephesus, *Lives of the Eastern Saints*. All three of these describe—however poetically—the instruction and rehearsing of female choirs for proper liturgical performance. Jacob and the author of the *Life of Ephrem* include these descriptions in their hagiographical accounts of Saint Ephrem, but they were writing more than a century after Ephrem's death in 373 and their accounts accord better with other evidence of their time than with that of Ephrem's day.

The *Life of Ephrem* provides in chapter 31 a fairly detailed description in all three of its extant recensions.[23] The text describes Ephrem's method for training the daughters of the covenant. Here, as in Jacob of Sarug, the author alleges that Ephrem's decision to train the women as a choir was motivated by his determination to fight heresy, and to do so by counteracting heretical hymns with his own orthodox compositions, to be sung by women's choirs. The account indicates the importance of the task:

> [Ephrem] prepared troops for battle against those heresies ... He appointed [female] teachers [*malphanyatha*] among all the Daughters of the Covenant who regularly came to the holy, catholic church, and taught

---

23 *Life of Ephrem* 31 (ed. and transl. Amar, 71–73 (text), 77–80 (transl.)). As Amar has demonstrated in this critical edition, the *Life of Ephrem* is a compilation of disparate Byzantine ascetic sources with little connection to the historical person of Ephrem. Because the three primary recensions are closely related but nonetheless distinct in their accounts, Amar's edition presents all three versions in parallel. The three are primarily based on manuscripts Vatican Syriac 117 dating to 1100 CE, Paris Syriac 235 copied early in the thirteenth century, and Damascus Syriac Orthodox Patriarchate 12/17, dated 1184/85. See the discussions in Amar, *The Syriac Vita Tradition*, CSCO 629 / Syr. 242, v–xvi; and CSCO 630 / Syr. 243, v–xxix. See also Sebastian P. Brock, "St. Ephrem in the Eyes of Later Syriac Liturgical Tradition," *Hugoye* 2 (1999): 5–25; Bernard Outtier, "Saint Éphrem d'après ses biographies et ses œuvres," *ParOr* 4 (1973): 11–33.

them hymns. Evenings and mornings they would gather in church before the liturgy on the feasts of martyrs, and for funeral processions, and they would sing.[24]

According to this anonymous text, Ephrem saw the women's choir as teachers (*malphanyatha*), and to that purpose met with them daily. Both the *Life of Ephrem* and Jacob of Sarug describe Ephrem as conducting the women "like an eagle perched among doves."[25] The *Life* implies that music was only part of what they needed to know: "All the Daughters of the Covenant would come down regularly to the church. [Ephrem] established instruction for them and taught them hymns as well."[26] The *Life* also indicates that Ephrem practiced with the women the kind of dialogical singing that characterized a variety of Syriac hymnography, not only in the pattern of alternating verses with sung refrains, but also the form of antiphonal choirs evidenced in the dialogue hymns favored by Syriac composers. Indeed, the most fulsome recension of the *Life* presents an entire range of liturgical hymnography mastered by the women's choir, and indicates the dialogical patterns involved:

> Seeing that all the people were attracted to singing and that (human) nature was drawn (to it), blessed Ephrem ... assembled and organized the Daughters of the Covenant and taught them hymns (*madrashe*) and songs (*seblatha*) and antiphons (*'onyatha*) and intercessions (*ba'watha*). He arranged songs (*qinyatha*) and verses (*mushhatha*) in rhythmic measures and transmitted his wisdom to all the learned and wise women. And he mixed in the hymns and chants sweet melodies which were pleasing and delightful to their hearers. He put in the hymns words of subtle meaning and spiritual knowledge .... Every day the Daughters of the Covenant would gather in the churches on the feasts of the Lord and on Sundays and for the commemoration of the martyrs. And he, like a father, would stand among them (as) a harpist of the Spirit, arranging various songs for them and demonstrating and teaching and alternating melodies until the entire city gathered around him.[27]

---

24 *Life of Ephrem* 31 (transl. Amar CSCO 630 / Syr. 243, pp. 77–78, following D).
25 *Life of Ephrem* 31 (transl. Amar, 78 (D)); Jacob of Sarug, *Homily on Ephrem*, vv. 98–101 (ed. and transl. Amar, 48–49).
26 *Life of Ephrem* 31 (transl. Amar, 78 (P)).
27 *Life of Ephrem* 31 (transl. Amar, CSCO 630 / Syr. 243, pp. 79–80 (v)). The different terminology for hymns in this passage may simply be literary elaboration: the words all signify

The results were impressive. According to Jacob of Sarug, "[Ephrem] taught the swallows to chirp, / and the church resounded with the pure voices of pious women."[28]

From other sources we know that Ephrem did indeed teach sons and daughters of the covenant and others who served the church in different capacities.[29] A number of his extant works attest to his labors in this regard. Several of his prose commentaries on biblical books survive and indicate that he led his students in close study of scripture and in exegetical method.[30] His *Commentary on the Diatessaron* shows evidence of repeated use, adaptation, and development by subsequent generations of students.[31] His polemical prose works show similar traits.[32] Some of the hymns attributed to Ephrem appear instead to be the work of his disciples, both those close to Ephrem's time and those following his style later.[33] Some of his students went on to become notable teachers and scholars in their own right (though only the names of male students are preserved).[34]

"song" or "hymn" or "melody." What is not clear is whether the terms might refer to specific types of hymns, in which case they would postdate the hymnography composed by Ephrem in the fourth century.

28   Jacob of Sarug, *Homily on Ephrem*, vv. 98–101 (ed. and transl. Amar, 48–49).
29   Jeffrey Wickes, "Between Liturgy and School: Reassessing the Performative Context of Ephrem's *Madrāšê*," *JECS* 26 (2018): 25–51.
30   Examples would be Ephrem's *Commentary on Genesis* and his *Commentary on Exodus*. These are translated with fine introductions and commentary in Joseph P. Amar and Edward G. Mathews, Jr., *St. Ephrem the Syrian, Selected Prose Works*, FC 91 (Washington, DC: Catholic University of America Press, 1994).
31   Christian Lange, *The Portrayal of Christ in the Syriac Commentary on the Diatessaron*, CSCO 616 / Subs. 118 (Leuven: Peeters, 2005), especially 162–173. For the reconstruction of Ephrem's commentary, see Carmel McCarthy, *Saint Ephrem's Commentary on Tatian's Diatessaron*, Journal of Semitic Studies Supplement 2 (Oxford: Oxford University Press, 1993).
32   E.g., C.W. Mitchell, A.A. Bevan, and F.C. Burkitt, eds. and transl., *S. Ephraim's Prose Refutations of Mani, Marcion, and Bardaisan*, 2 vols. (London: Williams and Norgate, 1912–1921, reprint Farnborough: Gregg, 1969).
33   Thus for example, did Edmund Beck consider all but the first four hymns in the cycle attributed to Ephrem on the holy man Julian Saba: Edmund Beck, *Des heiligen Ephraem des Syrers Hymnen auf Abraham Kidunaya und Julianos Saba*, CSCO 322 / Syr. 140, pp. v–xi, and CSCO 323 / Syr. 141, p. xv. For an example of the difficulties in differentiating authentic work by Ephrem from that perhaps composed by students soon after, see Sebastian P. Brock, "Ephremiana in Manuscript Sinai Syr. 10," *Le Muséon* 129 (2016): 285–322.
34   Sozomen, *Ecclesiastical History* 3.16, states: "It is said that [Ephrem] wrote three hundred thousand verses, and that he had many disciples who were zealously attached to his doctrines. The most celebrated of his disciples were Abbas, Zenobius, Abraham, Moras, and Simeon, in whom the Syrians and whoever among them pursued accurate learning make a

Ephrem's own writings hence provide a sense of the curriculum needed for liturgical training in a local church, as he himself designed it: how to read and interpret scripture; and how to understand "orthodox" theology over and against the teachings of heretics and Jews; how to perform and compose hymns. Jeffrey Wickes has argued that many of Ephrem's *madrashe*, such as the eighty-two *Hymns on Faith*, were composed for instructional rather than liturgical purposes.[35] In Ephrem's extant corpus, then, we see music as both a *method* of education (for example, in the *Hymns on Faith*), and also, in the form of liturgical hymns (such as the *Hymns on the Nativity* or the *Hymns on the Resurrection*), a *means* to disseminate that education to the congregation in a public liturgical context.[36] What I am arguing here supports Wickes' thesis and applies it further, extending it to the liturgy's performance as a complex ritual event. For those women and men who served as liturgical agents—as readers, chanters, singers, in addition to the diaconate and priests—it was important to perform one's ritual function effectively, *and also* to be able to understand church teaching correctly. Skilled singing was not sufficient for the task of choir or chanter; one had to know the content one was singing, and to understand it rightly. Proper performance of liturgy required serious biblical and theological training. Women's choirs, no less than other liturgical agents, needed that training. Ephrem's surviving corpus, as well as the brief testimonies in the anonymous *Life of Ephrem* and in Jacob of Sarug's homily on Ephrem, all attest that such was the case.

This picture is confirmed by the sixth-century hagiographer John of Ephesus in his account of Simeon the Mountaineer, a recluse who stumbled on a "heathen" semi-nomadic village at the eastern edge of the Roman Empire.[37] As a first act in establishing their church, Simeon rounded up eighteen boys and twelve girls whom he tonsured as sons and daughters of the covenant. Then,

---

great boast. Paulanas and Aranad are praised for their finished speech, although reported to have deviated from sound doctrine." Transl. Chester D. Hartranft, NPNF 2.2, p. 295. Variations on this list of disciples are given in several other late antique and medieval biographical notices of Ephrem. See Outtier, "Saint Éphrem d'après ses biographies et ses œuvres."

35 Wickes, "Between Liturgy and School."
36 Clearly intended for liturgical use, for example, were Ephrem's *Hymns on the Nativity* and *Hymns on the Resurrection*. These were sung during the vigil service prior to the liturgy of the feast, and the verses occasionally refer to the service and the occasion. By contrast, Ephrem's *Hymns on Faith* appear to indicate a non-liturgical, study-oriented setting, see Wickes, "Between Liturgy and School."
37 John of Ephesus, *Lives of the Eastern Saints* 16 (ed. and transl. Brooks, PO 17 (1923), 229–247).

he proceeded to train them. The process was not quick, but rather an education over some years:

> [For these girls and boys] he made tablets for writing, and wrote for them; and thus he would sit with patience as in a school (*eskole*), and would teach them, boys and girls together. And down to the time when they reached an age at which they might receive harm from one another, within four or five years, they learned the psalms and the scriptures; and thenceforward loud choirs were to be heard at the [church] service [*teshmeshta*].[38]

When Simeon died many years later, his covenanters were well established in their liturgical service, and engaged in training the children who followed after them: "when he was old and decrepit and these disciples of his also had become grown women and men, and they were now becoming readers and daughters of the covenant, and they were themselves teaching others also as well."[39] John's narrative is important because of its portrayal of the sons and daughters of the covenant as foundational to the liturgical life of the Christian community. But it is also significant as an account of the education necessary for their work of liturgical song to be performed well and effectively.

To my knowledge, these are the only Syriac sources that describe the training necessary for women's liturgical choirs. I suggest that we amplify the picture from three other areas for which we have more abundant Syriac evidence: (1) female literacy relevant to liturgical needs; (2) psalmody as an ascetic practice; and (3) the liturgical training provided to boys by the School of Nisibis and related village schools, where liturgical music was essential throughout the curriculum.

First, on female literacy and liturgical needs: there is strong Syriac evidence for women's literacy as part of ascetic training in late antiquity. Syriac sources on women ascetics indicate the ability to read scripture, hagiography, ascetic and theological literature, and the ability to chant psalms and prayers of the daily offices with knowledgeable skill.[40] The sixth-century widow Euphemia

---

38   John of Ephesus, *Lives of the Eastern Saints* 16 (ed. and transl. Brooks, 246–724).
39   John of Ephesus, *Lives of the Eastern Saints* 16 (ed. and transl. Brooks, 247).
40   On women's literacy in ancient Christianity generally, see Kim Haines-Eitzen, *The Gendered Palimpsest: Women, Writing, and Representation in Early Christianity* (Oxford: Oxford University Press, 2012); Amelia Brown, "Psalmody and Socrates: Female Literacy in the Byzantine Empire," in *Questions of Gender in Byzantine Society*, ed. Bronwen Neil and Lynda Garland (Farnham: Ashgate, 2013), 57–76. Specifically on the literacy and training

provided exactly this kind of instruction for her daughter Maria in the city of Amida, where their religious knowledge was widely admired in the civic community.[41] Some decades later, the solitary Shirin was renowned throughout northern Iraq for the sound of her long hours of psalmody and sung prayer services in her solitary dwelling, and also for the breadth and depth of religious reading through which she instructed the crowds of faithful who approached her for spiritual counsel.[42] Hagiography of women saints mentions reading together as a valued practice of women's monasteries, taking place in the context of sung prayer services as well as at other times of communal gathering; the *Life of Febronia* is a good example.[43]

A telling case of female literacy is that of the East Syriac nun Hanah-Ishoʿ, who, late in the sixth century, oversaw the education of her younger brother, the future saint Rabban Bar-ʿIdta, after they were orphaned. Over the course of his childhood and in two different schools, Hanah-Ishoʿ ensured that his training included liturgical music, hymnography, and the order and occasions of services.[44] The role of mothers and sisters in the education of children was a common theme in Syriac hagiography, as in Greek.[45] Still, it points to a culture where women valued and cared about serious religious education, including

necessary for Byzantine choir nuns, see Linda Garland, "'Till Death Do Us Part?' Family Life in Byzantine Monasteries," in *Questions of Gender in Byzantine Society*, 29–55. On the Syriac sources, see below.

41 John of Ephesus, *Lives of the Eastern Saints* 12 (transl. in Brock and Harvey, *Holy Women of the Syrian Orient* (Berkeley: University of California Press, 1998), 122–133, esp. 126, 128, 129).

42 Sahdona (Martyrios), *Book of Perfection* 69–79 (transl. Brock and Harvey, *Holy Women*, 177–181).

43 An especially prominent theme in the *Life of Febronia* (transl. Brock and Harvey, *Holy Women*, 150–176). For this aspect of Syriac women's monasticism, see Florence Jullien, "Le monachisme feminin en milieu syriaque," in *Le monachisme syriaque*, ed. F. Jullien, Études Syriaques 7 (Paris: Guethner, 2010), 65–87; Clémence Hélou, "La vie monastique féminine dans la tradition syriaque," in *Le monachisme syriaque du VIIe siècle à nos jours*, Patrimonie Syriaque: Actes du colloque, VI, vol. 1 (Antélias, Lebanon: Centre d'Études et de Recherches Orientales, 1999), 85–118.

44 *Life of Bar ʿIdta*, lines 59–120 (ed. and transl. Budge, 115–118 (text), 167–171 (transl.)).

45 Compare the accounts in the *Life of John Bar-Aphtonia*, sections 3–6 (ed. and transl. Nau, 114–118 (text), 123–130 (transl.)); Elias, *Life of John of Tella* (ed. and transl. Brooks, CSCO 7–8 / Syr. 7–8, pp. 39–43 (text), 27–30 (Latin transl.)); Thomas of Marga, *The Book of Governors* 2.34 (ed. and transl. Budge, 116–117 (text), 251–252 (transl.)). For comparative rabbinic evidence, see Susan Marks, "Bayit versus Beit Midrash: Jewish Mother as Teacher," in *A Most Reliable Witness: Essays in Honor of Ross Shepard Kraemer*, ed. S.A. Harvey, Nathaniel P. DesRosiers, Shira Lander, Jacqueline Z. Pastis, and Daniel Ulluci (Providence, RI: Brown Judaic Studies, 2015), 195–204.

knowledge of liturgy and its music, in addition to that of the classical curricula. The women themselves had to have appreciation for this kind of knowledge if they were to guide their youth to its pursuit.

Secondly, singing was an important part of ascetic practice for Syriac Christians in any social location. Constant singing and reading or intoning aloud for purposes of disciplined prayer and devotional practice also provided the opportunity for training, expertise, and the mastering of large bodies of liturgical song: hymns, prayers, psalms, litanies, invocations, supplications. Syriac sources mention that the sound of holy women singing their psalms and prayers was often heard by others.[46] I would suggest we understand resonance between this kind of singing and that of women's liturgical choirs. Further, I think we should hear these two kinds of singing—that of choirs in the church, and that of female ascetics performing their devotions—as interactive in the quality of authority they conveyed, and in the institutional recognition of that authority conferred by the ecclesiastical structure. Singing sacred song was a recognized part of the public activity of late antique Syriac women.

The third area of evidence pertinent here is the place of liturgical music within late antique Syriac religious education. The sizable corpus of materials extant for the (East Syriac) School of Nisibis affirms the importance as well as the challenges of instruction in liturgical music.[47] Statutes of the School identify liturgical music as a core part of the curriculum throughout a student's tenure. As was apparently the case for Ephrem's students, singing here was both

---

[46] For example, John of Ephesus, *Lives of the Eastern Saints* 12, on Euphemia and Maria (transl. Brock and Harvey, *Holy Women*, 122–133, esp. 126, 128, 129); and John of Ephesus, *Lives of the Eastern Saints* 31, on Elijah and Theodore (ed. and transl. Brooks, PO 18, 581–583). See also Sahdona's account of Shirin (transl. Brock and Harvey, *Holy Women*, 180); the *Life of Mary of Qidun* (transl. Brock and Harvey, *Holy Women*, 27–37, esp. 29, 36). The Daughter of Maʿnyo was remembered for the hours she spent singing prayers and hymns: *Sogitha*, v. 5 (transl. Sebastian P. Brock, "'The Daughter of Maʿnyo': A Holy Woman of Arbela," *Annales du Département des Lettres Arabes* 6-B (1991–1992 [1996]): 122.) The martyr Anahid sang psalms in the prison all night (transl. Brock and Harvey, *Holy Women*, 93–94).

[47] Adam H. Becker, *Fear of God and the Beginning of Wisdom: The School of Nisibis and the Development of Scholastic Culture in Late Antique Mesopotamia* (Philadelphia: University of Pennsylvania Press, 2006); idem, *Sources for the Study of the School of Nisibis*, TTH 50 (Liverpool: Liverpool University Press, 2008); Arthur Vööbus, *The Statutes of the School of Nisibis*, PETSE 12 (Stockholm: ETSE, 1961). Becker's groundbreaking work is now significantly supplemented by Ute Possekel, "Selbstverständnis und Bildungsauftrag der Schule von Nisibis," *ZAC* 19 (2015): 104–136; eadem, "'Go and Set Up for Yourselves Beautiful Laws': The School of Nisibis and Institutional Autonomy in Late Antique Education," in *Griechische Philosophie und Wissenschaft bei den Ostsyrern. Im Gedenken an Mār Addai Scher (1867–1915)*, ed. M. Perkams and A.M. Schilling (Berlin: de Gruyter, 2019), 29–47.

a mode of academic study and also a skill to be gained, refined, and mastered. Lessons were recited and sung with the students in formation as a choir: knowledge was conveyed in dialogic fashion through the singing or chanting of verses and responses. Faculty associated with the School over different centuries produced important scholarly works on the liturgy, including its different musical expressions.[48]

Teaching and learning were a musical exchange at the School of Nisibis. The great poet Narsai of Nisibis (ca. 399–502), older contemporary and rival of Jacob of Sarug, served as head of the School for twenty years, "while daily leading the choir and giving interpretation."[49] Subsequently Abraham of Bet Rabban "led the assembly for a period of sixty years, while interpreting, leading the choir, and resolving questions."[50] The *maqryane* were teachers of recitation and chant, and were among the distinguished ranks of instructors in the School.[51] The "recitation of the choirs" was required of the students in their studies, but evening and morning services were also mandated, as well as memorials for the dead. None were optional, except in cases of sickness or serious exigency.[52] According to the fourteenth-century *Nomocanon* of ʿAbdishoʿ bar Brika, the three-year curriculum at the School of Nisibis comprised mastery of the lectionary, the different services for Sundays, feasts, and commemoration days, the Psalms, and liturgical hymns including funeral hymns. These areas were distributed over the three years, with the final year including the reading of biblical commentaries by earlier theologians.[53] Learning the music of liturgy was hence deeply interwoven with learning the different services, their rubrics and correct celebration. It was also inextricable from learning correct ("orthodox") biblical interpretation and doctrinal instruction.

---

48 Becker, *Fear of God*, 89–94.
49 Barḥadbeshabba, *The Cause of the Foundation of the Schools* (ed. Scher, PO 4.4, 383:11–14, transl. Becker, *Sources*, 150–151); also cited and discussed in Becker, *Fear of God*, 89. Barḥadbeshabba, *Ecclesiastical History* 31, also comments on the musical qualities of Narsai's instruction (ed. Nau, PO 9.5, 612, transl. Becker, *Sources*, 69).
50 Barḥadbeshabba, *The Cause of the Foundation of the Schools* (ed. Scher, PO 4.4, 389:1–5, transl. Becker, *Sources*, 154–155); also cited and discussed in Becker, *Fear of God*, 89.
51 The *maqryane* are notably included among those who signed authorization and agreement to the different collections of canons that governed the School. See Vööbus, *Statutes of the School of Nisibis*, 52, 88, 92, 103–104; see also 83, n. 41.
52 *Canons of Narsai* 8 and 9 (ed. and transl. Vööbus, *Statutes*, 79); see also 79, n. 29; *Canons of Ḥenana* 5 and 11 (ed. and transl. Vööbus, *Statutes*, 94, 97).
53 For the portion of ʿAbdishoʿ, *Nomocanon*, labeled "On the School of Nisibis," as well as discussion of the historical problems apparent in the text, see Vööbus, *Statutes*, 107–111; and Becker, *Fear of God*, 92–94.

Related to the famed School of Nisibis were local, village schools (again, the surviving data here is East Syriac).[54] These appear to have functioned with different degrees of sophistication, but at the least included basic literacy, study of the psalms, and liturgical education. Church leaders not only participated in the education offered by the School of Nisibis, but also in the oversight and governance of these smaller village schools.[55] Local monks complained about the noise level when they heard students practicing their lessons and their "songs of hallelujahs, the psalms, the responses, [and] the harmonies of the youths and the vigilants."[56] Rival West Syriac church leaders complained about the sounds, as well as the efficacy, of these schools and their musical impact on local villagers and townspeople.[57]

Ephrem's teaching had included women, whereas the School of Nisibis was exclusively for male students. In fact, late-sixth-century canons from the School forbid the brothers of the community to teach women, or to interact with them, including daughters of the covenant.[58] Yet some kind of analogous instruction must have been available for the women's choirs and for those who served as their directors, including women deacons.[59] Convents may have provided it: the canons of John of Tella, like those ascribed to Maruta, encourage the education of sons (and daughters?) of the covenant in monastic schools.[60] But it seems likely that instruction also would have taken place in the local church, just as Ephrem had provided in the fourth century and as John of Ephesus in

---

54   Becker, *Fear of God*, 163–166. Becker argues persuasively for a typology of East Syriac schools in three categories: independent schools, monastic schools, and village schools (pp. 155–168). Music as a mode of study and as a skill to be mastered was important in all these locations: Becker, *Fear of God*, 89–90, 92–93, 189, 204–209.
55   Becker, *Fear of God*, 164–165.
56   Thomas of Marga, *Book of Governors* 2.8 (ed. and transl. Budge, 75–76 (text), 148–150 (transl.)). I cite following the translation in Becker, *Fear of God*, 170. Throughout the accounts in Thomas of Marga's *Book of Governors*, excellence of (liturgical) singing recurs as a skill or talent which could be edifying or problematic, inspiring or distracting to the monks of the different monasteries. In this case, of course, it was male voices that were the source of wonder or disturbance. E.g., Thomas of Marga, *Book of Governors* 2.2, 2.8, 2.11, 3.1, 3.2, 4.20, 5.17.
57   *Life of Maruta*, 65:10–66:2, transl. as cited in Becker, *Fear of God*, 90.
58   *Canons of Ḥenana* 18 (ed. and transl. Vööbus, *Statutes*, 100); see Becker, *Fear of God*, 86.
59   On the consecration and training of the daughters of the covenant, including their supervision by members chosen to be deaconesses: *Canons of Maruta* 26, 41 (ed. and transl. Vööbus, CSCO 439–440 / Syr. 191–192, pp. 76, 85 (text), 65, 72 (transl.)).
60   *Canons of Johannan bar Qursos* (John of Tella) 27 (ed. and transl. Vööbus, *The Synodicon in the West Syrian Tradition*, CSCO 367–368 / Syr. 161–162, p. 156 (text), p. 151 (transl.)).

the sixth century attributed to the monk Simeon the Mountaineer.[61] We must presume transmission of local traditions, consonant with the music, melodies, and performative patterns that generally prevailed or were popular across the regions in which Syriac liturgies were conducted.

Were the women's choirs always well trained? Apparently not. Syriac church canons admonish against poorly trained or uneducated clergy.[62] So, too, a liturgical commentary, attributed to George of Arbela but probably dating to the ninth century, twice likens the women's choir typologically to those who enslaved the people of God in the Hebrew Bible. The commentary compares the congregation seated at evening prayer to the humiliated Hebrew slaves, stating that the women's singing signified the enemy captors, Babylonians or Egyptians.[63] Did the commentator suffer an ill-trained or under-rehearsed women's choir? The passage stands in striking contrast to the happy description from the *Life of Ephrem*,

> My friends, who would not be astounded and filled with fervent faith to see the athlete of Christ [Ephrem] amid the ranks of the Daughters of the Covenant as they chanted songs, hymns, and melodies? Their songs resemble the songs and ethereal melodies of spiritual beings who chant to the spirits of humans with the sweetness of their songs.[64]

Our surviving evidence gives only the faintest glimpse of challenges and needs at the local parish level. Yet the insistence in late antique sources that Syriac women's choirs were valued for their ministry of teaching is itself indication of their education and training.

In an important article on the training of girls' choirs in Archaic Greece, Wayne Ingalls pointed out that choral training was not only a matter of preparing for performance. It was also a means of education for one's own place in society. The myths and local legends sung by young Greek girls served also to provide models for understanding their own significance, contributions, and roles in their communities.[65] The same could be said about the Syriac women's

---

61   John of Ephesus, *Lives of the Eastern Saints* 16 (ed. and transl. Brooks, PO 17 (1923), 229–247).
62   Consider the evidence in the rules distributed by John of Tella: Volker Menze, "Priests, Laity, and the Sacrament of the Eucharist in Sixth Century Syria," *Hugoye* 7 (2007): 129–146; idem, "The *Regula ad Diaconos*: John of Tella, his Eucharistic Ecclesiology and the Establishment of an Ecclesiastical Hierarchy in Exile," *OrChr* 90 (2006): 44–90.
63   Ps.-George of Arbela, as cited by Mateos, *Lelya-Ṣapra*, 408.
64   *Life of Ephrem* 31 (transl. Amar, CSCO 630 / Syr. 243, 80 (v)).
65   Wayne Ingalls, "Ritual Performance as Training for Daughters in Archaic Greece," *Phoenix*:

choirs. Often the hymns they performed told stories of biblical women, in terms that spoke to the needs, desires, and obligations of the present congregation.[66] As such, women's choirs and the women's stories they sang, highlighted women's significance for the church's health and flourishing, both liturgically and in the social order.

Women's choirs mattered in Syriac liturgies: it is important to understand how and why. While Syriac references to women's liturgical choirs are not frequent in the ancient sources, they are consistent in their indications that musical sound alone was not the value of these choirs. Theirs was not only an aesthetic adornment to worship. Rather, their offering was twofold. It comprised both the words they sang—the content of their hymns—and the manner of their expression: the sung performance. Theirs was a teaching ministry of song. As such, their contributions required—and deserved—a steady foundation, humbly gained through long hours of study, training, rehearsing, and well-practiced skills.

Acknowledgements

I am grateful to Ute Possekel for her valuable comments on an earlier draft of this essay, and for sharing her generous knowledge of the School of Nisibis. Any remaining errors are my own.

Journal of the Classical Association of Canada 54 (2000): 1–20. In Archaic Greece, the girls learned to sing the stories of important female figures of (often local) Greek mythology. Such stories contributed to the moral formation of these girls, inscribing messages of their proper place and conduct in society. These were reinforced through the bodily disciplines of memorization, melody, and dance. At the same time, these Greek hymns instilled in the girls' choirs a sense of their own significance: the importance of women for ensuring the continuation and healthy survival of their community, and the valuation of their performance for the community's wellbeing. See also Claude Calambe, *Choruses of Young Women in Ancient Greece: Their Morphology, Religious Role, and Social Functions*, transl. Derek Collins and Janice Orion (Lanham, MD: Rowman & Littlefield, 2001), 221–244.

66 E.g., S.A. Harvey, "Bearing Witness: New Testament Women in Early Byzantine Hymnography," in *The New Testament in Byzantium*, ed. Derek Krueger and Robert Nelson (Washington, DC: Dumbarton Oaks Research Library and Collection, 2016), 205–219.

Bibliography

Primary Sources

Barḥadbeshabba ʿArbaya. *Ecclesiastical History*. Ed. with French transl. François Nau, *La seconde partie de l'Histoire de Barḥadbešabba ʿArbaïa*. PO 9.5. Paris 1913. Partial English transl. in Adam Becker, *Sources for the Study of the School of Nisibis*, 47–85.

Barḥadbeshabba ʿArbaya. *The Cause of the Foundation of the Schools*. Ed. with French transl. Addai Scher, *Mar Barhadbeshabba ʿArabaya, Cause de la fondation des écoles*. PO 4.4. Paris, 1908. English transl. in Adam Becker, *Sources for the Study of the School of Nisibis*, 86–160.

Becker, Adam, transl. *Sources for the Study of the School of Nisibis*, TTH 50. Liverpool: Liverpool University Press, 2008.

Brock, Sebastian P., and Susan Ashbrook Harvey, transl. *Holy Women of the Syrian Orient*. Berkeley: University of California Press, 1998.

Canons of Johannan bar Qursos (John of Tella). Ed. with English transl. in Arthur Vööbus, *The Synodicon in the West Syrian Tradition*. Vol. 1. CSCO 367–368 / Syr. 161–162. Louvain: Secrétariat du CorpusSCO, 1975.

Canons of Maruta. Ed. with English transl. in Arthur Vööbus, *The Canons Ascribed to Maruta of Maipherqat and Related Sources*. CSCO 439–440 / Syr. 191–192. Louvain: Peeters, 1982.

Canons of Rabbula. Ed. with English transl. in Robert R. Phenix, Jr. and Cornelia B. Horn, *The Rabbula Corpus: Comprising the Life of Rabbula, His Correspondence, a Homily Delivered in Constantinople, Canons, and Hymns*. Atlanta: Society of Biblical Literature, 2017.

Egeria. *Diary*. English transl. George E. Gingras, *Egeria, Diary of a Pilgrimage*. ACW 38. New York: Paulist Press, 1970.

Elias. *Life of John of Tella*. Ed. with Latin transl. in E.W. Brooks, *Vitae virorum apud Monophysitas celeberrimorum*. CSCO 7–8 / Syr. 7–8. Paris: E typographeo reipublicae, 1907.

Ephrem. *Commentaries on Genesis and Exodus*. English transl. in Joseph P. Amar and Edward G. Mathews, Jr., *St. Ephrem the Syrian, Select Prose Works*. FC 91. Washington, DC: Catholic University of America Press, 1994.

Ephrem. *Commentary on the Diatessaron*. English transl. Carmel McCarthy, *Saint Ephrem's Commentary on Tatian's Diatessaron*. Journal of Semitic Studies Supplement 2. Oxford: Oxford University Press, 1993.

Ephrem. *Hymns on Faith*. Ed. with German transl. Edmund Beck, *Des heiligen Ephraem des Syrers Hymnen de Fide*. CSCO 154–155 / Syr. 73–74. Louvain: Secrétariat du CorpusSCO, 1955. English transl. Jeffrey Wickes, *St. Ephrem the Syrian: The Hymns on Faith*. FC 130. Washington, DC: The Catholic University of America Press, 2015.

Ephrem. *Hymns on Julian Saba*. Ed. with German transl. Edmund Beck, *Des heiligen*

Ephraem des Syrers Hymnen auf Abraham Kidunaya und Julianos Saba. CSCO 322–323 / Syr. 140–141. Louvain: Peeters, 1972.

Ephrem. *Hymns on the Nativity.* Ed. with German transl. Edmund Beck, *Des heiligen Ephraem des Syrers Hymnen de Nativitate (Epiphania).* CSCO 186–187 / Syr. 82–83. Louvain: Secrétariat du CorpusSCO, 1959. English transl. in Kathleen McVey, *Ephrem the Syrian: Hymns.* Mahwah, NJ: Paulist Press, 1989.

Ephrem. *Hymns on the Resurrection.* Ed. with German transl. Edmund Beck, *Des heiligen Ephraem des Syrers Paschahymnen (de azymis, de crucifixione, de resurrectione).* CSCO 248–249 / Syr. 108–109. Louvain: Secrétariat du CorpusSCO, 1964. Partial English transl. in Sebastian P. Brock and George A. Kiraz, *Ephrem the Syrian: Select Poems.* Provo, UT: Brigham Young University Press, 2006.

Ephrem. *Prose Refutations.* Ed. with English transl. C.W. Mitchell, A.A. Bevan, and F.C. Burkitt, *S. Ephraim's Prose Refutations of Mani, Marcion, and Bardaisan.* 2 vols. London: Williams and Norgate, 1912–1921; reprint Farnborough: Gregg, 1969.

Gregory bar Hebraeus. *Ethicon, Memra 1.* Ed. with English transl. Herman G.B. Teule, *Gregory bar Hebraeus, Ethicon, Memra 1.* CSCO 534–535 / Syr. 218–219. Leuven: Peeters, 1993.

Jacob of Sarug. *Against the Jews.* Ed. with French transl. Micheline Albert, *Jacques de Saroug, Homélies contre les Juifs.* PO 38.1. Turnhout 1976.

Jacob of Sarug. *Homily 4 on Elisha.* Ed. as *Homily* 119 in Bedjan, *Homiliae selectae.* Vol. 4, pp. 318–332. English transl. (with Bedjan's Syriac text) Stephen A. Kaufman, *Jacob of Sarug's Homilies on Elisha.* Piscataway, NJ: Gorgias Press, 2010.

Jacob of Sarug. *Homily on Ephrem.* Ed. with English transl. Joseph P. Amar, *A Metrical Homily on Holy Mar Ephrem by Mar Jacob of Sarug.* PO 47.1. Turnhout, 1995.

Jacob of Sarug. *On the Partaking of the Holy Mysteries.* Ed. as *Homily* 95 in Bedjan, *Homiliae selectae.* Vol. 3, pp. 646–663. English transl. (with Bedjan's Syriac text) Amir Harrak, *Jacob of Sarug's Homily on the Partaking of the Holy Mysteries.* Piscataway, NJ: Gorgias Press, 2009.

Jacob of Sarug. *Select Homilies.* Ed. Paul Bedjan, *Homiliae selectae mar-Jacobi Sarugensis.* 5 vols. Leipzig: Harrassowitz, 1905–1910. 2nd ed. in 6 vols. by Sebastian P. Brock. Piscataway, NJ: Gorgias Press, 2006.

John of Ephesus. *Lives of the Eastern Saints.* Ed. with English transl. E.W. Brooks. PO 17–19. Paris, 1923–1925.

Life of Bar-ʿIdtâ. Ed. with English transl. in E.A. Wallis Budge, *The Histories of Rabban Hormizd the Persian and Rabban Bar-ʿIdtâ.* 2 vols. Luzac's Semitic Text and Translation Series 9–10. London: Luzac, 1902.

Life of Ephrem. Ed. with English transl. Joseph P. Amar, *The Syriac Vita Tradition of Ephrem the Syrian.* CSCO 629–630 / Syr. 242–243. Leuven: Peeters, 2011.

Life of John bar-Aphtonia. Ed. with French transl. in François Nau, "Histoire de Jean bar Aphtonia." *Revue de l'Orient Chrétien* 7 (1902): 97–135.

McKinnon, James W., transl. *Music in Early Christian Literature*. Cambridge: Cambridge University Press, 1987.
Sogitha on the Daughter of Maʿnyo. English transl. in Sebastian P. Brock, "'The Daughter of Maʿnyo': A Holy Woman of Arbela," *Annales du Département des Lettres Arabes* 6-B (1991–1992 [1996]): 121–128.
Sozomen. *Ecclesiastical History*. English transl. Chester D. Hartranft, in *Socrates, Sozomenus: Church Histories*. NPNF, 2nd ser., vol. 2 (1890); reprint Peabody, MA: Hendrickson, 1995.
Statutes of the School of Nisibis. Ed. with English transl. Arthur Vööbus, *The Statutes of the School of Nisibis*. PETSE 12. Stockholm: ETSE, 1961.
Thomas of Marga. *The Book of Governors*. Ed. with English transl. E.A. Wallis Budge, *The Book of Governors: The Historia Monastica of Thomas Bishop of Marga A.D. 840*. 2 vols. London, 1893; reprint Piscataway, NJ: Gorgias Press, 2003.

Secondary Sources
Arentzen, Thomas. *The Virgin in Song: Mary and the Poetry of Romanos the Melodist*. Philadelphia: University of Pennsylvania Press, 2017.
Bakker Kellogg, Sarah. "Ritual Sounds, Political Echoes: Vocal Agency and the Sensory Cultures of Secularism in the Dutch Syriac Diaspora." *American Ethnologist* 42 (2015): 431–445. doi:10.1111/amet.12139.
Bakker Kellogg, Sarah. "Perforating Kinship: Syriac Christianity, Ethnicity, and Secular Legibility." *Current Anthropology* 60 (2019): 475–498.
Bakker, Sarah Aaltje. "Fragments of a Liturgical World: Syriac Christianity and the Dutch Multiculturalism Debates." PhD diss., University of California, Santa Cruz, 2013. http://escholarship.org/uc/item/4rr5t94m.
Becker, Adam H. *Fear of God and the Beginning of Wisdom: The School of Nisibis and the Development of Scholastic Culture in Late Antique Mesopotamia*. Philadelphia: University of Pennsylvania Press, 2006.
Brock, Sebastian P. "St. Ephrem in the Eyes of Later Syriac Liturgical Tradition." *Hugoye* 2 (1999): 5–25.
Brock, Sebastian P. "Ephremiana in Manuscript Sinai Syr. 10." *Le Muséon* 129 (2016): 285–322.
Brown, Amelia. "Psalmody and Socrates: Female Literacy in the Byzantine Empire." In *Questions of Gender in Byzantine Society*, ed. Bronwen Neil and Lynda Garland, 57–76. Farnham: Ashgate, 2013.
Calame, Claude. *Choruses of Young Women in Ancient Greece: Their Morphology, Religious Role, and Social Functions*. Translated by Derek Collins and Janice Orion. Lanham, MD: Rowman & Littlefield, 2001.
Cunningham, Mary, and Pauline Allen, eds. *Preacher and Audience: Studies in Early Christian and Byzantine Homiletics*. Leiden: Brill, 1998.

Frank, Georgia. "Romanos and the Night Vigil in the Sixth Century." In *A People's History of Christianity*. Vol. 3, *Byzantine Christianity*, ed. Derek Krueger, 59–78. Minneapolis: Augsburg Fortress Publishers, 2006.

Frank, Georgia. "Dialogue and Deliberation: The Making of the Sensory Self in the Hymns of Romanos the Melodist." In *Religion and the Self in Antiquity*, ed. David Brakke, Steve Weitzman, and Michael Satlow, 163–179. Bloomington, IN: Indiana University Press, 2005.

Gador-Whyte, Sarah. *Theology and Poetry in Early Byzantium: The Kontakia of Romanos the Melodist*. Cambridge: Cambridge University Press, 2017.

Garland, Lynda. "'Till Death Do Us Part?' Family Life in Byzantine Monasteries." In *Questions of Gender in Byzantine Society*, ed. Bronwen Neil and Lynda Garland, 29–55. Farnham: Ashgate, 2013.

Haines-Eitzen, Kim. *The Gendered Palimpsest: Women, Writing, and Representation in Early Christianity*. Oxford: Oxford University Press, 2012.

Harvey, Susan Ashbrook. "Bearing Witness: New Testament Women in Early Byzantine Hymnography." In *The New Testament in Byzantium*, ed. Derek Krueger and Robert Nelson, 205–219. Washington, DC: Dumbarton Oaks Research Library and Collection, 2016.

Harvey, Susan Ashbrook. "Liturgy and Ethics in Ancient Syriac Christianity: Two Paradigms." *Studies in Christian Ethics* 26 (2013): 300–316.

Harvey, Susan Ashbrook. "Performance as Exegesis: Women's Liturgical Choirs in Syriac Tradition." In *Inquiries into Eastern Christian Worship: Acts of the Second International Congress of the Society of Oriental Liturgy*, ed. Basilius J. Groen, Stephanos Alexopoulos, and Steven Hawkes-Teeples, 47–64. Eastern Christian Studies 12. Leuven: Peeters, 2012.

Harvey, Susan Ashbrook. *Scenting Salvation: Ancient Christianity and the Olfactory Imagination*. Berkeley: University of California Press, 2006.

Hattar, Renee Hanna. "Sacred Oriental Music: Preserving the Identity of Middle Eastern Christians." *ParOr* 44 (2018): 301–310.

Hélou, Clémence. "La vie monastique féminine dans la tradition syriaque." In *Le monachisme syriaque du VIIe siècle à nos jours*. Patrimonie Syriaque: Actes du colloque, VI. Vol. 1, pp. 85–118. Antélias, Lebanon: Centre d'Études et de Recherches Orientales, 1999.

Ingalls, Wayne B. "Ritual Performance as Training for Daughters in Archaic Greece." *Phoenix: Journal of the Classical Association of Canada* 54 (2000): 1–20. doi:10.2307/1089087.

Jarjour, Tala. *Sense and Sadness: Syriac Chant in Aleppo*. Oxford: Oxford University Press, 2018.

Jullien, Florence. "Le monachisme feminin en milieu Syriaque." In *Le monachisme syriaque*, ed. F. Jullien, 65–87. Études Syriaques 7. Paris: Guethner, 2010.

Krueger, Derek. *Liturgical Subjects: Christian Ritual, Biblical Narrative, and the Formation of the Self in Byzantium*. Philadelphia: University of Pennsylvania Press, 2014.

Lange, Christian. *The Portrayal of Christ in the Syriac Commentary on the Diatessaron*. CSCO 616 / Subs. 118. Leuven: Peeters, 2005.

Marks, Susan. "Bayit versus Beit Midrash: Jewish Mother as Teacher." In *A Most Reliable Witness: Essays in Honor of Ross Shepard Kraemer*, ed. Susan Ashbrook Harvey, Nathaniel P. DesRosiers, Shira Lander, Jacqueline Z. Pastis, and Daniel Ulluci, 195–204. Providence: Brown Judaic Studies, 2015.

Mateos, Juan. *Lelya-Ṣapra: Essai d'interprétation des matines chaldéennes*. OCA 156. Rome: Pontificium Institutum Orientalium Studiorum, 1959.

Maxwell, Jaclyn. *Christianization and Communication in Late Antiquity: John Chrysostom and his Congregation in Antioch*. Cambridge: Cambridge University Press, 2006.

Menze, Volker. "Priests, Laity, and the Sacrament of the Eucharist in Sixth Century Syria." *Hugoye* 7 (2007): 129–146.

Menze, Volker. "The *Regula ad Diaconos*: John of Tella, his Eucharistic Ecclesiology and the Establishment of an Ecclesiastical Hierarchy in Exile." *OrChr* 90 (2006): 44–90.

Outtier, Bernard. "Saint Éphrem d'après ses biographies et ses œuvres." *ParOr* 4 (1973): 11–33.

Page, Christopher. *The Christian West and Its Singers: The First Thousand Years*. New Haven: Yale University Press, 2010.

Possekel, Ute. "Selbstverständnis und Bildungsauftrag der Schule von Nisibis." *ZAC* 19 (2015): 104–136.

Possekel, Ute. "'Go and Set Up for Yourselves Beautiful Laws': The School of Nisibis and Institutional Autonomy in Late Antique Education." In *Griechische Philosophie und Wissenschaft bei den Ostsyrern: Im Gedenken an Mār Addai Scher (1867–1915)*, ed. M. Perkams and A.M. Schilling, 29–47. Berlin: de Gruyter, 2019.

Quasten, Johannes. "The Liturgical Singing of Women in Christian Antiquity." *Catholic Historical Review* 27 (1941): 149–165.

Rubenson, Samuel. "Monasticism and the Philosophical Heritage." In *The Oxford Handbook of Late Antiquity*, ed. Scott Fitzgerald Johnson, 487–512. New York: Oxford University Press, 2012.

Rubenson, Samuel. "Wisdom, Paraenesis, and the Roots of Monasticism." In *Early Christian Paraenesis in Context*, ed. James Starr and Troels Engberg-Pedersen, 521–534. Berlin: de Gruyter, 2004.

Rubenson, Samuel. *The Letters of Saint Antony: Monasticism and the Making of a Saint*. Minneapolis: Fortress Press, 1995.

Urbano, Arthur. *The Philosophical Life: Biography and the Crafting of Intellectual Identity in Late Antiquity*. Washington, DC: The Catholic University of America Press, 2013.

Watts, Edward. *City and School in Late Antique Athens and Alexandria*. Berkeley: University of California Press, 2006.

Wickes, Jeffrey. "Between Liturgy and School: Reassessing the Performative Context of Ephrem's *Madrāšê*." *JECS* 26 (2018): 25–51.

CHAPTER 11

Universal Wisdom in Defence of the Particular: Medieval Jewish and Christian Usage of Biblical Wisdom in Arabic Treatises

Miriam L. Hjälm

In 750 CE, the Umayyad Caliphate in Damascus was overthrown by the Abbasids. The new regime designated the newly established city of Baghdad as its capital and initiated a range of reforms, such as encouraging non-Arabs to convert to Islam and including them in the community. During this time in particular, Arabic became the everyday tongue of many urban people, Muslims and non-Muslims alike.[1] The pace with which this linguistic transformation took place was quite remarkable: whereas John of Damascus (d. 749 CE), who lived in the heart of the Umayyad Empire before settling in Palestine, wrote his theological tracts in Greek, his "ideological successor" Theodore Abū Qurra (d. ca. 825 CE), whose works circulated in Edessa, Palestine and Ḥarrān, wrote mainly in Arabic.[2]

The use of a shared language and the increased possibilities for contact offered by the urbanised settings spurred inter-religious engagement and facilitated access to a shared corpus of texts. At the dawn of the Islamic era, the Muslim holy Scriptures, the Qurʾān, appeared in a milieu partially shaped by Judaism and Syriac Christianity, much as the Christian Scriptures were embedded within a Jewish context in their early years. In the process of devel-

---

1 Arabic replaced Greek as the administrative language of the Empire at the time of ʿAbd al-Malik (d. 705 CE).
2 Abū Qurra's theological agenda resembles that of the Damascene; see Sidney H. Griffith, "'Melkites,' 'Jacobites' and the Christological Controversies in Arabic Third/Ninth-Century Syria," in *Syrian Christians Under Islam: The First Thousand Years*, ed. David Thomas (Leiden: Brill, 2001), 9–56, here 38–39. On the biography of Abū Qurra, see the introduction in John C. Lamoreaux, transl., *Theodore Abū Qurrah* (Provo, UT: Brigham Young University Press, 2005); John C. Lamoreaux, "Theodore Abū Qurra," in *The Orthodox Church in the Arab World 700–1700: An Anthology of Sources*, ed. Samuel Noble and Alexander Treiger (DeKalb: Northern Illinois University Press, 2014), 60–89; Alexander Treiger, "New Works by Theodore Abū Qurra," *JECS* 68 (2017): 1–51, and further references there. For an English translation of the Arabic *Vita* of John of Damascus, see Rocio Daga Portillo, "The Arabic Life of St. John of Damascus," *ParOr* (1996): 157–188.

oping and articulating the tenets of belief, the so-called ʿilm al-kalām, also known as Islamic scholastic theology, evolved in the early Abbasid era. Muslims requested translations of Greek philosophy from Christians who knew Greek, Syriac and Arabic, or at least two of these languages. The use and understanding of logic, or *rationalism*, which developed in the Muslim milieu, then returned to—or continued to be used in—the various Christian communities in the area and was adopted also by Jewish writers.[3]

Through intense polemical debates intended to prove the supremacy of their own religion, Muslim, Christian, and Jewish intellectuals contributed to the cultural flourishing commonly known as the Islamic Golden Age. To some extent these scholars engaged with one another using a common paradigm based on common topics, literary structures, methods, and authoritative sources. The present chapter will focus on how one such authoritative source, biblical wisdom, was extracted from its original context and utilized by Jewish and Christian Arabic-speakers to give a rational defence of their own faith traditions. In the ninth and tenth centuries, much of this intellectual activity focused on preventing members of their own communities from converting.[4] The apolo-

---

[3] For an overview on Christian kalām, see David Bertaina, "Christian Kalâm," in *Encyclopedia of Mediterranean Humanism*, ed. Houari Touati (2015), accessed 22 August 2018, http://www.encyclopedie-humanisme.com/?Christian-Kalam. See also Sidney H. Griffith, "Faith and Reason in Christian Kalām: Theodore Abū Qurrah on Discerning the True Religion," in *Christian Arabic Apologetics during the Abbasid Period (750–1258)*, ed. Samir Khalil Samir and Jørgen S. Nielsen (Leiden: Brill, 1994), 1–43. From the large amount of works on Jewish kalām, see for instance Haggai Ben-Shammai, "Kalām in Medieval Jewish Philosophy," in *History of Jewish Philosophy*, ed. Daniel Frank and Oliver Leaman (London: Routledge, 1997), 91–117; Gregor Schwarb, "Capturing the Meaning of God's Speech: The Relevance of uṣūl al-fiqh to an Understanding of uṣūl al-tafsīr in Jewish and Muslim kalām," in *A Word Fitly Spoken: Studies in Mediaeval Exegesis of the Hebrew Bible and the Qurʾan Presented to Haggai Ben-Shammai*, ed. Meir M. Bar-Asher et al. (Jerusalem: Ben-Zvi Institute, 2007), 111–156; Meira Polliack, ed., *Karaite Judaism: A Guide to its History and Literary Sources* (Leiden: Brill, 2003); Sarah Stroumsa, "Saadya and Jewish Kalam," in *The Cambridge Companion to Medieval Jewish Philosophy*, ed. Daniel H. Frank and Oliver Leaman (Cambridge: Cambridge University Press, 2003), 71–90.

[4] There are several examples of conversions among intellectuals. In the ninth century, Dāwūd ibn Marwān al-Muqammaṣ converted to Christianity and then back to Judaism; see Sarah Stroumsa, "On Jewish Intellectuals who Converted to Islam in the Early Middle Ages," in *The Jews of Medieval Islam: Community, Society, and Identity; Proceedings of an International Conference Held by the Institute of Jewish Studies, University College London 1992*, ed. Daniel Frank (Leiden: Brill, 1995), 179–197. Another famous example is ʿAlī b. Rabbān al-Ṭabarī (d. ca. 855–870 CE) who converted from Eastern Christianity to Islam; see Camilla Adang, *Muslim Writers on Judaism and the Hebrew Bible: From Ibn Rabban to Ibn Hazm* (Leiden: Brill, 1996), esp. 23–30; Ronny Vollandt, *Arabic Versions of the Pentateuch: A Comparative Study of Jewish, Christian, and Muslim Sources* (Leiden: Brill, 2015), 91–97. Intellectual Muslims took some interest in

gists, to whom we will soon turn, portray a society in which different creeds were constantly set against one another and in which people lacked sufficient tools to discern the truth; an atmosphere characterised by perplexity.[5] One cannot but notice that Theodore Abū Qurra, mentioned above, starts his work *Theologus Autodidactus* in a strikingly similar manner to how Friedrich Nietzsche commences his *Zarathustra*. *Theologus Autodidactus* describes a man who grew up in solitude on a mountain and one day felt compelled to descend to civilization, which he found divided between various religions. Abū Qurra, however, unlike Nietzsche, did not advocate a higher morality by arguing for the need of a "new" man, but was content with re-narrating the story of the once-and-for-all perfect man, Christ. He recapitulates fundamental Christian doctrines and, using reason as his chief weapon, aims at refuting other religions.[6]

Roughly a century later, the Jewish intellectual Saadia Gaon (d. 942 CE) assumed a similar role, seeking to save the perplexed among his people. He states, grievingly, in his magum opus *The Book of Beliefs and Opinions* (*Kitāb al-amānāt wa-l-iʿtiqādāt*, henceforth *The Book of Beliefs*):

> I saw, furthermore, men who were sunk, as it were, in seas of doubt and overwhelmed by waves of confusion and there was no diver to bring them up from the depths nor a swimmer who might take hold of their hands and carry them ashore.[7]

The present study will mainly focus on how these two men, religious leaders in an era of perplexity and conversion, used quotations from biblical wisdom books to prevent their flocks from losing faith in their ancient creeds.[8] Besides surveying some aspects of the reception of this corpus, I hope to add to our

---

Jewish and Christian writings, mostly to refute them, but this provides an interesting glimpse into inter-religious interactions; see for instance Nathan P. Gibson, "A Mid-Ninth-Century Arabic Translation of Isaiah? Glimpses from al-Jāḥiẓ," in *Senses of Scripture, Treasures of Tradition: The Bible in Arabic among Jews, Christians and Muslims*, ed. Miriam L. Hjälm (Leiden: Brill, 2017), 327–369. On *majālis*, see n. 55 below.

5 Cf. Stroumsa, "On Jewish Intellectuals," 196.
6 Abū Qurra, *Theologus Autodidactus*, transl. Lamoreaux, 1.
7 Saadia Gaon, *The Book of Beliefs and Opinions*, transl. Samuel Rosenblatt (New Haven: Yale University Press, 1948, 2nd ed. 1951), 7. For a more general discussion of Judaeo-Arabic polemical works, see Sarah Stroumsa, "Jewish Polemics against Islam and Christianity in the Light of Judaeo-Arabic Texts," in *Judaeo-Arabic Studies: Proceedings of the Founding Conference of the Society for Judaeo-Arabic Studies*, ed. Norman Golb (Amsterdam: Harwood Academic Publishers, 1997), 241–250.
8 Abū Qurra, transl. Lamoreaux; Saadia Gaon, *Book of Beliefs*.

understanding of how Jews and Christians interpreted their religious heritage in a meaningful way, and of the interaction between Jewish and Christian communities in the Islamic world.

1 Abū Qurra, Saadia Gaon, and the Bible

Spurred by the school of *kalām* and its demand for rational arguments, exegetical activity developed strongly among Jews in the Abbasid Caliphate. According to Haggai Ben-Shammai, the growth of exegesis, which became a hallmark of the Gaonic period (9th–11th cent.), was connected with the then novel idea that the Bible should be studied in its own right, independently from rabbinic tradition.[9] Conflicting views on the Bible, as well as which methods should be used in order to interpret and translate it in an Arabic-speaking context, culminated in a rift within Judaism between Rabbanites and Karaites. Whereas the former accepted the authority of the Oral Law, the latter rejected it.[10] As pointed out by Meira Polliack, in this new context the authoritative status of certain families or schools of rabbis and their orally received traditions was undermined and replaced by a new literacy which focused on the Bible "as a textual reference system and on the individual skills of the interpreter as one who interrogates this reference system."[11] It was in this intellectual context that Saadia al-Fayyūmī, who came from an undistinguished family, was appointed Gaon of the Sura Academy in Babylonia (near modern Baghdad) in 928 CE.[12] Saadia was a prolific author and a devout exegete who did not hes-

---

9   Haggai Ben-Shammai, "The Tension between Literal Interpretation and Exegetical Freedom," in *With Reverence for the Word: Medieval Scriptural Exegesis in Judaism, Christianity, and Islam*, ed. Jane D. McAuliffe, Barry D. Walfish, and Joseph W. Goering (Oxford: Oxford University Press, 2010), 33–50, here 33–34.
10 On Karaite Bible translations and views of the Bible, see for instance Meira Polliack, *The Karaite Tradition of Arabic Bible Translation: A Linguistic and Exegetical Study of Karaite Translations of the Pentateuch from the Tenth and Eleventh Century C.E.* (Leiden: Brill, 1997); Meira Polliack, "Inversion of 'Written' and 'Oral' Torah in Relation to the Islamic Arch-Models of Qur'an and Hadith," *Jewish Studies Quarterly* 22 (2015): 243–302; Marzena Zawanowska, "Religion in an Age of Reason: Reading Divine Attributes into the Medieval Karaite Bible Translations of Scriptural Texts," in *Senses of Scripture*, 153–181.
11 Meira Polliack, "Concepts of Scripture among the Jews of the Medieval Islamic World," in *Jewish Concepts of Scripture: A Comparative Introduction*, ed. Benjamin D. Sommer (New York: New York University Press, 2012), 80–101, here 81–82.
12 For overviews on Saadia, see for instance Henry Malter, *Saadia Gaon: His Life and Works* (Philadelphia: Jewish Publication Society of America, 1921).

itate to respond to the intellectual needs of his time.[13] In *The Book of Beliefs*, he explains that the biblical text must be understood literally unless the plain sense: 1) contradicts the experience of the senses; 2) contradicts reason; 3) contradicts the plain meaning of another (clearer) text within Scripture; or 4) is contradicted by reliable tradition, that is, as transmitted by the ancient rabbis.[14] In any of these four cases, the plain meaning of the biblical text should be replaced by an allegorical interpretation which harmonizes the meaning of the biblical text with these wider principles (i.e., sensual knowledge, reason, another text, or tradition). In this manner, Saadia brings Jewish interpretation in line with the requirements of *kalām* and refutes Karaism by emphasising the constant need to comprehend the meaning of Scripture in light of tradition.

The practice of writing commentaries on biblical books was widespread among Christians in patristic times, when crucial internal debates concerned the boundaries of non-literal interpretation such as allegory and typology. Discussions about Bible interpretation were often connected to other theological debates or to questions of identity and thus, at least partly, divided Christians along confessional lines. Yet methods and exegesis of specific passages were easily shared across such lines. Few early Christian Arabic commentaries or introductions to biblical works have as yet been edited, and we lack comprehensive studies on the type of changes in exegesis that Islamic influence might have had upon Arabic-speaking Christians, but on the whole it appears that Christian commentators remained heavily reliant upon their Syriac or Greek heritage.[15] Abū Qurra does not explicitly discuss interpretive methods, besides pointing out that understanding the Bible in a slavishly literal way is irrational (implying that this is what the Jews did);[16] and we are left to glean what we

---

13   For various aspects of Saadia's Bible translations, see, among others, Meira Polliack, "Arabic Translations, Rabbanite, Karaite," in *Textual History of the Bible*, vol. 1A, ed. Armin Lange and Emanuel Tov (Leiden: Brill, 2016), 289–308; Joshua Blau, "The Linguistic Character of Saadia Gaon's Translation of the Pentateuch," *Oriens* 36 (2001): 1–9; Amir Ashur, Sivan Nir, and Meira Polliack, "Three Fragments of Saʿadya Gaon's Arabic Translation of Isaiah Copied by the Court Scribe Joseph ben Samuel (c. 1181–1209)," in *Senses of Scripture*, 487–508, esp. 487–490, and further references there. The latter article discusses aspects of the reception of his translations.

14   Cf. Saadia Gaon, *Book of Beliefs*, transl. Rosenblatt, 232, 265–267.

15   A most helpful guide to Christian Arabic works and authors is the multi-volume *Christian-Muslim Relations: A Bibliographical History*, ed. David Thomas et al. (Leiden, Brill, 2009–). Georg Graf, *Geschichte der christlichen arabischen Literatur*, 5 vols. (Vatican: Biblioteca Apostolica Vaticana, 1944–1953), is still relevant.

16   Abū Qurra, *On the Councils*, transl. Lamoreaux, 63.

can about his approach to biblical interpretation from the way he uses biblical quotations.[17] Whereas Saadia translated the Hebrew Scriptures into Arabic, wrote commentaries on several biblical books, and composed both liturgical and theological-apologetical works, Abū Qurra focused on defending Orthodox Christianity. Abū Qurra was not an exegete proper in that he did not preoccupy himself with exegetical methods, and he did not even seem to have had access to all the Old Testament books.[18] In his treatises, he may have relied mainly on testimony collections, which assembled scriptural quotations on certain topics, as well as on apologetic writings from earlier times, as did many other Christian Arabic apologists.[19]

Abū Qurra probably does not cite biblical wisdom material extensively because of the universal nature of biblical wisdom books, which do not contain as much prophetic material as do the Psalms or prophetic books that he quotes in support of specific doctrines. Despite his frequent recourse to the Psalms, typical wisdom Psalms are not quoted, nor are Ecclesiastes, Wisdom of Solomon, or Ben Sira. The handful of quotes from biblical wisdom literature that we do find are from Proverbs, Song of Songs, Job and the "Praise of Wisdom" (Baruch 3:9–4:4), books quoted primarily for one of two reasons: either to argue for the

---

17 For articles on Abū Qurra's use of Scripture, see Sidney H. Griffith, "Arguing from Scriptures: The Bible in the Christian/Muslim Encounter in the Middle Ages," in *Scripture and Pluralism: Reading the Bible in the Religiously Plural Worlds of the Middle Ages and Renaissance*, ed. Thomas Heffernan and Thomas Burman (Leiden: Brill, 2006), 29–58; Samir Khalil Samir, "Note sur les citations bibliques chez Abū Qurrah," OCP 49 (1983): 184–191; Peter Tarras, "The Spirit Before the Letter: Theodore Abū Qurra's Use of Biblical Quotations in the Context of Early Christian Arabic Apologetics," in *Senses of Scripture*, 79–103; Alexander Treiger, "From Theodore Abū Qurra to Abed Azrié: The Arabic Bible in Context," in *Senses of Scripture*, 11–57; and Miriam L. Hjälm, "Psalms to Reason or to Heal? The Conceptualization of Scripture and Hermeneutical Methods in Early Rūm Orthodox Tracts" (submitted for publication).

18 Abū Qurra once states that he only quotes select passages from the Old Testament because "we do not have access to the majority of the Old Testament" (*On Our Salvation*, transl. Lamoreaux, 149).

19 On testimony collections, see David Bertaina, "The Development of Testimony Collections in Early Christian Apologetics with Islam," in *The Bible in Arab Christianity*, ed. David Thomas (Leiden: Brill, 2007), 151–173. In this very helpful study, the author argues that Abū Qurra's use of Bible quotations marks a shift away from earlier writings. The study is based on a later reception of Abū Qurra: *The Debate of Theodore Abū Qurra with Muslim Scholars in the Court of the Caliph al-Ma'mūn*. See David Bertaina, "An Arabic Account of Theodore Abu Qurra in Debate at the Court of Caliph al-Ma'mun: A Study in Early Christian and Muslim Literary Dialogues" (PhD diss., Catholic University of America, 2007). See also Mark Swanson, "Beyond Prooftexting (1): The Use of the Bible in Some Early Arabic Christian Apologies," in *The Bible in Arab Christianity*, 91–112, here 98–105.

eternality of the Christ, or for Abū Qurra to identify himself and his community with the righteous and the wise who are mentioned in these biblical books.

Despite their small number, Abū Qurra's quotations of wisdom material are of great interest, both for our understanding of how biblical wisdom material was utilized in a later era for the purpose of supporting contemporary doctrines and, ultimately, for the upholding of a community, as well as for demonstrating how interpretations of the Bible were exchanged between religious communities. Below we will examine Abū Qurra's quotations from wisdom books and, where possible, compare them with Saadia's use of the same or similar passages.

2   Biblical Wisdom in Arabic Treatises

In the context of arguing for the Eternal Son, Abū Qurra quotes Ps 110:3, "I begot you from the womb, before the light," and similar passages that were interpreted as maintaining the eternal existence of Christ.[20] He then asserts that Solomon labels the Eternal Son "Wisdom of God" in order to persuade his audience that the Eternal Son/Wisdom was always with God. Anyone who believes that the Eternal Son did not exist prior to time must therefore conclude that God at some point was without Wisdom, which would be irrational since it would imply that God lacked this quality and since it would imply a change in God. The logic of Abū Qurra's argument rests on the assumption that the Eternal Son may be identified with Wisdom. The identification of Wisdom with the Logos in the pre-Christian era, and subsequently in the Christian era with Christ, is well known (cf. John 1), and is taken by Abū Qurra as a generally accepted truth. In line with many patristic authors, he quotes Prov 8:22–30 as a proof for this identification:

> He [*al-ibn al-azlī* (the Eternal Son)] said, speaking in the voice of Wisdom, *The Lord created me at the beginning of his ways for his deeds. Before the ages, he established me in the beginning. Before the earth was made ... I was acting with him. I was daily his delight, and I was rejoicing in him always* (Prov 8:22–30).[21]

---

20   Abū Qurra, *On Our Salvation*, transl. Lamoreaux, 145, Arabic text ed. Qusṭanṭīn al-Bāshā, *Mayāmir Thāwdūrus Abī Qurrah usquf Ḥarrān: Aqdam ta'līf 'arabī naṣrānī* (Beirut: Maṭbaʻat al-Fawāʼid, 1904 [?]), 98.

21   Abū Qurra, *On Our Salvation*, transl. Lamoreaux, 145, Arabic text ed. al-Bāshā, 98. Cf. Maurice Dowling, "Proverbs 8:22–31 in the Christology of the Early Fathers," *Perichoresis* 8 (2010): 47–65.

Saadia deals with this Christian interpretation in the chapter on God's unity, where he states:

> Now I also encountered one of them [i.e., the Christians] who interpreted the passage, *The Lord made me as the beginning of his way* (Prov. 8:22), to indicate that God possesses an eternal word (*kalima qadīma*) that has always been in existence together with Him.[22]

Saadia then confirms the identification of (divine) Wisdom (*ḥikma*) as the referent of "me" in Proverbs 8:22, but criticizes the Christian understanding of its function. Rather than indicating that Wisdom was used as an instrument in creating the world, he claims that the wording indicates that God created it *wisely* (*muḥkam*).[23]

In the above passage Saadia is primarily concerned with the question of *creatio ex nihilo*. He is convinced that wisdom is one of God's attributes, and he previously argued at length that Christians mistake attributes for hypostases (i.e., persons).[24] He suggests that Christians arrive at this and other misunderstandings for two reasons, namely their failure to apply rational methods and their lack of knowledge of the Hebrew language. Thus, their problems are both rational and exegetical, and Saadia sometimes uses both accusations as a two-edged sword to dismantle an argument. In both cases, Saadia displays fairly good knowledge of Christian thought.

As for rational argument, Saadia states that Christians are ignorant of the methods of logical proof. He seemingly implies that they wrongly extend observations that are true for humans, for whom vitality and knowledge are distinct from essence, to what is true for God, for whom vitality and knowledge are

---

22 Prov 8:22 ff. was of great importance for Saadia since it seemingly contradicted the doctrine of *creatio ex nihilo*. In his work *Creation*, he dedicates an entire chapter to disproving the major interpretations of this verse known to him. He then develops his argument, evidently principally with Christians in mind, in section 6 of the chapter on God's unity (*Book of Beliefs*, transl. Rosenblatt, 103, 107–108).

23 Cf. Saadia Gaon, *Book of Beliefs*, transl. Rosenblatt, 55, 107. Here Saadia seems to be in dialogue with Midrash Genesis Rabba. For a discussion of the latter, see Susanne Plietzsch, "That Is What Is Written: Retrospective Revelation of the Meaning of a Verse," in *Narratology, Hermeneutics, and Midrash: Jewish, Christian, and Muslim Narratives from the Late Antiquity through to Modern Times*, ed. Constanza Cordoni and Gerhard Langer (Göttingen: V&R Unipress, 2014), 177–186.

24 Saadia Gaon, *Book of Beliefs*, transl. Rosenblatt, 103–107. He arrives at the conclusion that Christians erred since they do not reckon that if God is divided (into three persons), God must be a physical being (*jisman*), "for anything that harbours distinction within itself is unquestionably a physical being." Saadia Gaon, *Book of Beliefs*, transl. Rosenblatt, 103.

intrinsic to essence; and since only created beings harbour distinctions, the Christian argument on God's unity is flawed.[25] Saadia furthermore points out that it is inconceivable that there was a time when God was without life and knowledge, i.e., he uses the same argument as does Abū Qurra with regard to wisdom, but emphasizes that these are attributes of God's essence, not independent entities.[26]

Concerning exegesis, Saadia time and again comes back to the argument that Christians undermine the validity of their own exegesis, and hence the doctrinal conclusions they draw from it, by misunderstanding the Hebrew language. In the passage on divine attributes mentioned above, he states that God is "omniscient," or "wise" (*'ālim*). The Arabic word *'ālim* is an active participle that predicates something about its subject, i.e., God. In his discussion, he adds another eternal quality of God, namely *ḥayy* (alive), also predicated of God's essence.[27] Turning to the Christians' scriptural proofs for the Trinity, he apparently challenges the connection they assert between the biblical quotations and what he understands as attributes of God by claiming that spirit (*rūḥ*) and word (*kalima*), which are mentioned in Scripture in connection with God's activities, are in the form of nouns and thus designate entities created by God in order to convey his message to the prophets. He argues that it is their lack of knowledge of Hebrew that leads Christians to misinterpret these scriptural passages.[28]

It is quite reasonable to believe that Saadia knew that the terms *rūḥ* and *kalima*, on which he lingers, occur in the Qur'ān where discussions on the Trinity are apparently referenced: "The Messiah, Jesus, the son of Mary, was but a messenger of Allah and His word (*kalima*) which He directed to Mary and a spirit (*rūḥ*) from Him" (sūra 4:171; Sahih International, somewhat rephrased). The earliest Christian Arabic theologians used this and similar passages in the Qur'ān to argue that even in the Qur'ān the triune nature of God is evident.[29] One may surmise that Saadia did not passively repeat anti-Christian

---

25   Saadia Gaon, *Book of Beliefs*, transl. Rosenblatt, 104.
26   Saadia Gaon, *Book of Beliefs*, transl. Rosenblatt, 104. Since Saadia has already established that knowledge and, he adds, life are not hypostases but attributes (of which there are many), he wonders why Christians do not conclude that all attributes are persons.
27   Saadia Gaon, *Kitāb al-amānāt wa-l-i'tiqādāt*, ed. Samuel Landauer (Leiden: Brill, 1880), 86; Engl. transl. Rosenblatt, *Book of Beliefs*, 103.
28   Saadia Gaon, *Kitāb al-amānāt*, ed. Landauer, 88; transl. Rosenblatt, 105.
29   See Sidney H. Griffith, "The Qur'an in Christian Arabic Literature: A Cursory Overview," in *Arab Christians and the Qur'an from the Origins of Islam to the Medieval Period*, ed. Mark Beaumont (Leiden: Brill, 2018), 1–19; Mark Beaumont, "'Ammār al-Baṣrī: Ninth Century Christian Theology and Qur'anic Presuppositions," in *Arab Christians and the Qur'an*, 83–

polemics from earlier generations but engaged in debates with contemporary Christians. It should also be mentioned that of the six biblical passages which Saadia quotes as being used by Christians in support of the Trinity,[30] four are used in Abū Qurra's treatises *On the Trinity* and *On Salvation*.[31] These include a passage from Job, in which Job says, "The spirit of God is the one who created me" (Job 33:4). In refuting Christian exegesis of this passage, Saadia asserts that once again Christians misunderstand the language of Scripture because passages that speak of the spirit of God do not intend to suggest a separate entity within God, but seek to show that God created *with intent*, an interpretation that Saadia supports with another passage from Job, "But He is at one with Himself" (23:13).[32]

Saadia concludes his argument by pointing out that similar passages used by Christians in defence of their doctrines are in fact only "figures of speech and extensions of meaning."[33] Thus, Saadia accuses Christians of biblical lit-

---

105; David Thomas, "With the Qur'an in Mind," in *Arab Christians and the Qur'an*, 131–149. For similar arguments, see also Bertaina, "Testimony Collections," *passim*.

30   Job 33:4, Ps 33:6, Prov 8:22, and Gen 1:26 are used by Abū Qurra in connection to the Trinity, whereas 2 Sam 23:2 and Gen 18:1–2 are not found in the texts transl. by Lamoreaux or in Abū Qurra, *A Treatise on the Veneration of the Holy Icons*, transl. Sidney H. Griffith (Louvain: Peeters, 1997). Cf. Saadia Gaon, *Book of Beliefs*, transl. Rosenblatt, 105–108. Najib George Awad has discussed Abū Qurra's Trinitarian terminology at length in his *Orthodoxy in Arabic Terms: A Study of Theodore Abu Qurrah's Theology in Its Islamic Context* (Berlin: de Gruyter, 2015), 163–266.

31   The Christian topics discussed and refuted by Saadia are too general to suggest that he was directly refuting Abū Qurra's treatises, although in theory he could very well have had access to some of them. According to Daniel J. Lasker, who surveyed Saadia's attitude towards Christians in *The Book of Beliefs*, Saadia addresses three topics concerning Christians: the nature of God, whether Messiah has come or not, and the abrogation of Jewish law; see his "Saadya Gaon on Christianity and Islam," in *The Jews of Medieval Islam*, 165–178, here 166–168. In *Against the Jews*, Abū Qurra argues at length that since Jesus performed more miracles than Moses, he is more trustworthy (transl. Lamoreaux, 28–30). Lasker notes that Saadia rebuts this claim but points out that Origen brought up the question as well, and that it is a common topic in Christian polemics; see Lasker, "Saadya Gaon on Christianity and Islam," 172–173. Finally, one should point out that Abū Qurra accuses Jews of interpreting anthropomorphisms literally (transl. Lamoreaux, 63), a claim that Saadia refutes (cf. his principles on non-literal interpretation cited above).

32   Abū Qurra, *On the Trinity*, transl. Lamoreaux, 182; Saadia Gaon, *Book of Beliefs*, transl. Rosenblatt, 106.

33   Saadia Gaon, *Book of Beliefs*, transl. Rosenblatt, 107. Needless to say, the authors of polemical writings do not aim at presenting the opponent appropriately. For instance, Saadia claims that passages such as, *That the hand of the Lord has wrought this* (Job 12:9), according to the Christian system of logic should be interpreted as referencing another property of God, alongside spirit and word (*Book of Beliefs*, transl. Rosenblatt, 106–107). Such rea-

eralism.³⁴ Abū Qurra in turn concludes his *Against the Jews* by lamenting the Jews' inability to see what is good for them, and in support he quotes from the Song of Songs to defend the Christian appropriation of Scripture:

> for reason surely leads to Christ, and Christ confirms Moses and the prophets. Both the Old Testament and the New Testament thus belong to us, even as Solomon the son of David said in the Song of Songs, "On our doors are all fruits, both old and new (7:13)."³⁵

While Saadia rejects any christocentric exegesis of wisdom material, he shares with Abū Qurra the strategy of extending the moral argument of wisdom books to his own context, for they both apply the references to "the wise" and "the foolish," abundantly attested in this kind of literature, to their followers and opponents, respectively.³⁶ For instance, Abū Qurra quotes Prov 26:11, "returned to your vomit,"³⁷ and applies it to those who, he claims, get stuck in their faulty way of reasoning concerning God's triune nature. Saadia quotes the same passage and applies it to those who "constantly lapse back into sin," a statement which in this case is not directly polemical.³⁸ He quotes extensively from Proverbs and

---

soning is of course foreign to Christians, and Abū Qurra uses the example of God's hand and other anthropomorphisms as metaphors of the Trinity (*On the Trinity*, transl. Lamoreaux, 190–191).

34 Abū Qurra twice quotes from the wisdom part of the Book of Baruch (Baruch 3:35–37) as proof for the Incarnation of God: "This is our God; no other can be counted with him. He found the way of knowledge and gave it to Jacob his beloved and to Israel his friend. And after that he appeared on earth, and lived among human beings" (*Against the Jews*, transl. Lamoreaux, 37; and *On Our Salvation*, transl. Lamoreaux, 146) As expected, Saadia does not refer to this passage, which is not part of the Hebrew Bible.

35 Abū Qurra, *Against the Jews*, transl. Lamoreaux, 39.

36 This strategy of making Scripture relevant in a new context is comparable to Elizabeth A. Clark's category of "Changing the Audience" in her study on early Christian exegesis. In this study she focuses on how Scripture was interpreted for an ascetic audience. She claims that this methodology was used to bolster the audience's ascetic commitment; see her *Reading Renunciation: Asceticism and Scripture in Early Christianity* (Princeton: Princeton University Press, 1999), 136–138. This strategy can be compared to how the authors in our corpus encourage Christians to commit to their own creed in "times of confusion" (cf. Saadia's description of his society quoted above).

37 Abū Qurra, *On Our Salvation*, transl. Lamoreaux, 141. Abū Qurra also uses Proverbs to invoke common sense, such as Prov 20:10.23, "My soul hates a balance that is too big or to small" (*Greek Fragments*, transl. Lamoreaux, 232). In *On the Venerations of Icons*, Abū Qurra makes use of a proverb from Prov 19:17, "Whoever gives to the poor makes a loan to God," which again is a saying of a more universal kind (transl. Griffith, 95).

38 Saadia Gaon, *Book of Beliefs*, transl. Rosenblatt, 233.

other wisdom books in which "the righteous one" is contrasted with "the fool," and he identifies the former with those who follow his own "rational" argument on the right religion, and the latter with his adversaries. For instance, he suggests that those who abandon one system of thought for another as soon as they find some flaw in it, are like a person who wants to enter a city but does not know the way there. He writes, "Of him does Scripture say, *The labor of fools wearieth every one of them, for he knoweth not how to go to the city* (Eccl 10:15),"[39] and, "Any person, then, who follows this course of giving his cognitive faculty dominion over his appetites and impulses, is disciplined 'by the discipline of the wise,' as Scripture says, *The fear of the Lord is the discipline of wisdom* (Prov 15:33) ... *But the foolish despise ... discipline* (Prov 7:22)."[40]

As mentioned above, Abū Qurra did not occupy himself with biblical exegesis proper. There are, however, early compositions of a more exegetical character. The earliest attested introduction to a Christian Arabic translation of Proverbs, for instance, is commonly attributed to al-Ḥārith ibn Sinān.[41] I have argued elsewhere that this prologue, and the version of Proverbs that follows, have been wrongly attributed to al-Ḥārith.[42] The earliest attestation of this Christian Arabic translation of Proverbs, without the prologue, is the tenth- or early eleventh-century manuscript Sinai Ar. 597. The earliest extant witness to the prologue is a manuscript dated to around the eleventh century, part of which now is in Birmingham and part of which is in Milan.[43]

---

[39] Saadia Gaon, *Book of Beliefs*, transl. Rosenblatt, 7.
[40] Saadia Gaon, *Book of Beliefs*, transl. Rosenblatt, 361.
[41] For al-Ḥarith, see Joseph Nasrallah, "Deux versions Melchites partielles de la Bible du IXe et du Xe siècles," *OrChr* 64 (1980): 202–215. Cf. Vollandt, *Arabic Versions*, 60, n. 60. Here we will focus on the content of the prologue, which has been edited and transl. by Joseph Sadan, "In the Eyes of the Christian Writer al-Ḥāriṯ ibn Sinān: Poetics and Eloquence as a Platform of Inter-Cultural Contacts and Contrasts," *Arabica* 56 (2009): 1–26, here 13–25. Sadan did not have access to the earliest manuscript. See n. 43 below.
[42] Miriam L. Hjälm, "Texts Attributed to al-Ḥāriṯ b. Sinān b. Sinbāṭ al-Ḥarrānī: Notes on Prologues, Translation Techniques and New Manuscripts" (submitted for publication).
[43] The earliest manuscript is in two parts, one of which is located in Milan (Biblioteca Ambrosiana, X 200 Sup., usually dated 11th–12th cent.), and the other in Birmingham (Mingana Christian Ar. Add. 199 [121], dated to around 950 CE). As to the difference in date, based on a survey of ninth-century manuscripts, this manuscript is datable to the long eleventh century; see Hjälm, "Texts Attributed to al-Ḥāriṯ." Cf. Miriam L. Hjälm, "The Hazy Edges of the Biblical Canon: A Case Study of the Wisdom of Solomon in Arabic," in *The Embroidered Bible: Studies in Biblical Apocrypha and Pseudepigrapha in Honour of Michael E. Stone*, ed. Lorenzo DiTommaso, Matthias Henze, and William Adler (Leiden: Brill, 2017), 569–187.

In the prologue to Proverbs, the author informs his audience that Solomon composed the book of Proverbs for two reasons: first, because the reader would find pleasure in reading it, and second, because of Solomon's

> desire to be like his father; for his father's words in Psalms have meter [rhythm]. [Therefore king Solomon] gave his words the form of *amṯāl* [spelled: *amṯāl*, proverbs], the form of *qawāriʿ* (exhortations), and the form of *awābid* (lessons, past experiences).[44]

Towards the end of the introduction, the author provides his audience with various riddles found in the last part of Proverbs and concludes by stating,

> And after all these matters, he [Solomon] compares the man who possesses benevolence and fear of God with a virtuous and industrious woman, of whom he says that she has sent forth her maidens to work [cf. Prov 29:15, LXX][45]

The passage to which he alludes describes the "Woman of Valour," a stereotypical picture of the good wife, which the king wishes for his son to marry. Unless they interpret it literally as reference to a good Christian wife,[46] patristic commentators often understand the woman in this passage as a type of the Church.[47] In this Christian Arabic prologue, however, the description becomes an allegory of a righteous man. Interestingly, the same interpretation of this passage was offered by Saadia. In a recent study, Ilana Sasson has commented on his exegesis of this passage:

> [Saadia] begins his introduction to the poem by saying that the biblical author presents at the end of the book a metaphor of the good wife in order to compare her with every wise and proper man ... Saadia explains that the author (Solomon) crafted his metaphor describing the skills of a woman, and not a man, out of reverence for men. The

---

44 Sadan, "In the Eyes," 22.
45 Sadan, "In the Eyes," 25.
46 See for example, *Apostolic Constitutions* 1.3.8; Gregory of Nazianzus, *On his Sister St. Gorgonia* (Oration 8.9), transl. in Robert J. Wright and Thomas C. Oden, eds., *Proverbs, Ecclesiastes, Song of Solomon*, Ancient Christian Commentary on Scripture, Old Testament, vol. 9 (Downers Grove, IL: InterVarsity Press, 2005), 186.
47 Origen, *Exposition on Proverbs*, Fragment 31.16; Caesarius of Arles, *Sermon* 139:1; Augustine, *Sermon* 37.4–5; excerpts transl. in Wright and Oden, *Proverbs, Ecclesiastes, Song of Solomon*, 186–187.

underlying supposition in Saadia's commentary is that the description of a woman's body is allowable, while the description of a man's body is ill-mannered.[48]

Sasson further notes that Yefet ben 'Elī, who polemicized against Saadia even though he sometimes also relied on him, presents a very different account. Suggesting that Lemuel's mother, understood by him to be Bathsheba, is the author of this passage, Yefet interprets the text literally as Bathsheba's advice to Solomon concerning the type of woman she, his mother, would like him to marry.[49] In contrast to Yefet, Saadia was of the opinion that Solomon composed all of Proverbs, a common assumption, which was also shared by the Christian Arabic author of the introduction to the translation discussed above.

3 Exegesis and Jewish-Christian Relations

It remains to discuss whether or not Saadia and the Christian author of this introduction to Proverbs relied on a common source. The practice of "gender-bending" was quite common in early Christian exegesis as a method of making Scripture relevant for a specific (male) audience.[50] Our author must have been active in or around the eleventh century, and might thus have been a contemporary of Saadia (d. 942 CE). Of course, the two writers could have reached the same conclusion independently. Yet it is not unlikely that this interpretation resulted from an inter-religious exchange at some point. According to Sarah Stroumsa, exegesis constitutes a genre most suitable, methodologically, for the tracing of inter-religious encounters.[51] Already in 1991, she demonstrated that

---

48 Ilana Sasson, "The Book of Proverbs between Saadia and Yefet," *Intellectual History of the Islamicate World* 1 (2013): 159–178, here 174.

49 Sasson, "Book of Proverbs," 175.

50 "Changing sex: gender-bending" is another category developed by Clark in her study on the early Christian use of Scripture (*Reading Renunciation*, 138–140). She does not mention this specific biblical passage, but the method is frequently applied in biblical interpretation by early Christian authors, including on Prov 5:3–4. It seems as if some sort of gender-bending took place within the Hebrew Scriptures as well: Esther may be seen as a female equivalent to Joseph, and Judith to David, cf. Irmtraud Fischer, "Reception of Biblical Texts within the Bible: A Starting Point of Midrash?" in *Narratology, Hermeneutics, and Midras*, 15–24, here 21.

51 Sarah Stroumsa, "The Impact of Syriac Tradition on Early Judaeo-Arabic Bible Exegesis," *Aram* 3 (1991): 83–96, here 83–85. I have previously noted such interpretation in the Book of Daniel, where the Christian translation in Sinai MS Ar. 1 and Yefet's commentary on the

the commentary on the first verses of Genesis by the tenth-century Jewish convert Dāwūd ibn Marwān al-Muqammiṣ must be explained as the result of influence from Syriac Christian sources, such as *Mimra* 1, 96H by the eighth-century exegete Theodore bar Khōnī. She also showed how this and other interpretations were then transmitted through various Judaeo-Arabic works, including those by the tenth-century Karaite Jacob al-Qirqisānī. For instance, Maimonides' commentary on Gen 1 exhibits the influence of the ninth-century East Syriac author Ishoʿdad of Merv, who in turn relied on Theodore of Mopsuestia (d. 428 CE).[52] Thus, it is clear that Christian exegesis played a role in forming the Judaeo-Arabic exegetical tradition. Recently, Arye Zoref has followed Stroumsa's careful method of tracing Christian influence, and has provided additional instances of the influence of Syriac exegetes (e.g., Ephrem and Ishoʿdad) upon the Genesis commentaries by Yefet and al-Qirqisānī and, indirectly, upon Yeshʿuah ben Yehudah, another Karaite active in the eleventh century.[53] Zoref concludes that Judaeo-Arabic authors accessed Christian material in written form.[54] Thus, written works may have circulated among various religious communities, parallel to disputes about theological topics that occurred in inter-religious oral settings known as *majālis*[55] and in personal meetings.[56] In particular methods of biblical exegesis could be transferred from one com-

---

same verse exhibit a similar non-literal translation, see Miriam L. Hjälm, *Christian Arabic Versions of Daniel: A Comparative Study of Early MSS and Translation Techniques in MSS Sinai Ar. 1 and 2* (Leiden: Brill, 2016), 219–121.

52   Stroumsa, "Impact of Syriac Tradition."
53   Arye Zoref, "The Influence of Syriac Bible Commentaries on Judeo Arabic Exegesis as Demonstrated by Several Stories from the Book of Genesis," *Studies in Christian-Jewish Relations* 11 (2016): 1–18.
54   Zoref, "Influence of Syriac Bible Commentaries," 17.
55   Muslim leaders invited representatives from various creeds to defend their theological and philosophical stance in a so-called *majlis* (sing.) "sitting." This phenomenon gave rise to a genre among Muslim, Christian and Jewish apologetics where the debate took place in such a setting. Although the surviving records of such debates themselves are often fictional, these kinds of *majālis* were most likely taking place in the early Abbasid era, cf. Hava Lazarus-Yafeh et al., eds., *The Majlis: Interreligious Encounters in Medieval Islam* (Wiesbaden: Harrassowitz, 1999).
56   A famous example of a religious leaders consulting other religious leaders is the statement in *The Fihrist* by Ibn al-Nadīm (d. 995 CE) that Muslims visited a Christian named Pethion concerning a theological statement by a certain Ibn Kullāb; see Ibn al-Nadīm, *Kitab al-Fihrist mit Anmerkungen*, 2 vols., ed. Gustav Flügel (Leipzig: Vogel, 1871–1872, reprint Beirut: Khayats, 1964), ١٨٠. See also the account on the Jewish Hai Gaon (d. 1038) who reportedly summoned a Katholikos for the interpretation of a Psalm verse; see Stroumsa, "Impact of Syriac Tradition," 93–95, who quotes Ibn Aqnin's commentary on the Song of Songs.

munity to another due to the similarity between East Syriac and (especially) Karaite approaches to the Bible. Both typically shared an interest in viewing the Bible at least partly as a self-contained text in its own right and placed value on its literal and historical sense. Yet exegetical exchange is notable also between Rabbanites and various Christian communities. Furthermore, such exchange soon went beyond commentaries on specific verses and extended to the adoption of complete books, the most important example of which are the Coptic and Syriac Orthodox adaptions of Saadia's Arabic translation of the Pentateuch.[57]

Whereas Saadia seems to be quite up-to-date with contemporary Christian Arabic topics, the same is not true for Abū Qurra. When writing passages critical of the Jewish religion, Abū Qurra exhibits poor knowledge of, or a disinterest in, contemporary Jewish communities, and on the whole he repeats polemics from earlier times. But Abū Qurra belonged to the first generation of Christian Arabic writers, a time when access to material from other traditions was comparatively limited.[58] Later Christian authors display more knowledge of Jewish writings. For instance, Agapius of Manbij shows at the least an awareness of the fact that (Rabbanite) Jews adhere to an oral Torah, contrary to the impression given by Abū Qurra.[59]

Daniel Lasker's observation that Saadia seems more interested in criticizing Christians rather than Muslims in *The Book of Beliefs* draws attention to the comparatively little studied topic of Jewish-Christian relations in the Mus-

---

[57] Graf, *Geschichte*, vol. 1, pp. 101–103 and further references there; Vollandt, *Arabic Versions*, 221–242 and *passim*.

[58] It could also be a strategy Abū Qurra adhered to in order to minimize the attraction of the Jewish creed. Portraying an opponent's views too accurately could attract readers to those views and thus prove counter-productive.

[59] See, for instance, Agapius of Manbij, *Universal History*, ed. and transl. Alexandre Vasiliev, *Kitāb al-ʿunwān/Histoire Universelle*, PO 5 (1910), 559–691, here 665. The text was translated into English by Roger Pearse as *Universal History* (Ipswich, UK, 2009), accessed 21 August 2018, http://www.tertullian.org/fathers/agapius_history_01_part1.htm. For studies on Agapius, see John C. Lamoreaux, "Agapius of Manbij," in *The Orthodox Church in the Arab World*, 136–159. Agapius was also well aware of the fact that the Hebrew and Greek versions of the Old Testament sometimes differed, and he readily blamed the Jews for having tampered with the literal sense of the Scriptures (cf. *taḥrīf*), an accusation brought by Muslims against both Christians and Jews in their arguments that the Qurʾān contains the true version of God's words; see Treiger, "From Theodore Abū Qurra to Abed Azrié," 24–26; Yonatan Moss, "Versions and Perversions of Genesis: Jacob of Edessa, Saadia Gaon and the Falsification of Biblical History," in *Intersections between Judaism and Syriac Christianity*, ed. Aaron M. Butts and Simcha Gross (Tübingen: Mohr Siebeck, forthcoming); Hjälm, "Psalms to Reason."

lim empires.[60] Several scholars have argued that Abū Qurra criticized Jews when he primarily intended to target Muslims, with whom he did not wish to engage overtly. This may of course be true, but such a conclusion should not prevent us from examining more deeply the relations between Christians and Jews and investigate further how they may have reflected on, and engaged with, each other in their common Islamic context, and how their texts and ideas circulated, either to be refuted or to be incorporated into the other tradition.

The challenges faced by Jews and Christians in the early Islamic period resembles in many ways those they encountered during the first centuries CE. Until the early third century, Jews and Christians had to defend their religions not only against "Gnostic" streams and paganism but also against one another.[61] Under Islam, *ahl al-kitāb*, the people of the book,[62] once again found themselves defending this book, this *kitāb*, which in the early Islamic period meant not only a physical text, but also a system of thought.[63] Indeed, the ultimate meaning of sacred texts are provided by the paradigm in which they are interpreted. Thus, Abū Qurra used a range of scriptural proofs against other creeds, including the Jews, in support of his system of thought; and Saadia, in defence of his arguments and in order to refute Christian exegesis, built testimony collections of his own. The practice of refuting scriptural proof-texts with other scriptural proof-texts is characteristic of Christian apologetics and can be traced back to the gospels themselves where we read of Jesus refuting the Devil's interpretation of Ps 91:11–12 by quoting Deuteronomy 6:16, during his temptation in the wilderness (cf. Matt 4:6–7).[64]

---

60   He argues for instance that the abrogation of the Law, which is commonly assumed to be directed at Muslims, is in fact directed towards Christians (hence the use of biblical quotations). See Lasker, "Saadya Gaon on Christianity and Islam," esp. 168–169.
61   Marc Hirshman, *A Rivalry of Genius: Jewish and Christian Biblical Interpretation in Late Antiquity*, transl. from Hebrew by Batya Stein (Albany: State University of New York Press, 1996), 1–12.
62   As Jews and Christians are often referred to in the Qurʾān.
63   Abdulla Galadari, paper presented at the Society of Biblical Literature, Helsinki, July–August 2018. Many thanks to the author for sharing the paper with me. Galadari attributes this view to Daniel A. Madigan, *The Qurʾān's Self-Image: Writing and Authority in Islam's Scripture* (Princeton: Princeton University Press, 2001).
64   Cf. "Talking Back," another category developed by Clark in her study of early Christian exegesis, which she connects with rabbinic exegesis. This technique was typically used in debates; see Clark, *Reading Renunciation*, 128–132.

4   Concluding Remarks

The examples provided in this study hopefully suffice to demonstrate how ancient wisdom was used in a new context to answer the changing needs of two competing religions. On this journey, biblical wisdom literature became less universal in nature and more particular. Quotations from this genre were employed by Abū Qurra and Saadia in matters of exegetical controversy in support of or against particular theological doctrines. Other quotations were used to assure the reader or listener that he or she belonged to the "wise and righteous" and that adherents of other faiths were the "fools." This kind of "identification technique" as an exegetical strategy is of immense importance, for while being a technique that is correctly seen by the modern (and postmodern) eye as a "disparaging" of the other, it also functions as an identity-solidifying technique which assures the relevance of Scripture to each community. It creates solidarity within a group, which strengthens that community's identity and sense of purpose. Whereas linguistic-contextual, literary and historical exegesis may, at least theoretically, be settled by diligent biblical scholarship, the task of deepening a community's sense of identification with the narratives and moral imperatives of Scripture is an ongoing process, which needs to be renewed in every generation. This ongoing, often challenging and sometimes uneasy process of identifying with the biblical texts is, in a way, what makes Scripture sacred in a community of believers, rather than it simply being a collection of historical documents whose original meaning and historical context are, in any case, often beyond our full reach.[65]

Acknowledgements

This chapter was composed with support of the Swedish Research Council (2017-01630). I stand in deep gratitude to Professor Samuel Rubenson who was one of the scholars who initiated me into the field of Christian Arabic studies, and who thereafter constantly supported, advised and encouraged me. For

---

65   The words of Samuel Rubenson regarding the sayings of the Desert Fathers, "Instead of grieving for the lack of authenticity in the sense of true and pure snapshots of, or windows, into a historical situation, we ought to ask ourselves why we want to isolate sayings that we hopefully can claim are authentic sources for the first generations of monks, or why we think that the desert monks of fourth-century Egypt are more important than the monks of the sixth century," apply also, in some sense, to the study of biblical texts and their later reception. See Rubenson, "The Formation and Re-Formations of the Sayings of the Desert Fathers," *StPatr* 55 (2013): 5–22, here 19–20.

similar reasons and for her valuable comments on an earlier version of this paper, I also wish to thank Professor Meira Polliack. Finally, I wish to express my gratitude to Dr. Ute Possekel for carefully reading and commenting on the present paper.

Bibliography

Primary Sources

Abū Qurra, Theodore. Ed. Qusṭanṭīn al-Bāshā [Constantin Bacha], *Mayāmir Thāwdūrus Abī Qurrah usquf Ḥarrān: Aqdam ta'līf 'arabī naṣrānī*. Beirut: Maṭba'at al-Fawā'id, 1904 [?].

Abū Qurra, Theodore. Transl. John C. Lamoreaux, *Theodore Abū Qurrah*. Provo, UT: Brigham Young University Press, 2005.

Abū Qurra, Theodore. *On the Veneration of the Holy Icons*. Transl. Sidney H. Griffith, *A Treatise on the Veneration of the Holy Icons written in Arabic by Theodore Abū Qurrah, Bishop of Ḥarrān (c. 755–c. 830)*. Louvain: Peeters, 1997.

Agapius of Manbij. *Universal History*. Ed. with French transl. Alexandre Vasiliev, *Kitāb al-'unwān/Histoire Universelle*. PO 5 (1910), 559–691. English transl. Roger Pearse, http://www.tertullian.org/fathers/agapius_history_01_part1.htm. Accessed 21 August 2018.

Ibn al-Nadīm. *Fihrist*. Ed. Gustav Flügel, *Kitab al-Fihrist mit Anmerkungen*. 2 vols. Leipzig: Vogel, 1871–1872, reprint Beirut: Khayats, 1964.

Saadia Gaon. [*Book of Beliefs and Opinions*]. Ed. Samuel Landauer, *Kitāb al-amānāt wa-l-i'tiqādāt*. Leiden: Brill, 1880.

Saadia Gaon. *Book of Beliefs and Opinions*. Transl. Samuel Rosenblatt, *Saadia Gaon: The Book of Beliefs and Opinions*. New Haven. Yale University Press, 1948, 2nd ed. 1951.

Secondary Sources

Adang, Camilla. *Muslim Writers on Judaism and the Hebrew Bible: From Ibn Rabban to Ibn Hazm*. Leiden: Brill, 1996.

Ashur, Amir, Sivan Nir, and Meira Polliack. "Three Fragments of Sa'adya Gaon's Arabic Translation of Isaiah Copied by the Court Scribe Joseph ben Samuel (c. 1181–1209)." In *Senses of Scripture*, ed. Hjälm (see below), 487–508.

Awad, Najib George. *Orthodoxy in Arabic Terms: A Study of Theodore Abu Qurrah's Theology in Its Islamic Context*. Berlin: de Gruyter, 2015.

Beaumont, Mark. "'Ammār al-Baṣrī: Ninth Century Christian Theology and Qur'anic Presuppositions." In *Arab Christians and the Qur'an from the Origins of Islam to the Medieval Period*, ed. Mark Beaumont, 83–105. Leiden: Brill, 2018.

Ben-Shammai, Haggai. "Kalām in Medieval Jewish Philosophy." In *History of Jewish Philosophy*, ed. Daniel Frank and Oliver Leaman, 91–117. London: Routledge, 1997.

Ben-Shammai, Haggai. "The Tension between Literal Interpretation and Exegetical Freedom." In *With Reverence for the Word: Medieval Scriptural Exegesis in Judaism, Christianity, and Islam*, ed. Jane D. McAuliffe, Barry D. Walfish, and Joseph W. Goering, 33–50. Oxford: Oxford University Press, 2010.

David Bertaina, "An Arabic account of Theodore Abu Qurra in debate at the court of Caliph al-Ma'mun. A study in early Christian and Muslim literary dialogues," Washington DC, 2007 (PhD Catholic University of America).

Bertaina, David. "Christian Kalâm." In *Encyclopedia of Mediterranean Humanism*, ed. Houari Touati. 2015. Accessed 22 August 2018. http://www.encyclopedie-humanisme.com/?Christian-Kalam.

Bertaina, David. "The Development of Testimony Collections in Early Christian Apologetics with Islam." In *The Bible in Arab Christianity*, ed. David Thomas, 151–173. Leiden: Brill, 2007.

Blau, Joshua "The Linguistic Character of Saadia Gaon's Translation of the Pentateuch." *Oriens* 36 (2001): 1–9.

Clark, Elizabeth A. *Reading Renunciation: Asceticism and Scripture in Early Christianity*. Princeton: Princeton University Press, 1999.

Dowling, Maurice. "Proverbs 8:22–31 in the Christology of the Early Fathers." *Perichoresis* 8 (2010): 47–65.

Fischer, Irmtraud. "Reception of Biblical Texts within the Bible: A Starting Point of Midrash?" In *Narratology, Hermeneutics, and Midrash: Jewish, Christian, and Muslim Narratives from the Late Antiquity through to Modern Times*, ed. Constanza Cordoni and Gerhard Langer, 15–24. Göttingen: V&R Unipress, 2014.

Gibson, Nathan P. "A Mid-Ninth-Century Arabic Translation of Isaiah? Glimpses from al-Jāḥiẓ." In *Senses of Scripture*, ed. Hjälm (see below), 327–369.

Graf, Georg. *Geschichte der christlichen arabischen Literatur*. 5 vols. Vatican: Biblioteca Apostolica Vaticana, 1944–1953.

Griffith, Sidney H. "Arguing from Scriptures: The Bible in the Christian/Muslim Encounter in the Middle Ages." In *Scripture and Pluralism: Reading the Bible in the Religiously Plural Worlds of the Middle Ages and Renaissance*, ed. Thomas Heffernan and Thomas Burman, 29–58. Leiden: Brill, 2006.

Griffith, Sidney H. "Faith and Reason in Christian Kalām: Theodore Abū Qurrah on Discerning the True Religion." In *Christian Arabic Apologetics during the Abbasid Period (750–1258)*, ed. Samir Khalil Samir and Jørgen S. Nielsen, 1–43. Leiden: Brill, 1994.

Griffith, Sidney H. "'Melkites,' 'Jacobites' and the Christological Controversies in Arabic Third/Ninth-Century Syria." In *Syrian Christians Under Islam: The First Thousand Years*, ed. David Thomas, 9–56. Leiden: Brill, 2001.

Griffith, Sidney H. "The Qur'an in Christian Arabic Literature: A Cursory Overview." In *Arab Christians and the Qur'an from the Origins of Islam to the Medieval Period*, ed. Mark Beaumont, 1–19. Leiden: Brill, 2018.

Hirshman, Marc. *A Rivalry of Genius: Jewish and Christian Biblical Interpretation in Late Antiquity*. Translated from Hebrew by Batya Stein. Albany: State University of New York Press, 1996.

Hjälm, Miriam L. *Christian Arabic Versions of Daniel: A Comparative Study of Early MSS and Translation Techniques in MSS Sinai Ar. 1 and 2*. Leiden: Brill, 2016.

Hjälm, Miriam L. "The Hazy Edges of the Biblical Canon: A Case Study of the Wisdom of Solomon in Arabic." In *The Embroidered Bible: Studies in Biblical Apocrypha and Pseudepigrapha in Honour of Michael E. Stone*, ed. Lorenzo DiTommaso, Matthias Henze, and William Adler, 569–587. Leiden: Brill, 2017.

Hjälm, Miriam L. "Psalms to Reason or to Heal? The Conceptualization of Scripture and Hermeneutical Methods in Early Rūm Orthodox Tracts" (submitted for publication).

Hjälm, Miriam L., ed. *Senses of Scripture, Treasures of Tradition: The Bible in Arabic among Jews, Christians and Muslims*. Leiden: Brill, 2017.

Hjälm, Miriam L. "Texts Attributed to al-Ḥāriṯ b. Sinān b. Sinbāṭ al-Ḥarrānī: Notes on Prologues, Translation Techniques and New Manuscripts" (submitted for publication).

Lamoreaux, John C. "Agapius of Manbij." In *The Orthodox Church in the Arab World 700–1700: An Anthology of Sources*, ed. Samuel Noble and Alexander Treiger, 136–159. DeKalb: Northern Illinois University Press, 2014.

Lamoreaux, John C. "Theodore Abū Qurra." In *The Orthodox Church in the Arab World 700–1700: An Anthology of Sources*, ed. Samuel Noble and Alexander Treiger, 60–89. DeKalb: Northern Illinois University Press, 2014.

Lasker, Daniel J. "Saadya Gaon on Christianity and Islam." In *The Jews of Medieval Islam: Community, Society, and Identity: Proceedings of an International Conference Held by the Institute of Jewish Studies, University College London 1992*, ed. Daniel Frank, 165–178. Leiden: Brill, 1995.

Lazarus-Yafeh, Hava, et al., eds. *The Majlis: Interreligious Encounters in Medieval Islam*. Wiesbaden: Harrassowitz, 1999.

Malter, Henry. *Saadia Gaon: His Life and Works*. Philadelphia: Jewish Publication Society of America, 1921.

Moss, Yonatan. "Versions and Perversions of Genesis: Jacob of Edessa, Saadia Gaon and the Falsification of Biblical History." In *Intersections between Judaism and Syriac Christianity*, ed. Aaron M. Butts and Simcha Gross. Tübingen: Mohr Siebeck, forthcoming.

Nasrallah, Joseph. "Deux versions Melchites partielles de la Bible du IXe et du Xe siècles." *OrChr* 64 (1980): 202–215.

Plietzsch, Susanne. "That Is What Is Written: Retrospective Revelation of the Meaning of a Verse." In *Narratology, Hermeneutics, and Midrash: Jewish, Christian, and Muslim Narratives from the Late Antiquity through to Modern Time*, ed. Constanza Cordoni and Gerhard Langer, 177–186. Göttingen: V&R Unipress, 2014.

Polliack, Meira. "Arabic Translations, Rabbanite, Karaite." In *Textual History of the Bible*. Vol. 1A. Ed. Armin Lange and Emanuel Tov, 289–308. Leiden: Brill, 2016.

Polliack, Meira. "Concepts of Scripture among the Jews of the Medieval Islamic World." In *Jewish Concepts of Scripture: A Comparative Introduction*, ed. Benjamin D. Sommer, 80–101. New York: New York University Press, 2012.

Polliack, Meira. "Inversion of 'Written' and 'Oral' Torah in Relation to the Islamic Arch-Models of Qur'an and Hadith." *Jewish Studies Quarterly* 22 (2015): 243–302.

Polliack, Meira, ed. *Karaite Judaism: A Guide to its History and Literary Sources*. Leiden: Brill, 2003.

Polliack, Meira. *The Karaite Tradition of Arabic Bible Translation: A Linguistic and Exegetical Study of Karaite Translations of the Pentateuch from the Tenth and Eleventh Century C.E.* Leiden: Brill, 1997.

Portillo, Rocio Daga. "The Arabic Life of St. John of Damascus." *ParOr* (1996): 157–188.

Rubenson, Samuel. "The Formation and Re-Formations of the Sayings of the Desert Fathers." *StPatr* 55 (2013): 5–22.

Sadan, Joseph. "In the Eyes of the Christian Writer al-Ḥārit ibn Sinān: Poetics and Eloquence as a Platform of Inter-Cultural Contacts and Contrasts." *Arabica* 56 (2009): 1–26.

Samir, Samir Khalil. "Note sur les citations bibliques chez Abū Qurrah." *OCP* 49 (1983): 184–191.

Sasson, Ilana. "The Book of Proverbs between Saadia and Yefet." *Intellectual History of the Islamicate World* 1 (2013): 159–178.

Schwarb, Gregor. "Capturing the Meaning of God's Speech: The Relevance of *uṣūl al-fiqh* to an Understanding of *uṣūl al-tafsīr* in Jewish and Muslim *kalām*." In *A Word Fitly Spoken: Studies in Mediaeval Exegesis of the Hebrew Bible and the Qur'an Presented to Haggai Ben-Shammai*, ed. Meir M. Bar-Asher et al., 111–156. Jerusalem: Ben-Zvi Institute, 2007.

Stroumsa, Sarah. "The Impact of Syriac Tradition on Early Judaeo-Arabic Bible Exegesis." *Aram* 3 (1991): 83–96.

Stroumsa, Sarah. "Jewish Polemics Against Islam and Christianity in the Light of Judaeo-Arabic Texts." In *Judaeo-Arabic Studies: Proceedings of the Founding Conference of the Society for Judaeo-Arabic Studies*, ed. Norman Golb, 241–250. Amsterdam: Harwood Academic Publishers, 1997.

Stroumsa, Sarah. "On Jewish Intellectuals who Converted to Islam in the Early Middle Ages." In *The Jews of Medieval Islam: Community, Society, and Identity: Proceedings of an International Conference Held by the Institute of Jewish Studies, University College London 1992*, ed. Daniel Frank, 179–197. Leiden: Brill, 1995.

Stroumsa, Sarah. "Saadya and Jewish Kalam." In *The Cambridge Companion to Medieval Jewish Philosophy*, ed. Daniel H. Frank and Oliver Leaman, 71–90. Cambridge: Cambridge University Press, 2003.

Swanson, Mark. "Beyond Prooftexting (1): The Use of the Bible in Some Early Arabic Christian Apologies." In *The Bible in Arab Christianity*, ed. David Thomas, 91–112. Leiden: Brill, 2007.

Tarras, Peter. "The Spirit Before the Letter: Theodore Abū Qurra's Use of Biblical Quotations in the Context of Early Christian Arabic Apologetics." In *Senses of Scripture*, ed. Hjälm (see above), 79–103.

Thomas, David. "With the Qurʾan in Mind." In *Arab Christians and the Qurʾan from the Origins of Islam to the Medieval Period*, ed. Mark Beaumont, 131–149. Leiden: Brill, 2018.

Thomas, David et al., eds. *Christian-Muslim Relations: A Bibliographical History*. Leiden, Brill, 2009–.

Treiger, Alexander. "From Theodore Abū Qurra to Abed Azrié: The Arabic Bible in Context." In *Senses of Scripture*, ed. Hjälm (see above), 11–57.

Treiger, Alexander. "New Works by Theodore Abū Qurra." *JECS* 68 (2017): 1–51.

Vollandt, Ronny. *Arabic Versions of the Pentateuch: A Comparative Study of Jewish, Christian, and Muslim Sources*. Leiden: Brill, 2015.

Wright, Robert J., and Thomas C. Oden, eds. *Proverbs, Ecclesiastes, Song of Solomon*. Ancient Christian Commentary on Scripture. Old Testament. Vol. 9. Downers Grove, IL: InterVarsity Press, 2005.

Zawanowska, Marzena. "Religion in an Age of Reason: Reading Divine Attributes into the Medieval Karaite Bible Translations of Scriptural Texts." In *Senses of Scripture*, ed. Hjälm (see above), 153–181.

Zoref, Arye. "The Influence of Syriac Bible Commentaries on Judeo Arabic Exegesis as Demonstrated by Several Stories from the Book of Genesis." *Studies in Christian-Jewish Relations* 1 (2016): 1–18.

Rubenson on the Move: A Biographical Journey

Thomas Arentzen, Henrik Rydell Johnsén and Andreas Westergren

Samuel Rubenson (b. 1955) grew up in Ethiopia. His parents had gone as missionaries, but with time the mission changed. His father, Sven Rubenson, became a student of Ethiopian history and came to play an influential role in developing the field of Historical Studies in Ethiopia. Rubenson the Younger first went to Scandinavia at the age of sixteen. He has often mentioned what a strange culture shock it was to go north, "home" to a world that was supposed to be his, but which was, in fact, foreign to this teenage boy from Addis Ababa. He still travels regularly to Ethiopia, and anyone following him and his wife Inga-Lill on one of their many journeys to the Middle East and the Horn of Africa, will soon notice to what extent he is at home in the region. Although Samuel Rubenson has spent his academic career beyond Ethiopia, and his research has focused primarily on fields other than Ethiopian traditions, his early years in the African highlands were no minor biographical detail; rather, they seem like a center around which much of his research has revolved.

With hindsight, one might see Rubenson's interpretation of Antony of Egypt prefigured in his own experience of contemporary monasteries in Ethiopia and Egypt. Although a solitary, Antony is not on his own, but part of an ancient heritage that is continually developing, constantly crossing borders, moving from the city to the cell—and back. Academically, Antony and the ascetic legacies of Egypt have driven Rubenson's research. His doctoral thesis, *The Letters of St Antony* (Lund 1990), argued that contrary to the scholarly consensus Antony was not the unlearned peasant Athanasius of Alexandria had suggested in the *Life of Antony*. Rather, Rubenson's close study of Antony's letters in several ancient languages revealed an ascetic schooled in the heritage of Origen. Rubenson's position is now generally accepted by the scholarly community, and the monograph has become a standard for the interpretation of the early monastic movement. In subsequent publications, Rubenson argued further that Athanasius intentionally shaped Antony into the antithesis of Pythagoras and other ancient philosophers: instead of studying and travelling, as they had done, Antony found the truth in an inner journey, by divine grace.

Rubenson himself has followed a long journey of learning. In the 1970s he completed bachelor and master degrees in theology and philosophy at Lund University; in the 1980s he continued his studies in Lund, Tübingen and Cairo. During 1980–1981, he studied Arabic in Egypt. The year allowed him to visit the

St. Macarius monastery in Wadi Natrun on a regular basis and to come to know a living desert tradition where the monks read the *Paradise of the Fathers* daily. Oriental languages would prove vital to his research on Antony's letters, and in Germany he continued the study of Georgian, Armenian, Syriac and Coptic, before completing his doctoral degree in Lund in 1990.

With his thesis defended, Rubenson returned to Egypt, into the monastic desert, the place where Antony had fought demons and battled death. This time, his task was to lead a group of European travelers by foot across the desert wilderness between the monasteries of St. Antony and St. Paul, a distance of approximately 35 miles (55 km). As if to rival the monastic tales of old, the group encountered unexpected challenges in the desert and faced what they believed to be their own imminent death, and finally their own salvation when the lost and desperate group finally stumbled to safety. Having survived the desert, one of his companions, Bishop Martin Lönnebo, insisted on ordaining him a priest in the Church of Sweden. Their journey and Rubenson's teaching about the desert also inspired Lönnebo to compose the *Wreath of Christ*, a meditative rosary which has become hugely popular in Nordic churches.

During the 1990s, Rubenson held a long-term research position at Lund University which allowed him to broaden his network, develop his skills, and continue his work both on monastic history and, more generally, on the history and contemporary state of the Eastern Orthodox and Oriental Orthodox churches. While Lund became his academic base, his travels continued. During the first years (1991–1992) he spent time in the Middle East, primarily in Egypt and Jerusalem. A variety of European institutions also benefitted from his scholarly expertise as guest professor: the Central European University in Budapest (1998), the University of Bergen (1999–2002), and the University of Kiel (2004–2005). Furthermore, the Centre for Advanced Study in Oslo and the University of Göttingen both gained from his research visits. In 1999 Samuel Rubenson became Professor of Church History at Lund University, a position he still holds.

Between 2009 and 2015, Rubenson directed a group of scholars in a major international research project funded by the *Riksbankens jubileumsfond: The Swedish Foundation for Humanities and Social Sciences*. With this project— *Early Monasticism and Classical Paideia* (abbreviated MOPAI)—Rubenson was able to continue his work on the reception of the classical and philosophical heritage in monastic sources, studying how wisdom traditions moved diachronically.

Perhaps Rubenson's most important work during these years has gone largely unnoticed, namely the continued, daily effort to translate the experience of the desert into the digital age, so that the stories of the saints could be tracked and traced and compared—even as their transmission continues across languages as varied as Sogdian and Swedish. The realization that the Sayings-tradition is so diverse that it cannot be traced back to one single source, or published in a traditional critical edition, led to genre-bending work with a highly complex database. This database, in turn, spurred a new research endeavor, *Formative Wisdom: The Reception of Monastic Sayings in European Culture (Scholarly Collaboration on a Digital Platform)*. Rubenson was in charge of this project from its launch in 2016 until its completion in 2019.

At the same time, younger academics have found an engaged listener and advisor in Rubenson. As one of the initiators of the Nordic master's program *Religious Roots of Europe*, he has worked to attract new students to the study of early Christianity, early Islam and late ancient Judaism. His efforts continue to draw students from around the world.

As these projects exemplify, Rubenson has been involved in many collaborations. He is also a member of various scholarly associations, including the *Association Internationale des Études Patristiques*, which he served as vice president from 1999 to 2007. Closest to his heart, or at least closest to home, is the *Collegium Patristicum Lundense*. Although not one of the founding fathers, he soon joined the ranks of this illustrious association whose love for late antiquity stretches beyond the confines of academic disciplines. In 1993, Rubenson was elected *preses* (president), and under his leadership the *Collegium* in Lund has emerged as a hub for patristic studies in the Nordic region.

After his return from Egypt in 1981, Rubenson met the Swedish patristic scholar Per Beskow. The latter casually mentioned a Swedish translation of the *Apophthegmata Patrum* in his possession. Rubenson had just spent time in the ascetic desert and heard these sayings recited in a living monastic context; in Scandinavia, however, the entire *Apophthegmata* tradition was largely unknown at this point. Through the years, Rubenson has taken an active interest in translating the early Christian heritage into Swedish. Together with Tomas Hägg, he translated the *Life of Antony*. He founded the series Swedish Patristic Library (SPB), still actively publishing, and he has taken an active part in Lund's patristic seminar and in the translation circles at St. John's Academy in Linköping. His endeavors have contributed significantly to the fact that translations of early Christian wisdom literature, and other patristic sources, are widely accessible on the Swedish book market. Although a university professor, Rubenson has always felt a duty to share his knowledge with a broader audience; he is a popular writer and lecturer, especially in ecclesiastical contexts. When asked what he considers his most important publication, he has been known to reply that it must be the small Swedish book from 1983, *Ett odelat hjärta: En studie i ökenfädernas vishet*, a work that requires no degree in theology from the reader.

Rubenson is a historian with a keen sense of the present. His study of the past is intrinsically connected to contemporary communities in the Middle East and in Scandinavia that—as any community—live with their past. The object of church history, he once wrote, is the Church. The fact that he has been involved in ecumenical work throughout his career, then, is no coincidence. He has been especially engaged in dialogues with the Orthodox. A position in the diocese of Strängnäs in 1990 allowed him to work directly with Oriental Orthodox communities in Sweden. He currently serves as Senior Professor of Eastern Christian Studies at the Stockholm School of Theology, a university college connected to St. Ignatios College, and supports its ambition to build an academic environment for Eastern Orthodox and Oriental Orthodox traditions together in Scandinavia.

Since his father's death in 2013 at the age of 92, Samuel has assumed the responsibility of continuing Sven's work in Ethiopian history. He has taken over the editorship of the series *Acta Æthiopica* and become chairman of *The Society for the Conservation of the Ethiopian Cultural Heritage*, a collaboration between local authorities in Ethiopia, the patriarchate, and universities in Ethiopia and beyond. With this project Rubenson returns to the beginning of his journey, while yet opening a door to the future.

List of Publications by Samuel Rubenson

1983
Ett odelat hjärta: En studie i ökenfädernas vishet. Religio: Skrifter utgivna av Teologiska institutionen i Lund 10. Lund: Teologiska institutionen i Lund, 1983.

1984
Ett odelat hjärta: En studie i ökenfädernas vishet. Revised edition. Skellefteå: Artos, 1984.

1986
"The Arabic Version of the Letters of St. Antony." In *Actes du deuxième congrès des études arabes chrétiennes (Oosterhesselen, septembre 1984)*, ed. K. Samir, 19–29. OCA 226. Rome: Pontificium Institutum Studiorum Orientalium, 1986.

1987
"The Antonian Material in the Library of the Monastery of St. Antony." *Journal of Arab Christian Studies* 2 (1987).
"Självkännedom och frälsning: Huvudlinjer och spänningar i det tidiga munkväsendets människosyn." *Svensk teologisk kvartalskrift* 63 (1987): 49–58.

1990
The Letters of St. Antony: Origenist Theology, Monastic Tradition and the Making of a Saint. Bibliotheca historico-ecclesiastica Lundensis 24. Lund: Lund University Press, 1990.
"Arabic Sources for the Theology of the Early Monastic Movement in Egypt." *ParOr* 16 (1990): 33–47.

1991
(translated with Tomas Hägg) *Athanasios av Alexandria: Antonios liv.* Skellefteå: Artos, 1991.
(edited with Gösta Hallonsten and Sten Hidal) *Florilegium patristicum: En festskrift till Per Beskow.* Delsbo: Åsak, 1991.

1992
(edited) *Öppna gränser: Ekumeniskt och europeiskt i Strängnäs stift genom tiderna. En samling uppsatser.* Stockholm: Proprius, 1992.
"Kyrka eller folk: Den syrisk-ortodoxa kyrkan och det svenska samhället." *Svensk teologisk kvartalskrift* 68 (1992): 71–79.

"St. Antony, 'The First Real Coptic Author'?" In *Actes du IVe congrès copte, Louvain-la-Neuve, 5–10 septembre 1988*, ed. M. Rassart-Debergh and J. Ries, 16–27. Louvain-la-Neuve: Université catholique de Louvain, Institut orientaliste, 1992.

1993

"Evagrios Pontikos und die Theologie der Wüste." In *Logos: Festschrift für Luise Abramowski zum 8. Juli 1993*, ed. H.C. Brennecke, E.L. Grasmück and C. Markschies, 384–401. Berlin: de Gruyter, 1993.

1994

(edited with Amsalu Aklilu and Merid Wolde Aregay) *Acta Æthiopica*. Vol. 2, *Tewodros and his contemporaries 1855–1868*. Lund: Lund University Press, 1994.

1995

The Letters of St. Antony: Monasticism and the Making of a Saint. Minneapolis: Fortress Press, 1995.
(edited) *Patristica Nordica 4. Föreläsningar hållna vid det fjärde Nordiska patristikermötet i Lund 17–20 augusti 1993*. Religio: Skrifter utgivna av Teologiska institutionen i Lund 44. Lund: Teologiska institutionen, Lunds universitet. 1995.
"Att måla sin tro: Möte med ikonmålare." In *Lunds stiftsbok*, 54–59. Malmö: Lunds stiftsbok, 1995.
"Christian Asceticism and the Emergence of the Monastic Tradition." In *Asceticism*, ed. V.L. Wimbush and R. Valantasis, 49–57. Oxford: Oxford University Press, 1995.
"The Egyptian Relations of Early Palestinian Monasticism." In *The Christian Heritage in the Holy Land*, ed. A. O'Mahony, G. Gunner and K. Hintlian, 35–46. London: Scorpion Cavendish, 1995.
"Kampen om Origenes." In *Patristica Nordica 4. Föreläsningar hållna vid det fjärde Nordiska patristikermötet i Lund 17–20 augusti 1993*, ed. S. Rubenson, 57–73. Religio: Skrifter utgivna av Teologiska institutionen i Lund 44. Lund: Teologiska institutionen, Lunds universitet, 1995.

1996

"Church between Society and Association: The Case of the Syrian Orthodox Church in Sweden." In *Church and People in Britain and Scandinavia*, ed. I. Brohed, 231–245. Bibliotheca historico-ecclesiastica Lundensis 36. Lund: Lund University Press, 1996.
"The Transition from Coptic to Arabic." *Égypte/Monde arabe*, première série, 27–28 (1996): 77–92.
"Translating the Tradition: Some Remarks on the Arabization of the Patristic Heritage in Egypt." *Medieval Encounters* 2 (1996): 4–14.

1997

"Helighet i tid och rum: Aspekter på religionens roll i konflikten." In *Drömmen om fred*, ed. A. Svalander and K.-A. Elmquist, 70–82. Lund: Studentlitteratur, 1997.

1998

(edited with Getatchew Haile and Aasulv Lande) *The Missionary Factor in Ethiopia: Papers from a Symposium on the Impact of European missions on Ethiopian Society, Lund University, August 1996*. Frankfurt: Peter Lang, 1998.

"Eros och agape: Om himmelsk åtrå i den tidiga kyrkan." *Vår Lösen* 8 (1998): 587–595.

"Den hemlighetsfulla kyssen: Sångernas sång hos Gregorios av Nyssa." *Vår Lösen* 2 (1998): 134–138.

"The Interaction between the Missionaries and the Orthodox: The Case of Abune Selama." In *The Missionary Factor in Ethiopia: Papers from a Symposium on the Impact of European Missions on Ethiopian Society, Lund University, August 1996*, ed. G. Haile, A. Lande and S. Rubenson, 71–84. Frankfurt: Peter Lang, 1998.

"Kyrkan, staten och religionsfriheten ur invandrarkyrkans perspektiv." In *Möte med människor av annan tro*, ed. S.A. Flodell and H. Eilert, 46–62. Skellefteå: Norma, 1998.

1999

(edited with Sten Hidal) *Patristica Nordica 5. Föreläsningar hållna vid det femte Nordiska patristikermötet i Lund 20–23 augusti 1997*. Religio: Skrifter utgivna av Teologiska institutionen i Lund 51. Lund: Teologiska institutionen, Lunds universitet, 1999.

"Origen in the Egyptian Monastic Tradition of the Fourth Century." In *Origeniana Septima: Origenes in den Auseinandersetzungen des 4. Jahrhunderts*, ed. W.A. Bienert and U. Kühneweg, 319–337. Leuven: Peeters, 1999.

"Pelarhelgonets hemlighet." *Bulletin* 17 (1999): 15–26.

2000

(edited with A. Aklilu and M. Welde Aregay) *Acta Æthiopica*. Vol. 3, *Internal Rivalries and Foreign Threats 1869–1879*. Addis Ababa: Addis Ababa University Press, 2000.

(edited with Anders Jarlert) *Kyrkohistoria i Lund: Fyra föreläsningar*. MKHA, n. s., 2. Lund: Lunds universitets kyrkohistoriska arkiv, 2000.

(edited) *Martyrer och Helgon*. Svenskt Patristiskt Bibliotek 2. Skellefteå: Artos, 2000.

(edited and translated) *Matta Al-Miskîn: Enhet ger liv*. Sturefors: Silentium, 2000.

"Bibelspridare, biskopar och botgörare—kyrkohistoriska kulturkrockar i kolonialismens tidevarv." In *Kyrkohistoria i Lund: Fyra föreläsningar*, ed. S. Rubenson and A. Jarlert, 25–38. MKHA, n. s., 2. Lund: Lunds universitets kyrkohistoriska arkiv, 2000.

"The Correspondence between the Coptic Patriarchs and the Rulers and Metropolitans of Ethiopia 1800–1881." *ParOr* 25 (2000): 715–725.

"Katekumenatet: Katekese, dåb og medlemsoptagelse i oldkirken." In *Dåb og medlemskab i folkekirken*, ed. H. Raun Iversen, 31–42. Copenhagen: Anis, 2000.

"Kyrkohistoriens objekt." In *Kyrkohistoria i Lund: Fyra föreläsningar*, ed. S. Rubenson and A. Jarlert, 17–23. MKHA, n. s., 2. Lund: Lunds universitets kyrkohistoriska arkiv, 2000.

"Philosophy and Simplicity: The Problem of Classical Education in Early Christian Biography." In *Greek Biography and Panegyric in Late Antiquity*, ed. T. Hägg and P. Rousseau, 110–139. The Transformation of the Classical Heritage 31. Berkeley, CA: University of California Press, 2000.

2001

Betraktelser över ökenfädernas tänkespråk. Göteborg: Cordia, 2001.

"Inledning." In *Makarios andliga homilier*, ed. O. Andrén, 7–22. Skellefteå: Artos, 2001.

"Kroppens uppståndelse i martyrakter och helgonbiografier." In *Kropp og opstandelse*, ed. T. Engberg-Pedersen and I.S. Gilhus, 134–154. Oslo: Pax Forlag, 2001.

"När Bibeln ersatte Homeros." *RIT: Religionsvetenskaplig Internettidskrift* 1 (2001). Accessed 22 November 2019. https://www.ctr.lu.se/fileadmin/user_upload/ctr/pdf/rit/1/rubenson.pdf.

2002

Omvändelsens väg: Att med fruktan och bävan arbeta på sin frälsning. Sturefors: Silentium, 2002.

"Ensamhet och gemenskap: Några drag i Evagrios av Pontus mystik." *Mystiker mitt i världen*, ed. A. Geels, 99–113. Lund: Teologiska institutionen, Lunds universitet, 2002.

"Hotet från islam. Kolonialismen och de förändrade islamisk-kristna relationerna i Etiopien på 1800-talet." *Svensk religionshistorisk årsskrift* 11 (2002): 160–170.

2003

"Hänförelsens språk: Mysteriets liturgiska språkdräkt i fornkyrklig teologi." *Svenskt gudstjänstliv* 78 (2003): 9–23.

2004

"Hett material? Religion och politik i de egyptiska arkiven." In *Arkiv, fakultet, kyrka: Festskrift till Ingmar Brohed*, ed. A. Jarlert, 423–431. Lund: Lunds universitets kyrkohistoriska arkiv, 2004.

"Ökenfädernas väg från söndring till helhet." *Finsk tidskrift: Kultur, ekonomi, politik* 255–256 (2004): 81–95.

"Reading Origen in the Egyptian Desert." *MCPL* 19 (2004): 44–50.

"Wisdom, Paraenesis and the Roots of Monasticism." In *Early Christian Paraenesis in Context*, ed. J. Starr and T. Engberg-Pedersen, 521–534. Berlin: de Gruyter, 2004.

2005

(edited) *Imago Dei: Poesi och bildspråk i fornkyrkan.* Patristica Nordica 6. Skellefteå: Artos, 2005.

(edited with Anders Jarlert) *Kyrkohistoriska omvärderingar.* MKHA, n. s., 7. Lund: Lunds universitets kyrkohistoriska arkiv, 2005.

"Kristendomens hellenisering—ett märkligt missförstånd." In *Kyrkohistoriska omvärderingar*, ed. S. Rubenson and A. Jarlert, 9–18. MKHA, n. s., 7. Lund: Lunds universitets kyrkohistoriska arkiv, 2005.

"Medeltiden—medel för vad och för vem." In *Kyrkohistoriska omvärderingar*, ed. S. Rubenson and A. Jarlert, 19–28. MKHA, n. s., 7. Lund: Lunds universitets kyrkohistoriska arkiv, 2005.

2006

"Anthony and Pythagoras: A Reappraisal of the Appropriation of Classical Biography in Athanasius' *Vita Antonii*." In *Beyond Reception: Mutual Influences Between Antique Religion, Judaism, and Early Christianity*, ed. A.-C. Jacobsen, D. Brakke and J. Ulrich, 191–208. Frankfurt: Peter Lang, 2006.

"Är bilder farliga—frågor till kristen bildkonst." *Kirke og kultur* 111 (2006): 181–190.

"The Cappadocians on the Areopagus." In *Gregory of Nazianzus: Images and Reflections*, ed. J. Børtnes and T. Hägg, 113–132. Copenhagen: Tusculanum, 2006.

"Mångfald och enhetssträvanden." In *Jesus och de första kristna: Inledning till Nya testamentet*, ed. D. Mitternacht and A. Runesson, 370–385. Stockholm: Verbum, 2006.

2007

"Äktenskapet i den tidiga kyrkan." In *Uppdrag samliv*, ed. M. Lindfelt and J. Gustafsson Lundberg, 179–224. Stockholm: Verbum, 2007.

"Argument and Authority in Early Monastic Correspondence." In *Foundations of Power and Conflicts of Authority in Late-Antique Monasticism: Proceedings of the International Seminar Turin, December 2–4, 2004*, ed. A. Camplani and G. Filoramo, 75–87. OLA 157. Leuven: Peeters, 2007.

"Asceticism and Monasticism, I: Varieties of Eastern Monasticism." In *Cambridge History of Christianity*. Vol. 2, *Constantine to c. 600*, ed. A. Casiday and Frederick W. Norris, 637–668. Cambridge: Cambridge University Press, 2007.

2008

(edited) *Asketer och munkar.* Svenskt Patristiskt Bibliotek 5. Skellefteå: Artos, 2008.

"Matta al-Miskîn." In *Moderne teologi: Tradisjon og nytenkning hos det 20. århundrets teologer*, ed. S. Kristiansen and S. Rise, 430–443. Kristiansand: Høyskoleforlaget, 2008.

2009

(edited with Per Rönnegård) *Paradiset: Ökenfädernas tänkespråk. Den systematiska samlingen.* Vol. 1, *De heliga fädernas råd för den som söker fullkomlighet.* Silentium Apophthegmata 1. Sturefors: Silentium, 2009.

"'As Already Translated to the Kingdom While Still in the Body': The Transformation of the Ascetic in Early Egyptian Monasticism." In *Metamorphoses: Resurrection, Body and Transformative Practices in Early Christianity*, ed. T.K. Seim and J. Økland, 271–289. Berlin: de Gruyter, 2009.

"The European Impact on Christian-Muslim Relations in the Middle East During the Nineteenth Century: The Ethiopian Example." In *The Fuzzy Logic of Encounter: New Perspectives on Cultural Contact*, ed. S. Juterczenka and G. Mackenthun, 117–126. Münster: Waxmann Verlag, 2009.

"From School to Patriarchate: Aspects on the Christianisation of Alexandria." In *Alexandria: A Cultural and Religious Melting Pot*, ed. G. Hinge and J.A. Krasilnikoff, 144–157. Aarhus: Aarhus University Press, 2009.

"Himmelsk åtrå—Höga visan i tidigkristen mystik." In *Eros och Agape: Barmhärtighet, kärlek och mystik i den tidiga kyrkan*, ed. H. Rydell Johnsén and P. Rönnegård, 105–127. Skellefteå: Artos, 2009.

"Det koptiska arvet." In *Innanför och utanför: Arv, identitet och nyorientering hos armenier och kopter i Sverige*, ed. S. Halvardson, 15–25. Tro & Liv 6. Stockholm: Teologiska högskolan, 2009.

"Kyrkohistoria som teologi." In *Kyrkohistoria—perspektiv på ett forskningsämne*, ed. A. Jarlert, 87–93. Kungliga Vitterhets historie och antikvitets akademien 70. Stockholm: Kungl. Vitterhets historie och antikvitets akademien, 2009.

"Martyrdom and Identity: Reflections on a Coptic Martyrdom under Muslim Rule." *Swedish Missiological Themes* 96 (2009): 235–247.

"Power and Politics of Poverty in Early Monasticism." In *Prayer and Spirituality in the Early Church.* Vol. 5, *Poverty and Riches*, ed. G.D. Dunn, D. Luckensmeyer and L. Cross, 91–110. Strathfield, New South Wales: St Paul's Publications, 2009.

"Den tidiga kyrkan." In *Kyrkohistoria—perspektiv på ett forskningsämne*, ed. A. Jarlert, 13–21. Kungliga Vitterhets historie och antikvitets akademien 70. Stockholm: Kungl. Vitterhets historie och antikvitets akademien, 2009.

2010

(edited with Per Rönnegård) *Paradiset: Ökenfädernas tänkespråk. Den systematiska samlingen.* Vol. 2, *Om nödvändigheten av att hängivet sträva efter stillheten.* Silentium Apophthegmata 2. Sturefors: Silentium, 2010.

"Det gyllene Athen: Vältalighetens lockelse och bildningens förförelse i den tidiga kyrkan." In *Flumen saxosum sonans: Studia in honorem Gunnar af Hällström*, ed. M. Ahlqvist, A.M. Laato and M. Lindfelt, 211–225. Åbo: Åbo Akademis förlag, 2010.

2011

"Antony and Ammonas: Conflicting or Common Tradition in Early Egyptian Monasticism." In *Bibel, Byzanz und christlicher Orient: Festschrift für Stephan Gerö zum 65. Geburtstag*, ed. D. Bumazhnov, 185–201. Leuven: Peeters, 2011.

"The Apophthegmata Patrum in Syriac, Arabic and Ethiopic. Status Questionis." *ParOr* 36 (2011): 319–328.

"Athanasius und Antonios." In *Athanasius Handbuch*, ed. P. Gemeinhardt, 141–145. Tübingen: Mohr Siebeck, 2011.

"Ikonen—spegel och närvaro." In *Ikonen—närvaro och källa: Essäer om ikonen som liturgisk konst och personlig dialogbild*, ed. L. Gerdmar, 11–20. Lund: Sekel Bokförlag, 2011.

"Kroppen är frälsningens nav." *Pilgrim* 18, no. 3 (2011): 6–11.

2012

"Monasticism and the Philosophical Heritage." In *Oxford Handbook of Late Antiquity*, ed. S. Johnson, 487–512. Oxford: Oxford University Press, 2012.

"Mönchtum I (Idee u. Geschichte)." In *Reallexikon für Antike und Christentum: Sachwörterbuch zur Auseinandersetzung des Christentums mit der antiken Welt*, vol. 24, ed. G. Schöllgen et al., 1009–1064. Stuttgart, Hiersemann, 2012.

"Tradition and Renewal in Coptic Theology." In *Between Desert and City: The Coptic Orthodox Church Today*, ed. N. Van Doorn-Harder and K. Vogt, 35–51. Oslo: Novus, 1997.

2013

"Apologetics of Asceticism: The *Life of Antony* and Its Political Context." In *Ascetic Culture: Essays in Honor of Philip Rousseau*, ed. B. Leyerle and R.D. Young, 75–96. Notre Dame: University of Notre Dame Press, 2013.

"The Formation and Re-Formations of the Sayings of the Desert Fathers." In *StPatr* 55, ed. M. Vincent and S. Rubenson, 5–22. Leuven: Peeters, 2013.

"Matta el-Meskeen." In *Key Theological Thinkers: From Modern to Postmodern*, ed. S. Kristiansen and S. Riise, 415–426. Farnham: Ashgate, 2013.

"To Tell the Truth: Fact and Fiction in Early Monastic Sources." *Cistercian Studies Quarterly* 48 (2013): 317–324.

2014

"A Database of the *Apophthegmata Patrum*." In *Analysis of Ancient and Medieval Texts and Manuscripts: Digital Approaches*, ed. T. Andrews and C. Macé, 203–212. Turnhout: Brepols, 2014.

"Transformative Light and Luminous Traditions in Early Christian Mysticism and Monasticism." *Svensk teologisk kvartalskrift* 90 (2014): 179–187.

2015

"The Letter-Collections of Antony and Ammonas: Shaping a Community." In *Collecting Early Christian Letters: From the Apostle Paul to Late Antiquity*, ed. B. Neil and P. Allen, 68–79. Cambridge: Cambridge University Press, 2015.

2016

"Antonius Abba, 251?–356 CE." In *Oxford Classical Dictionary*, ed. T. Whitmarsh. Oxford: Oxford University Press, 2016. doi: 10.1093/acrefore/9780199381135.013.8083.

"Athanasius av Alexandria: En missionär." In *Ad Fontes: En feststkrift till Olof Andrén på 100-års dagen*, ed. C.J. Berglund and D. Gustafsson, 253–265. Skellefteå: Artos, 2016.

(co-authored with Jesper Blid, Maximous El-Antony, Hugo Lundhaug, Jason Zaborowski, Meira Polliack and Mengistu Gobezie Worku) "Excavations at the Monastery of St Antony at the Red Sea: The Monastery in Literary Sources during the Period of Study." *Opuscula: Annual of the Swedish Institutes at Athens and Rome* 9 (2016): 133–215.

Det tidiga klosterväsendet och den antika bildningen: Slutrapport från ett forskningsprogram. Göteborg: Makadam förlag, 2016.

2017

"Matta el Meskin e la Riscoperta dei Padri nella chiesa Copta." In *Matta el Meskin: Un padre del deserto contemporaneo*, ed. E. Di San Macario, S. Rubenson, A.Y. Sidarus and N.H. Abu Zayd, 129–140. Magnano: Edizioni Qiqajon, Comunità di Bose, 2017.

"Textual Fluidity in Early Monasticism: Sayings, Sermons and Stories." In *Snapshots of Evolving Traditions: Jewish and Christian Manuscript Culture, Textual Fluidity, and New Philology*, ed. L. Ingeborg Lied and H. Lundhaug, 178–200. TU 175. Berlin: de Gruyter, 2017.

"Vitas Patrum as Material for Revival and Reform in Medieval Monasticism, the Reformation and Pietism." In *Classics in Northern European Church History Over 500 Years: Essays in Honour of Anders Jarlert*, ed. D. Gudmundsson, A. Maurits and M. Nykvist, 23–40. Frankfurt: Peter Lang, 2017.

2018

(edited with Lillian Larsen) *Monastic Education in Late Antiquity: The Transformation of Classical Paideia*. Cambridge: Cambridge University Press, 2018.

"Early Monasticism and the Concept of a 'School.'" In *Monastic Education in Late Antiquity: The Transformation of Classical Paideia*, ed. L. Larsen and S. Rubenson, 13–32. Cambridge: Cambridge University Press, 2018.

2019

"Preface." In *More Sayings of the Desert Fathers: An English Translation and Notes*, ed. J. Wortley, xiii. Cambridge: Cambridge University Press, 2019.

"Det senantika Mellanöstern, ökenfäderna och Palladios." In *Vägar till Bysans*, ed. O. Heilo, 35–43. Skellefteå: Artos, 2019.

Index

Abraham of Bet Rabban 214
Abu Nu'aym 178
Abū Qurra, Theodore 224, 226, 228–230, 232, 234, 235, 239, 240, 241
adab collections 172–173
Against the Jews (Theodore Abū Qurra) 234
'Anazī, Ḥātim al- 180
Anub 65
Aesop 4
Amoun of Nitria 41, 45
Anaxagoras 92
Antony 1, 2, 45, 47, 111, 247, 248
 See also Life of Antony
Aphthonius 103
Apollo 109
Apollos 112–113
apomnēmoneuma, anecdotes 75, 85, 87
 and *apophthegm(ata)* 75, 91
apophthegm(ata), saying(s) 3–4, 20, 54–70, 75–93, 104, 109, 120, 132–142, 148, 176–177, 179, 181
 and *apomnēmoneuma* 75, 91
 and *bios*, *vita* 4, 83–84, 88–90, 122–123, 140
 and *chreia* 75, 82–83, 85, 87–88, 89, 104
 and *gnōmē* 3–4, 75, 79–81, 85, 86–87, 91
 and non-Christian *apophthegm(ata)* 90–92
 and *paroimia* 75, 86–87
 collections of 83–86, 90–91, 92, 122, 163
 meaning of 75–77, 81, 92
 kinds of 86–88
Apophthegmata Patrum 1, 5, 6, 7, 13, 16, 19, 24, 36, 54, 55, 57–70, 75, 91, 104, 109–111, 114, 119–142, 147–163, 166, 175–180, 249
 and *bios*, *vita* 122–123, 140, 148, 149–163
 and non-Christian *apophthegmata* 91
 and John Cassian 109–111, 114
 collections of 58, 60, 62, 63
 translations of, Arabic 175–179
 translations of, Armenian 147–163
 translations of, Slavonic see paterikon, Slavonic
Aristotle 78–81, 82, 83, 86
Arsenius 58, 63
Ascetica see Paralipomena

ascetics in Islam see zuhhād
Aṣmaʿī, al- 174
Athanasius 37, 39, 40, 43, 44, 46, 47, 49, 247
Athenaeus 77, 82, 87
Avot (tractate) 5

Barsanuphius and John the Prophet, correspondence of 54–70
 identity of 'fathers' 54–57
Bartholomew 147
Basil the Great 15, 59
Basra 166–181
Baṣrī, Ḥasan al- 167–169
Bible 58, 67–70, 168, 170, 175–176, 189, 191, 192–197, 216, 224–241
 and prooftexting 240
biography, *vita*, *bios* 122, 123, 140, 180
 and *apophthegm(ata)* 4, 83–84, 88–90, 122–123, 140
 and *Apophthegmata Patrum* 148
Book of Beliefs and Opinions, The (Saadia Gaon) 226, 228, 239
Bunānī, Thābit al- 169
Bustān al-Ruhbān (*The Garden of the Monks*) 166

Callisthenes 83
Cassian the Sabaite 97–98
Cassius Dio 77
choirs, Syriac women's 203–217
Cicero 81–82
chreia 103
 and *apophthegm(ata)* 75, 82–83, 85, 87–88, 89, 104
Clitarchi sententiae 5
Commentary on the Diatessaron (Ephrem the Syrian) 209
Corpus Dionysiacum 14
Cyril of Alexandria 39
Cyril of Scythopolis 97

De gentibus Indiae et Bragmanibus (Palladius of Helenopolis) 124, 127
Demetrius of Phalerum 83
Dicaearchus 81

INDEX

Diogenes Laertius 77, 81, 82, 84, 87, 88, 89–90
Diogenes the Cynic 84
Diogenianus 86
Dionysius Exiguus 21
Dorotheus of Gaza 54, 56, 57, 58, 59–60, 63, 66

Egypt *see* Lower Egypt; Upper Egypt
ʿElī, Yefet ben 237
Elianus 69–70
Ephesus, council of 39
Ephrem the Syrian 205, 207–210, 215, 216
    See also Life of Ephrem
Epictetus 4
Epicurus 4
Euripides 86, 87
Euthymius 56
ergasia, elaborations 103, 104, 106
Evagrius of Pontus 1, 47n47, 59, 64, 99–108
    and John Cassian 99–108, 114

Favorinus 87

Gaza 54, 56, 57–58
gentiles and Jews 187–200
George of Arbela 216
gnōmē, maxim 103, 104, 107
    and *apophthegm(ata)* 3–4, 75, 79–81, 85, 86–87, 91
    and *paroimia* 75, 82
gnomologia 79–81, 85–86, 90, 173
Gnomologium Vaticanum 87
Gregory Bar Hebraeus 205n8
Gregory of Nazianzus 14, 55n6, 59
Gregory of Nyssa 55n6
Gregory the Illuminator 147

hadīths 169, 171, 172–173, 177, 140, 180–181
hagiography 6, 20, 23, 120, 122, 123, 127, 140, 180, 212, 247
Hanah-Ishoʿ 212
Hermogenes 103
Historia Lausiaca (Palladius) 41, 48–49, 61, 91, 124, 127
Historia monachorum in Aegypto 55, 57–61, 124, 126, 127
Ḥilyat al-awliyāʾ waṭabaqāt al-aṣfiyāʾ (Abū Nuʿaym al-Iṣfahānī) 172, 179, 180

Homily on Ephrem the Syrian (Jacob of Sarug) 207, 210
Horsiesius 36, 39, 43, 46
hymnography, hymns 203–217
Hymns on Faith (Ephrem the Syrian) 210
Hymns on the Nativity (Ephrem the Syrian) 210
Hymns on the Resurrection (Ephrem the Syrian) 210

Ibn Aḥmad, ʿAbdallāh 180
Ibn al-Jawzī 169
Ibn al-Mubārak 171, 172
Ibn Dīnār, Mālik 169, 177–178
Ibn Dīnār, Salama 169
Ibn Ḥanbal, Aḥmad 172, 180
Ibn Kaysān, Ṭāwūs 169
Ibn Munabbih, Wahb 174
Ibn Sinān, al-Ḥārith 235–236, 237
Instructions (Dorotheus of Gaza) 59–60, 63
Isaiah of Gaza 56, 57
    Asceticon 61
Iṣfahānī, Abū Nuʿaym al- 172
isnād, chain of transmission 173, 180
isrāʾīliyyāt 174, 175, 179

Jacob of Sarug 205, 206, 207, 208, 209, 210, 214
Jāḥiẓ, al- 174
Jewish-Christian relations 237–240
Jews and gentiles 187–200
Jesus 167, 168, 175, 188, 189, 193, 194, 195–197, 226, 230, 232
    and Moses 175, 187, 190–192, 195, 199, 200, 234
John Cassian 97–114
    and *Apophthegmata Patrum* 98, 109–111
    and Evagrius of Pontus 99–108, 114
John of Damascus 224
John of Ephesus 207, 210, 211, 215–216
John of Tella 215
John the Persian 178
Judaeo-Arabic 226, 237–239
Justinian I 40

K. al-Zuhd wa-l-raqāʾiq (Ibn al-Mubārak) 171
kalām 225, 227, 228

kephalaia 5, 67
Kievan Rus' 119, 128, 129

Lamprias 84–85
Letter of Ammon 22, 36, 38, 39, 45, 47, 48–49
Life of Antony (*Vita Antonii*) 36, 40–41, 42, 43, 247, 249
Life of Ephrem 206, 207–209, 210, 216
  See also Ephrem the Syrian
Life of Febronia 212
Life of Methodius 120
Life of Pachomius 13–32, 20, 35–50
  Vita altera (G2) 20–21, 22, 49
  Vita brevis 21
  Vita prima (G1) 13–32, 40–41, 45–46, 48, 49
Life of Shenoute 41
Life of Theodorus 21
literacy, female 211–213
liturgy 203–217
  and liturgical training 211
Lives of the Eastern Saints (John of Ephesus) 207
Lower Egypt 35–50, 125
Lynceus 83

Maruta Canons 206, 215
Menander 4, 87
Methodius 119, 120, 125, 126–127
Metrocles 89
monasticism 5–6, 35, 36–46, 47, 48, 49, 50, 56–57, 107–108, 147–148, 166, 170, 175, 176, 247, 248
Moses 175, 193, 194
  and Jesus 175, 187, 190–192, 195, 197, 199, 200, 234
Moses (Abba) 111–113

Narsai of Nisibis 214
Nicaea, council of 55n6
Nisteros the Cenobite 58, 65, 67
Nomocanon ('Abdishoʿ bar Brika) 214

Old Church Slavonic 119, 126
onomatomania 174
On Salvation (Theodore Abū Qurra) 233
On the Trinity (Theodore Abū Qurra) 233
orality 2, 50, 58, 60, 90, 167, 176, 177, 180, 192, 195, 197, 227, 238

Origen 46–47, 49, 70, 247
Origenism 49, 59, 62

Pachomius 13–32, 35–50
  See also Life of Pachomius; Rule of Pachomius
Palamon 42
Paralipomena (*Ascetica*) 20, 21, 22, 36, 45, 47, 48–49
paroimia, proverb
  and *apophthegm(ata)* 75, 86–87
  and *gnōmē* 75, 82
paterikon, Slavonic 120–140
  Azbučno-Ierusalimskij Paterik 124–125
  Egipetskij 124, 127
  Rimskij Paterik 124, 126–127
  secondary collections 127–128
  Sinajskij Paterik 124, 126, 127
  Skitskij Paterik 124, 125–126, 127, 128, 129
Paul of Samosata 204n6
Petronius 43
Philo of Alexandria 77
Photios 84
Plato 78
Plutarch 1, 81, 82, 84, 87, 88–90
Poemen 58, 62–66
Pratum spirituale (John Moschos) 91, 124, 126
progymnasmata 82, 87, 103
prooftexts 240
Psalms, psalmody 175–176, 206, 211, 213, 214, 229
Pseudo-Clementine *Homilies* 187–200
  and Clement of Rome 188
  and Peter 187, 188, 192, 193–195, 197, 199
  and Pharisees 193–197
  and the Prophet of truth 187, 188, 193–194, 195
Pythagoras 4, 86–87, 247

Qurʾān 3, 167, 170, 172, 175, 224, 232
quṣṣāṣ, Islamic storytellers 169, 173–174, 177–178, 180
Qūt al-qulūb (Abū Ṭālib al-Makkī) 180

Rabbinic Judaism 192–200, 227–228
Rāzī, Ḥātim al- 172
renunciants see *zuhhād*
rhēma 78

INDEX

Rubenson, Samuel   247–258
    list of publications   251–258
Rule of Pachomius   21, 22, 48–49
Rus' *see* Kievan Rus'
Russian literature   119, 120, 122–128

Saadia Gaon   226, 227–228, 229, 230, 231–235, 236–237, 239, 240, 241
Sabākhī, Farqad al-   169, 170
Sayings of the (Desert) Fathers see Apophthegmata Patrum
Scala paradisi (John Climacus)   91
School of Nisibis   211, 213–215
schools, village   211, 215
Sentences of Pseudo-Phocylides   5
Sentences of Sextus   5, 100
Sententiae ad virginem (Evagrius of Pontus)   107–108
Sententiae Pythagoreum   5
Seridus   56, 60, 61
Seven Sages   4, 77, 78, 83
Sextus   87
Shenoute   45
    See also Life of Shenoute
Simeon the Mountaineer   210–211, 216
Socrates   83–84
Sopater   84
Sotion   77
Stesichorus   81
Stobaeus   81, 82, 84

Testament (Horsiesius)   43
textual doublets   121, 132–142
Thaddeus   147
Theodore the Sanctified   36, 39, 43, 46, 47
Theodosius, Archbishop of Alexandria   45
Theologus Autodidactus (Theodore Abū Qurra)   226
Theon   82, 103
Theophilus, Pope of Alexandria   38–39, 43
Theophrastus   81
theosebeis   189, 198, 200
Timothy I   167
Timothy of Alexandria   40
Tiridates III, king of Armenia   147
Trinity   232–234

Upper Egypt   36, 38–39, 41, 42, 43, 45, 46, 47–48

Wisdom   230–231
wisdom literature, biblical   3, 5, 175–176, 224–241
wisdom traditions   3–7, 247, 248
women as teachers   203–217

Xenophon   77–78, 81, 82, 87

Zenobius   86
Zosimas   56, 60
Zuhd al-thamāniyya min al-tābi'īn (Ḥātim al-Rāzī)   172
zuhhād, Islamic renunciants   166–181

Printed in the United States
By Bookmasters